W9-ADN-280

DATE DUE

JUL 1 9 1995

COLLABORATION WITH PARENTS OF EXCEPTIONAL CHILDREN

Marvin J. Fine, Editor

CPPC

4 Conant Square
Brandon, VT 05733

HG
773
5
C59
1991

Library of Congress Catalog Card Number: 90-82413

ISBN: 0-88422-109-1

CPPC   4 Conant Square
        Brandon, Vermont 05733

Cover design: Thomas Hannan

Printed in the United States of America.

CONTENTS

v

LIST OF CONTRIBUTORS

Mary Wysopal Bolger
Waismann Early Childhood Program
University of Wisconsin—Madison
Madison, WI

Harriet C. Cobb
Department of Psychology
James Madison University
Harrisonburg, VA

Vivian I. Correa
Department of Special Education
University of Florida
Gainesville, FL

Donald D. Deshler
Institute for Research in Learning
    Disabilities
University of Kansas
Lawrence, KS

Beth Doll
Division of Educational
    Psychology/Special Education

University of Colorado at Denver
Denver, CO

Carl J. Dunst
Center for Family Studies
West Carolina Center
Morganton, NC

Craig R. Fiedler
Department of Special Education
University of Wisconsin—Oshkosh
Oshkosh, WI

Marvin J. Fine
Department of Educational
    Psychology and Research
University of Kansas
Lawrence, KS

Marian C. Fish
Graduate Program in School
    Psychology
Queens College of the City
    University of New York
Flushing, NY

Reva C. Friedman (Jenkins)
Department of Educational
    Psychology and Research
University of Kansas
Lawrence, KS

Thomas J. Gallagher
Department of Educational
    Psychology and Research
University of Kansas
Lawrence, KS

J. Stephen Hazel
Institute for Research in Learning
    Disabilities
University of Kansas
Lawrence, KS

Mindy Sloan Kohler
Department of Educational and
    Counseling Psychology
University of Kentucky
Lexington, KY

Roberta Krehbiel
Family Consultant to Project T.I.M.E.
Division of Neonatology
University of New Mexico
Department of Pediatrics
Albuquerque, NM

Roger L. Kroth
Department of Special Education
University of New Mexico
Albuquerque, NM

Lou Ann Kruse
School Psychologist and Family
    Counselor
Lexington, KY

Steven W. Lee
Department of Educational
    Psychology and Research
University of Kansas
Lawrence, KS

Edward M. Levinson
Department of Educational
    Psychology
Indiana University of Pennsylvania
Indiana, PA

Emanuel J. Mason
Department of Educational and
    Counseling Psychology
University of Kentucky
Lexington, KY

Lynne M. McKee
School Psychologist Intern
ARIN Intermediate Unit #28
Shelocta, PA

Kathleen D. Paget
Department of Psychology
University of South Carolina
Columbia, SC

H. Thompson Prout
Department of Human Services and
    Studies
Florida State University
Tallahassee, FL

Susan M. Prout
School Psychologist
Schalmont (NY) Central Schools
Schenectady, NY

Ronald E. Reeve
Department of Psychology
University of Virginia
Charlottesville, VA

Jean Bragg Schumaker
Institute for Research in Learning
  Disabilities
University of Kansas
Lawrence, KS

Richard L. Simpson
Department of Special Education
University of Kansas
Kansas City, KS

Sue Vernon
Institute for Research in Learning
  Disabilities
University of Kansas
Lawrence, KS

Peggy Jo Wallis
Consultant in Training and Program
  Design
Wallis Associates
Clifton Park, NY

Chriss Walther-Thomas
Department of Special Education
College of William and Mary
Williamsburg, VA

Jo Webber
Department of Curriculum and
  Instruction
Southwest Texas State University
San Marcos, TX

Jeanne Weismantel
Consultant in Bilingual Education
University of Florida
Gainesville, FL

PREFACE

The last several decades have witnessed dramatic changes in society's perception and treatment of exceptional individuals. The increased sophistication of early diagnosis of problematic conditions, the deinstitutionalization of handicapped persons, the growth of community-based services, and the legislative mandates for public school involvement all have contributed to the care, training, and education of exceptional individuals, with direct implications for their parents.

Numerous myths have affected not only the community's perception of parents of exceptional individuals, but also the perceptions and behaviors of professional persons. Although it is true that these parents typically undergo a process of adjustment, there is evidence that they often demonstrate effective coping skills in dealing with the problems that their children present, are able to maintain a functional integrity within their families, and can be proactive and advocacy oriented in efforts on behalf of their children. The perception by professionals that parents are often in need of extensive psychotherapy, unable to accept the realities of their child, or recalcitrant receivers of professional services needs to be replaced by a more constructive view. "Exceptional" parents are often eager to learn as much as they can about their child's exceptionality, able to acquire specific skills necessary to facilitate the growth and development of their child, and able to participate in partnership with professionals in the care, treatment and education of their child.

These optimistic observations are not meant as a denial that there are some parents who are in need of ongoing therapeutic assistance and who continue to struggle with the nature of the child's problems and with their relationship to the child. However, there is evidence, even for those parents for whom the presence of the exceptionality has been problematic, that they can be helped to assume a partnership role with professionals. It is in the theme of viewing parents as collaborators or partners with the professional community in the care, treatment, and education of their exceptional child that this book has been written. Professionals, and particularly persons in training to assume a professional role that will put them in contact with parents of exceptional children, can benefit from the sympathetic and collaborative orientation of this book.

It has been observed many times that the greatest gift that can be given to persons in need is the skill necessary for them to meet their own needs, so they become less dependent upon others. This book is presented in exactly that theme—the education and the empowerment of parents so they can become active partners with the professional community in meeting the needs of their own children.

The first section, "The Family and Exceptionality," includes four chapters that underscore the theme of the book and set the stage for the subsequent sections. The introductory chapter by Fine reviews the literature on parental and family response to a handicapped child, presents implications for professionals, and describes a collaborative/empowerment model.

The concept of family empowerment is superbly elaborated by Dunst and Paget in Chapter 2. They examine the dynamics of helping behavior, consider a social systems perspective, and detail a model of both enablement and empowerment.

Much of the existing literature on handicapped children speaks as if intact, two-parent families were the norm. This stance ignores what for many families is the reality of variations to the parenting/family structure. The important chapter by Fish focuses very sensitively on the issues and needs of single-parent, stepparent, foster-parent, and adoptive parent families. It also touches briefly on families wherein one or both parents are physically or mentally disabled.

Chapter 4 on siblings, by Mason, Kruse, and Kohler, brings our attention to often-forgotten members of the family. These children can be at risk for, if not already experiencing, stress regarding their place in the family and struggling with related personal adjustment issues. The more immediately evident parental concern with the exceptional child can capture the professional's attention, while the less obvious needs of the siblings are ignored.

Section two focuses on important educational and intervention considerations. The section begins with the chapter by Correa and Weismantel on multicultural issues. The value of this chapter cannot be overstated in its attempts to sensitize the reader to the potential cultural/ethnic variability among families with a handicapped child.

Krehbiel and Kroth bring their rich backgrounds of professional contact with parents and families to the chapter on communication. The "how, what, and when" of the professional's communication are inextricably connected to facilitating a collaborative partnership with parents.

Chapter 7 on counseling approaches, by Cobb and Reeve, argues for sensitivity and caring by professionals. Models of counseling and a range of counseling issues that parents, siblings, and families may experience are well delineated. The final chapter in this section, by Fine, describes an intervention model for parents who already have or may develop the potential for abusing their handicapped child. These parents need to be understood sympathetically and assisted in a variety of ways to strengthen positive parenting attitudes and skills.

Section three examines the impact of different exceptionalities on the family and discusses specific ways in which parents can be assisted. The emphasis again is on educating, collaborating with, and empowering parents.

The exceptionalities discussed include the mentally retarded child (Prout and Prout), the young developmentally disabled child (Doll and Bolger), the chronically ill child (Lee), the learning disabled child (Walther-Thomas, Hazel, Schumaker, Vernon, and Deshler), and the autistic child (Simpson and Webber). The last chapter in this section, by Friedman (Jenkins) and Gallagher, expands the spectrum of exceptionality by discussing the gifted child. Although this book deals mainly with handicapping conditions, the gifted child may also affect the family in ways that require professional interventions.

The last section of the book considers three very important topics about which all professionals need to be informed: sexuality, transitions, and advocacy. Chapter 15, by Wallis, brings sexuality and the handicapped into a more normal, healthy focus. In the past not only parents but often professionals have acted as if the handicapped were not sexual beings or as if their sexuality was somehow aberrant.

Levinson and McKee address the crucial area of the child transitioning from the more sheltered school/family setting into the world of job training and employment, as well as into a more independent style of living. This can be a time of stress for parents that invites the support and assistance of professionals.

The last chapter, by Fiedler, concerns the extremely important area of professionals advocating for parents. Despite legislation that has created a role for parent involvement, the research reveals rather limited parent participation in educational programs and life planning for their handicapped child. Fiedler's framework for parent advocacy is education oriented and includes procedures for assisting parents to achieve fuller participation in their child's educational life.

It is hoped that this book will substantially influence its readers to use their own creativity and initiative on behalf of a productive parent–professional partnership. Long after a given professional has terminated contact with the parents, those parents will continue to be involved in the life of their handicapped or exceptional child. Each of us needs to view our contribution as part of a continuity of sensitive and caring parent–professional involvement that supports the empowerment of parents.

Marvin J. Fine

SECTION ▌

The Family and Exceptionality

1

THE HANDICAPPED CHILD AND THE FAMILY: IMPLICATIONS FOR PROFESSIONALS

Marvin J. Fine

A substantial increase in parent participation in the education and care of handicapped children has come about in the last several decades. These changes have occurred as a result of trends such as deinstitutionalization and in relation to significant legislation affecting the care and treatment of handicapped individuals (Newman, 1983; Peterson & Cooper, 1989; Simpson & Fiedler, 1989). Considerable parent efforts have occurred over the years to influence national policy and community attitudes toward the handicapped. Public Law 94-142 (Education for All Handicapped Children Act), which has been in existence since 1975, and the more recent P.L. 99-457, which essentially extends services to younger children with a substantial emphasis on parental participation, offer greater assurance that handicapped children will receive appropriate educational services and that their parents will be actively involved.

There is evidence, however, that the dream of effective and comprehensive services for all handicapped children and the active inclusion of their parents has not yet been realized (Simpson & Fiedler, 1989; Turnbull & Leonard, 1981; Yoshida, Fenton, Kaufman & Maxwell, 1978). Many problems have surfaced related to parent involvement. The point has even been made that policy makers' ideas on parent involvement may miss the realities of parental readiness or preference for involvement and that a different way of looking at parental involvement is needed (Turnbull & Turnbull, 1982). It is recognition of the value of parent involvement on behalf of the handicapped child, along with the awareness of recurrent problems in parent involvement, that has prompted the preparation of this book.

This chapter will focus on the implications for parents, families, and involved professional persons of the presence of a handicapped child in the family. There are a number of specific issues for professionals related to the manner in which they work with parents; this chapter will include a description of a model of collaborative involvement that can serve as a framework for professionals who are convinced that it is appropriate for parents to be empowered to work effectively on behalf of their own children.

Professional persons who do not have an adequate frame of reference may be inclined to "sniff out" pathology in families of handicapped children. This inclination may be based on several factors, including misconceptions regarding the impact of a handicapped child on the family, unfamiliarity or even a sense of alienation with the positive image of parents working on behalf of their handicapped child, and an inadequate understanding regarding normal family functioning. As has been pointed out by a number of authors, it is not the existence of stress within a family that constitutes dysfunctionality, it is the manner in which the family organizes itself, over time, to cope with stressful events (Lewis, 1986; McCubbin & Figley, 1983; Selye, 1974).

With these observations in mind, the first section of this chapter will be a discussion of families and how they function; this should offer the reader a background against which to understand the nature of parental response to and involvement with a handicapped individual in the family.

What Are Families and How Do They Function?

Although there are numerous definitions of the family, from a pragmatic point of view a family seems to be a collection of individuals who are connected to each other by blood ties or strong emotionality and who, for the most part though not under all circumstances, reside together (e.g., a child off to college is still considered to be a member of that family). The nuclear family is understood as the parents and children in the home setting, with the extended family including relatives and others of very close emotional ties who are probably outside of the home and may transcend different generations. It is more common now to think in terms of blended or reconstituted families, given the frequency of remarriages that include "yours," "mine," and "ours." By the year 2000, it is estimated that the majority of families will involve some kind of "reconstruction" (Glick & Lin, 1986).

These observations may have projected a stereotyped view of the two-parent, middle-class family. Indeed, Foster, Berger, and McLean (1981) have criticized existing conceptual models of parent involvement because they assume the prevalence of two-parent families, mother having a primary child-care rather than employment role, and father eager to be involved in community activities. The divorce figures make it evident that there will be many single-parent families, and the economic realities speak to the frequent necessity of both parents or the single parent working. Single-parent families are more likely to experience financial hardship than two-parent families.

Also, there are a growing number of couples who prefer to establish careers and an adequate income before having children. The implications of having a handicapped child for a couple in their late 30s, planning to have only one child, may be quite different from those affecting a family with two "normal" children whose third child has a handicap. A handicapped child will have a different impact on a family with financial resources to access private services, to employ support caretakers, and to allow the parent(s) time for vacations than on a family of more limited finances.

Several aspects of family functioning will be discussed, followed by a family analysis questionnaire for the reader.

The Family as a System

It is important to understand the family as a system and the reciprocal impact of persons within a family. The essence of the family as a "system" is that persons establish roles and relationships and grow, develop, and change in interaction with each other. Any change in the family, whether it be a teenager starting to drive or the presence of a handicapped child, will have an impact on the family. Seldom is it "business as usual" for family members when changes occur in another part of the family. Families have rules; communication, affection, and power patterns; and ways of dealing with problems and stress. A handicapped child is not just an issue for the parents, but has an impact throughout the family system, influencing, for example, economics, vacations, social relationships, and family satisfaction, among other areas. It is encouraging to see the literature on handicapped children assuming more of a family systems perspective (Bailey & Simeonsson, 1988; Foster, 1988; Foster et al., 1981; Seligman & Darling, 1989; Simpson & Fiedler, 1989; Turnbull, Summers, & Brotherson, 1986; Turnbull & Turnbull, 1986).

Ethnic/Cultural Considerations

A family is rooted in a matrix of influences and traditions, including of course the ethnic/cultural background of that family. The traditions influencing parent–child relationships and values within the family of a first-generation Japanese-American family are likely to vary considerably from those of a more "typical" middle-class American family. Ethnicity is an important consideration in understanding the dynamics of a particular family (McGoldrick, Pearce, & Giordano, 1982). As an example germane to the theme of this book, in some cultures the event of a handicapped infant is considered to mean that the family has been somehow cursed or victimized (see Correa and Weismantel, Chapt. 5).

In some instances cultural values make it easier for a family to accommodate a handicapped child. Winton (1988a) observed that, "The values of some cultures encourage passivity and ascribe events to fate or outside uncontrollable sources. For these families, a simple acceptance of the handicapped child may be their natural response; reliance on outside help may be minimal" (p. 313).

Along with particular culturally based perceptions of handicapped conditions, some groups may feel more insulated and self-protective regarding opening up to outsiders. A strong "we-they" attitude might persist that can affect help seeking and help acceptance. This is not to say that such group members will not accept help, but rather that the involved professionals need to be aware of such cultural or ethnic values and to proceed in an appropriate way. Special efforts at relationship building and the development of trust may be necessary before the parents willingly ask for help or follow directions.

The ignoring of or insensitivity to such cultural/ethnic considerations by professionals can impair the relationship with the parents and reinforce negative stereotypes. The family may become more convinced that "others" don't understand them, and the professional may confirm the suspicion that "those people" reject services.

Life Cycle Considerations

Families also reflect a life cycle, and this should be understood by any professional person interacting with that family (Carter & McGoldrick, 1980; Foster et al., 1981). Consider the "young" family composed of husband and wife in their 20s, attempting to establish an economic base and career direction. Children often arrive in the context of the parents trying to move forward as well as just cope economically with the demands on the young family. As the children grow older, so of course do the parents, and their needs and aspirations become modified by the realities of their lives; all the while the children are learning and developing within the microsystem of the family as well as in contact, progressively so, with outside influences such as school and community.

It is not unusual at some point in time to see a family extended over a range of age and developmental positions, including, for example, a preschool child and an elementary child. In a matter of years the same family may have a child at the secondary level and a child already moving out of the home into young adulthood. The parents by this time have usually grown into that status referred to as "middle age" and are dealing with related personal, social, and economic issues.

One observation of the impact of a handicapped child in the family is that the maturation of the family unit can become slowed (Farber, 1959). When families without a handicapped child reach a point of greater individual independence, the family with a handicapped child may be behaving as if it still had a young, dependent child.

The importance of family life cycle considerations for professionals cannot be overstated. One can only fully appreciate the implications of the handicapped child by being aware of the family context and how the perceived demands or responsibilities of that child interface with the ongoing development and functioning of the family.

Boundaries and Hierarchies

The term *boundary* refers to the delineation of roles and relationships within a family that seem necessary in order to have a functional unit. The term boundary also implies that there are subsystems within the family that are differentiated from each other (Minuchin & Fishman, 1981). For example, we can conceptualize a parent subsystem and a child subsystem having a different hierarchical status within a family. The parent subsystem subsumes certain roles and responsibilities including, or course, the leadership function and protection function for the family. The parent role can be expanded to include many tasks, from assuring the economic survival of the family to the imparting of values and all the other elements that go into the raising of children. The child subsystem is differentiated in terms of power, authority, and responsibility, although as children become older they would assume more prerogatives as they move toward maturity and independence.

In instances where parents are unsure of themselves in their parenting role, it is not unusual to find one of the children becoming a "parental child" and assuming more power than is really appropriate. We can think of parental over- or underfunctioning as contributing toward children who are implicitly and explicitly encouraged to take on a parental role versus children who are held back from progressing in relation to normal increases of responsibility and decision making within the family. The demands on the family of caretaking a handicapped child might move the normal siblings into a more responsible role than would otherwise occur. Such added responsibilities might be accepted well by the siblings and even contribute toward greater family solidarity. In some instances the siblings may want to expand their responsibilities into other areas of decision making that challenge parental authority ("If I'm old enough to take care of Susy while you run errands, I'm old enough to decide who my friends are!").

Healthy, functional, or strong families have reasonably clear boundaries and lines of authority. There is some flexibility to accommodate changes and shifts as children grow, but there remains a clear executive, leadership position for the parents. Especially at times of stress, the parents are able to work together to support each other and to serve as models for and give support to the rest of the family.

Single parenting and other parenting configurations present some challenges to the development of appropriate boundaries. These considerations are discussed in Chapter 3.

Enmeshment-Disengagement

Families can reveal considerable differences in the degree of emotional close-ness versus distance among family members (Minuchin & Fishman, 1981; Minuchin, Rosman, & Baker, 1978). Some families have a very strong "we" nature, where everyone is expected to behave and think and feel in certain ways. In these instances, a whole range of forces are exercised within the family to ensure that this happens. It may be difficult for siblings of the handicapped child to express their frustrations or resentments because of the family value of "we accept and love the handicapped child." The sibling may grow in resentment and feel alienated within the family.

Children growing up in enmeshed families may fail to achieve reasonable differentiation from the family; this is exemplified by the kinds of shared and overlapping decision making that occur and the ways in which family or parental approval is constantly sought. Even after the children reach a point at which one would expect them to be functioning somewhat more autonomously, their emotional binds/bonds to the nuclear family are so great as to extend into their attempts to function as an adult in terms of establishing a home and family. Achieving a functional adulthood requires the person to adequately differentiate self from the family of origin; emotional enmeshment can be understood as interfering with this necessary differentiation.

Some family members may disengage from the family as a way of achieving some degree of independence. In instances where a sibling of the handicapped child might feel overwhelmed by the responsibilities he or she was forced to assume, the sibling might seek ways of separating emotionally from the family.

There should be a certain amount of warm connectedness within families to allow children to internalize values and to develop a sense of being a part of the unit. As children increase in their maturity and capacity to reason, there should be opportunities allocated for them to differentiate themselves appropriately from the family and to gain a greater sense of individuality.

Intimacy and Communication

Although both intimacy and communication have been dealt with extensively by writers on family structure and style, it seems that there are close parallels between these two factors (Roman & Raley, 1980; Stinnett & DeFrain, 1989). That is, families that are characterized by a high degree of intimacy in the forms of caring and positive feeling for each other that are expressed, also have fairly effective communication patterns. This seems to follow logically. It would be difficult to think of many situations in which there is a high degree of intimacy without a reasonably high degree of communication among the family members.

There are instances where parents feel very strongly in their love for their children, but yet their style of communication is one of holding back from tangible expressions of those feelings. In these families where one holds back expressing feelings, even physically, there is likely to be a reticence to talk about one's feelings and concerns; this can lead to a blunting or limiting of expressing empathy and sensitivity to the feelings and inner psychological life of the other person.

In a family where the parents model and children develop reasonably open and intimate patterns of communication, it is easier for the family to cope with normal crises as they might arise. In families that are characterized by limited or inadequate communication, there is no background to draw upon as readily to talk about and understand some new event impacting on the family, such as a handicapped child. There is greater potential for persons to feel confused, scared, or alienated when family members are unable to deal openly and supportively with the new events.

Some Thoughts for Professionals

These aspects of family functioning that have been touched on only briefly are some ways in which families can be differentiated. It is important for professionals to keep in mind that many families may be equipped, by way of family structure and functioning, including affectional ties, communication, and problem-solving skills, to cope adequately with most crises including those presented by a handicapped child.

Other families, already conflicted or marginal in adjustment, may react more destructively under stress. Such families may not have developed the kinds of dynamics that can tolerate increased stress. In these vulnerable or marginally functional families, the presence of a handicapped child is more likely to precipitate personal catastrophic reactions including divorce or separation, alienation of family members, and other severe emotional and behavioral reactions.

It is additionally important for professionals to acknowledge that while the presence of the handicapped child brings special stresses to a family, no family is exempt from experiencing stress. The Social Readjustment Rating Scale (Holmes & Rahe, 1967) is an index of stress that individuals or families might experience. It seems that almost any kind of change has a stress value to it. The breadwinner being fired is certainly stressful, but achieving a promotion can also be quite stressful. When we talk about stress and adaptation in the family, we are not talking about the absence of stress but the family's historic ways of mobilizing itself and its resources to cope with stressful events.

The handicapped child's impact on a family and the implications for professionals will be subsequently discussed in more detail. But before moving on to the next section, which will focus more specifically on the handicapped child in the family, there is a useful exercise the reader can complete. The following questions provide an opportunity for you to analyze your own family background. This activity can enhance your appreciation of the rich variations across families, enabling you to develop a broader perspective on how families function.

Family Analysis Questionnaire

1. Describe your family's cultural/ethnic background. What family values, behaviors, attitudes, and customs have been handed down?
2. What was happening in your family at the time of your birth (e.g., economic status, membership, housing, employment)?
3. What was the significance of your birth (e.g., long-awaited child, financial burden, etc.)?
4. What role(s) did you assume within your family as compared to other persons (e.g., the studious child, the bad child, etc.)?
5. What subgroups existed in your family and how clear were the boundaries (e.g., parent subsystem–child subsystem, older vs. younger children, etc.)?
6. What rules (implicit and explicit) existed in your family?
7. What alliances existed and how did they shift (e.g., mother and son vs. father on discipline, mother and father vs. daughter on school issues)?
8. How and by whom were decisions made (e.g., money, child management, vacations)?
9. How was affection expressed (physically, verbally, by whom, to whom, etc.)?
10. What kinds and patterns of communication existed? (Were there family secrets?)
11. In what ways and in what areas were you and your siblings able or unable to establish independence or interdependence?
12. How did your family connect and interact with the extended family?
13. How did your family connect and interact with the community?
14. How was spirituality or religiosity treated in the family? (Was there active church affiliation?)
15. How did family patterns shift as the children got older?
16. Were there characteristic ways that your family responded to crises? (You can organize your thoughts around specific crises.)
17. How do you think your family would have reacted to a handicapped child? You might speculate in terms of which child (oldest or youngest), and the nature and severity of the handicap.

The Impact of the Exceptional Child

The foregoing section on families presented a systemic view—that of persons reciprocally interacting, affecting others, and being affected by others—of people assuming roles and relationships, and all of this happening against the background of individual and family development, life cycle, and ethnic considerations. The point was made that historical family patterns include ways of responding and coping with stressful events; also, some families are precariously balanced in terms of their functionality so that a particularly stressful event can unbalance the family. It is in consideration of this range of background information and concepts that professionals can develop a sensitive and sympathetic understanding of the reciprocal impact of handicapped/exceptional children in the family.

The research literature can be extremely useful in depicting "typical" patterns or effects of certain events, but research findings can also lead us into generalizations where "believing is seeing." It is also important to note that in many studies on the effects of a handicapped child on the family there has been difficulty with research methodology (Foster, 1988; Foster & Berger, 1985). Examples of such problems would include studies without adequate control groups, studies that focused on a wide range of ages (which increases the difficulty in generalizing results to a single age group or degree of severity), examining parental responses rather than looking at family dynamics, and ignoring some of the considerations that might mediate the effects that the parents experience.

Awareness of research limitations should support a cautious stance in concretely applying specific findings to "all parents." Parents in fact respond differentially and uniquely to their situations. There may be enough similarities to give us some sense of anticipation and to sharpen our sensitivities, but as professionals we need to remain open to the individuality of each situation.

We will now consider two questions that are often of concern to professionals working with parents and families, followed by a discussion of intervention implications.

Are There Stages Parents Go Through on Learning of Their Child's "Handicap"?

Blacher (1984) reviewed the literature on parental reactions and concluded that there is a general pattern of parental adaptability to the handicapped child, but individual family differences also exist. One of her concerns was with the methodological problems of studying parental reactions that can lead to different conclusions. Of great importance, however, were the mediating considerations. For example, there may be dramatically different implications for a single-parent versus a two-parent family (Schilling, Kirkham, Snow, & Schinke, 1986; see also Fish, Chapt. 3). The availability of two parents to support each other emotionally and physically paints a more viable picture of functionality than a single parent struggling with the logistics of family life, employment, and what may be the added demands of a handicapped child. The presence of normal children and the solidity of the marital relationship as mentioned earlier also become factors influencing the impact on the parent and in turn the parent's response to the child. The observation of the importance of the strength of the marital relationship in the family's positive adaptation to a handicapped child was again underscored in a recent research report by Trute and Hauch (1988).

In some instances the etiology of the child's handicap and condition is clearly established and in many other instances it is only inferred. The parents may vary in terms of their sense of personal responsibility and accountability for the child's condition depending on what they learn and have been told. For example, a mother who was deliberately abusing drugs which seems to have resulted in the development of a birth defect may respond differently to the subsequent birth of the handicapped child than a parent for whom either the cause is not known or the cause was somehow considered to be outside of the parent's control.

Numerous other factors can mediate parental reaction to a handicapped child, including religiosity (Zuk, 1959), severity of the problem (Fewell & Gelb, 1983; Grossman, 1972), socioeconomic level (Hampson, Hulgus, Beavers, & Beavers, 1988), and, most important, the family's support network (Dunst, Trivette, & Cross, 1986; Kazak, 1986). And of course there are the important ethnic/cultural and life cycle influences discussed earlier.

With these considerations in mind, to conclude that all parents go through some common sequence such as denial, anger, bargaining, depression, and finally acceptance (Huber, 1979) or shock, denial, sadness/anger/anxiety, adaptation, and finally reorganization (Drotar, Baskiewicz, Irvin, Kennell, & Klaus, 1975) may miss the uniqueness of a given family.

It may be more useful for a professional to anticipate that there will indeed be some process that family members will go through in their attempts to come to terms with the events, but that there will likely be individual family variations. The professional's ability to listen, explore, and interact with the family members will be necessary in order for that person to appreciate the family's process of adaptation and where individual families are in that process. A danger is that the professional may conclude that the family or family members are "stuck" at a hypothetical point in the adaptation process; in fact, different family members may be involved in their own idiosyncratic way of progressing through a process.

Is Acceptance the Endpoint of the Process of Family Adjustment?

One of the problematic notions of the stages of adjustment view of looking at families is that some idealized acceptance stage is often implicitly if not explicitly promoted as where healthy families should end up. The literature, however, suggests that "chronic sorrow" (Olshansky, 1962; Searle, 1978; Wikler, Wasow,

& Hatfield, 1981) is not unusual, and reflects the family's continued need to adapt to changes in circumstances. Although the parents may move from some shock or grief position to a more proactive and adaptive position, there will be many life events and transitions that prompt the parents to reappraise the child's limitations and to again come to terms with what is and what may never be.

Consider the hypothetical situation of parents with a preschool developmentally handicapped child. Their initial concerns on behalf of the child relate to determining and then acquiring appropriate educational and developmental experiences for that child. Within several years there will be the transition from community to school services with a host of new issues surrounding the transition. Because of the mandates under which public schools must operate to serve handicapped children, the labeling process becomes more explicit and categorical. Parents who may have adapted to notions of "developmental delays" even with implications of retardation are now going to face a whole new set of diagnostic and placement criteria, some of which may appear to be in conflict with their earlier understanding of the child's handicap (Peterson & Cooper, 1989). This also means that the child is now going to a different setting with new issues around transportation and time management.

As the child enters adolescence, questions related to sexuality often arise. What normal leeway should the adolescent be allowed in dating and socializing, and when do the parents need to assume a more controlling, supervisory stance? How does sexual information get communicated to the child (Wallis, Chapt. 15)? Eventually the child's transition from a public school setting into the community by way of field-based training or sheltered workshop types of facilities may arise, and, for a number of handicapped children, the question of whether they will ever be able to function independently in the community looms prominent (Levinson and McKee, Chapt. 16). With most handicapping conditions, as the child gets older there is a need for parents progressively to "let go." And as the handicapped child becomes less central in the lives of the parents, they may have to face some relationship issues they were able to avoid earlier because of the constant focus on the handicapped child.

This brief review of some developmental and educational milestones was meant to underscore that there are a number of recurring points at which the parents will have to confront the handicapped child's limitations, as well as capabilities, and work with the child and school and community persons in aspects of life planning. On these occasions the parents may find themselves struggling again with feelings of sadness or grief over the realities of the child's condition as compared to what the parents hoped and wished for at different times. This way of viewing the extended periods of adjustment and readjustment has argued for a continuum of services over the life span of the handicapped individual (Werth & Oseroff, 1987; Wikler et al., 1981).

Professionals in Their Contacts with Parents

A starting point for professionals is not to assume automatically that parents are "pathological," overwhelmed, or inadequate. As mentioned earlier, there is a growing body of literature that presents fairly positive findings on how many families are responding to the experience of raising a handicapped child (Hampson et al., 1988; Kazak & Marvin, 1984; Longo & Bond, 1984; Palfrey, Walker, Butler, & Singer, 1989; Trute & Hauch, 1988). Longo and Bond (1984) completed their extensive review of the literature with the observation that there is

> . . . sufficient evidence to suggest that more optimistic attitudes and frameworks can be employed when working with families of handicapped children. Overall, many families cope adequately with the added complications of the disabled member; marriages are not necessarily torn apart by the presence of a chronically ill child nor do parents automatically become dysfunctional under these circumstances. (p. 64)

Widerstrom and Dudley-Marling (1986) reviewed the literature on living with a handicapped child in terms of what they felt were some myths possibly held by professionals. Their findings were similar to those of Longo and Bond in supporting the conclusions that families of handicapped individuals seem to be managing much better than some of the early literature would have predicted. Their concern is that professionals who interact with families from a negative anticipation may in different ways interfere with the family's progress. They go on to state that:

> If, on the other hand, families are generally seen as capable of dealing effectively with the stress of having a handicapped child, it is more likely that the prophecy will self-fulfill and good adjustment will result. (Widerstrom & Dudley-Marling, p. 366)

The presence of a support network also becomes a frequently noted major mediating factor in how the parents respond to the potential stress of raising the handicapped child (Dunst et al., 1986; Kazak, 1986; Trute & Hauch, 1988). There may be a need for some parents to seek and or develop a support system. Professionals can be a helpful resource in identifying existing support groups, community services, and organizations that the parent can contact.

Rubin and Quinn-Curran (1983) have written on institutional impediments that parents will often confront, and the nature of professionals' biases has been described by many authors (Darling, 1983; Swap, 1984); it seems apparent that the "helping" systems can in some instances become a major source of stress on parents and the family. Parents who "scout out" different options for services may be seen as shopping for more optimistic feedback, rather than attempting to represent the best interests of the child and family. The view by professionals of assertive parents as "aggressive," "disturbed," or "overemotionally involved" may again discount the legitimate role of a parent.

Professionals unfamiliar with the life cycle aspects of the handicapped individual and family might not appreciate the sadness that often recurs as parents have to work with the child and the "system" in relation to new developmental or social milestones. Parents might be seen as "stuck" at some point in the hypothesized process of adaptation, without regard for the often cyclical nature of the adaptation process, and in relation to the manner in which the family organizes itself regarding the handicapped individual.

The data on siblings also seem to be somewhat problematic; there is documentation of siblings benefiting or at least not being notably negatively affected by the presence of a handicapped child, as well as research that presents the normal sibling experiencing difficulties. Perhaps the best way for professionals to consider the questions regarding the siblings of handicapped children is, as Hannah and Midlarsky (1985, 1987) suggest, to consider them as potentially at risk for some problems within the family, but not to make the automatic assumption that there must be problems. There certainly will be instances in which parents can benefit from examining the demands on normal siblings, whether the family has become overly focused on the exceptional child, and how everyone in the family can work together to get their needs met.

It is interesting how in families without a handicapped individual we find any number of instances where one child might believe that the parents favor another child, or that parental expectations of different children in the family are unfair, etc. These occurrences are often dealt with by the parents by talking it out and examining how in fact different children are being treated. For the most part we can understand these concerns from a normal, developmental, sibling rivalry point of view without being concerned about family dysfunctionality. But given the family of a handicapped child, professionals may be inclined to look at the same kinds of complaints by the normal child in a very different light. These observations again underscore the need for the professional to have a "normal family" frame of reference so as not to pathologize certain events.

A recent study by Palfrey et al. (1989) involved interviews with parents of 1,726 special education students. To the authors' surprise, the majority of parents did not report any particular stress because of the handicapped child. The authors, while wondering about parental denial, also considered that many parents might have reached a reasonable point of acceptance and had learned how to cope adequately with the child's disability.

The Palfrey et al. study did break down parental reports of stress in relation to numerous variables. The prior mention that the majority of parents did not report any particular stress was not meant as a "whitewash" of the potential stressful effects of raising a handicapped child. For example, 63% of the parents of children with physical/multiple handicaps reported relatively more stress on the family, whereas only 23% of parents of children with speech or learning problems reported family stress. Also, parents with a higher educational background reported more stress than parents of lower educational and socioeconomic backgrounds. The area of marital satisfaction was least affected of all the domains that were considered.

Those parents experiencing stress could benefit from a range of counseling, educational, and support programs. The authors felt that greater involvement by parents in their children's educational program enhanced their sense of empowerment. Professionals may need to develop new strategies to promote greater parental participation and also need to become more involved with families to understand better the specific sources of stress and how to assist those families.

A sensitive and comprehensive interview with parents can help to identify specific sources of stress as well as family needs (Seligman & Darling, 1989; Turnbull & Turnbull, 1986; Winton, 1988b). Although checklists and rating scales can be useful, the involved professionals should consider a follow-up interview to explore indicated areas of stress or concern, as well as to encourage discussion of concerns not identified on the instruments. Most important, the professional should be prepared to identify strengths that can be incorporated into subsequent collaborative intervention efforts. There are also checklists and rating scales available for parents to complete that can reveal areas of concern, stress, and need (Bailey, 1988; Holroyd, 1987; Seligman & Darling, 1989).

Normal family considerations can assist the involved professionals in maintaining a perspective on the family with a handicapped member. Concepts of healthy family functioning can also precipitate some directions for professionals to move with specific families. Families who have become excessively enmeshed around the handicapped child may need help in "loosening up," involving others in the child care picture, and reaching for social support. Siblings may have been moved into inappropriate roles by way of becoming "parental," and the family might benefit from a clearer demarcation of subsystem boundaries.

Increased communication about the handicapped person within the family may be helpful to all family members and can encourage a diminishment of secrets and stigma associated with the handicapped person. Open communication can help family members to learn that their various reactions are normal and appropriate.

More community support services are becoming available in the forms of library materials, parent discussion groups, and individual, family, and group counseling. Assisting parents and families to assess their needs and to seek out appropriate services and resources becomes an important focus for the involved professionals.

Palfrey et al. (1989) observed that the past decade has witnessed a greater emphasis on individualizing approaches to handicapped children and their families. These authors believe that individualization, which includes an appreciation of the needs and characteristics of a given family, can lead to a fuller use of human services programs. Such individualization is consistent with the theme of this book, that of productive collaboration by professionals with parents of handicapped children.

A Collaborative Model of Parent Involvement

When helping professionals such as mental health workers and educators relate with parents of exceptional children, the potential is present for those interactions to serve an educative and strengthening function for the parents in terms of their developing capacity to act on behalf of their children. But the professional's beliefs about the parents' capacity to help themselves can influence perceptions and behaviors and strongly affect the helping relationship for better or worse (Brickman et al., 1982).

The collaborative model being proposed represents a frame of reference that can guide mental health professionals and educators in their contacts with parents of exceptional individuals. The model represents a value stance and conveys a positive view of parent involvement including some important perceptions of potential parental competency and effectiveness. A number of writers have influenced the conceptualization of the proposed model, and their works can serve as helpful resources to the reader (Bailey & Simeonsson, 1988; Dunst et al., 1986; Ehly, Conoley, & Rosenthal, 1985; Seligman & Darling, 1989; Simpson & Fiedler, 1989; Turnbull & Turnbull, 1986).

There are four main objectives to the collaborative model of parent involvement; these can be acted out creatively and with varying emphases by the involved professional persons. The four objectives are:

1. To include parents in decision making regarding their exceptional child;
2. To educate parents for participation in the decision-making process regarding their exceptional child;
3. To assist parents therapeutically as needed so they will be better able to cope with specific issues that may be impeding their participation regarding their exceptional child; and
4. To enable and empower parents to work actively on behalf of their exceptional child.

Functional Aspects of the Model

The model should prove useful and applicable for professionals working in different contexts with parents; however, it is probably most effectively implemented by professional persons who view themselves operating out of a flexible, consultative orientation. Several functional aspects of the model will be discussed.

1. *The model initially represents an existential stance that the helping professional can take toward parents.* There are likely to be a set of attitudes and attributes that any professional will process in relation to parents of exceptional individuals that represents a kind of worldview. When professionals respond to parents as potential partners and collaborators, a different set of attitudes, expectations, and behaviors on the part of the professional exist than when parents are seen as overly emotionally involved, adversaries, or patients. Different "messages" are likely to be sent and received by the parents and responded to in various ways.

Being on the receiving end of somebody's negative attributions is not a particularly pleasant experience and may precipitate a hostile reaction or, perhaps even worse, convince the parents of their inadequacies. The helping professional can be a significant person in the life of parents and, as such, can strongly influence the parents' concept of self as someone who can participate actively and responsibly on behalf of their child.

2. *The model is developmental* in the sense that it recognizes that parents may not be prepared for full collaborative participation at any point in time, but can be assisted toward greater future involvement. The important element here is that parents not be viewed in some kind of static and unchangeable posture, but as persons who are capable of expanding their understanding and skills. This position leads logically to the next aspect of the model.

3. *The model is proactive* in its recognition that activities may need to occur that can help the parents move toward greater participatory capabilities in the future. These activities, while often prompted at the time of a problem or crisis, should be more a part of the ongoing relationship between the helping professional and parents so that parents are assisted toward greater readiness to deal with the range of needs and issues that may subsequently arise. The proactive aspect of the model can focus on three areas: educational, therapeutic, and organizational.

The *educational* dimension relates to the input of needed information as well as the training of specific skills. The skills can focus on many areas from child management issues to more effective communication within the family or between the parents or even to specific preparations for parent participation in staffing or IEP meetings.

The *therapeutic* dimension occurs as professionals assist parents in processing and understanding their feelings and experiences. The broad goals of the therapeutic dimension are to support the parents in working through whatever personal issues may exist in relation to the child and helping them gain a greater sense of objectivity and awareness in the parenting role.

The *organizational* dimension recognizes the social support needs of parents both in terms of their own emotional well-being and also as a vehicle for organizing parental efforts on behalf of exceptional children. The notion of networking is extremely important, and it has been demonstrated that parents working together are able to construct organizational vehicles that can serve them and their children well. Examples of such organizational vehicles are clearinghouses for information on community resources, identification of individuals who can assist with specific kinds of parental problems such as estate planning, and the development of advocacy, planning, or educational programs.

4. *The model is family-ecologically oriented* in its sensitivity to implications of the family constellation and the day-to-day realities of the parents living with an exceptional or handicapped child. For example, advising parents "to get out and relax" without regard for the difficulties in finding a sitter for a severely and multiply handicapped child may miss an important point in the parents' reality. This especially becomes the case when we are dealing with a single-parent situation.   *parents ←→ organizations*

The model recognizes that the parents may need help in problem solving a number of family issues in order for them to be able to enact a decision such as taking time for themselves. What are the baby-sitter problems, financial issues, as well as the attitudes toward child care that impede or support the parents' ability to take time for themselves? What are the implications of decisions on other family members? For example, how are older siblings used and what is the impact of the baby-sitting requirements on sibling-family relationships?

Tied in with the notion that there is a broad ecology within which the parents and child interact is awareness of the importance of parents developing an appreciation of institutional issues. For example, it may be necessary to help parents increase their sensitivity to teacher needs such as for appropriate planning time and time for in-service and emotional renewal experiences.

5. *The model requires multiple roles on the part of the helping professional.* As stated earlier, a consultative stance can represent a useful orientation for the professional in affording the flexibility to pursue a range of activities selectively. As an example, in instances where the parent and school might be experiencing some conflict, the helping professional could assume the role of *mediator* and arrange some sessions that involve the parents and school personnel.

There may also be a need for the professional to take a more *advocacy-oriented* stance by way of contributing educational and training inputs so that the parents can be better able to confront school personnel or to participate in planning meetings. From a *therapeutic* stance, the professional may at times feel it appropriate to schedule sessions with one or both parents, possibly siblings, or even the whole family, in order to help them deal with different issues. And finally, there may be a need for the helping professional to assume the role of *expert* by way of giving specific information, opinions, or recommendations.

Assuming these multiple roles has the potential of precipitating role confusion on the part of the helping professional with concomitant loss of objectivity and neutrality. In a sense there are always such dangers for professionals when they assume a caring and helping attitude toward a client. When mental health professionals are aware they will be assuming multiple roles, they can be more aware of how the roles are shifting and can even communicate explicitly to the parents about role shifts. The more open and direct the relationship can be, the less likely it is that there will be confusion or misperceptions.

6. *The model promotes a constructive and positive stance* rather than an adversarial one with side-taking that can lead to a polarization of positions. This constructive and positive stance not only reflects the helping professional's relationship with the parents of exceptional children, but also speaks to the kind of view that the model attempts to promote in those parents in their dealings with other professionals and agencies.

This focus on the positive will require certain skills on the part of the professional including the most important skill of being able to reframe events in a positive and constructive light. This kind of stance encourages people to work together, to see each other as contributors, and to engage in networking and group planning.

7. *The model has a problem-solving emphasis.* The energy direction in the interaction between the helping professional and parents is on such questions as "What can we do now?" and "Where do we go from here?" Some parents may have a litany of complaints against the systems with which they have had to deal. Although the parents may need to be heard and to have their feelings and thoughts validated, the helping professional should avoid supporting the parents' obsessing or remaining fixated at the level of complaint or hurt. One of the easiest ways to resolve a person's old complaints and hurts is to do something about them. From this position the focus is more constructively on "what can be" rather than on "what should have been."

Also, this approach to problem solving ought to be more than just an attempt to push people into action. It should involve some step-by-step thinking along the lines of setting goals or objectives, evaluating resources, deciding what steps need to be taken and what other logistical issues have to be dealt with, determining who else needs to be involved in what ways, and, finally, establishing a reasonably concrete timeline for activity. Opportunities for evaluation, feedback, and processing also need to be built into an effective problem-solving approach.

8. *The model views parents as teachers as well as learners.* Collaboration implies that people not only work together in a mutually supportive fashion but that they teach and learn from each other. Many assumptions that professionals hold about what is best for the child or how the parents can accomplish a particular goal need to be checked out with the parents. The parents may have learned how to deal with specific child management or training issues in different and creative ways. The professional community has much to learn from parents who live day to day with a handicapped child and have had to cope over time with the child in home and school as well as with the "helping" service bureaucracies.

Many professionals who are eager to advise others such as parents of a handicapped child would do well to listen and observe carefully before recommending other strategies or approaches to a problem situation. What the professional sees as a problem may not be one for the parents; what the parents believe to be a problem is one for the parents. A collaborative partnership requires a valuing of the beliefs and perceptions of parents by professionals, and an appreciation of the parents' insights, ideas, and experiences with the handicapped child.

Summary

This chapter has approached the handicapped child in the family from the perspective of the need of involved professionals to (a) understand normal family development, (b) appreciate individual variations among families with a handicapped member, and (c) develop a collaborative orientation to working with parents and families. There is documentation of professionals, through attitudes and beliefs, impeding the active and proactive participation by parents in the care and education of their handicapped child.

The literature has become progressively more optimistic about parents being able to cope satisfactorily with a handicapped child. Parent involvement continues to receive legislated support, although it is acknowledged that individual parents may need assistance in learning how to be effectively involved. The rights of parents to limit formal involvement in certain programs also need to be accepted and appreciated by professionals. After all, not every parent of "normal" children is enthusiastic about attending school functions and parent–teacher conferences or serving on parent advisory, curriculum, or school policy committees.

We may be approaching a new era of awareness and response to the needs of handicapped individuals and their families. It is hoped that helping professionals such as psychologists, social workers, psychiatrists, counselors, rehabilitation personnel, and educators will assume leadership roles rather than acting out less positive or more adversarial roles.

References

Bailey, D. B. (1988). Assessing family stress and needs. In D.B. Bailey & R. J. Simeonsson (Eds.), *Family assessment in early intervention* (pp. 95-118). Columbus, OH: Merrill.

Bailey, D. B., & Simeonsson, R. J. (1988). *Family assessment in early intervention.* Columbus, OH: Merrill.

Blacher, J. (1984). Sequential stages of parental adjustment to the birth of a child with handicaps: Fact or artifact? *Mental Retardation, 22,* 55-68.

Brickman, P., Rabinowitz, V., Karuza, J., Coates, D., Cohn, E., & Kidder, L. (1982). Models of helping and coping. *American Psychologist, 37,* 368-384.

Carter, E., & McGoldrick, M. (1980). *The family life cycle: A framework for family therapy.* New York: Gardner Press.

Darling, R. B. (1983). Parent-professional interaction: The roots of misunderstanding. In M. Seligman (Ed.), *The family with a handicapped child* (pp. 95-121). Orlando, FL: Grune & Stratton.

Drotar, D., Baskiewicz, A., Irvin, N., Kennell, J., & Klaus, M. (1975). The adaptation of parents to the birth of an infant with congenital malformation: A hypothetical model. *Pediatrics, 56,* 710-717.

Dunst, C. J., Trivette, C. M., & Cross, A. (1986). Mediating influences of social support: Personal, family, and child outcomes. *American Journal of Mental Deficiency, 90,* 403-417.

Dyson, L., & Fewell, R. R. (1986). Stress and adaptation in parents of young handicapped and nonhandicapped children: A comparative study. *Journal of the Division of Early Childhood Education, 10,* 25-35.

Ehly, S., Conoley, J., & Rosenthal, D. (1985). *Working with parents of exceptional children.* St. Louis, MO: Mosby.

Farber, B. (1959). Effects of a severely mentally retarded child on family integration. *Monographs of the Society for Research in Child Development, 24* (Whole no. 71).

Fewell, R. R., & Gelb, S. A. (1983). Parenting moderately handicapped persons. In M. Seligman (Ed.), *The family with a handicapped child: Understanding and treatment* (pp. 175-202). Orlando, FL: Grune & Stratton.

Foster, M. (1988). A systems perspective and families of handicapped children. *Journal of Family Psychology, 2,* 54-56.

Foster, M., & Berger, M. (1985). Research with families with handicapped children: A multi-level systemic perspective. In L. L'Abate (Ed.), *The handbook of family psychology and therapy* (Vol. 11, pp. 741-780). Homewood, IL: Dorsey.

Foster, M., Berger, M., & McLean, M. (1981). Rethinking a good idea: A reassessment of parent involvement. *Topics in Early Childhood Special Education, 1,* 55-65.

Glick, P., & Lin, S. (1986). Recent changes in divorce and remarriage. *Journal of Marriage and the Family, 48,* 737-747.

Grossman, F. K. (1972). *Brothers and sisters of retarded children: An exploratory study.* Syracuse, NY: Syracuse University Press.

Hampson, R., Hulgus, Y., Beavers, W., & Beavers, J. (1988). The assessment of competence in families with a retarded child. *Journal of Family Psychology, 3,* 32-53.

Hannah, M. E., & Midlarsky, E. (1985). Siblings of the handicapped: A literature review for school psychologists. *School Psychology Review, 14,* 510-520.

Hannah, M. E., & Midlarsky, E. (1987). Siblings of the handicapped: Maladjustment and its prevention. *Techniques, 3,* 188-195.

Holmes, T. H., & Rahe, R. H. (1967). The Social Readjustment Rating scale. *Journal of Psychosomatic Research, 2,* 213-218.

Holroyd, J. (1987). *Questionnaire on Resources and Stress for families with chronically ill or handicapped members.* Brandon, VT: Clinical Psychology.

Huber, C. H. (1979). Parents of the handicapped child: Facilitating acceptance through group counseling. *Personnel and Guidance Journal, 57,* 267-269.

Kazak, A. E. (1986). Families with physically handicapped children: Social ecology and family systems. *Family Process, 25,* 265-281.

Kazak, A. E., & Marvin, R. S. (1984). Differences, difficulties and adaptation: Stress and social networks in families with a handicapped child. *Family Relations, 33,* 67-76.

Lewis, J. (1986). Family structure and stress. *Family Process, 25,* 235-247.

Longo, D., & Bond, L. (1984). Families of the handicapped child: Research and practice. *Family Relations, 33,* 57-65.

McCubbin, H. I., & Figley, C. (1983). Bridging normative and catastrophic family stress. In H. McCubbin & C. Figley (Eds.), *Stress and the family, Vol. 1: Coping with normative transitions* (pp. 218-228). New York: Brunner/Mazel.

McGoldrick, M., Pearce, J., & Giordano, J. (Eds.). (1982). *Ethnicity and family therapy.* New York: Guilford.

Minuchin, S., & Fishman, H. (1981). *Family therapy techniques.* Cambridge, MA: Harvard University Press.

Minuchin, S., Rosman, B., & Baker, L. (1979). *Psychosomatic families: Anorexia nervosa in context.* Cambridge, MA: Harvard University Press.

Newman, J. (1983). Handicapped persons and their families: Philosophical, historical, and legislative perspectives. In M. Seligman (Ed.), *The family with a handicapped child: Understanding and treatment* (pp. 3-25). Orlando, FL: Grune & Stratton.

Olshansky, S. (1962). Chronic sorrow: A response to having a mentally defective child. *Social Casework, 43,* 190-193.

Palfrey, J., Walker, D., Butler, J., & Singer, J. (1989). Patterns of response in families of chronically disabled children: An assessment in five metropolitan school districts. *American Journal of Orthopsychiatry, 59,* 94-103.

Peterson, N. L., & Cooper, C. (1989). Parent education and involvement in early intervention programs for handicapped children: A different perspective on parent needs and the parent-professional relationship. In M. Fine (Ed.), *The second handbook on parent education: Contemporary perspectives* (pp. 197-234). New York: Academic Press.

Public Law 94-142, The Education for All Handicapped Children Act of 1975.

Public Law 99-457, The Education of the Handicapped Act.

Roman, M., & Raley, P. (1980). *The indelible family.* New York: Rawson, Wade.

Rubin, S., & Quinn-Curran, N. (1983). Lost, then found: Parents journey through the community service maze. In M. Seligman (Ed.), *The family with a handicapped child* (pp. 63-94). Orlando, FL: Grune & Stratton.

Schilling, R. F., Kirkham, M. A., Snow, W. H., & Schinke, S. P. (1986). Single mothers with handicapped children: Different from their married counterparts? *Family Relations, 35,* 69-77.

Searle, S. (1978). Stages of parent reaction. *The Exceptional Parent, 8,* 23-27.

Seligman, M., & Darling, R. B. (1989). *Ordinary families, special children: A systems approach to childhood disability.* New York: Guilford Press.

Selye, H. (1974). *Stress without distress.* New York: Lippincott.

Simpson, R. L., & Fiedler, C. R. (1989). Parent participation in individualized educational program (IEP) conferences: A case for individualization. In M. Fine (Ed.), *The second handbook on parent education: Contemporary perspectives* (pp. 145-170). New York: Academic Press.

Stinnett, N., & DeFrain, J. (1989). The healthy family: Is it possible. In M. J. Fine (Ed.), *The second handbook on parent education* (pp. 53-74). New York: Academic Press.

Swap, S. M. (1984). Ecological approaches to working with families of disturbing children. In W. O'Connor & B. Lubin (Eds.), *Ecological approaches to clinical and community psychology* (pp. 107-144). New York: Wiley.

Trute, B., & Hauch, C. (1988). Building on family strengths: A study of families with positive adjustment to the birth of a developmentally disabled child. *Journal of Marital & Family Therapy, 14,* 185-194.

Turnbull, A. P., & Leonard, J. (1981). Parent involvement in special education: Emerging advocacy roles. *School Psychology Review, 10,* 32-44.

Turnbull, A. P., Summers, J., & Brotherson, M. (1986). Family life cycle: Theoretical and empirical implications and future directions for families with mentally retarded members. In J. Gallagher & P. Vietze (Eds.), *Families of handicapped persons: Research, programs, and policy issues* (pp. 45-65). Baltimore: Brookes.

Turnbull, A. P., & Turnbull, H. R. (1982). Parent involvement in the education of handicapped children: A critique. *Mental Retardation, 20,* 115-122.

Turnbull, A. P., & Turnbull, H. R. (1986). *Families, professionals, and exceptionality: A special partnership.* Columbus, OH: Merrill.

Werth, L., & Oseroff, A. (1987). Continued counseling intervention: Lifetime support for the family with a handicapped member. *The American Journal of Family Therapy, 15,* 333-342.

Widerstrom, A., & Dudley-Marling, C. (1986). Living with a handicapped child: Myth and reality. *Childhood Education, 62,* 359, 362, 364-67.

Wikler, L., Wasow, M., & Hatfield, E. (1981). Chronic sorrow revisited: Parent vs. professional depiction of the adjustment of parents of mentally retarded children. *American Journal of Orthopsychiatry, 51,* 63-70.

Winton, P. J. (1988a). Effective communication between parents and professionals. In D. Bailey & R. Simeonsson (Eds.), *Family assessment in early intervention* (pp. 207-228). Columbus, OH: Merrill.

Winton, P. (1988b). The family-focused interview: An assessment and goal setting mechanism. In D. Bailey & R. Simeonsson (Eds.), *Family assessment in early intervention* (pp. 185-205). Columbus, OH: Merrill.

Yoshida, R., Fenton, K., Kaufman, M., & Maxwell, J. (1978). Parent involvement in the special education pupil planning process: The school's perspective. *Exceptional Children, 44,* 531-534.

Zuk, G. (1959). The religious factor and the role of guilt in parental acceptance of the retarded child. *American Journal of Mental Deficiency, 64,* 139-147.

2

PARENT–PROFESSIONAL PARTNERSHIPS AND FAMILY EMPOWERMENT

Carl J. Dunst and Kathleen D. Paget

The words *partnerships* and *empowerment* are now part of the lexicon of professionals working with families and their special needs children (Buswell & Martz, 1987; Dunst, 1985; Dunst & Trivette, in press-a; Lombana, 1983; Mulick & Pueschel, 1983; Nelkin, 1987; Schulz, 1987). The use of these terms suggests a new or alternative way of *helping* special needs children and their parents and clearly conveys the message that traditional "parent involvement" practices have been ineffective and leave a lot to be desired. In this chapter we define the meaning of both partnerships and empowerment and describe the implications of these concepts for practice. These concepts and their implications are discussed within a helping model framework that explicitly attempts to specify the parameters of helping relationships that are necessary to promote participatory involvement and informed decision making on the part of parents of special needs children. We begin with a brief discussion of a dilemma of helping that must be resolved before partnerships between parents and professionals can truly become a reality.

A Dilemma of Helping

Professionals who provide help to their clients do so with the intent that it will be beneficial. There is evidence, however, that certain types of help, and the manner

This chapter is based upon a presentation made at the symposium "Working Collaboratively with Parents of Handicapped Children" held at the annual meeting of the American Psychological Association, Atlanta, Georgia, August 1988. Appreciation is extended to Pat Condrey for assistance in preparation of the manuscript.

in which they are provided, can and often do have debilitating consequences (DePaulo, Nadler, & Fisher, 1983; Dunst & Trivette, 1988; Fisher, Nadler, & DePaulo, 1983a; Nadler, Fisher, & DePaulo, 1983). For example, help giving is likely to create dependencies when professionals take relative, and in some cases absolute, control over their clients' fates. Because the "professional consulted when the client needs help may never [have] seen the client in a state of general well-being, [the help giver] can therefore have only an indirect sense of the client's capabilities and strengths. This limited perspective reinforces the already ingrained tendency for the professional to exercise paternalistic authority" (Merton, Merton, & Barber, 1983, p. 21).

Surrender or usurpation of active control and autonomy to "powerful others" is one of the major determinants of dependency (Brickman et al., 1982; Merton et al., 1983). Dependency, in turn, is likely to result in a sense of helplessness, hopelessness, depression, or alienation on the part of the help seeker (Reid, 1984). Research on patterns of help giving has consistently produced findings demonstrating that dependency and its consequences are often induced by certain types of professional practices (e.g., Brickman et al., 1982; Reid, 1984; Schopler & Bateson, 1965; Taylor, 1979). The care of children with special needs oftentimes results in child and parental dependency upon professionals (Kohrman & Diamond, 1986). This is the case even though the literature abounds with references to the need for active involvement of families in meeting the special needs of their handicapped children (e.g., National Center for Clinical Infant Programs, 1985).

The plea for more active involvement of family members in the education and treatment of children with special needs has been voiced on a number of fronts. A common theme of these pleas has been a call for increased family involvement in education decision making and promotion of a family's sense of control over efforts to meet the special needs of their children. Despite apparent advances, why have families of children with special needs not been more frequently given the rightful role to be involved in discussions and decisions regarding what is in the best interest of their children? The answer, in part, comes from the failure of proponents of increased family involvement to recognize a dilemma of helping that must be explicitly acknowledged and addressed if partnerships are to become remotely possible, let alone a reality.

The dilemma that must be resolved is the disparity between the model of helping typically employed by professional help givers and the beliefs, attitudes, and behaviors necessary to promote greater participatory involvement on the part of the family. According to Merton et al. (1983), most professionals have been socialized to believe that they must have all the right answers regarding the care and treatment of clients. To suggest that clients may be capable of managing events that professionals have been trained to deal with as experts becomes a direct threat to professionals' sense of competence. Thus, despite calls for more involvement, many professionals would rather have clients succumb to their decisions concerning the course of care and treatment.

> Assuming an attitude of need, dependency, and trust can be a powerful means of influencing others' behavior. . . . When joined with the legitimized role expectations that the professional is going to improve the client's lot, it takes on an added force. It makes the professional feel important, responsible, and—at least by comparison with the client—capable. A client who fails to play the complementary role of dependent in some sense deprives the professional of a tool of the trade. . . . Thus, *the prospect of clients' taking a more active and responsible role in their own care is unnerving* in part because it seems that the less helpless the client, the less helpful the professional can be. (Merton et al., 1983, pp. 21-22, emphasis added)

To the extent that this position and stance are embraced by a professional helper, they are in direct conflict with the conditions necessary for more active involvement of parents in the care, education, and treatment of their special needs children.

How are we to resolve the dilemma between these apparently contradictory alternatives? We believe the predicament can be resolved by employing a conceptual framework of helping relationships that on the one hand permits greater understanding of the types of helping styles that have health- and competency-promoting influences, and on the other hand expands the legitimized roles of help givers to include those necessary for helping relationships to have enabling and empowering consequences. In this chapter we describe at least one way of doing so which has proved beneficial in enabling and empowering families to become more actively involved in the care and management of special needs children (Deal, Dunst, & Trivette, 1988; Dunst & Trivette, 1987, in press-a; Dunst, Trivette, & Deal, 1988). By *actively involved* we mean parents' increased understanding of child and family needs, their ability to deploy competencies to meet those needs, and self-attributions about the role family members played in meeting needs. It should be noted that our model and its corollaries are based upon a philosophy of human behavior that explicitly aims to support and strengthen family functioning (Hobbs et al., 1984) as a way of empowering the family (Rappaport, 1981, 1987) to acquire the competencies necessary to negotiate its developmental course in response to both normative and nonnormative life events (Dunst, 1987). Because we use the terms *partnerships* and *empowerment* to refer to specifiable processes and outcomes pertaining to participatory involvement on the part of the family, we begin with a detailed discussion of these terms to place our helping model in proper perspective.

Definition of Terms

The terms partnerships and empowerment are often used without any operational definition of their meaning. Without such definitions, it is difficult to specify the characteristics of the phenomena, and even more difficult to operationalize these notions at the direct service level. Therefore, more precise definitions and specification of the components of partnerships and empowerment are a necessary first step before application can proceed in a way that insures positive consequences.

Partnerships and Collaboration

The terms partnerships and collaboration are often used interchangeably, although we prefer the use of partnerships because it carries additional meaning and useful information not conveyed by the term collaboration. We define partnership as the *association* of two or more people in pursuit of a common goal or joint interest, and collaboration as *cooperation* among two or more people concerning a particular undertaking. The operatives that distinguish partnerships and collaboration are, respectively, association and cooperation. Association implies a long-term union between people, whereas cooperation implies a combination of efforts designed to produce a short-term or immediate effect. As will become clear in a moment, all partnerships involve collaboration, but not all collaborative relationships meet the requisite criteria for defining partnerships.

Legal partnerships. We have found the legal and business definition of partnership helpful in our work because it has explicit meaning and implication for human service practices (e.g., Clifford & Warner, 1987). According to the Uniform Partnership Act (Section 6[1]), the legal definition of a partnership is "an association of two or more persons to carry on as co-owners of a business for profit." Although the concept of partnership is very broad and includes varied enterprises such as syndicates, joint ventures, resource pools, and unincorporated organizations, the rights, responsibilities, and expectations imposed upon partners are explicit and clear cut regardless of what the collaborative arrangement is called.

Characteristics of business partnerships. "A *partnership* is in effect when more than one person is in business, and the people have an *agreement about their mutual roles*" (Phillips & Rasberry, 1981, p. 145, emphasis added). Once a partnership arrangement has been entered into, there are legally required and binding rights and responsibilities that guide the operation of the business.

First, a partnership does not exist unless each partner actually *contributes* something — money, services, resources, etc. — to the partnership. This requirement must be met before any collaborative arrangement is recognized as a partnership.

Second, "To have a partnership, each person must *volunteer* to be a partner, they can't be drafted against their will" (Clifford & Warner, 1987, p. 19). The voluntary, active joining of interests makes people partners where each member stands to benefit from the collaborative arrangement.

Third, partnerships require that partners are *fiduciaries* toward one another. This means that all partners owe complete loyalty to the partnership. Trust and honesty are expected at all times, no partner can engage in any activity that in any way conflicts with the partnership, and each partner must fully disclose to the other(s) any and all information that relates to the common interest or joint venture of the partnership. According to one court decision, the *punctilio of honor* is the standard of behavior of partnerships (*Meinhard v. Salmon*, 1928).

Fourth, the *powers* of any partner in the partnership are determined by the members themselves, and decisions made by the duly recognized partners are legal and binding. "Equal partnerships" give each partner full power to speak and make decisions on behalf of other partners and the partnership and are the reason why loyalty, trust, and honor are so vital in a joint venture.

These exacting, legally binding conditions have their roots in the Babylonian Code of Hammurabi dating back to 2300 B.C. Their usefulness has stood the test of time for more than 4,000 years, and countless court decisions have upheld their value for businesslike collaborative arrangements. As Clifford and Warner (1987) advise,

> The courts often rule that those who've seriously discussed a partnership must adhere to the same exacting standards of good faith that bind partners, even if an actual partnership agreement is never signed. Just when this "partner-like" responsibility arises isn't totally clear, but once real negotiating begins, that probably means there are fiduciary duties involved. *Since you'll have to trust your partners, eventually, it makes sense to start building that trust by full disclosure and square dealing right from the start.* (p. 16, emphasis added)

The latter could not be more true for help givers who work with families in cases where parents and professionals decide to work collaboratively.

Parent–professional partnerships. The legal definitions of partnerships and the rights and responsibilities of partners have proved useful in drawing parallel descriptors and criteria for defining parent–professional partnerships. Operationally, a parent–professional partnership can be defined as an association between a family and one or more professionals who function collaboratively using agreed-upon roles in pursuit of a joint interest and common goal. The minimal requirements of such a venture include *all* of the following:

1. *Both the family and professional contribute resources and expertise (knowledge, skills, time, etc.) to the partnership that are pooled and employed collaboratively.* A partnership does not exist unless this condition is met. This excludes certain collaborative arrangements, including situations in which professionals provide a family advice, but it is the family who must act independently upon the

recommendation; and situations in which a family makes known their wants or desires, but the professional, without any significant or ongoing contributions from the family, mobilizes resources or procures services to meet needs on behalf of the family. A parent–professional partnership exists when, and only when, the partners act in concert and contribute time, resources, and expertise in pursuit of a mutually agreed upon goal or interest.

2. *Both the family and professional want and agree to enter into a collaborative arrangement.* A partnership exists only in cases where the potential partners recognize the benefits of a collaborative arrangement and openly agree to pool their resources (knowledge, skills, etc.) and work toward a mutually agreed upon goal or interest. Although the active pooling of resources in pursuit of a common goal or interest implies that the parties have entered into a partnership arrangement, not every active joining of interests makes people partners. Both the parent and professional must discuss the joint venture, volunteer to be participants, and then proceed to define the mutually agreed upon roles that will be used in pursuit of the "business" of the partnership.

3. *The partnership must be built upon loyalty, trust, and honesty and must involve full disclosure of any and all "material facts" affecting the joint venture.* Honesty, trust, and commitment are the backbone of any effective helping relationship and are, as well, absolutely necessary for partnerships to be effective. Professionals who enter into collaborative arrangements with families must give complete loyalty to the partnership, be honest and trustworthy at all times, provide families with any and all information concerning the "business" of the partnership, and not engage in any activity that conflicts with the explicit, agreed-upon roles and expectations of the partners. Anything less would be a violation of the *sine qua non* standard of behavior of the partnership. This responsibility, more than any other, is essential if the partnership is to be conducted in good faith and in the best interest of the partners in pursuit of their goals and interests.

4. *The powers of the partners must be established at the point of entry into a collaborative arrangement, and the locus of decision making clearly stated.* Partners do not have to share equally in decision-making power for a partnership to exist. Inasmuch as parents have a rightful role to decide what is in the best interest of their family and its members, the locus of decision making in parent–professional partnerships must clearly rest with the family itself. To the extent that the well-being and rights of all family members are protected, the family alone bears responsibility for deciding its goals and course of development (Hobbs et al., 1984). In parent–professional partnerships, a major duty and responsibility of the professional is to provide all necessary information to assist the family to evaluate different options so that the parents can make *informed decisions* regarding their child and family. The final decision, however, about what goals and interests should be pursued, and what courses of action will be taken to attain stated intentions, rests solely with the "senior" partners—namely, the parents.

For those who decide to use partnerships as a mechanism for promoting participatory involvement of families in the education and treatment of special needs children, the above standards of behavior can be used to guide the conduct of joint ventures between parents and professionals. Although not as exacting as the "rules" of business partnerships, these principles can structure the ways in which collaborative arrangements are entered into and used effectively toward a desired goal or interest. Parent–professional partnerships are serious business, and we have a responsibility to treat them as such; otherwise, conflict and dissolution are highly likely to occur.

Enablement and Empowerment

Partnerships *enable* partners to accomplish a mutually agreed upon goal or interest by *empowering* one another to act on behalf, and in the best interest of, the partnership. The term enable connotes making something possible by creating a means or opportunity. Empower implies providing power or authority to make decisions or offer judgment. Thus, partnerships create opportunities for partners to become empowered to make *informed decisions* about the best course of action to achieve a common goal or interest.

The idea of empowerment has come of age in the human services field (Rappaport, Swift, & Hess, 1984). Much of the current interest in empowerment can be traced to Rappaport's (1981) seminal paper on the topic. He proposed empowerment as an alternative to the paternalism that has for so long dominated the ways in which help is provided to clients, and as an approach for resolving the dilemma with which we began this chapter. According to Rappaport (1984), empowerment is viewed both as a process and an outcome and can be understood as either an internalized psychological state or as an observable set of behavior. "Empowerment is easy to define in its absence; powerlessness, real or imagined; learned helplessness; alienation; loss of a sense of control over one's own life. It is more difficult to define positively only because it takes on a different form in different people and contexts" (p. 3). Inasmuch as business and parent–professional partnerships are formed for different purposes, one would expect that empowerment would take on different forms within the context of these collaborative arrangements.

A Social Systems Perspective of Empowerment

The ways in which Rappaport (1981, 1984, 1987) has conceptualized empowerment suggest the need to consider the broader-based systems and social contexts that affect human behavior and the bidirectional and transactional influences that people have on each other's behavior (Bronfenbrenner, 1979). Any *complete* definition of empowerment should recognize these conditions and take them into consideration when operationalizing the concept in practice.

A number of definitions of empowerment can be found in the literature (e.g., Brickman et al., 1982; Dunst, 1985; Hobbs et al., 1984; Soloman, 1985), although few reflect these social systems considerations. Three characteristics of these definitions have guided the ways in which most investigators have typically defined and attempted to operationalize the empowerment construct. These characteristics include the help seeker's: (a) access and control over needed resources, (b) decision-making and problem-solving abilities, and (c) acquisition of instrumental behavior needed to interact effectively with others in order to procure needed resources. Although this approach to defining empowerment has stimulated interest in the concept, it has nonetheless constrained our understanding of what it means to be empowered and *how we can go about enabling and empowering people.* Indeed, we would go so far as to say that the problem-solving/decision-making approach to conceptualizing empowerment, which focuses almost entirely on the help seeker's behavior without consideration of the help giver's role in helping relationships, has restricted our understanding of empowerment because it fails to consider explicitly a number of broader-based issues as part of help seeker (client) and help giver (professional) exchanges. More specifically, it fails to consider how people become empowered through social transactions (e.g., partnerships) designed to achieve mutually agreed upon goals or interests.

A more complete understanding of empowerment requires that we take a broader-based perspective of the conditions that influence the behavior of people during help seeker and help giver exchanges. A social systems perspective offers this type of framework and is perhaps best reflected in Rappaport's (1981) contention that

> [e]mpowerment implies that many competencies are already present or at least possible. . . . Empowerment implies that what you see as poor functioning is a result of social structure and lack of resources which make it impossible for the existing competencies to operate. It implies that in those cases where new competencies need to be learned, they are best learned in a context of living life rather than in artificial programs where everyone, including the person learning, knows that it is really the expert who is in charge. (p. 16)

This set of assertions includes three characteristics that we believe reflect the way in which we need to think about helping relationships and empowerment.

1. *Proactive stance toward help seekers.* This characteristic of an empowerment philosophy assumes that people are already competent or have the capacity to

become competent. Partnerships are built upon this assumption by the voluntary pooling of resources in pursuit of an agreed-upon goal or interest. The belief that families have existing capabilities and strengths as well as the capacity to become more competent must be held by professionals before help givers are likely to enter into partnership arrangements with families. As noted by Clifford and Warner (1987), "the most important attribute of any shared business is the competence of the co-owners and the trust they have in one another" (p. 10). Recognition of the mutual strengths (competence) and loyalty (trust) of partners in a partnership is essential if the venture is to get started in the right direction and eventually succeed.

2. *Enabling experiences are the cornerstone for promoting competence.* This characteristic explicitly states that the failure to display competence is not due to deficits within the help seeker but rather the failure of social systems to create opportunities for competencies to be displayed. It concerns the potential and unrealized capabilities that all people have if afforded the necessary opportunities to learn and grow. A partnership is precisely the type of collaborative experience that creates opportunities for persons to work in concert in pursuit of a goal or interest, and which promotes each partner's capabilities and capacities. The planning, decision making, joining of interests, actions, etc. that are the fundamental ingredients of partnerships are the types of enabling experiences that support and strengthen individual and group functioning.

3. *Empowerment is the sense of control and meaningful contributions resulting from enabling experiences.* This characteristic of empowerment states that the person who is the learner, client, etc. must be able to deploy competencies to obtain resources to meet needs and attribute behavior change to his or her own actions, if one is to acquire a sense of both control over important aspects of one's life and meaningful contribution to family and community (Hobbs et al., 1984). The active participation expected and required by partners in partnership is highly likely to enhance a sense of control and self-efficacy (Bandura, 1977) as well as promote a sense of meaningful contributions to the operation of the partnership to the extent that the "business" succeeds in achieving its aim and goals. Parent–professional partnerships provide the context for help seeker and help giver alike to learn and grow from one another in ways that are mutually beneficial.

Taken together, these three characteristics provide a basis for viewing empowerment from a broader-based social systems perspective. They also suggest the importance of the help giver's behavior in empowering families and the role partnerships can play as an enabling experience in achieving this outcome. Additionally, this philosophical stance toward helping relationships suggests a new and expanded definition of effective helping that explicitly considers the conditions necessary for help giver–help seeker exchanges to have positive results. Based upon the major features of the above perspective of empowerment, Dunst (1987) defined effective helping as the

act of enabling individuals or groups (e.g., family) to become better able
to solve problems, meet needs, or achieve aspirations by promoting
acquisition of competencies that support and strengthen functioning in
a way that permits a greater sense of individual or group control over
its developmental course. (p. 1)

This definition has been used to propose an enabling model of helping that specifies
the particular types of help-giving behavior that are likely to have empowering
consequences. The majority of the help giver characteristics subsumed under the
model are precisely the behaviors that define partnerships and are expected by
partners that are in business together. The model makes concrete what professionals can do to create collaborative interactions with families that promote the
pooling and sharing of resources in ways that have family-strengthening and
growth-producing influences central to an empowering philosophy (Dunst et al.,
1988; Hobbs et al., 1984; Rappaport, 1981, 1987). The model, in a nutshell,
attempts to specify the professional roles and help-giving behaviors that reverse

[t] he pervasive belief that experts should solve all of [the help seeker's]
problems in living . . . which [only] extends the sense of alienation and
loss of ability to control [one's] life. . . . This is the path that the social
as well as the physical health experts have been on, and we need to
reverse this trend. (Rappaport, 1981, p. 17)

An Enablement Model of Helping

Accumulated evidence from the help-giving literature (e.g., DePaulo et al.,
1983; Fisher et al., 1983a; Nadler et al., 1983) strongly suggests the types of
helping behaviors that are likely to be enabling and have positive consequences
(Dunst, 1987; Dunst & Trivette, 1987, 1988; Dunst, Trivette, Davis, & Cornwall,
1988). Conceptually and temporally, there are three clusters of variables that both
contribute to effective helping and promote a sense of family empowerment: (1)
Prehelping attitudes and beliefs, (2) help-giving behavior, and (3) posthelping
responses and consequences. Prehelping attitudes and beliefs refer to the help
giver's posture and stance toward help seekers and helping relationships. Help-
giving behavior refers to the interactional styles employed by help givers as part
of helping relationships. Posthelping responses and consequences refer to ensuing
influences of the help giver's behavior on the help seeker.

Figure 2.1 shows the temporal relationship among the three clusters of attributes
and the influences these attributes have on help seeker behavior. According to this
model, prehelping attitudes and beliefs influence help giver behavior, and help
giver attitudes, beliefs, and behaviors influence posthelping responses and consequences. (The feedback loops from posthelping responses and consequences to

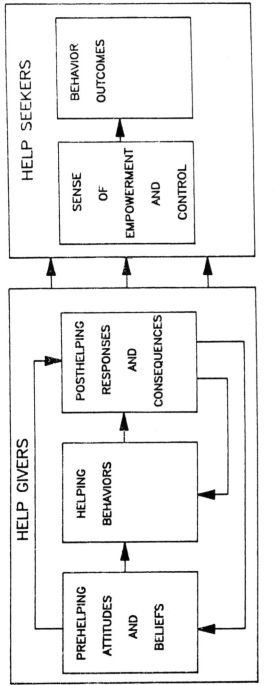

Figure 2.1. A Model for Depicting the Influences of Prehelping, Helping, and Posthelping Behavior on Help-Giver Outcomes.

35

the other two process phases reflect the fact that help-giving experiences are likely to influence the subsequent attitudes, beliefs, and behaviors of help givers toward help seekers.) Collectively, prehelping, helping, and posthelping characteristics define the help giver's contributions to helping relationships. These three clusters of variables are seen as determinants of a help seeker's sense of control and self-efficacy (Bandura, 1977) resulting from help seeker–help giver exchanges

Table 2.1

Help Giver Attitudes, Beliefs, and Behaviors Associated with Empowering and Competency-Producing Influences

Prehelping attitudes and beliefs	Helping behaviors	Posthelping responses and consequences
1. Positive attributions toward help seekers and helping relationships.	1. Employs active and reflective listening skills.	1. Accepts and supports help seeker decisions.
2. Emphasis on help seeker responsibility for meeting needs and solving problems.	2. Helps client clarify concerns and needs.	2. Minimizes the help seeker's sense of indebtedness.
3. High expectations regarding the capacity of help seekers to become competent.	3. Pro-offers help in response to help seeker needs.	3. Permits reciprocity as part of help giver–help seeker exchanges.
4. Emphasis upon building on help seeker strengths.	4. Offers help that is normative.	4. Minimizes the psychological response costs of accepting help.
5. Proactive stance toward helping relationships.	5. Offers help that is congruent and matches the help seeker's appraisal of needs.	5. Enhances a sense of self-efficacy regarding active involvement in meeting needs.
6. Promotion emphasis as the focus of help giving.	6. Promotes acquisition of competencies to meet needs, solve problems, and achieve aspirations.	6. Maintains confidentiality at all times; shares information only with help seeker's permission.
	7. Employs partnerships and parent–professional collaboration as the mechanism for meeting needs.	
	8. Allows locus of decision making to rest with the help seeker.	

which, in turn, are seen as exerting influence on physical and psychological health outcomes of the person receiving help (e.g., well-being).

Table 2.1 lists the particular help giver attitudes, beliefs, behaviors, and responses that are most consistent with positive, competency-producing influences. Direct and corroborative theoretical and empirical evidence shows that individual help-giving characteristics within and across clusters tend to occur simultaneously and exclude the use of characteristics incongruent with competency-producing attitudes, beliefs, and behaviors (e.g., Brickman, Kidder et al., 1982; Brickman, Rabinowitz et al., 1983; DePaulo et al., 1983; Dunst & Trivette, 1988; Fisher et al., 1983a; Fisher, Nadler, & Whitcher-Alagna, 1983b; Hobbs et al., 1984; Nadler et al., 1983; Rappaport, 1981, 1987).

Prehelping Attitudes and Beliefs

The preconceived notions that help givers hold toward help seekers and helping relationships set the occasion for whether or not helping acts are likely to have empowering or usurping consequences. The predispositional posture most consistent with an empowerment stance toward help seekers and helping relationships is characterized by certain attitudes and beliefs. Help giving will be more effective if help givers (a) assume a positive stance toward help seekers and helping relationships; (b) employ helping models that emphasize help seekers' acquisition of competencies necessary to solve problems or meet needs rather than ones that emphasize causes of problems; (c) assume that help seekers have the capacity to understand, learn about, and manage significant events in their lives; (d) build upon help seeker strengths rather than correct deficits as the primary way of strengthening family functioning; (e) approach helping relationships from a proactive rather than a reactive posture; and (f) employ promotion as opposed to either prevention or treatment models for helping families become more capable and competent. Collectively, these six different but highly related attitudes and beliefs constitute the underlying assumptions of an enabling approach to helping relationships (Dunst & Trivette, 1987, in press-a). The term enablement reflects the underlying rationale of the model; that is, help seekers create opportunities for competencies to be acquired by assuming a stance that is positive, proactive, and competency producing. Nearly all the prehelping attitudes and beliefs are also the attributes, albeit described in different terms, that form the backbone of partnership arrangements (Clifford & Warner, 1987).

Help-Giving Behavior

In addition to the preconceived notions that help givers bring to helping relationships, the ways in which attitudes and beliefs are translated into help-giving practice can either promote or impede acquisition of a sense of help seeker understanding and control over managing life events. Table 2.1 shows the cluster of interactional behaviors that are most likely to have competency-producing influences. Help giving will be more effective if help givers (a) employ active and reflective listening skills as a basis for understanding help seeker concerns and needs, (b) enhance the help seeker's ability to clarify concerns and prioritize needs, (c) pro-offer rather than wait for help to be requested, (d) offer aid and assistance that is normative and nondemeaning, (e) offer assistance that matches the help seeker's appraisal of his or her problem or need, (f) promote acquisition of effective behavior that makes the help seeker more capable and competent, (g) employ help seeker–help giver partnerships as the basis for mobilizing resources to meet needs and enhance competence, and (h) allow final decision making to rest entirely with the help seeker, including decisions about the need for help, the options for meeting needs, and whether or not to accept or reject help that is offered. The help-giving style embodied within these eight behavior characteristics is necessary if helping acts are to be both effective and empowering. This helping style places major emphasis upon truly understanding the needs and concerns of help seekers, being responsive to what is important to help seekers, promoting acquisition of competencies that permit help seekers to become better able to manage life events and negotiate their developmental courses, and using partnerships as the mechanism for both promoting acquisition of competencies and strengthening functioning.

Posthelping Responses and Consequences

One aspect of help giving and helping relationships often overlooked as part of assessing the extent to which helping acts have either positive or negative influences is the posthelping responses and consequences of the help giver and help giving, respectively. The competency-producing attitudes, beliefs, and behaviors of help givers can be undone by what happens as a result of, and following help giver–help seeker exchanges. Table 2.1 shows the cluster of responses and consequences that are likely to contribute to effective helping. Help giving will be more effective if help givers (a) accept and support the decisions made by help seekers, (b) minimize the sense of indebtedness felt by the help seeker toward the help giver, (c) sanction and approve reciprocity but do not expect help seekers to provide assistance or advice in return, (d) minimize the psychological response costs of accepting help, (e) promote and enhance the help seeker's psychological sense of involvement and control over life events, and (f) maintain and preserve confidentiality at all times by sharing information with others only with the explicit permission of the help seekers. Reactions to help giving are major determinants of whether or not aid and assistance will have positive or negative influences. Therefore, help givers must be cognizant about how their responses to help seeker decisions and actions influence help seeker reactions, and interact with help seekers in ways that are accepting, supportive, and empowering.

Many of the characteristics of this enablement model of helping are the same as the attributes described above that are fundamental to both business and parent–professional partnerships. The overlap and similarities are not surprising given the fact that helping and business relationships, to be successful, must be based upon certain beliefs and attitudes regarding the competencies each "partner" brings to the relationship and the types of trust and confidence that are necessary for the relationship to grow and become the foundation for achieving agreed-upon goals and interests. Partnerships are in many ways synonymous with effective helping, at least as we have defined it in this chapter.

Implications for Practice

The concepts and material presented in this chapter can be found as part of numerous efforts to improve communication and working relationships between professionals and their clients, including families of children with special needs. Lombana (1983) has devoted an entire volume to home–school partnerships, with particular attention to the methods and strategies that can be used to promote a variety of collaborative and participatory parent–professional relationships. She describes a model for conceptualizing different types of home–school partnerships and then proceeds to detail how opportunities can be created to enhance increased collaborative arrangements.

Both Schulz (1987) and Farkas (1981) address the ways in which professionals can employ enabling experiences to promote participatory involvement on the part of parents of children with special needs. Schulz's treatment of parent–professional relationships is taken from the perspective of the special education teacher, whereas Farkas focuses on what school principals can do to increase the involvement of families in their children's education. Farkas' (1981) "guide" includes a number of useful checklists for determining whether school policy and the ensuing behavior of school personnel are consistent with the belief that families can and should function as informed decision makers in their children's education.

One of the most useful documents available for encouraging professionals to include families as partners in the care of their children is *Family-Centered Care for Children with Special Health Care Needs*, published by the Association for the Care of Children's Health (Shelton, Jeppson, & Johnson, 1987). Shelton and her colleagues describe eight elements of family-centered care, one of which is parent–professional collaboration. The essentials of collaboration are detailed at the help giver–help seeker, service delivery, and policy levels. The book includes a number of useful checklists for assessing if family-centered care practices are consistent with a participatory philosophy regarding meaningful family involvement in the care of their children. Among the checklists included in the Shelton et al. book, one specifically addresses the characteristics of collaborative parent–

professional relationships and another considers the ingredients of collaboration and family-centered care from the perspective of state-level policy and program developers. The Shelton et al. (1987) book is essential reading for anyone committed to parent–professional partnerships as a mechanism for empowering families and strengthening family functioning.

Buswell and Martz (1987), as part of their discussion of the meaning of partnership within the context of P.L. 99-457 (Education of the Handicapped Act) and multidisciplinary team functioning, describe four key ingredients necessary for parent–professional partnerships to become a reality.

> First, everyone on the team must accept the fact that the roles of the various team members are different, and as such, there undoubtedly will be differences of opinion as to what the child's needs are. . . . In this kind of situation, however, the "conflicts" can be the catalyst for all the "experts" . . . to create the kind of individualized program that the child really needs.
>
> Second, people must be honest and share what they are thinking directly [with] each other. Parents must tell professionals their thoughts . . . [and] professionals have an obligation to be honest with parents as well.
>
> Third, . . . everyone needs to listen carefully [to everyone else]. . . . It is important to ask questions to try to clarify issues rather than replay it over and over and not participate actively.
>
> Fourth, . . . partners need to be effective collaborators in their ability to negotiate and compromise. . . . Give and take in compromise is an essential part of the [empowering] process. (Buswell & Martz, 1987, pp. 3-4)

On the one hand, these key ingredients mirror the attributes and characteristics of both partnerships and effective helping as described above; on the other hand, they provide a concrete set of recommendations regarding how to put the principles into practice.

Dunst and his colleagues (Deal, Dunst, & Trivette, 1988; Dunst, 1985, 1987; Dunst & Trivette, in press-a; Dunst et al., 1988) have employed the material presented in this chapter as a foundation for (a) delineating an empowerment philosophy regarding early intervention and family support practices, (b) implementing a family-centered approach to working with families, (c) specifying the necessary roles and functions for an enabling approach to case management, and (d) operationalizing partnerships within the context of developing and implementing individualized family support plans. These various applications have been formulated at the Family, Infant and Preschool Program (FIPP; Dunst, 1985; Dunst & Trivette, in press-b) and specifically aim to support and strengthen family functioning vis à vis enabling and empowering experiences.

The methods and approaches used at FIPP for supporting families are guided by a philosophy called Proactive Empowerment through Partnerships (PEP). The PEP philosophy places major emphasis on (a) recognizing and strengthening child and family capabilities using a proactive rather than a deficit approach; (b) enabling and empowering parents with the necessary knowledge, skills, and resources needed to perform family and parenting functions in a competent manner; by (c) using partnerships between parents and professionals as the means to strengthen, enable, and empower families. FIPP is proactive in the sense that the program takes a positive stance toward children and their families. A proactive approach focuses on the child's and family's strengths and not their weaknesses and promotes positive functioning by supporting families. FIPP enables and empowers families by creating opportunities that permit greater understanding and control over resources and decision making. This is done within the context of partnerships between families and professionals that avoids the paternalism characteristic of most client–professional relationships. As noted by Rappaport (1981), enabling and empowering families "requires a breakdown of the typical role relationship between professionals and community people" (p. 19). Partnerships are used at FIPP for accomplishing this breakdown and building collaborative arrangements between staff and families.

The family-centered intervention model used at FIPP to operationalize this philosophy includes a set of four principles that guide practices designed to enable and empower families (Dunst et al., 1988). The model is implemented in the following way: (1) Identify family needs to determine the things to which the family considers it important enough to devote time and energy, (2) build upon family strengths and capabilities as a basis for promoting the family's ability to mobilize resources to meet needs, (3) strengthen the family's personal social network and mobilize potential but untapped sources of aid and assistance necessary to meet needs, and (4) function in a number of different roles to enable and empower the family to become more competent in mobilizing resources to attain stated outcomes and achieve desired goals.

The particular roles, or case management practices, that are used at FIPP to enable and empower families include expanded functions and responsibilities that help givers employ as part of helping relationships and parent–professional partnerships (Dunst & Trivette, 1988; Dunst et al., 1988). As noted by Hobbs et al. (1984), policies and practices that operate according to enabling and empowering principles are by far the preferred strategies for strengthening family functioning. Accordingly, "Parents become able to develop and to become effective decision makers when they are treated as capable adults and are helped by service organizations and professionals to become even more capable" (Hobbs et al., 1984, p. 51). Therefore, case management may be considered effective only to the extent that families become more capable, competent, and empowered as a result of the help-giving acts of case managers.

Last, all of the above are put into practice and operationalized at the direct service level by the ways in which individualized family support plans (IFSPs) are developed and implemented. The IFSP used at FIPP is a "working" document that guides needs specification and resource mobilization. It includes: (1) A list of family-identified needs, aspirations, projects, etc., in order of priority; (2) a series of statements regarding the sources of support and resources that will be mobilized to meet needs; (3) a series of statements regarding the actions that will be taken by the family and early intervention practitioner to mobilize resources; and (4) procedures for evaluating the extent to which needs are met. The "steps" that are taken to mobilize resources to meet needs are listed for both the family and early intervention practitioner and are stated in terms of what will be done by each "partner" to actualize the plan. Doing so emphasizes shared responsibility (partnership) between the family and early intervention practitioner.

Collectively, the family-centered philosophy, assessment and intervention model, case management practices, and IFSP procedures and practices used at FIPP represent a "system" that places major emphasis upon *partnerships* and *empowerment* as the mechanisms for supporting and strengthening family functioning. This integrated system has proved useful as a framework for operationalizing the concepts and notions described in this chapter. The interested reader should consult the major reference sources describing this system and its components for additional information regarding the FIPP model (Deal et al., 1988; Dunst, 1987; Dunst & Trivette, in press-a; Dunst et al., 1988).

Conclusion

The purpose of this chapter was to describe the meaning of partnerships and empowerment and how these notions, when couched within the context of helping relationships, can be used to support and strengthen family functioning. This was preceded by a discussion of a dilemma of helping that has prevented families of special needs children from having increased decision-making power regarding the care, education, and treatment of their children. The resolution of this dilemma will require new models and new approaches to conceptualizing parent involvement. The material presented in this chapter offers at least one alternative viewpoint from which to see and operationalize parent-involvement practices.

References

Bandura, A. (1977). Self-efficacy: Toward a unifying theory of behavioral change. *Psychological Review, 84*, 191-215.

Brickman, P., Kidder, L. H., Coates, D., Rabinowitz, V., Cohn, E., & Karuza, J. (1983). The dilemmas of helping: Making aid fair and effective. In J. D. Fisher, A. Nadler,

& B. M. DePaulo (Eds.), *New directions in helping: Vol. 1. Recipient reactions to aid* (pp. 18-51). New York: Academic Press.

Brickman, P., Rabinowitz, V., Karuza, J., Coates, D., Cohn, E., & Kidder, L. (1982). Models of helping and coping. *American Psychologist, 37,* 368-384.

Bronfenbrenner, U. (1979). *The ecology of human development: Experiments by nature and design.* Cambridge, MA: Harvard University Press.

Buswell, B., & Martz, J. (1987). The meaning of partnerships: Parents' perspectives. *Mainstream.* Washington, DC: The Legal Center.

Clifford, D., & Warner, R. (1987). *The partnership book* (3rd ed.). Berkeley, CA: Nolo Press.

Deal, A. G., Dunst, C. J., & Trivette, C. M. (1988). A flexible and functional approach to developing individualized family support plans. *Infants and Young Children, 1*(4), 32-43.

DePaulo, B., Nadler, A., & Fisher, J. (Eds.). (1983). *New directions in helping: Vol. 2. Help-seeking.* New York: Academic Press.

Dunst, C. J. (1985). Rethinking early intervention. *Analysis and Intervention in Developmental Disabilities, 5,* 165-201.

Dunst, C. J. (1987, December). *What is effective helping?* Paper presented at the biennial meeting of the National Clinical Infants Program Conference, Washington, DC.

Dunst, C. J., & Trivette, C. M. (1987). Enabling and empowering families: Conceptual and intervention issues. *School Psychology Review, 16,* 443-456.

Dunst, C. J., & Trivette, C. M. (1988). Helping, helplessness, and harm. In J. Witt, S. Elliott, & F. Gresham (Eds.), *Handbook of behavior therapy in education* (pp. 343-376). New York: Plenum Press.

Dunst, C. J., & Trivette, C. M. (in press-a). An enablement and empowerment perspective of case management. *Topics in Early Childhood Special Education.*

Dunst, C. J., & Trivette, C. M. (in press-b). A family systems model of early intervention with handicapped and developmentally at-risk children. In D. P. Powell (Ed.), *Parent education and support programs: Consequences for children and families.* Norwood, NJ: Ablex.

Dunst, C. J., Trivette, C. M., & Deal, A. G. (1988). *Enabling and empowering families: Principles and guidelines for practice.* Cambridge, MA: Brookline.

Dunst, C. J., Trivette, C. M., Davis, M., & Cornwall, J. (1988). Enabling and empowering families of children with health impairments. *Children's Health Care Journal, 17,* 71-81.

Farkas, S. (1981). *Taking a family perspective: A principal's guide for working with families of handicapped children.* Washington, DC: Family Impact Seminar Center.

Fisher, J. D., Nadler, A., & DePaulo, B. M. (Eds.). (1983a). *New directions in helping: Vol. 1. Recipient reactions to aid.* New York: Academic Press.

Fisher, J. D., Nadler, A., & Whitcher-Alagna, S. (1983b). Four theoretical approaches for conceptualizing reactions to aid. In J. D. Fisher, A. Nadler, & B. M. DePaulo (Eds.), *New directions in helping: Vol. 1. Recipient reactions to aid* (pp. 51-84). New York: Academic Press.

Hobbs, N., Dokecki, P. R., Hoover-Dempsey, K. V., Moroney, R. M., Shayne, M. W., & Weeks, K. H. (1984). *Strengthening families.* San Francisco: Jossey-Bass.

Kohrman, A. F., & Diamond, L. (1986). Institutional and professional attitudes: Dilemmas for the chronically ill child. *Topics in Early Childhood Special Education, 5*(4), 82-91.

Lombana, J. (1983). *Home-school partnerships.* New York: Grune & Stratton.

Meinhard v. Salmon (1928). 164 N.E. 545.

Merton, V., Merton, R. K., & Barber, E. (1983). Client ambivalence in professional relationships: The problem of seeking help from strangers. In B. DePaulo, A. Nadler, & J. Fisher (Eds.), *New directions in helping: Vol. 2, Help-seeking* (pp. 13-44). New York: Academic Press.

Mulick, J., & Pueschel, S. (1983). *Parent–professional partnerships in developmental disability services.* Cambridge, MA: Academic Guild Publishers.

Nadler, A., Fisher, J. D., & DePaulo, B. M. (Eds.). (1983). *New directions in helping: Vol. 3. Applied perspectives on help-seeking and -receiving.* New York: Academic Press.

National Center for Clinical Infant Programs. (1985). *Equals in this partnership: Parents of disabled and at-risk infants and toddlers speak to professionals.* Washington, DC: National Center for Clinical Infant Programs.

Nelkin, V. (1987). *Family-centered health care for medically fragile children: Principles and practice.* Washington, DC: Georgetown University, National Center for Networking Community Based Services.

Phillips, M., & Rasberry, S. (1981). *Honest business.* New York: Random House.

Public Law 99-457, the Education of the Handicapped Act.

Rappaport, J. (1981). In praise of paradox: A social policy of empowerment over prevention. *American Journal of Community Psychology, 9,* 1-25.

Rappaport, J. (1984). Studies in empowerment: Introduction to the issues. In J. Rappaport, C. Swift, & R. Hess (Eds.), *Studies in empowerment: Steps toward understanding and action* (pp. 1-7). New York: Haworth Press.

Rappaport, J. (1987). Terms of empowerment/Exemplars of prevention: Toward a theory for community psychology. *American Journal of Community Psychology, 15*(2), 121-128.

Rappaport, J., Swift, C., & Hess, R. (Eds.) (1984). *Studies in empowerment: Steps toward understanding and action.* New York: Haworth Press.

Reid, D. W. (1984). Participatory control and the chronic-illness adjustment process. In H. M. Lefcourt (Ed.), *Research with the Locus of Control construct* (Vol. 3, pp. 361-389). Orlando, FL: Academic Press.

Schopler, J., & Bateson, N. (1965). The power of dependence. *Journal of Personality and Social Psychology, 3,* 247-254.

Schulz, J. (1987). *Parents and professionals in special education.* Boston: Allyn & Bacon.

Shelton, T. L., Jeppson, E. S., & Johnson, B. H. (1987). *Family-centered care for children with special health care needs.* Washington, DC: Association for the Care of Children's Health.

Soloman, M. (1985). How do we really empower families? *Family Resource Coalition Report, 3,* 2-3.

Taylor, S. E. (1979). Hospital patient behavior: Reactance, helplessness or control? *Journal of Social Issues, 35*(1), 156-184.

3

EXCEPTIONAL CHILDREN IN NONTRADITIONAL FAMILIES

Marian C. Fish

The recent literature, both scholarly and popular, on establishing partnerships between professionals and parents of exceptional children has been primarily directed at two-parent households with, most often, the natural mother as caregiver (e.g., Turnbull & Turnbull, 1986). A 4-year review of an established journal for parents of exceptional youngsters uncovered only three articles about nontraditional family situations, in each case concerning a single mother with an exceptional child (Barnes, 1986; Cline, 1985; "Demands," 1984). Although the intact nuclear family is still representative of a majority of American households, an increasing percentage of exceptional children are being raised in nontraditional families, such as single-parent, blended, foster, adoptive, and disabled-parent homes (Carlson, 1985; Glick, 1984; Lombana, 1983). Current statistics indicate that half of first marriages are expected to end in divorce and over 50% of divorces will involve children (Sauer & Fine, 1988). It is estimated that one out of six children in school is a stepchild (Prosen & Farmer, 1982), one out of every six babies is born out of wedlock (Golden & Capuzzi, 1986), and that close to half a million children in the United States are under the auspices of the child welfare system (Lewis, 1984). Thus, there is great urgency for professionals to develop knowledge about these families. Looking across *all* nontraditional families with exceptional children, it seems fair to say that the stresses encountered are greater than those in traditional households (Simpson, 1982). Indeed, Lombana (1983) suggests that parents in these families have even greater needs for positive relationships with professionals than do other parents.

45

Working with Nontraditional Families

The basic principles in a collaborative relationship between professionals and parents of exceptional children apply across all types of families; yet, an understanding by the professional of characteristics and concerns relevant to nontraditional families may enhance the relationship. Just as family cultural background or ethnicity is an important consideration in working with parents, nontraditional family units have special issues that may need to be addressed. Of course, even among these subgroups of exceptional families, there is much diversity, and generalizations should be made with care. Nonetheless, there are common needs and experiences shared by parents in each type of nontraditional family.

This chapter examines five nontraditional family types: single-parent, blended or stepfamilies, foster, adoptive, and families with a disabled parent. The chapter (1) identifies characteristics and issues associated with these families and (2) provides guidelines for professionals who work with these parents.

Single Parents: Characteristics and Issues

The single-parent family in the United States today arises from diverse origins, including separation (70%), death (14%), parent never married (10%), and temporary circumstances (6%) (Golden & Capuzzi, 1986). Four critical variables for professionals to consider are: (a) sex of parent remaining with the family, (b) reason for only one partner (death, divorce, separation, or never married), (c) permanent or temporary absence, and (d) total or partial absence (Young & Ruth, 1983). Research in this area is muddled and does not address specific subgroups (Young & Ruth, 1983). Yet, it is possible that the manner in which one becomes a single parent may affect functioning (Golden & Capuzzi, 1986). For example, blame of the spouse may be prevalent in separation cases, whereas the child may be blamed when the mother was never married. Or, when a spouse in an intact marriage dies, the widow(er) often has continued support and functions as a representative of the couple (Golden & Capuzzi, 1986).

Virtually all studies view single parents from a deficit model, looking for evidence that single parenting results in unhappy children while ignoring positive outcomes. Contrary to this commonly held belief, Atlas (1981) found that 75% of single-parent families report they are doing well and that the children are well adjusted. Common characteristics and needs of the single-parent household are identified below.

An overwhelming majority of single parents, 95%, are mothers who work outside the home (Lombana, 1983). Further, a high proportion of single mothers are Black, as 55% of Black babies are born to unmarried mothers (Cordes, 1984).

Numerous authors have described common characteristics of these families (Carlson, 1985; Golden & Capuzzi, 1986; Simpson, 1982; Weiss, 1979; Young & Ruth, 1983). Carlson (1985) sees single-parent families as having the same functions as two-parent households, but with fewer participants to carry out these functions resulting in role strain. One mother describes her feelings: "Being a single, divorced parent under the best of circumstances is very demanding and often frustrating and unrewarding" ("Demands," 1984, p. 48). The situation resulting when the custodial parent attempts to fulfill two roles is often charac-terized by financial constraints, family management overload (both child care and household), and emotional overload (Weiss, 1979).

Financial constraints. One of the major problems faced by single parents is economic survival (Simpson, 1982). A female-headed family after a divorce or an unwed teenage mother are both vulnerable to financial problems. In fact, 25% of single-parent, female-headed households are below the poverty line (Golden & Capuzzi, 1986). For parents with exceptional youngsters, there are reports of additional expenses, including laundry or structural modifications for the home to accommodate an exceptional child or to repair damage (Horne, 1985). Frequently, expenses covered by a spouse such as insurance and/or health benefits are not available. Of note, too, is that children may hold the mother responsible for the change in life-style (Simpson, 1982).

Family management. When the parent is single, family structure and function-ing are altered. The parent is expected to assume responsibilities of the absent partner and may have to learn or relearn tasks (Young & Ruth, 1983). For example, if a father always handled automobile repair and maintenance, the single mother may need to assume this role. Similarly, a single father who never cooked would need to explore the kitchen. These additional household tasks do not excuse the single parent from the major responsibility of child care. It is known that boys are especially vulnerable to discipline problems in families headed by women (Simpson, 1982). When there is an exceptional child in the household, child care responsibilities are often greater and might include trips to specialists or direct physical care. One mother describes her life with a retarded daughter:

> It is not a one-time demand. . . . Each day presents . . . the challenge of figuring out how to do everything . . . while managing the handicapped child. . . . That might entail, for instance, grocery shopping with the retarded child in tow. When Beckie was little, such an excursion required only the extra energy needed to carry her on my hip and choose groceries one handed. . . . But, when she hit her teens a completely new ingredient was added to the challenge. (Turnbull & Turnbull, 1985, pp. 143-144)

It is often hard to find baby-sitters for exceptional children. At times the parent may use another sibling to take over some of the roles of the missing parent. Care must be taken not to exploit these youngsters or assign them inappropriate tasks. (A discussion of siblings of exceptional children can be found in Chapter 4.)

Emotional overload. Along with financial and household burdens is the emotional overload. One single mother wrote, "I am tired, lonely and isolated" (Barnes, 1986, p. 47). Feelings of being emotionally overwhelmed and angry are commonly reported. When stressed, a single parent may attribute blame to the child for a marital breakup, particularly if there is an exceptional child. Feelings of social isolation are probably the most widely reported. The restrictions an exceptional child places on the social life of two parents have been well documented. The parents engage in far fewer leisure time activities and interact socially less with friends (Horne, 1985). For single mothers there is great difficulty establishing new relationships and developing a social support network. When describing her mentally retarded child, one mother said, "Sometimes I felt very lonely. Weekends were even harder. I was still the caretaker, and it was hard to find sitters, no neighbor offered to take her" ("Demands," 1985, p. 48). Another mother said, "I felt sorry for myself" (Barnes, 1986). These economic, management, and personal experiences often result in decreased efficiency and a reassessment of priorities by single parents because it is not possible for them to assume the roles of two parents.

Single Parents: Guidelines for Professionals

When working collaboratively with single parents of exceptional children, it is important to begin by recognizing the overwhelming responsibilities that they face daily. With time at a premium and child care for the exceptional child often difficult to arrange, flexibility in scheduling appointments, including evenings and/or weekends, is helpful. Some professionals may be able to schedule home meetings as well; if not, phone calls may be effective. At the least, do not get discouraged at cancelled appointments or spotty attendance; they do not indicate a lack of interest or caring, but rather that a more crucial priority has arisen. Understanding on these occasions will enhance, and perhaps save, a relationship with a single parent.

To counter the isolation of the single parent, professionals can work with them to find and/or help them develop a support network. Parents without Partners, for example, is a volunteer agency with chapters throughout the country where single parents can meet. A less formal network is one of extended family, old friends, and neighbors. It is important to locate other single parents either to share baby-sitting or to join the mother and child on a trip or outing. Social and recreational outlets for parents and children provide relief from isolation. Respite care, the provision of temporary relief services for exceptional children, is a highly valued service, but one that is not available in many states or is available only on a limited basis (Blacher, 1984). Also, if a child has excessive medical needs or severe behavioral problems, he or she may not be eligible. A local Association for Retarded Citizens may have a list of respite care providers. Professionals must be careful in identifying these resources, however, that they do not become engaged in fulfilling some of the functions of the absent parent; single parents must be allowed to accept these responsibilities (Young & Ruth, 1983).

With regard to family management, it is important to work with parents to establish guidelines for their relationship with their children. Help organize domestic responsibilities so that children are not asked to assume parental roles. Boundaries between parent and child(ren) must be clearly delineated, roles defined, and lines of authority specified. Additionally, encourage parents to take care of themselves physically and to take time for their personal needs. It will not be enough simply to give them this information; where necessary, teach them skills necessary to accomplish these tasks (e.g., relaxation training, time management, behavior management).

There is considerable evidence that positive postdivorce parental relationships are a major factor in a child's successful adjustment. Whenever possible, professionals should involve the noncustodial parent in the collaborative planning.

In general, when working with single-parent families with exceptional children, the information and support provided should take into consideration these unique characteristics.

Stepparents: Characteristics and Issues

In a stepfamily, either one or both partners have been previously married with at least one of the partners having children from that previous marriage (Katz & Stein, 1983). It is estimated that 1,300 new stepfamilies are being formed each day in the United States and that there are approximately 35 million stepparents (Jarmulowski, 1985). Over 13% of all families with children under 18 in the United States are stepfamilies (Visher & Visher, 1979). Also known as reconstituted, blended, or remarried families, the nontraditional makeup of stepfamilies has widespread ramifications in everyday life, for example, when sending greeting cards, when filling out school record forms, and on holidays and special occasions. Although the stepfamily seems similar to the nuclear family, it is more complex because it joins (at least) two households with children living in one home and visiting another.

The uniqueness of a stepfamily stems from its formation out of a past that has involved the experience of loss, either from death or loss of a previous family unit, and the disruption of attachment (Golden & Cappuzi, 1986). All members of a stepfamily bring with them histories of how families are supposed to function based on experiences they have had in their prior families. One stepfather describes a dinner table scene as follows: "Sometimes we sit around the dinner table and the children chatter to their mother with great excitement about events before they knew me—the family gatherings, the celebrations, the vacations—the usual family experiences I once shared with my own boys. I want to be part of it, but can't. It is their history" (Giordano, 1985, p. 78).

The relationship between the biological parent and children predates the new marriage (Visher & Visher, 1979). This leads to a number of common features of ways of functioning that distinguish stepfamilies from other family types (Katz & Stein, 1983). There is, unfortunately, no research on the exceptional child in stepfamilies from which to draw information. It is necessary to extrapolate from the many discussions of nonexceptional stepfamilies to those with an exceptional child.

Unrealistic expectations of family members is probably the most cited characteristic of stepfamilies. The sprouting of instant love between stepparents and stepchildren resulting in one big, happy family (e.g., "The Brady Bunch") is one myth, while the wicked stepmother of fairy tales is the other common myth. One stepmother illustrated these feelings as follows: "I want his children to love me and be with us all the time. I do not want them at all" (Maglin, 1985, p. 40). Conflicts may result when a stepparent tries to assume the role of the "absent" parent prematurely. This is a particular burden for stepmothers who have the cultural expectation of caregiver and try to live up to it. One mother describes her feelings when her husband's mentally retarded son comes to live with them: "For one who thought she knew a lot, the last three years have . . . been a humbling experience" (Turnbull & Turnbull, 1985, p. 128). She reports one experience shopping and says: "As the screams became louder and the crowds larger, I felt more and more helpless and inept. My image of being a model mother able to handle difficult situations was beginning to crumble" (Turnbull & Turnbull, 1985, p. 128). Conflicts may be intensified with an exceptional child in the family if the noncustodial, biological parent is especially concerned about how the stepparent will parent and conveys this message to the child. Competition may arise between parents, resulting in problems over visitation, life-style, and/or discipline.

Parenting skills comprise an area in which issues arise. Because the new marital couple has not developed as a team, there is no shared history of child-rearing. A stepparent may not know what is appropriate discipline, and this may easily be exacerbated with an exceptional child. The stepparent not only has to understand developmental stages and age-appropriate behavior but also must modify and adjust expectations for an exceptional child. This can be made more complex by differing guidelines in custodial and noncustodial households.

The lack of clear role definition inherent in stepfamilies underlies all of these characteristics. Though the manpower is available in terms of number of family members, there is role ambiguity as members assume instant multiple roles.

Complicating these situations is the lack of established patterns and rituals to help families with this transition (McGoldrick & Carter, 1980). One stepmother says: "I experience a complex emotional package of jealousy, anger, and fear. I am jealous of his ex-wife. I am jealous of his children, especially his two daughters. I feel inadequate" (Maglin, 1985, p. 40).

There is some preliminary evidence that remarriage is harder on girls than on boys (Kutner, 1988). Younger children usually adapt to stepfamilies more quickly than older children, and, generally, adolescents have the most difficult time.

Stepparents: Guidelines for Professionals

The major emphasis in collaboration with stepparents should be on clarification of roles and boundaries. Subsystems that must be established include the remarried couple, the divorced couple(s), the custodial parent–child, and the stepparent–stepchild (Carlson, 1985). It is important to explore and dispel false expectations stepparents can develop about their role as a parent that lead to feelings of being overburdened, unappreciated, or left out (Golden & Capuzzi, 1986). The special parenting issues unique to this type of family structure can be pointed out. Generally, the biological parent retains the primary parenting role. It can take 4 years or longer for the stepparent to be accepted in an equal parenting role. The professional must be aware of the stages of the parent–child relationship and adjust expectations accordingly. Roles and boundaries need to be clarified, not only within the remarried family, but also with regard to the noncustodial parent and/or family. This is especially important when an exceptional child is involved, for example, when educational decisions must be made. The constructive involvement of noncustodial parents assures the child of the continued support of his or her parents, regardless of the changed marital status. The child knows that in case of emergency the parents can be relied upon. If this doesn't occur, a child may "develop" problems to keep the two biological parents in a relationship (Carlson, 1985).

Professionals can help parents negotiate and develop new traditions (Visher & Visher, 1982). For example, discussion may center on how to address family members, what to do on holidays and special occasions such as Mother's and Father's Day, and how to fill out school forms. Children may have some pragmatic issues such as how friends will find them if their parents have a different last name. An interesting fact is that a stepparent is not legally related to his or her stepchildren (adoption changes the legal relationship, but it is uncommon); they cannot make medical decisions about them, for example, if the school calls with an emergency, or even educational decisions. Though new alliances are formed, old ones that are still important should be preserved (Visher & Visher, 1982). As was suggested above, noncustodial parents should be included in decision making for the child, for example, in school conferences and meetings. The professional might want to encourage the institutions with which the family interacts to send information to *all* involved adults.

A key aspect in working with remarried families is to solidify the couple's relationship. An exceptional child who requires much attention from the biological custodial parent can truly stress the marital relationship. It is not uncommon to find that social networks are restricted and recreational activities limited. Established organizations such as Remarried, Inc. (Santa Ana, California) and the Stepfamily Association of America, Inc. are one source of support. Also, there are a number of books written in comprehensible language that help parents understand the uniqueness of stepparenting (e.g., Visher & Visher, 1979; Weiss, 1979). Finally, several programs have been developed, for example, *Strengthening Stepfamilies* (Albert & Einstein, 1986), to give information and skills to adults in stepfamilies. On the positive side, there are often a wide circle of interested family members who can be counted on for support.

The exceptional child in a stepfamily provides a special challenge to the stepparent. As one mother points out, "Retardation is chronic; that is one of the fundamental problems for families. I am just beginning to realize the impact of lifelong responsibilities and the need to fortify my coping abilities for the adult years" (Turnbull & Turnbull, 1985, p. 140). The stepparent of an exceptional child is accepting a role that is even more challenging than the role of stepparenting a nonexceptional child.

Foster Parents: Characteristics and Issues

The child welfare system in the United States is responsible for over 400,000 children; foster family care is provided when a child's own family is unable to care for him or her (Lewis, 1984). The placement of children into foster homes occurs for reasons including (1) child abuse and neglect; (2) poor physical and/or mental health of the parent; (3) arrest or incarceration of the parent; (4) family violence, drug abuse, or alcoholism; and (5) following political and/or economic upheaval (e.g., Vietnamese boat children). Most of the foster youngsters do not return to their biological parents nor are they adopted (Lewis, 1984). Recently, the placement of exceptional children in foster (and adoptive) homes has increased with the realization of the negative effects of institutional living on a child's development. There are estimates that 40% of children in foster care have physical, emotional, or mental handicaps (Lombana, 1983). In general, foster parents are not responsible for medical expenses and receive a stipend for their services (Nazarro & Warfield, 1975). Those who choose to become foster parents do so for a variety of reasons, and often the financial situation of the foster placement is only marginally better than that of the family of origin (Triseliotis, 1980).

Of primary interest is the role ambiguity that foster parents experience. The status of the foster parents is unclear as they are expected to provide care for an exceptional child in a normal family setting, and yet they have limited authority over the child. Ultimate responsibility for the child rests with the child welfare agency and its representative, the caseworker. Thus, decisions about an exceptional child's education or medical care are always made after conferring with the agency. In fact, many decisions are made by the agency alone without consultation with the foster parents who live with the child. This is problematic as there is often a high turnover of casework staff that leads to a lack of continuity in planning. Lombana (1983) points out that foster parents are pulled in many directions; they are supposed to be advocates of the child, collaborators with the welfare agency, and supportive of the natural parents, yet frequently these three have conflicting needs.

A major characteristic of a foster family is that the duration of placement is temporary, or at least uncertain. Foster children change homes on average 2.7 times (Lombana, 1983). This results in a lack of historical perspective on a child's development and lack of expectation of participating in a child's future. This sense of temporariness may restrain parents from becoming overly involved with the child as the relationship can be terminated at any time. For an exceptional child with physical, emotional, or educational problems, the upheaval and future uncertainty may contribute to insecurity and low self-esteem (Lombana, 1983). It is not uncommon for children to blame themselves when they are moved around from home to home. Inconsistency of care is a serious problem for exceptional children who need structure and regularity of daily life.

Foster Parents: Guidelines for Professionals

As with single parents and stepparents, clarification of role responsibilities is a major objective for foster parent–professional collaboration. Initially, the collaboration may be three-way, that is, foster parent–professional–caseworker. If adoption is unlikely, it is generally helpful for the professional to reframe the foster family as the child's "permanent" family, giving them greater authority and decision-making power (Lewis, 1984). Thus, the caseworker's role is reduced, and control is placed in the hands of the foster parents. This shift may be more difficult to implement when there is an exceptional child, as the foster parents frequently need permission from the agency for medical, tutoring, and/or therapeutic services, which are costly; this means greater reliance on the caseworker. Or the natural parents, if available, may be especially involved with an exceptional child. Still, it is critical that foster parents are fully in charge of exceptional children, who require consistency and certainty. In particular, if the children have come from

institutions, it is important that the permanency of the relationship be acknowledged. When there are disagreements between caseworker and foster parents, it is
advisable for professionals not to make decisions as they will be viewed as siding
with one and against the other (Lewis, 1984).

It seems that many of the foster parents with exceptional children have limited
knowledge and/or training about parenting skills despite good intentions. One of
the major roles in a collaboration is to facilitate skill acquisition, whether within
the relationship or through parent education programs. Again, if the foster parents
are not as familiar with exceptional children and services available to them, the
professional can serve, initially, as a translator of language, roles, and procedures,
particularly for institutions such as schools (e.g., IEP, CSE, least restrictive
environment) or hospitals (e.g., EEG, CAT scans, Ritalin). Parent groups for
special youngsters are often held in the school. Encouraging foster parents to gather
more complete information about the child will help them to understand the child's
needs. For example, instructional methods for a retarded child that were successful
in one school were never shared with the new school until the foster parents called
the original teacher who provided suggestions for both the new teacher and the
foster parents. In another case, one sensitive foster mother did not use the foster
child's native language with him, though she was fluent in it, as she realized that
he felt the language intruded on his relationship with his natural mother which he
wanted to keep separate (Walsh, 1982). Thus, greater knowledge of the child's past
can help foster parents in their present situation. Contact with former caretakers
and family members is generally recommended. In fact, it has recently been
suggested that foster families become a resource in permanency planning for
children. Rather than competing with biological families for a child's affection,
foster parents can give emotional support and model healthy family relationships
and parenting skills for biological families (Ryan, McFadden, & Warren, 1981).
Of course, this applies to situations where children will be returning to birth
parents.

Although all foster parents have to deal with normal fears and fantasies of
children removed from their natural parents, the foster parents of a retarded child
may find he or she has greater difficulty understanding the situation and may blame
him- or herself. There is very limited literature on the exceptional child in a foster
family despite the prevalence of this type of placement, and books you can
recommend to parents are not specifically aimed at these special children (e.g.,
Felker, 1977; Sarason, Lindner, & Crnic, 1976).

Foster parents are often treated as pariahs by others in the community who
suspect their motives or who simply avoid those who are different. As with other
nontraditional parents, social isolation may occur, and the establishment or
reestablishment of a support network is a priority. Again, extended family,
neighbors, and friends provide a good place to start.

Adoptive Parents: Characteristics and Issues

Children previously considered unadoptable can be adopted, and there are people willing to be parents to such children and prepared to work hard to build a family in this different way (James, 1980). Although childless couples are still adopting, so are couples with birth children and singles. Babies are being placed as are older children, sibling groups, and exceptional children with physical and mental handicaps (Gilman, 1987). The growing number of families with non-traditional structure in our society, combined with interracial and other child adoptions in which biological simulation is impossible, have paved the way for sharing rather than concealing differences of adoptive families from other families (Haley, 1973).

Adoption is a different way of building a family but is neither better nor worse than other ways (Gilman, 1987). It provides permanency, something that foster care cannot promise. Still, adoptive parenthood is often seen by societal values as "second best" after biological parenthood (Lewis, 1984). Although the literature suggests that adoptive parents are psychologically diverse, these parents do share some common characteristics. For example, they share a history of waiting for a child, often having had a series of raised expectations and dashed hopes (Ross, 1964). Though the age of adoption, current age of child, type of handicap, and sibling situation all influence the adjustment of the adoptive family, there are certain issues that cut across all groups. These include children's concerns about separation, clinging to old roles, knowledge of the past, and family integration. Further, family issues, particularly with an exceptional child, include the reaction of the extended family and neighbors and responses by other children in the family. Practical concerns abound, for example, health insurance, wills, and life insurance, which parents must be sure apply to an adopted child. At times, society gives mixed messages to adoptive families regarding such issues. However, to ease financial burdens, all states have developed adoption subsidies for special needs children (Gilman, 1987).

It has been suggested that more successful adoptive parents of exceptional youngsters are those who have experienced some trauma or difficulty themselves; this enables them to put themselves in the child's place, face criticism, and cope with painful experiences (James, 1980). Still, as one mother describes, the difficulties can be overwhelming:

> Before Adam came I had read everything I could get my hands on about cerebral palsy. I was prepared for his not walking and speech difficulties. However, reading about a disability and living with a child on a daily basis who has that disability are two different things. . . . I was overwhelmed with it all . . . fear and guilt and tremendous feelings of failure. (Gilman, 1987, p. 211)

Adoptive Parents: Guidelines for Professionals

The collaboration between professionals and adoptive parents with exceptional youngsters has as its goal the successful functioning of the family. The professional supports parental competencies as they talk to their children about separation from birth or foster parents, what happened in the past, what is happening now, and making new attachments. Obviously, the stage at which you see the parents will determine the particular concerns. For children, learning to become a member of the family is probably hardest if they have spent long periods in institutional care. Their adjustment may be precarious, and behaviors may be inappropriate. It is estimated that adoptive families take about 2 years before they "feel right together" (James, 1980). The childless couple who adopts an exceptional child must move from an adult-centered world to a unit with a child. There is some evidence that adoptive parents react to ordinary crises in child-rearing in an extraordinary fashion (Ross, 1964). Professionals can help adoptive parents be realistic in their expectations. Some adoptive parents are uniquely capable of dealing with a specific disability, such as a teacher of the deaf adopting a hearing-impaired child; others must be helped to learn about the disability and, perhaps, how to parent. Again, locating parent education programs or developing new ones collaboratively can be beneficial. As with other nontraditional families, helping to locate community resources and facilitating social supports are important aims of the collaboration and have been discussed above. Helpful agencies and organizations include the Child Welfare League of America (Washington, DC), the North American Council on Adoptable Children (NACAC) (Minneapolis, MN), and Families and Adopting Children Everywhere (FACE) (Baltimore, MD). The National Resource Center for Special Needs Adoption (P.O. Box 337, Chelsea, MI 48118) has as its focus special needs children.

Exceptional children in adoptive families have the same basic needs as all children though they require some additional care. Parents will need to explore future resources for the child who as an adult may require a sheltered environment or special services. Also, if there are normal siblings, rivalries and jealousies may arise, and parents may be faced with loyalty conflicts (see Chapter 4 on siblings).

In all cases, parents and professionals need as much information as possible about the child and his or her background. As with foster children, often the information relevant to current education or medical care is lost or buried; there are frequent examples of misdiagnosis, as when a child labelled retarded was actually hearing impaired.

Finally, the emotional and physical exhaustion common to all parents with exceptional children can be addressed by identifying or developing respite care as was discussed in the section on single parents.

Exceptional Parents

A final form of nontraditional family that professionals may encounter is one where one or both parents of the exceptional child are physically or mentally disabled. Parents who have a handicap do not necessarily have characteristics different from other parents of an exceptional child. There are, however, some special considerations when working with each type of exceptional parent. The first area of concern is with logistical issues (Turnbull & Turnbull, 1986). For example, for a physical disability where a parent uses a wheelchair, transportation and physical access to offices and meeting rooms have to be worked out. Home visits and/or telephone conference calls may be especially appropriate with these parents. With limited physical mobility, taking care of some exceptional youngsters can be more difficult, and home care workers can provide assistance with child care. There are also transport services for parents and children throughout the local area.

Professionals can still work toward joint decision making and collaboration with parents who are limited intellectually. The language used by the professional should avoid difficult and abstract terminology (Seligman, 1979). It may be necessary to repeat information; also, it is frequently useful to have parents take notes and keep records of contacts. For example, when visiting the school or doctor, parents should write down the name, address, telephone number, and specialty area along with simply worded recommendations or outcomes of the meeting. This can facilitate later retrieval of information.

Finally, as with other families, modeling of appropriate parenting behaviors through pairing with neighbors and/or parent education programs is suggested when skills are limited. The Association for Retarded Citizens generally has a wide variety of services in this area.

Summary

Successful professional–parent collaboration involves joint decision making, mutual respect, recognizing and acknowledging strengths, skill acquisition, and empowering parents to work actively on behalf of their exceptional children. This chapter focused on working with nontraditional families, where professionals may need to modify their approach in some way to recognize the special characteristics and needs of these families.

References

Albert, L., & Einstein, E. (1986). *Strengthening stepfamilies.* Circle Pines, MN: American Guidance Service.

Atlas, S. L. (1981). *Single parenting: A practical resource guide.* Englewood Cliffs, NJ: Prentice-Hall.

Barnes, K. (1986). Surviving as a single parent. *The Exceptional Parent, 16,* 47-49.

Blacher, J. (Ed.). (1984). *Severely handicapped young children and their families.* Orlando, FL: Academic Press.

Carlson, C. (1985). Best practices in working with single-parent and stepfamilies. In A. Thomas & J. Grimes (Eds.), *Best practices in school psychology* (pp. 43-60). Kent, OH: National Association of School Psychologists.

Cline, B. (1985). Raising Alan alone. *The Exceptional Parent, 15,* 44-46.

Cordes, C. (1984, August). The rise of one-parent black families. *APA Monitor,* 16-18.

Demands on single parents. (1984). *The Exceptional Parent, 14,* 43-49.

Felker, E. H. (1977). *Foster parenting young children: Guidelines from a foster parent.* New York: Child Welfare League of America.

Gilman, L. (1987). *The adoption resource book.* New York: Harper & Row.

Giordano, J. (1985, February). A stepfather tries to find his role. *Ms,* pp. 50, 78.

Glick, P. (1984). Marriage, divorce and living arrangements: Prospective changes. *Journal of Family Issues, 5,* 7-26.

Golden, L. B., & Capuzzi, D. (1986). *Helping families help children.* Springfield, IL: Charles C. Thomas.

Haley, J. (1973). *Uncommon therapy.* New York: W. W. Norton.

Horne, M. D. (1985). *Attitudes toward handicapped students: Professional, peer and parent reactions.* Hillsdale, NJ: Erlbaum.

James, M. (1980). Home-finding for children with special needs. In J. Triseliotis (Ed.), *New developments in foster care and adoption* (pp. 178-195). London: Routledge & Kegan Paul.

Jarmulowski, V. (1985, February). The blended family: Who are they? *Ms,* pp. 33-34.

Katz, L., & Stein, S. (1983). Treating stepfamilies. In B. B. Wolman & G. Stricker (Eds.), *Handbook of family and marital therapy* (pp. 387-420). New York: Plenum.

Kutner, L. (1988, June). Parent and child. *New York Times,* p. C10.

Lewis, H. C. (1984). Child welfare agencies. In M. Berger & G. J. Jurkovic (Eds.), *Practicing family therapy in diverse settings* (pp. 180-210). San Francisco, CA: Jossey-Bass.

Lombana, J. H. (1983). *Home-school partnerships.* New York: Grune & Stratton.

Maglin, N. B. (1985, February). It could not be more complicated. *Ms,* pp. 40-45.

McGoldrick, M., & Carter, E. A. (1980). Forming a remarried family. In E. A. Carter & M. McGoldrick (Eds.), *The family life cycle* (pp. 265-294). New York: Gardner.

Nazzaro, J. N., & Warfield, G. J. (Eds.). (1975). The parent-professional partnership [Special issue]. *Exceptional Children, 41,* (8).

Prosen, S., & Farmer, J. (1982). Understanding stepfamilies: Issues and implications for counseling. *The Personnel & Guidance Journal, 60*(7), 393-397.

Ross, A. O. (1964). *The exceptional child in the family.* New York: Grune & Stratton.

Ryan, P., McFadden, E. J., & Warren, B. (1981). Foster families: A resource for helping parents. In A. N. Maluccio & P. Sinanoglu (Eds.), *The challenge of partnership: Working with parents of children in foster care* (pp. 189-199). New York: Child Welfare League.

Sarason, I. G., Lindner, K. C., & Crnic, K. (1976). *A guide for foster parents.* New York: Human Science Press.

Sauer, L. E., & Fine, M. A. (1988). Parent-child relationships in stepparent families, *Journal of Family Psychology, 1,* 434-445.

Seligman, M. (1979). *Strategies for helping parents of exceptional children.* New York: Free Press.

Simpson, R. L. (1982). *Conferencing parents of exceptional children.* Rockville, MD: Aspen.

Triseliotis, J. (1980). *New developments in foster care and adoption.* London: Routledge & Kegan Paul.

Turnbull, A. P., & Turnbull, H. R. (1986). *Families, professionals, and exceptionality: A special partnership.* Columbus, OH: Merrill.

Turnbull, H. R., & Turnbull, A. P. (Eds.). (1985). *Parents speak out.* Columbus, OH: Merrill.

Visher, E. B., & Visher, J. S. (1979). *Stepfamilies: A guide to working with stepparents and stepchildren.* New York: Brunner/Mazel.

Visher, E. B., & Visher, J. S. (1982). Stepfamilies and stepparenting. In F. Walsh (Ed.), *Normal family process* (pp. 331-353). New York: Guilford Press.

Walsh, F. (Ed.). (1982). *Normal family process.* New York: Guilford Press.

Weiss, R. (1979). *Going it alone.* New York: Basic Books.

Young, H. H., & Ruth, B. M. (1983). Special treatment problems with the one-parent family. In B. B. Wolman & G. Stricker (Eds.), *Handbook of family and marital therapy* (pp. 377-386). New York: Plenum.

4

EXCEPTIONAL CHILDREN AND THEIR SIBLINGS: OPPORTUNITIES FOR COLLABORATION BETWEEN FAMILY AND SCHOOL

Emanuel J. Mason, Lou Ann Kruse, and Mindy Sloan Kohler

Families with a handicapped child often expend enormous amounts of energy and resources to meet the needs of the disabled member. This investment in the disabled child may come at great cost to other members of the family. An indication of this cost to nonhandicapped siblings is the finding that psychiatrists and other mental health professionals often report that they treat more of these children for adjustment and school-related problems than their handicapped brothers or sisters (Pozanski, 1969; Wikler, 1981). Many of these nonhandicapped siblings of the handicapped bring difficulties to the classroom that other children would not.

Any child may be considered to be a member of two overlapping systems, the home and the school. Viewing the home and school in this way provides a perspective for recognition of shared responsibilities for a child's experiences and how these experiences may have an impact across settings. We will first consider the structure of a well-functioning family and how this structure may be affected by the presence of a handicapped child. In doing this, we will look at how such factors as age and gender of the children and socioeconomic status of a family can influence family dynamics, growth, and development. The school can also be viewed as a complex system that creates pressures and dynamics affecting the members of the school population. With this foundation in structure and dynamics of home and school, we then develop a basis for discussing ways that professional school staff and parents can work collaboratively to help reduce naturally occurring pressures that affect nonhandicapped siblings. It must be emphasized at the outset that although the nonhandicapped sibling may be "at risk" for various types of learning and adjustment difficulties, many of these children do not experience any difficulty. Thus, our focus is on the nonhandicapped child who is experiencing difficulties due to the pressures and conditions resulting from having a handicapped sibling.

The Family as a System

A family may be viewed as a social system that is structured by rules, patterns of communication, and positions of relative power. This structure permits the family to function as a unit and provides support for each member's role (Goldenberg & Goldenberg, 1980). Within the family structure, subsystems may be formed based on gender, interests, environmental contexts or function, and every family member plays unique roles in these subgroupings. Some members might be more heavily involved in some subgroupings than others. For example, in a family subgroup that is devoted to hiking and other outdoor activities, the mother may or may not participate regularly, or may be involved only to pack lunches for the weekly outings.

Roles of individual family members are influenced by culture, tradition, social patterns, and family structure. In the well-functioning family, these roles are mutually supportive and permit growth, satisfaction, expression, and development of a sense of self-efficacy, competence, and personal worth in all family members. Figure 4.1 shows in diagram form how each member's position in the family is balanced by the position and roles of the other family members. The roles and structure are maintained in response to ongoing communication between family members, and the various contexts and functions of the family.

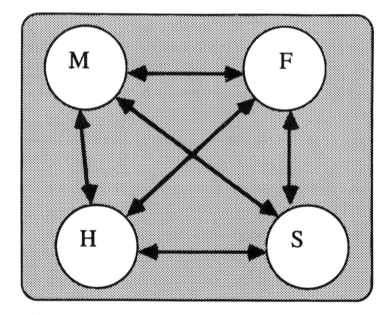

Figure 4.1. The Well-Functioning Family with a Handicapped Child Has Balance and Reciprocity Between All Family Members (M = Mother, F = Father, H = Handicapped Child, S = Sibling of Handicapped Child).

When channels of communication break down due to the focusing of energy and resources on the disabilities of one child, the structure of the family breaks down. The ensuing reduction in the quality of supportiveness in the environment can produce unfavorable effects on self-concept in children with handicapped siblings (Ferrari, 1984; Harvey & Greenway, 1984). Further, increased stress and fatigue experienced by the parents can reduce the quantity and quality of their interactions with their nonhandicapped child (Brody & Stoneman, 1986). On the other hand, the presence of a handicapped brother or sister may afford opportunities for the normal child to expand the sibling role to include helping, teaching, and caregiving, and this could lead to an increased sense of competence, independence, and feelings of self-worth.

Birth Order, Age, and Gender

Although the effects of birth order alone seem negligible (Gath, 1974; Tew & Laurence, 1975), when considered in the context of age and gender, some interesting consistencies appear in the literature. Generally, nonhandicapped older sisters were depended upon to a greater extent than other siblings to assume responsibilities for managing and giving care to the handicapped child (Cleveland & Miller, 1977; Gath, 1972, 1974; Grossman, 1972; Stoneman, Brody, & MacKinnon, 1986). Thus, the older sister may feel more stress and resentment toward the handicapped child, often leading to feelings of guilt and anger directed toward the parents for loss of her childhood and freedom, and for not recognizing or for ignoring her needs. Teachers have reported these older sisters to be less social at school than their peers, but to be better adjusted when the handicapped child did not live at home. On the other hand, when the sister is younger than the handicapped child, the adjustment problems tend to be no greater than those of the younger male sibling (Breslau, 1982; Breslau, Weitzman, & Messenger, 1981).

Male siblings seem to be affected differently than females. When a brother is older or a sister is younger than the handicapped sibling, adjustment may be more difficult for the normal child (Lavigne & Ryan, 1979). Breslau (1982), on the other hand, found that younger males exhibited more symptoms of poor mental health, particularly when the handicapped sibling is male, close in age to the younger brother, and the handicap is severe (Trevino, 1979). Older brothers may be the least involved and consequently the most isolated of the siblings.

The effects of birth order, age, and gender can be compounded by the handicapping condition. For example, brothers seem to become less involved than sisters when the handicap is retardation and the male is the older sibling (Cleveland & Miller, 1977; Grossman, 1972). Further, as the retarded child grows older, his or her younger brothers pass him or her in abilities and knowledge, thus prompting role reversal between the siblings which can lead to resentment and rejection directed toward the older handicapped sibling (Simeonsson & McHale, 1981).

When the handicapping condition is cystic fibrosis, it has been suggested that family structure will be most severely affected when the handicapped child is the first born (Johnson, Muyskens, Bryce, Palmer, & Rodnan, 1985).

Socioeconomic Status of the Family

The less financially secure a family is, the greater the demands upon family members to meet the needs of the handicapped child because fewer resources are available to pay for outside help and services (Featherstone, 1980; Grossman, 1972; Seligman, 1983; Simeonsson & McHale, 1981). In the context of such sacrifice, the handicapped child might be blamed by family members, particularly siblings, for the family's financial condition. Lower socioeconomic status families, often heavily invested in basic economic survival, are not in a position, psychologically, physically, or financially, to deal with the added responsibilities of a handicapped child (McHale, Simeonsson, & Sloan, 1984).

On the other hand, more affluent families who take advantage of their better resources to secure assistance in the care of the handicapped child (e.g., residential programs, summer camps, and professional services) often feel guilty about leaving responsibility for the care of their child to others (Grossman, 1972). Further, these parents may feel that they are neglecting the nonhandicapped child and attempt to compensate for this by indulging this child with material goods instead of attention and emotional support. Middle-class families' problems were often linked to the disappointment of the parents in terms of their aspirations for the handicapped child, and their worries about her or his ability to assume independence at maturity.

Family Size

In larger families, the hopes and aspirations of the parents can be spread over several children, thus dispersing the pressures to compensate for the handicapped member. Further, the more children present, the less obvious the handicapped child becomes in the family constellation (Trevino, 1979). In addition, caretaking responsibilities can be shared by more children in larger families. For these reasons, nonhandicapped siblings from larger families are usually better adjusted than members of small families (Gath, 1973; Grossman, 1972; Trevino, 1979).

Disability Type and Severity

The type of disability may not significantly affect the adjustment of the nonhandicapped siblings (Breslau et al., 1981). For example, Lobato (1983) has summarized a number of studies of siblings of children with Down's Syndrome, hearing impairment, autism, cerebral palsy, and childhood cancers and noted that the type of disability alone did not significantly appear to contribute to the siblings' adjustment. Individual traits such as temperament and behavior of the handicapped or nonhandicapped child might override the influence of a particular disability (McHale et al., 1984).

When severity is defined as the amount of help needed in such basic activities of daily life as toileting, eating, and dressing, siblings of handicapped children show greatest negative effects when the degree of disability is mild or severe. Moderate disability does not produce as strong effects in nonhandicapped siblings (Farber, 1960; Grossman, 1972; Hewitt, Newsom, & Newsom, 1970; Tew & Laurence, 1975). The mechanisms underlying the better situation posed by moderately handicapping conditions are not clear. However, it might be speculated that resentment and jealousy directed toward the handicapped child by the nonhandicapped sibling may result from what appears to be parental favoritism toward a child who does not appear to be very disabled or incapacitated. But, the presence of a severe disability places more of the responsibility on the handicapped sibling leading to complex feelings and pressures.

Family Dynamics

It is clear from the material just reviewed that a handicapped child has definite effects on family relationships. A family that functions well will presumably make better adaptation to the pressures resulting from the presence of the disabled child. *Disengagement* is a common form of adaptation among families with disabled children. A disengaged family is one that is isolated, autonomous, independent, and striving for mastery of the difficulties it faces. Disengagement tends to limit warmth, affection, nurturance, and social support within the family, particularly toward the nonhandicapped children. The parents may rest all their hopes and aspirations on their normal child (or children). However, the nonhandicapped siblings may not be psychologically or intellectually suited to attain these lofty levels and, when they fail to meet the expected standards, these children frequently react with anger, irritation, aggression, and disobedience (Barragan, 1976). On the other hand, when they succeed, they often feel ignored and unappreciated. The feelings of anger resulting from the parental push to excel may be compounded by resentment toward the parents and handicapped siblings over money spent for caregiving and other services that could have been used for family activities, comforts, education, or other needs.

How the parents perceive, feel about, and react to their handicapped child is extremely important (Grossman, 1972). Parents with a mildly handicapped child often display more disengaged reactions and stronger neglect reactions (Perosa & Perosa, 1981). For example, mothers may indulge their learning disabled child in material ways, while at the same time rejecting him or her emotionally (Faerstein, 1981). Parents who overindulge, overprotect, and become otherwise overinvolved with their handicapped children, without dealing with their own feelings of shame, rejection, and anxiety, establish a pattern of confusion for the family. Their contradictory messages toward the handicapped child leave the normal sibling with little support in resolving his or her own confused feelings about the situation. Another common pattern is for the nonhandicapped child to feel left out of discussions or deliberations on family matters and to resent being omitted. The feelings of parents and children alike are complex and conflicting. Without proper opportunity for communication between family members, these confused feelings will remain troubling and unresolved.

Communication among family members is crucial to the preservation of effective functioning. The negative consequences of having a handicapped child in the family will be reduced when family members understand the nature of the handicap and can communicate within the family about it and themselves. This communication would be most effective when conversation concerning the handicapped child involves all family members. However, participation of the mother appears to be most important in family discussions of the handicap (Grossman, 1972).

The School as a System

In school the child is in a system similar to the family. The child must meet obligations and perform according to standards established by others, participate with peers, and respond to pressures to fill a role as student and social member. Because of the number of students in a class, the teacher may not be able to respond effectively and appropriately to the needs of each child at every minute of the school day. This nonresponse can increase behavior that will pressure the teacher to respond and also affects others in the classroom. At the same time, teachers look to the children for recognition and approval of their efforts and investment in the classroom. Further, teachers and administrators are engaged in a mutually dependent relationship in which each one's perceived success relies to some extent on how the other seems to be accepting them. In this way the dynamics of the school are formed and stabilized. Viewing the school setting as a system in which elements—teachers, students, administrators, and others—interact, influence each other, and find roles within, and become invested in, the system permits consideration of ways to destabilize and realign destructive interactive patterns that might form.

In situations in which the school system is functioning effectively, channels of communication are open between the child, his or her peers, and the teacher. (See Figure 4.2.) A child who brings problems from home into the classroom will seek

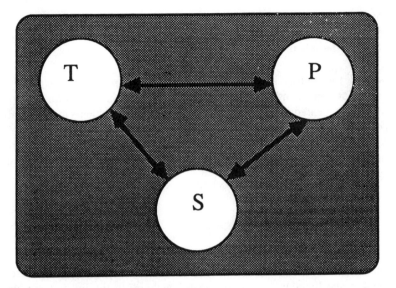

Figure 4.2. Dynamics in a Well-Functioning School Structure (T = Teacher, P = Peer Group, S = Sibling of the Handicapped Child).

ways to express pent-up anger, frustration, or needs for recognition. Teachers may not recognize the child's activity as expressing needs and may respond in such a way as to reinforce the withdrawal, aggression, or other undesirable behavior patterns.

Home and School: Collaborative Overlapping Systems

Minuchin, Rosman, and Baker (1979) used the term "psychofamilial" to describe the connection between school disorders and family functioning. Events that occur in one of these arenas may have direct consequences for the other. Thus, home and school may be viewed as overlapping systems, and the school may become the location of the child's transferred and displaced family struggles (Ehrlich, 1983; Fine & Holt, 1983). Further, examining school-related problems can serve as a diversion from stress factors for family members.

Because the child is a member of two systems, his or her behavior must be viewed within the contexts of these systems. Collaboration between home and school:

1. Provides for a more complete perspective and understanding of the child's problem,

2. promotes direct parent involvement in the solution, and
3. encourages a more comprehensive treatment plan that will have consequences beyond the school setting.

Plas (1986) as well as several contributors to the present book have suggested methods for implementing the systemic approach in schools and for overcoming the inertia of the traditional ways of viewing children's problems that predominate in school settings. Power and Bartholomew (1985) presented an illustration of how the collaborative approach may be implemented through a systems perspective in which the difficulties of crossing the boundaries between school and home spheres of control are discussed.

Three Hypothetical Illustrations

Figure 4.3 contains diagrams of the structural dynamics in three different disengaged families. Each of these illustrations was composed from cases described in the literature or familiar to the authors. In the illustrations, we see Nathan, a child who is frozen out of the lines of communication of the family and left to fend for himself; Jennifer, apparently a very responsible young lady who cares for her handicapped brother after school while her parents both work to meet their medical bills and other expenses; and Tommy, a high-achieving "super kid" whose performance level is determined by unrelenting pressure from his family to compensate for his disabled sibling. As you read the brief family descriptions, it might help to compare the structural diagrams in Figure 4.3, which represent how each family is communicating and relating, to the well-functioning family and school situations depicted in Figures 4.1 and 4.2. In addition to the family structure, the diagrams depict the overlapping school setting and the adjustment the child has made to the family disengagement. The darker the line, the more overloaded the relationship. These illustrations can help the school-based professional understand what must be accomplished to elicit a collaborative effort between family and school to help the child.

It should be remembered when working with these families that there are rarely any real villains. No one is deliberately and individually responsible for causing the family's difficulties. Rather, everyone is mired in a system that is not working, even though the dysfunction is not recognized by all family members. Furthermore, awareness that the family is struggling might increase defensiveness in parents, and this defensiveness will impede their cooperative involvement with the school. Thus, the children need help to break with the roles they find themselves filling, the parents need help to change what they are doing, and teachers and perhaps others in the school who might work with the child will need help to change what

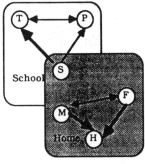

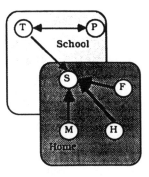

(a) The Isolate   (b) The Overloaded Child

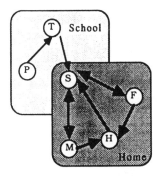

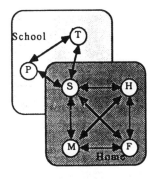

(c) Mandatory Super Kid   (d) Balanced Adjustment

Figure 4.3. The Dynamics of Three Disengaged Families with the Overlapping School Situation (darker lines reflecting higher intensity).

they are doing in response to the child's behavior. Because the intention of a school professional is to improve the adjustment and learning of the child, the examples and recommendations in the next section were devised to support, but not replace, family therapy or other direct intervention outside of the school setting when such action is necessary.

1. The Isolate (Figure 4.3a)

Nathan is 11 years old. His sister is 9 and has been severely handicapped from birth. Since the beginning of the school year, Nathan has been experiencing difficulties in the classroom and has been kept after school for disciplinary reasons several times. Teachers complain that Nathan is aggressive, disrespectful, and stubborn. He frequently draws attention to himself in class by calling out. In addition, Nathan is often tardy for class or skips classes. He seems to have no close friends. Nathan's teachers report that he shows limited social skills on the playground. In conferences with teachers, Nathan's parents indicated a very different perception of their son. His parents reported that he was independent and confident and they displayed little concern about his emotional adjustment or ability in social situations. Their expectations for Nathan's achievement seemed vague. Family activities are almost nonexistent. Usually one parent or the other will do something with the handicapped child while Nathan is left to amuse himself. The family rarely does anything as a unit. The parents were reluctant to discuss the future with teachers and have not considered who will assume responsibility for caring for their handicapped daughter when they become too old to be her primary caregivers. The parents seem very busy with their handicapped child and admit to not having discussed their daughter's handicaps with Nathan ("He is only a kid!"). They further admit that they do not talk to him (or each other) very much about anything.

2. The Overloaded Child (Figure 4.3b)

Jennifer is the 14-year-old sister of a 12-year-old handicapped boy. Jennifer's parents both have to work to keep the family out of financial difficulty. Therefore, Jennifer is the primary caregiver to her brother after school. Her brother attends a special school and is brought home by the school bus at 3:45. Jennifer must meet her brother's bus each day, clean the house, do physical therapy with her brother, and prepare dinner before her parents arrive home from work. She has few friends, does not participate in extracurricular activities after school, and has a very limited social life. Her teachers report that they like Jennifer very much, but that she seems withdrawn, quiet, and distracted when compared to the other children. A couple of her teachers even said they felt she was depressed, and one said that "Jennifer does not seem to be a happy person." The teachers report that Jennifer's grades are average, that she accepts responsibility, and that she follows orders and does everything asked of her. Jennifer states that she enjoys taking care of her brother, but sometimes resents being the only one who is available to provide care.

3. The Mandatory Super Kid (Figure 4.3c)

Tommy, 10 years old and 7 years younger than his severely handicapped brother, has an A average in academic subjects and excels in all the major seasonal sports at school. His teachers and coaches all report that although Tommy seems to excel at everything he tries, he does not seem to be enjoying himself. Rather, as one of his teachers said, "Tommy is grimly devoted to excellence." In other words, Tommy seems to feel he has no choice but to do well in everything. His homework assignments are often turned in late, but are perfectly done. Work done in class is seldom completed within the time allotted, but the work that is done is always perfect. Group cognitive assessments suggest that Tommy's current academic performance exceeds the level at which he should be expected to perform. Although Tommy plays team sports, and is always chosen as a teammate because of his athletic ability, he seems to have few friends off the athletic field. Both Tommy and his parents have high, and somewhat unrealistic, expectations and aspirations for him. His mother expects him to be "a famous physician," while his father expects him to ". . . at least be a state governor." Although Tommy has few friends among his peers, his parents happily report that he mixes very well in adult company.

Establishing Collaborative Relationships Between School and Home

The three illustrations show how family dysfunction centering around a handicapped child can affect school performance of the nonhandicapped sibling. They also show how school-related difficulties are often extensions of problems experienced in the home environment. Effective attempts at reducing these patterns, once established, will require cooperation between school and home. However, one of the strongest barriers to eliciting this cooperation may be conflicts in power that both structures exercise over the child. For example, it is difficult for parents to discuss responsibility for events that occur at school, and for the school to share responsibility for events that happen in school. In addition, educators will rarely commit to any obligations to their students beyond the walls of the school. In other words, problems of territory and power may require attention before a collaborative relationship can be established. In view of these barriers, the overall strategy for establishing collaborative relationships to deal with the problem should include the following elements:

1. *Education of all concerned*—Parents may need help to understand the dynamics of family interaction and the role each member plays in the family constellation. They should be made aware of the unique pressures to perform, assume responsibility, and succeed placed upon nonhandicapped siblings and the frustration, deprivation, jealousy, guilt, and isolation these pressures can produce. In addition, school personnel should be prepared to understand the role the nonhandicapped sibling plays in the family, and how this role may be translated into behavior that reflects learning or adjustment problems these children might be experiencing. Further, both should be prepared to avoid natural barriers and territorial issues as they pursue a collaborative effort in which school and home support cooperative goals.

2. *Parents included as partners in the decision making and planning for the nonhandicapped child*—Parents and school personnel should come to recognize that each has as its primary concern the interests of the child and, further, that neither is trying to usurp the authority of the other. Parents should realize that school personnel are concerned about their children, see them for a significant part of the day, and are willing to work cooperatively, while school personnel should recognize that parents are concerned and can have something to offer. By planning interventions together, a more integrative approach can be achieved.

3. *Family counseling or consultation*—Parents may require therapeutic consultation to recognize the character of the problem in their own family and be able to take action to destabilize destructive patterns, particularly in terms of issues extending beyond school.

4. *Parents become empowered*—By being involved in the planning and decision making for their child, parents are given the power to work actively to assist in the reduction of school learning, behavioral, and adjustment problems. This will contribute to increased support from the child's home for school interventions.

Implementation of a collaborative effort between the school and the parents would probably be done by a school-based helping professional such as a school psychologist or guidance counselor. However, anyone able to function on behalf of the child, and with the confidence of both the school staff and the parents (such as a physician, pastor, or community mental health worker), could probably play an active role in the implementation. This professional can act initially as consultant and informational conduit between parents and school and in this manner bring the two together to establish the collaboration. This may require a slightly different stance than other forms of consultative services in that the initial goal of the consultant is to bring the two not always congruently oriented groups into a productive, collaborative relationship, rather than to provide information directly to help the parents or school personnel work out the problems on their own.

Later consultative activities might require more therapeutic involvement as the collaborative process progresses and the nature of the problem changes. Further, during the course of the collaborative relationship, the consultant might assume different roles and positions within the consultative system. For example, initially the helping professional might act as a mediator between the school and home, later serving more of an information resource function, and still later taking an advocacy position for the handicapped or nonhandicapped child as the situation changes. Other roles might be relatively more based in therapeutic intervention.

The activities and strategies presented below may be considered as a list of ideas that can be applied when a nonhandicapped child with a handicapped brother or sister presents a pattern similar to one of the three illustrations discussed earlier. First, five general goals are listed that may be applicable to any situation in which a child is experiencing school difficulties because of the pressures of coming from a home in which there is a handicapped sibling. Then more specific suggestions are given for the isolated, overloaded, and mandatory super kid patterns described earlier. When faced with similar cases, the helping professional may use these suggestions to help formulate a strategic plan that provides sufficient flexibility for implementation of an effective collaborative relationship between the parents and the school.

Goals for Home–School Collaboration

1. Break the dysfunctional patterns of behavior in the family and at school.
2. Establish and reinforce new patterns of behavior for members of both the home and school systems.
3. Open channels of communication between teachers and parents.
4. Open channels of communication between the child and other family members.
5. Involve parents actively and constructively in the planning and decision making regarding their child's school experiences.

Strategies for the School-Based Professional to Establish Collaboration Between Parents and School

The following strategies would be helpful in establishing a collaborative relationship between the school and the family of a nonhandicapped child who has a handicapped brother or sister. These general strategies may be useful in a variety of situations. More specific strategies to use with families of children who resemble the Isolate, Overloaded Child, or Super Kid follow. The strategies discussed below are not presented in any particular order and are only suggested. Implementation should be determined by the settings and people involved, and the collaborative process.

1. Recognizing that a complex assortment of tradition, personal feelings and investment, social expectation, and well-established rules exist in both parents and school workers regarding the performance of the child, both should be separately prepared to enter the collaborative relationship before the first joint meetings are held. Both parents and teachers should recognize that neither intends to usurp the power of, or undermine, the other within their respective domain (home or school), and that both are interested in helping the child. It should be evident from the outset that each party has something to gain from cooperating with the other.

2. In preparing the parents, what the parents would like the school to do and what they themselves might be prepared to do if the school would permit them should be discussed. Similar planning with the teachers and relevant school personnel could facilitate progress at the first meeting between parents and school.

3. Help both parents and school personnel understand the home–school dynamics of the nonhandicapped child's situation.

4. Arrange for regular and periodic follow-up contacts between parents and teachers to update the collaborative relationship and change strategies and activities at home and in school as the child's behavior changes with the goal of further establishing the child's effective adjustment and learning.

5. The school-based consultant might place him- or herself in a neutral role, collaborative to both parents and school staff, monitoring progress at home and in school, and promoting communication and coordination between the two settings.

Goals and Strategies for the Isolated Nonhandicapped Sibling

General Goals: At home the goals are to increase involvement of Nathan in the family; strengthen family interaction and communication, improve quality and quantity of Nathan's interactions with his peers; reduce the amount of family energy focused on the handicapped sibling, set clearer objectives and expectations for Nathan at home. In school, the goals are to identify responsibilities for Nathan and reward successful performance, increase constructive participation in class and social interaction with classmates, increase level of verbal expression and communication.

Specific Strategies:

1. Parents and teachers hold regular meetings to discuss Nathan and his activities at home and school.
2. Parents and teachers provide honest answers to Nathan's questions about his sister and what is expected of him and, when they do not know the answer to a particular question, they will say so.
3. Parents spend time with Nathan in family activities (e.g., hobbies, homework, outings) and include him in family discussions.

4. Parents provide Nathan with a sense of his own importance by giving him opportunities to participate in family planning and decision making.

5. Teachers agree to design small group classroom activities in which any child, including Nathan, will find it difficult to avoid participation, such as group learning activities in which each member of the group is responsible for some part of a lesson.

6. Teachers agree to appoint Nathan to classroom committees and responsibilities that would involve him with his peers (e.g., committee planning a class Christmas party, committee planning class production of a play, etc.).

7. Teachers agree to try to get Nathan to speak or write about his feelings, home, handicapped sister, but to do this in ways that would avoid involving the whole class and might embarrass him.

8. Teachers agree to contact the parents regularly to discuss Nathan's performance in class when something out of the usual occurs and will try to involve both the mother and the father in these contacts.

9. Teachers recognize that they should not reveal information to the parents that Nathan provides in confidence without discussing the situation first with Nathan (unless not to reveal the information might put him in some sort of danger).

10. Parents agree to help Nathan understand his sister's condition and the long-term implications of it. They might have to begin the dialogue by asking the first questions.

11. Parents agree to provide material about their daughter's handicaps for Nathan to read and then discuss these materials with him. They may obtain this material from the library or their physician's office.

12. Parents agree to talk about the future together and to include Nathan in these discussions. Topics might include such things as who will care for their daughter when she is an adult. What will her life be like, and what will Nathan's responsibilities for her be.

13. Parents agree that when they cannot answer a question, they should tell Nathan, and seek help with these questions from school professionals (school psychologist, social worker, teacher, guidance counselor, etc.), their family physician, or other families with handicapped children.

14. Parents agree to schedule regular family discussions in which Nathan takes part. At these discussions, parents should ask for Nathan's opinions about family plans and decisions.

15. Parents agree to show interest in Nathan's school activities by asking him what his day was like, and about his activities. They will also show him that they are concerned about his activities outside of school by discussing with him his friends, preferences, and interests.

16. Parents agree to encourage Nathan's participation in team sports (such as soccer, Little League, etc.), scouts, or other group activities outside of school.

17. Parents agree to regular meetings with the teacher to learn about Nathan's performance in school, on the playground, and with peers and to relate to the teacher any significant changes in behavior or performance at home.
18. Both parents agree to discuss together how to bring Nathan into family discussions and activities and recognize him for his efforts in school and at home.

Goals and Strategies with the Overloaded Child

General Goals: To decentralize the focus from the overloaded child, to establish more communication between all the family members, to create more balance in the distribution of responsibilities within the family, and to increase participation and involvement in class and extracurricular activities. Additional goals are: to improve the opportunity for experiences more typical of adolescence by reducing some of Jennifer's caregiving and family responsibilities and to increase the time the family spends together as a unit.

Specific Strategies:

1. Parents and teachers agree to encourage Jennifer to participate in extra-curricular activities that they feel she would enjoy.
2. Teacher agrees to regular meetings with parents regarding Jennifer's participation in school settings.
3. Teacher agrees to help parents arrange to meet with the school social worker to help find community resources for caregiving and services to handicapped children.
4. Parents agree to help Jennifer identify interests (e.g., reading, hobbies, etc.) that can be engaged in while she is at home with her handicapped brother.
5. Teacher agrees to encourage Jennifer to work with other students on class projects and to organize small group activities in class in which Jennifer will have to participate.
6. Parents agree to prepare a list of responsibilities and chores with Jennifer and assign them on a rotational basis.
7. Parents agree to initiate a "day off" for the overloaded child so that she can participate in activities with her peers outside of the home.
8. Members of the family agree to schedule weekly meetings to discuss problems, feelings, and successes of each member because there is so little opportunity for the family to meet informally and spontaneously to discuss these matters. Activities involving the whole family may be planned at these meetings.
9. Parents agree to contact the school to discuss Jennifer's progress and performance with her teachers. They will ask for teachers' assistance in

identifying things that Jennifer should be doing which should be built into her schedule of responsibilities.

10. Parents agree to encourage Jennifer to express her feelings and frustrations to them and provide a model for this by discussing their own feelings with her.

Goals and Strategies with the Super Kid

General Goals: To help Tommy develop social skills and foster relationships that are more reciprocal with his handicapped sibling, parents, and peers; to redirect intense pressure for achievement and excellence that Tommy perceives focusing on him and encourage parents to make their expectations for Tommy more realistic.

Specific Strategies:

1. Teachers agree to maintain a realistic perspective about Tommy's capabilities while not confronting his parents about their views because the parents are probably at least as invested as Tommy in Tommy's overcompensating for his brother's handicap.

2. Teachers agree to communicate to parents information about test scores, grades, work performance, and peer interaction objectively and, at the same time, to sound favorably disposed toward the child and recognize frankly and objectively how hard he works to achieve his level of performance. The teachers further agree to avoid sounding too accusative to the parents in order not to arouse unnecessary defenses.

3. Teachers will suggest that parents ask the school psychologist or counselor to explain in greater depth the meaning of test scores and other information if this seems necessary.

4. Teachers agree to arrange for Tommy's feelings and interests to be explored by the counselor or school psychologist and then enlist their aid in explaining these interests to the parents and Tommy.

5. Teachers agree to be warm and supportive of Tommy, even when he is late with homework or assignments, or on the rare occasion that his work is not outstanding, and will encourage the parents to recognize his efforts regardless of the outcome. Tommy is hard enough on himself without additional pressure from teachers and parents.

6. The school psychologist agrees to discuss with the parents the implications of Tommy's need to excel in terms of its effects on his future growth and emotional development, self-concept, self-esteem, and social relationships.

7. Parents agree to suggest ways that their son involve himself more with his peers in his various activities.

8. Parents agree to explore with Tommy any interests beyond schoolwork and sports that would not put him in competition with his peers (e.g., model airplane

building, studying birds or insects, or learning to play a musical instrument). These should be activities that would provide opportunity for enjoyment and making friends with children his own age who have similar interests.

9. Parents agree to schedule times for family activities, picnics, outings, etc., in which all members participate and which provide times to discuss feelings, goals, and aspirations and other matters of importance to individual family members.

Summary

The nonhandicapped sibling of a handicapped child lives in a setting that contains potential for more intense pressures, unresolved expectations, and conflicting feelings than if that family had no disabled members. Increased pressure from financial needs, caregiving responsibilities for the handicapped child, and lack of opportunity for communication and self-expression within the family can become major sources of conflict for the normal sibling and may lead to disengagement and dysfunction in the family system. Often the behavior resulting from disruption to family functioning is brought to school in some form by the child. When school-based professionals provide mental health and psychological services for these children, a collaborative family–school systems approach can assist parents and school personnel to help more effectively to reduce the problems and frustrations of the nonhandicapped sibling.

References

Barragan, M. (1976). The child centered family. In P. J. Guerin (Ed.), *Family therapy: Theory and practice* (pp. 232-248). New York: Gardner.

Breslau, N. (1982). Siblings of disabled children: Birth order and age spacing effects. *Journal of Abnormal Child Psychology, 10,* 85-96.

Breslau, N., Weitzman, M., & Messenger, K. (1981). Psychological functioning of siblings of disabled children. *Pediatrics, 61,* 344-353.

Brody, G. H., & Stoneman, Z. (1986). Contextual issues in the study of sibling socialization. In J. J. Gallagher & P. M. Vietze (Eds.), *Families of handicapped persons: Research, programs and policy issues* (pp. 197-217). Baltimore, MD: Paul H. Brookes.

Cleveland, D. W., & Miller, N. (1977). Attitude and life commitments of older siblings of mentally retarded adults. *Mental Retardation, 15,* 38-41.

Ehrlich, M. I. (1983). Psychofamilial correlates of school disorders. *Journal of School Psychology, 21,* 191-199.

Faerstein, L. W. (1981). Stress and coping in families of learning disabled children: A literature review. *Journal of Learning Disabilities, 14,* 420-423.

Farber, B. (1960). Family organization and crises: Maintenance of integration in families with a severely mentally retarded child. *Monographs of the Society for Research in Child Development, 25* (Serial No. 75) 1-95.

Featherstone, H. (1980). *A difference in the family: Life with a disabled child.* New York: Basic Books.

Ferrari, M. (1984). Chronic illness: Psychosocial effects on siblings. I. Chronically ill boys. *Journal of Child Psychology and Psychiatry, 25,* 459-476.

Fine, M. J., & Holt, P. (1983). Intervening with school problems: A family systems perspective. *Psychology in the Schools, 20,* 59-66.

Gath, A. (1972). The mental health of congenitally abnormal children. *Journal of Child Psychology and Psychiatry, 13,* 211-218.

Gath, A. (1973). The school-age siblings of mongol children. *British Journal of Psychiatry, 123,* 161-167.

Gath, A. (1974). Siblings' reactions to mental handicap: A comparison of brothers and sisters of mongol children. *Journal of Child Psychology and Psychiatry, 15,* 187-198.

Goldenberg, I., & Goldenberg, H. (1980). *Family therapy: An overview.* Monterey, CA: Brooks/Cole.

Graliker, B., Fishler, K., & Koch, R. (1962). Teenage reaction to a mentally retarded sibling. *American Journal of Mental Deficiency, 66,* 838-843.

Grossman, F. K. (1972). *Brothers and sisters of retarded children: An exploratory study.* Syracuse, NY: Syracuse University Press.

Hannah, M. E., & Midlarsky, E. (1985). Siblings of the handicapped: A literature review for school psychologists. *School Psychology Review, 14,* 510-520.

Harvey, D. H. P., & Greenway, A. P. (1984). The self-concept of physically handicapped children and their nonhandicapped siblings: An empirical investigation. *Journal of Child Psychology and Psychiatry, 25,* 273-274.

Hewitt, S., Newsom, J., & Newsom, E. (1970). *The family and the handicapped child.* London: George Allen & Unwin.

Johnson, M. C., Muyskens, M., Bryce, M., Palmer, J., & Rodnan, J. (1985). A comparison of family adaptations to having a child with cystic fibrosis. *Journal of Marital and Family Therapy, 11,* 305-312.

Lavigne, J., & Ryan, M. (1979). Psychological adjustment of siblings with chronic illness. *Pediatrics, 63,* 616-627.

Lobato, D. (1983). Siblings of handicapped children: A review. *Journal of Autism and Developmental Disorders, 13,* 347-364.

McHale, S. M., Simeonsson, R. J., & Sloan, J. L. (1984). Children with handicapped brothers and sisters. In E. Schopler & G. Mesibov (Eds.), *The effects of autism on the family.* New York: Plenum.

Minuchin, S., Rosman, B. L., & Baker, L. (1979). *Psychosomatic families: Anorexia nervosa in context.* Cambridge, MA: Harvard University Press.

Perosa, L. M., & Perosa, S. L. (1981). The school counselor's use of structural family therapy with learning disabled students. *The School Counselor, 29,* 152-155.

Plas, J. M. (1986). *Systems psychology in the schools.* New York: Pergamon Press.

Power, T. J., & Bartholomew, K. L. (1985). Getting uncaught in the middle: A case study in family-school system consultation. *School Psychology Review, 14,* 222-229.

Pozanski, E. (1969). Psychiatric difficulties in siblings of handicapped children. *Pediatrics, 8,* 232-234.

Seligman, M. (1983). *Family with a handicapped child: Understanding and treatment.* New York: Grune & Stratton.

Simeonsson, R. J., & McHale, S. W. (1981). Review: Research on handicapped children: Sibling relationships. *Child Care, Health, and Development, 7,* 153-171.

Stoneman, Z., Brody, G. H., & MacKinnon, C. E. (1986). Same-sex and cross-sex siblings: Activity choices, roles, behavior, and gender stereotypes. *Sex Roles, 15,* 495-511.

Tew, B., & Laurence, K. (1975). Mothers, brothers, and sisters of patients with spina bifida. *Developmental Medicine and Child Neurology, 15,* 69-76.

Trevino, F. (1979). Siblings of handicapped children: Identifying those at risk. *Social Casework, 60,* 488-493.

Wikler, L. (1981). Chronic stresses of families of mentally retarded children. *Family Relations, 30,* 281-288.

SECTION ▌▌

Educational and Intervention Considerations

5

MULTICULTURAL ISSUES RELATED TO FAMILIES WITH AN EXCEPTIONAL CHILD

Vivian I. Correa and Jeanne Weismantel

Involving families in the education of their children has become a major goal for professionals working with handicapped students. The benefits associated with involving the families in planning and implementing interventions have been documented by many researchers (Comer, 1980; Epstein, 1985, 1986; Morgan, 1982; Turnbull & Turnbull, 1986). With the increased incidence of culturally and linguistically diverse students entering mainstream U.S. school programs, professionals have become aware of their responsibilities in meeting the needs of students and families from different cultural backgrounds. Cultural and ethnic backgrounds are important aspects of how a family conceptualizes, understands, and reacts to having a child with a disability, with implications in terms of the extended family's (a) acceptance and support, (b) willingness to acknowledge a disability, and (c) perception of and response to agencies and mental health professionals.

The purpose of this chapter is to present a model for developing culturally sensitive home–school partnerships among culturally diverse families with handicapped children and mental health and special education personnel. The chapter will (a) provide an overview of the present demographic changes related to culturally diverse families in the United States, (b) discuss cultural attributes associated with various ethnic groups that have an impact on the families' adjustment to having a handicapped child, (c) review the changing role of school professionals' meeting the needs of culturally diverse children and encouraging family involvement in school, and (d) provide a step-by-step model that guides the professional in developing effective special education partnerships with culturally diverse families.

Changing Demographics

The need for professionals to work effectively with families from varying cultural backgrounds is becoming crucial as numbers of minority populations continue to increase. The foreign-born population in the United States may currently exceed 15 million (National Coalition of Advocates for Students, 1988). Predictions are that by the turn of the century, minority cultures will be in the majority in many urban centers (Lynch & Stein, 1987). One estimate is that the numbers of Hispanic immigrants into the United States will average 250,000 a year for the foreseeable future (Nicolau & Valdivieso, 1988). Currently, immigration into the United States from war-torn countries like Nicaragua continues at a high rate. Trauma, time away from school, and poor diet are experienced by youth fleeing such conditions. This background puts them at risk of school failure in the United States. Immigrants seeking economic betterment continue to cross the Rio Grande. Many native-born Mexican-American families as well as some other Hispanic groups are poorer than and have higher birth rates than do mainstream U.S. persons. The incidence of teenage child-bearing mothers is high among some Hispanic groups, and infants born to these mothers are at risk for medical and educational problems. Asian populations also continue to immigrate to the United States. Some Asian groups like the Hmongs from Cambodia bring with them two difficulties: stresses due to war experiences and educational problems due to being from a nonliterate background. Unquestionably, professionals who can work effectively with culturally diverse students and their families are greatly needed. Within the public schools the need for personnel who can work with students who are both handicapped and from culturally and linguistically varied backgrounds is becoming critical.

Cultural Variations

Today, special education professionals are aware that their job responsibilities will require that they provide intervention programs that are sensitive to culturally and linguistically different students and their families. For example, mental health professionals who work with seriously emotionally disturbed children and youth expressed concern about meeting the needs of the increasing number of minority children referred for consultation. In a workshop in 1986 of the Child and Adolescent Service System Program of the National Institute for Mental Health, professionals delineated stresses that have an impact on the mental health of minority youth in school systems:

• social environment in which the natural, familiar helping and support systems of cultural groups are not utilized by professionals;

- poverty, including lack of employment opportunities and poor urban housing and neighborhoods;
- intergroup conflict;
- intergenerational conflicts, as young students adopt values and choose life-styles of the new culture faster than do older members of families;
- difference in family structure between minority extended family and dominant nuclear family of the majority culture;
- alcohol and substance abuse;
- negative perceptions held by minority groups about mental health care and other types of medical care in the mainstream culture;
- lack of sensitivity of professionals to factors such as level of acculturation of members of minority cultures, degree of proficiency in English, and the fact that many families have multiple problems.

Although stresses contributing to the families' and individual family members' inability to function were seen as having similarities across minority groups, differences among the groups and their reactions to life in the United States were noted.

It is critical that special education and mental health professionals become acquainted with the families' individual cultural life-style, including values, beliefs, and practices associated with having a child with a disability. Unfortunately, many professionals have typically gained this knowledge through exposure to multicultural materials that offer a smattering of stereotypical elements of cultures. Glenn (1989) warns that "[W]e must never speak of culture as an occasion for reinforcing stereotypes—negative or positive—about ethnic groups" (p. 779). Culture is dynamic and requires from professionals that they understand the "lived culture" of the family, not the fiestas and folklore that had meaning for older generations but are not part of the lives of families currently immigrating to the United States and adapting to the Anglo-American mainstream culture (Glenn, 1989).

Furthermore, the general labels "Hispanic" and "Asian-American," for example, can conceal the differences that exist among national groups. Cuban-Americans, Mexican-Americans, and Puerto Ricans are the largest groups among Hispanics. Cuban-Americans are a refugee population who came under duress to the United States and who cannot return to Cuba. Many Mexican-Americans and Puerto Ricans are among those who migrate to find better opportunities. Mexican-Americans include both native-born persons and recently arrived immigrants. Many immigrants enter illegally and have had minimal experience in school and in urban life. Puerto Ricans are U.S. citizens, who frequently move between the island and the mainland United States. Asian-Americans are often pictured as models for minority populations by the media that report Asian educational achievements. The term "Asian" includes some national groups from Southeast

Asia who are refugees unaccustomed to urban life. These groups often experience grave problems in U.S. public schools. For the mental health worker to assume that persons who are Chinese, Japanese, Korean, Vietnamese, or Filipino can all be neatly fit under the label of Asian-Americans would ignore some important cultural and familial differences.

An added difficulty with labels is stereotyping. For example, labeling Asians as models of success obscures the very real problems many Asian students from all the national groups experience, especially in trying to master English (Yao & Houng, 1987). Stereotyping obscures recognition of personal traits. Some Hispanics are quiet, independent persons, and there are both outgoing and relaxed Asians.

Providing professionals with cultural profiles of ethnic groups will be effective *only* if the professional can affirm that the cultural pattern does indeed exist within an individual family and that it may be affecting the way the family is coping with a disabled child. For example, parents and family members should be the first source of information about their child's behavior and cause of a disability. A second source of information is those persons whose opinions are valued by the families, such as *compadres* (godparents) in the Hispanic family and elders in the Asian family. Including the families' respected support person in decision making assists professionals and minority culture persons in determining if students' behaviors indicate problems, the degree of illness, and appropriate therapy. Once a cultural belief is validated within the family, mental health and special education personnel can work to modify the traditional client–therapist relationship in order to incorporate the informal network of the minority culture students (Katz-Levy, Laurie, & Kaufmann, 1987). Using cultural information wisely and carefully in working with ethnically different families empowers professionals to provide more effective services. Valuable resources on cultural profiles of minority group children and their families are provided by McGoldrick, Pearce, and Giordano (1982) and by Powell (1983).

Specific cultural characteristics that may provide mental health and special education personnel with valuable insight into the family of a disabled child vary among ethnic groups. For example, many Hispanics report that for them, the U.S. mental health system seems irrelevant and oppressive. They see the family as the source of problem solving, and of value setting. Frequently, they perceive the U.S. system as being in conflict with traditional Hispanic family values, including their spiritual beliefs. In some Hispanic cultures, for example, the belief that a child's handicap resulted from *mal ojo* (evil eye) can influence the family adjustment to special education intervention (Seligman & Darling, 1989). The family may believe it is pointless to provide special education services and instead provide the child with spiritual healing sessions from a *curandero* (folk healer) (Spector, 1979).

Asian-American families generally place great value in conformity to authority and tranquility. Acting in harmony, being humble about one's abilities, and showing deference to authority figures are appropriate behaviors. In working with Asian-American troubled students, counselors and mental health caregivers are learning to consider the degree to which mental and emotional stresses have physical manifestations. Students do not wish to display emotions, but may experience deeply felt shame and guilt when they fail to achieve at a high level. Asian-American students may feel that they have brought shame on their families; students' painful headaches may be symptoms of inner stress. Furthermore, Chinese parents have been reported as having high educational aspirations for their children, and the birth of a child with severe mental handicaps may be problematic to the family's acceptance of the child (Seligman & Darling, 1989). If the family appears to ignore or deny the child's special educational needs, school personnel can at least understand the family's reactions and ask them to speak with other Chinese families who have adjusted to the special needs of their children.

Table 5.1 provides selected examples of cultural beliefs that may assist school personnel and mental health personnel in working with culturally diverse families of exceptional children. The list is by no means representative of all aspects of cultural beliefs within the ethnic groups. It serves only as a way to demonstrate areas that may be considered when providing culturally sensitive intervention programs for families and their exceptional children. Again, professionals are warned not to stereotype families on the basis of ethnicity (Seligman & Darling, 1989).

Even among other school professionals, such as librarians, modifying an existing practice is becoming a way to meet the needs of culturally diverse groups. A report of the Task Force on Library and Information Services to Cultural Minorities stated that librarians should reach out to members of diverse groups who may fear what they perceive to be institutions that are government operated (Allen, 1988). Others cannot believe that library service is free, without obligation to the user. In Fresno County, California, an area with a large population of Hispanic farm workers who mainly lacked transportation to the city library, librarians called the bookmobile a "barriomobile." Complete with a mural painted on the sides of the vehicle and providing appropriate materials in English and in Spanish, the Biblioteca Ambulante provides library services to Hispanic families (Allen, 1988).

These reports by mental health practitioners, special educators, and librarians indicate that working effectively with families from diverse cultural backgrounds requires that professionals have a positive, accepting attitude toward persons of minority language and culture. A willingness to adapt practices to meet the needs of changing populations is essential. Being informed about the background and characteristics of a particular group enables professionals to assess the needs of the group and of the individual members better. The task is challenging and complex.

Table 5.1
Examples of Cultural Beliefs Affecting Intervention with Culturally Diverse Families of Exceptional Children

Ethnic group	Cultural beliefs	Implication for services
Mexican-American	• spiritual healing (*curanderos*)	• understand that health-related, special education, or mental health services may be secondary to the family's hope of a cure for the disabled child • healers may be a support system for the family
Puerto Rican	• *machismo*	• respect the role of the father in family governance • understand that the father may be uncomfortable with the child care role • provide "male-oriented" activities for parent involvement • use male professionals when possible • respect the mother's need to postpone decision making until she speaks with her husband
	• *compadres*	• extended family system may include godparents, close friends, and neighbors • respect the involvement of nonfamily members in the decision-making process for the child's services • use extrafamilial subsystems to provide support for parents
Japanese	• avoid confrontation	• parents are not likely to challenge professionals in a meeting, even if they are unhappy with the recommendations
Native American	• acceptance of fate	• acceptance of the handicapped child and focus on the child's strengths

Evaluating and refining ways of working with families as professional knowledge accumulates through experience is important.

The Changing Role of School Professionals

As far back as the 1950s educators commented on the need to construct bridges between home and school (Hymes, 1953). The bridge was seen in the 1950s as a modern concept of a link that allows parents and teachers, through proven techniques, to achieve a unity for children. The goal was to define an area of common understanding between parents and teachers. The first area was a definition of what children are—the roles they play; how they grow and develop; and how to help them learn. The second area was to determine what good *education* is—what to look for in schools and how to obtain the desired educational programs within communities. If educators and parents could agree on this common area, then they could form a team, reinforce each other, and work to assist the student.

Common areas were defined, at least in some schools, especially in suburbia, where, in the 1950s, mothers were home and were often school volunteers, PTAs flourished, dads came home in the evening, families ate dinner at the table together, and the children did homework. Few families had the small black and white televisions of the era. The schools saw such families as providing the background needed for the education of youth. Suburban mothers, with their station wagons for field trips and their cakes for school parties, were defined as supportive of school efforts. Parents saw the local public schools as the important elements of a democratic society, often with bright new buildings and enthusiastic teachers and coaches, who guided the students toward social and economic success. The support system arising from the common understanding of students and education by school personnel and parents worked, at least for white, middle-class students with no special needs.

In the 1950s, however, cracks appeared in the common area. From *Brown vs. the Board of Education,* a series of challenges to the nation's education system appeared. Where were the common areas when black parents entered previously all-white schools, or when white parents found that their children had a black teacher? In the 1960s and 1970s, where were the common areas when parents of handicapped children in regular classrooms came to confer with the teacher? In the 1970s and 1980s the question arose again, when teachers found that increasing numbers of limited English proficient (LEP) people from a variety of backgrounds were the real-life parents in the school community.

Traditionally in the United States, which is a nation of immigrants, the public schools have had major responsibility for assisting students and their families through the transition from their native culture to that of mainstream U.S. school culture. Such a change may be particularly difficult for families of handicapped children. A family from a culturally diverse group may not understand the nature of the child's handicap, the appropriate educational services available to the child, or the expectations of the professionals working with the child (Heron & Harris, 1987). The following scenario serves to illustrate this point.

> Hue is a 6-year-old student who has just arrived in the United States from Vietnam. His first grade teacher, Ms. Johnson, has noticed that Hue is extremely withdrawn and has episodes of crying during the

school day. Ms. Johnson contacts the school psychologist, Mr. Ramirez, referring Hue to the special education program for emotionally handicapped students. Ms. Johnson also makes a home visit to talk with Hue's mother and father. The family speaks very little English. Ms. Johnson tries to explain to the parents that she needs their permission to have Hue tested for special education placement. Only parts of the conversation are understood by the family. Ms. Johnson does manage to get the father to sign the school consent forms for evaluation. She leaves the home shortly after arriving. Ms. Johnson speaks with Mr. Ramirez about proceeding with the referral into special education. Mr. Ramirez asks Ms. Johnson to try some strategies to help Hue feel more comfortable in her classroom by placing Hue with another Vietnamese first grader from another class, in a buddy-system. Ms. Johnson is opposed. She thinks Hue is emotionally handicapped and should be removed from her class. Mr. Ramirez provides Ms. Johnson with an article on student behaviors associated with assimilation to a new culture and second language acquisition. He asks Ms. Johnson to be patient and try some positive strategies for helping Hue adjust to the new situation.

School-based professionals like Mr. Ramirez who take on the role of advocates serve as culture brokers between the majority and minority cultures (Correa, 1989). Culture brokers are mediators in dealing with the mainstream culture for the culturally diverse family. Knowledge of both minority and majority cultures and language, and the ability to interpret from one group to the other, are essential characteristics of effective culture brokers. Culture brokers assist school personnel in empowering culturally diverse families by developing family members' skills for adapting to and coping with the U.S. school system, which may be very different from the educational systems they have experienced in their former countries.

Building Blocks to Home–School Partnerships

Research continues to show that when parents are involved, students of all backgrounds and capabilities benefit (Met, 1987). Teachers want parent involvement and have reported that lack of parental support is their number one problem (Stern & Chandler, 1987). Furthermore, school personnel are under legal mandate to involve parents. For example, any school receiving Title VII funds to provide special language services (those provided by the federal government under the Bilingual Education Act) are required to inform parents of their child's educational program and progress in that program (Cubillos, 1988). Parents must be invited to participate in conferences where decisions are made about students in special education. If parents do not understand English, federal law requires that translated materials and an interpreter be provided. Even with provision of materials and interpreters, finding common areas that allow teachers and parents to become partners in the educational process is difficult when school personnel are linguistically and culturally different from the parents of the students.

A problem in defining common areas is that school personnel have not approached the issue from a perspective of knowing about the parents' point of view (Hymes, 1953). Some school personnel may not have developed a way of incorporating those parents who may themselves have had difficulties in school or not attended school into the educational system as partners. Often school personnel obtain information about parents from only a few sources:

- *memory:* what their parents or friends' parents were like;
- *personal experience:* what they themselves and their friends are like as parents, or what they perceive parents to be like;
- *media:* television, newspapers, magazines;
- *general information:* information in the professional's background that may tend to be general in nature.

Memory, one's perception of oneself as a parent, the media, and general information may combine to give an idealized mental picture of what a parent is or, perhaps, should be. School personnel who have an image of middle-class parents as school volunteers during the day and supervisors of homework at night expect to involve parents in school by planning an Open House as discussed in many education courses. The image of parents held by middle-class school personnel may be far from the reality of non-English speaking parents of a handicapped child. When the immigrant parents fail to respond to the traditional written school material, they are perceived as being nonsupportive and disinterested.

On the other hand, parents from another culture have images of education drawn from their memories, experiences, and media. There may be little match between their image of school and the reality of U.S. classrooms. For parents from another culture, the freedom, openness, even the wealth and beauty of a U.S. classroom, may not fit with their conception of what an ideal educational situation is. The informality of the teacher may indicate a lack of professional ability to a parent from an authoritarian society. The U.S. school's expectations that the parents participate in the education process may be completely outside the experience of some parents. Images on television of teenagers' behavior in schools frighten parents who believe in their right to control their children's behavior and to make decisions for their children. For parents of minority language and culture, the trip to school is at best difficult due to lack of comprehension of both language and the ways of doing things. At worst, the trip may evoke painful memories of their own failure in school, or indicate the seeming failure of their children. Finding common areas is a difficult task when school personnel and parents are very different.

Yet, there is a base on which to begin to build common areas: the desire of parents and school personnel to have students experience success. Parents make a great investment in their children. Many immigrants give as a major reason for leaving their countries the opportunity for education that their children will have in the United States. Immigrant parents have reported that they value education, and most wished to be involved in their children's education (NCAS, 1988). School personnel, representing those persons who are knowledgeable about the United States, the culture, the language, and the school system, are the leaders in the effort to build partnerships with culturally diverse parents based on the common ground of desiring student success. Schools and teachers should take the initiative in involving parents (Met, 1987). Research results indicate that it is the differences in teachers, not parents, that determine the level of parents' involvement in school.

Unfortunately, school personnel generally are not succeeding in attempts to involve multicultural immigrant families in the educational process. Schools not only fail to reach out to these parents, but, in many cases, school personnel are indifferent to attempts at involvement by parents whose language and values are unlike their own. At times in the schools there is even hostility and resentment due to school personnel perceiving attempts by culturally different groups to express their beliefs about education as threats to the education professionals' established methodology (NCAS, 1988).

Fortunately, the lack of success of school personnel in reaching out to parents of diverse backgrounds is not universal. There are educational leaders, teachers and school personnel, in the area of parent involvement. These leaders are able to involve parents as supporters of school efforts and as volunteers regardless of parents' educational and cultural background. These leaders are able to involve single and married parents equally and to rate the contributions of all parents equally. In fact, these leaders organize and get good results from the involvement of all parents (Becker & Epstein, 1982). Believing that building a mutually beneficial partnership with multicultural parents is possible and desirable is the first step in reaching out to any family. The model of parent involvement (Figure 5.1) describes six building blocks needed to bridge the gap of school and home to meet the common goal of educating children.

Promote the Attitude of School Personnel

In developing a parent program that meets the needs of diverse parents, the first building block is to promote a positive attitude in school personnel. Recognizing that parents of all backgrounds do want to support the education of their children and have high hopes for their children is an attitude that must prevail among school personnel. For example, Hispanic families often encourage their children to study and apply themselves in school. To many of these minority families, an education

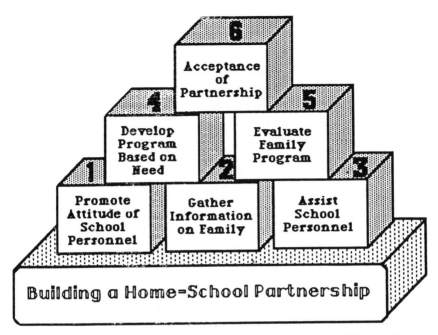

Figure 5.1. Six Building Blocks Needed to Form a Home–School Partnership.

means a way to improve their way of life (Florida Department of Education, 1983). The following vignette depicts an inaccurate perception of a Hispanic family by a professional.

Rosa, a 12-year-old Cuban student, was not performing well in her social studies class at her middle school. Her teacher, Ms. Smith, had sent a note home asking the mother to come meet with her regarding the school problem. Ms. Smith had not received a reply to the note. One afternoon in the teacher's lounge, Ms. Smith commented to the school psychologist that Rosa's mom had not responded to the note and that it was obvious that this mother didn't care about her child's education. "You know those Hispanic people, they have little education themselves, and don't see any value in giving their children a good education," commented Ms. Smith. She further stated that many Hispanic families feel as though education will never get them out of their *barrios* (local housing projects). The school psychologist, who was knowledgeable about the Cuban community, interrupted Ms. Smith and stated that he had found the opposite attitude among the Cuban families he had worked with. In fact, he found that Cuban families were very eager to see their children succeed in education and

encouraged good performance in school. The school psychologist
asked Ms. Smith if she had sent the note home in Spanish, and if she
knew that Rosa's mom worked full-time in a local grocery store.

Attitudes of school personnel that reflect faulty thinking or inaccurate stereotyping toward families of diverse cultures must be changed if a collaborative
relationship is to work. It is hoped that Ms. Smith will learn from this experience
and contact Rosa's mom via a Spanish-speaking interpreter and schedule a
conference during the mother's lunch hour or after work.

School personnel must first understand their own images of parenting, and their
own values and beliefs, before they can effectively integrate the values and beliefs
of others. Culture brokers assist in helping school personnel understand how the
majority culture values and beliefs are perceived by minority culture persons and
what modifications of the mainstream culture of school will assist the minority
person in feeling part of the school community. When professionals realize that
integrating others' values and beliefs into the mainstream generally means
modification of existing practices, and not necessarily radical change, then
professionals feel less threatened. They are more willing to make adaptations to
meet the needs of minority culture and language students and their families.
Helping school personnel to become both sensitive to cultural groups and willing
to enter into partnership is only the first step in building a solid relationship with
families and students.

Gathering Family Information

The second building block for school personnel is learning about the family. One
way to begin gathering information is to develop a parent profile that consists of
questions regarding (a) socioeconomic characteristics, (b) cultural and linguistic
characteristics, and (c) reactions to having a handicapped child. Many authors
provide excellent surveys for use with parents (Sandhu, 1988; Turnbull &
Turnbull, 1986). Table 5.2 is provided as a guideline for developing a parent
profile.

The information in Table 5.2 can be acquired through interviewing parents,
providing professional in-services, talking with persons knowledgeable about the
community, and talking with persons who understand the needs of handicapped
children from diverse cultures. Often, local clergy or community leaders can
provide school personnel with insight into family customs and beliefs. Local public
libraries may have resources describing cultural patterns of particular minority
groups. School personnel are encouraged to spend time in the community,
including making home visits, attending local art or musical events, dining in local
restaurants, and listening to local radio or television broadcasts (Correa, 1989).

Table 5.2
Guidelines for Developing a Family Profile

Socioeconomic Characteristics:
1. How old are the parents?
2. What is the occupation of the parents?
3. How much education do the parents have?
4. Who is the primary caretaker of the children, if parents work?
5. What is the number and age of the siblings?
6. Who are the other family members in the home?
7. What general resources are available to the family?

Linguistic and Cultural Characteristics:
1. What is the culture group?
2. What is the family's national origin?
3. What is the native language?
4. How much English is spoken in the home?
5. What is the literacy level of parents?
6. What are the family's religious practices?
7. How long have the group and family been in this country?
8. If the culture group migrated, why?
9. Does the family return to their native country for visits?
10. If they were refugees, did they flee war?
11. Are culture group members poor?
12. What reasons did the group have for settling in the particular school area?
13. What roles are assigned to family members?
14. Did the children previously have an opportunity to go to school?
15. What was school like in the country of origin?
16. What aspirations do the family have for their children, especially in terms of education?
17. What special customs and beliefs of the group may affect the behavior of their children in school?

Perceptions of the Handicapped Student:
1. How long has the handicap been suspected or known to parents?
2. What is the medical history?
3. How does the family react to the handicapped child?
4. What resources does the family have to cope with the handicapped child?
5. How do members of the cultural group view handicapped children?
6. What are the medical practices in the culture (e.g., folk medicine)?
7. What are the family's beliefs as the cause of the handicap?

Gathering information about the particular cultures represented within a school community can be a complex task. Developing in-service components, bringing in speakers, planning excursions to ethnic restaurants, and sharing the materials and information obtained from reading and travel can be collegial experiences for school personnel. Learning about other cultures' foods, music, and beliefs is an enlarging experience for individuals. The following vignette helps illustrate this point.

> Carmen, a Salvadoran mother whose 3-year-old child is blind due to prematurity, will be receiving services for her daughter by the local public school system within a few months. The school social worker and early childhood/special education teacher make a home visit for the purpose of orienting the mother to the special services provided by the school program. In talking with the mother, the social worker asks for a description of her daughter's medical diagnosis. Carmen describes what the physicians have told her about retinopathy of prematurity, but Carmen states that she believes evil spirits had caused the problem. She further states that she is glad the schools are going to teach her daughter, but she would continue to take her daughter for spiritual (*espiritual-istas*) treatments. After the home visit, the social worker volunteered to gather information on the spiritual and religious beliefs of Salvadorans. She contacted a local Catholic clergyman and asked him to share information that would be relevant to understanding Carmen's case.

School administrators provide leadership by initiating and participating in the information gathering and sharing. Including English-speaking, mainstream culture community leaders and parents of handicapped and nonhandicapped students extends the learning opportunity and demonstrates that the school as a community wishes to incorporate all families into the education process.

Assist School Personnel

The third building block is to assist school personnel in working with individual parents by providing them skills in how to communicate and conduct conferences with families from culturally diverse groups. The parent profile developed at the school level provides general information about the family's culture and their perceptions of the handicapped child. It is important to understand the potential barriers that may prevail in getting families involved in school programs. Barriers may include the facts that:

- the burden of family care is on elderly family members who are in poor physical condition to travel to school;
- poverty prohibits transportation and requires long hours of work;
- lack of baby-sitting support prevents school visits;
- inability to speak or read English prevents understanding of school policies and procedures;

- lack of literacy skills in native language hinders the use of materials written in native language; or
- lack of legal documents for citizenship deters entry into school for fear of exposure.

A school professional must first establish if any of the above barriers are an explanation for lack of school involvement by the culturally diverse families of handicapped students. Once the barriers are identified, resources must be utilized to overcome those barriers including providing transportation, day care for siblings at school, native language interpreters, or meetings outside of the school facilities.

Once families have agreed to interact with school personnel, the next step is to provide school personnel with assistance in understanding how to communicate effectively with families from diverse cultures. Initially, it is beneficial for professionals to understand that persons from different cultures may have different nonverbal communication skills. For example, it has been reported that persons from the Hispanic culture will stand closer to and touch others more often than will persons from white Anglo-American groups (Sandhu, 1988; Torres, 1983). Additionally, some Asian groups will avoid eye contact as a form of respect toward authority figures such as school personnel (Kumabe, Nishida, & Hepworth, 1985).

Furthermore, many professionals often mistakenly perceive the family who speaks very little or no English as inferior, or as lacking awareness of conceptual knowledge (Kumabe et al., 1985). For example, the perception that families cannot understand the complex jargon related to special education is not reason enough for not involving them in conferences and informal meetings. By providing the family with information in their native language and utilizing interpreters during meetings, school personnel can begin to bridge the linguistic and communication gap between families and schools. Remembering that culturally diverse families come to school with many apprehensions and are often shy to ask questions is critical in understanding the home–school interaction. Sandhu (1988) suggests the following ways for school personnel to work effectively with families of minority culture groups:

- Make a positive first impression by having staff welcome and accommodate parents when enrolling their children.
- Maintain positive communication directly with parents by calling or providing informal meetings, instead of sending written notes home with children.
- Familiarize parents with school buildings and school policies by providing interpreters at a Special Open House for families of LEP students.
- Provide frequent and flexible opportunities for parent conferences by inviting them to attend school meetings before or after work, or attend special events at school which coincide with holidays of cultural importance.

It is necessary to provide school personnel with positive communication skills including active listening that are sensitive to families from diverse cultures. As mentioned previously, providing in-services on multicultural issues and learning about cultural groups through community contacts are excellent ways in which to enhance the professional's knowledge and encourage family involvement in school-related activities.

Additionally, school personnel must be knowledgeable about the culturally diverse child's learning styles and behaviors. For example, a school psychologist must provide assessment instruments that are culturally nonbiased and adapt administration of those instruments for the child who does not speak English. Teachers must provide classroom environments and activities that match the learning styles of minority students (Gilbert & Gay, 1985; Westby & Rouse, 1985). There is sufficient research that supports the notion that many LEP students are often referred to special education primarily because of behavior that is reflective of a child adjusting to a new culture and secondary to learning a second language (Hoover & Collier, 1985).

Develop a Program Based on Need

The fourth building block is planning a parent involvement program based on the needs of the particular student and family. There are numerous ways in which school personnel can develop positive partnerships with families. The following are some examples.

- If there are a sizeable number of poor, female-headed families, having an inexpensive supper to which the mothers can bring all their children can be a way to begin parent involvement.
- If a particular culture group in the school has a national holiday or hero, school personnel can provide a program on or near the day and invite parents to assist.
- Materials can be added to the school library about the particular group.
- Parents may serve as bilingual aids, and community volunteers who speak the language and/or are acquainted with the culture group can be enlisted to assist at school.
- Schools might offer English classes and/or citizenship classes on a regular basis.
- Schools can provide a community bulletin board notifying parents of special services (baby-sitting, transportation, employment openings, church activities, etc.).
- Parents of other handicapped children can meet with minority parents and assist them in understanding special education policy and procedures.
- Parents can be given information on basic child development and disciplining techniques, as well as information on handicapping conditions.

- Parents can be trained in simple special education instructional strategies and methodologies that can be adapted for the home (e.g., behavior management programs, precision teaching, behavioral contracts, story telling).
- Parents can be trained in advocacy and leadership skills and serve on advisory councils for bilingual and special education programs.

Developing a program to meet the needs of the families within the school can be the responsibility of a committee of faculty, parents, and community members. Once needs of families are ascertained, then resources can be found that enable the school to provide programs that meet the needs. Community agencies as well as those who provide informal support services to cultural groups can be asked to assist in providing programs, transportation, and other services.

Evaluate the Parent Program

Professionals working with parents from culturally diverse populations increase the effectiveness of their efforts through continual evaluation of their parent-involvement activities. Parents' needs may change throughout the school year; parents from a different cultural group may become involved; parents of students with a certain type of handicap may request assistance. School personnel then add to the existing parent involvement program, or change emphasis. Monitoring the parent involvement program can be informal. School personnel maintain records of conversations with parents about the parent-involvement program. Formal monitoring by means of telephone and written questionnaires can be beneficial. Asking parents either personally or through a newsletter to recommend new ideas for planning programs encourages their participation. Educators monitor three areas of parent involvement: (a) whether the planned activities meet parents' needs, (b) whether the level of parent involvement has increased, and (c) whether parents are better informed about the educational program (Sandhu, 1988). If the school has identified culture brokers and informal support network persons, then asking these resource people to review the program would assist school personnel in evaluation.

Acceptance of the Partnership

The final block in developing a collaborative relationship with multicultural families of handicapped students is that of acceptance of the partnership. The previous blocks provide the school professional with skills to construct and to enhance the home–school relationship. Parents are provided with opportunities to become knowledgeable about and to participate in the education of their children. The final phase requires cooperative efforts of both school professionals and parents in reaching consensus as to what educational success is for each student and what is the appropriate instructional plan for that student. Consensus in each situation depends on school and parents developing areas across cultures for understanding children and education. This consensus depends on both sides changing to some degree. By absorbing some of the values and traditions about children held by members of a minority cultural group, the school opens the door to cooperation in the education of diverse students and their families. This process of absorbing values applies equally to culturally diverse students and their families. It is their responsibility to come to understand the U.S. school system and to participate in working toward the fundamental goals of education in a democracy. School personnel as professionals have the right and responsibility to insist on the policies that are effective in the instruction of students. They have the obligation to see that students acquire the knowledge and understanding of the rights and duties of citizens of this nation. A two-way paradigm of involvement is necessary if common ground is to be found between home and school.

Summary

Developing a cross-cultural partnership of home and school is a challenging task. The shared desire to have students enjoy educational success provides the basis on which to construct such partnerships. School personnel engaged in this task are assisted by collaborating with each other in the sharing of knowledge and experiences. They can work together on case studies, visit ethnic neighborhoods of the families, attend workshops to develop active listening and communication skills, set aside time to reflect and evaluate their efforts. Administrators can offer encouragement through personally welcoming minority-culture parents and by supporting faculty and other personnel efforts to establish school–parent programs that are effective. The task has been described in this chapter as a process like that of erecting a structure out of building blocks. In the end the successful completion of the task depends on school professionals' patience, commitment, and belief that incorporating parents of diverse backgrounds into the educational process is a part of modern school life.

School personnel need to be told that theirs is a most important role in determining the future of the nation. A multicultural, humanistic environment in which all students and their families gain understanding in how to work and live in a nation of diverse persons can flourish with school leadership. Welcoming parents of students who differ from the mainstream into the school community, encouraging them to participate, giving them a voice in decisions about the education of the children, and providing them with programs that meet their instruction needs are actions that public schools can assist all parents to take. Learning how to participate in schools enables multicultural families to participate as citizens in the broader community of city, state, and nation. Schools can thus continue to fulfill their traditional role of educating and empowering families of all backgrounds. In this era of continued high levels of immigration of persons of diverse backgrounds into the United States, the public schools that find common areas where mainstream and minority-culture persons share in planning and decision making set an example for other democratic institutions.

References

Allen, A. (1988). Library services for Hispanic young adults. *Library Trends, 37*(1), 80–105.

Becker, H. J., & Epstein, J. L. (1982). Parent involvement: A study in teacher practices. *The Elementary School Journal, 83,* 85–102.

Comer, J. P. (1980). *School power: Implications of an intervention project.* New York: The Free Press.

Correa, V. I. (1989). Involving culturally diverse families in the educational process. In S. Fradd & M. J. Weismantel (Eds.), *Meeting the needs of culturally and linguistically different students: A handbook for educators* (pp. 130–144). San Diego: College-Hill Press.

Cubillos, E. (1988). *The bilingual education act: 1988 legislation.* Wheaton, MD: National Clearinghouse for Bilingual Education.

Epstein, J. (1985). *Effects of teacher practices of parent involvement on change in student achievement in reading and math.* Unpublished manuscript, Johns Hopkins University.

Epstein, J. (1986). Parents' reactions to teacher practices of parent involvement. *The Elementary School Journal, 86,* 277–294.

Florida Department of Education. (March, 1983). *A resource manual for the development of evaluation of special programs for exceptional children: Vol III-B, Evaluating the Non-English speaking handicapped.* Tallahassee, FL: Bureau of Exceptional Education Services.

Gilbert, S. E., & Gay, G. (1985). Improving the success in school of poor black children. *Phi Delta Kappan, 67,* 133–137.

Glenn, C. L. (1989). Just schools for minority children. *Phi Delta Kappan, 10*(70), 777–779.

Heron, T. E., & Harris, K. C. (1987). *The educational consultant: Helping professionals, parents, and mainstreamed students.* Austin, TX: Pro-Ed.

Hoover, J. J., & Collier, C. (1985). Referring culturally different children: Sociocultural considerations. *Academic Therapy, 20,* 503–509.

Hymes, J. I. (1953). *Effective home-school relations.* New York: Prentice Hall. (Republished in 1974, Sierra Madre, CA: Southern California Association for the Education of Young Children)

Katz-Levy, J., Laurie, I. E., & Kaufman, R. (1987). Meeting the mental health needs of disturbed minority children and adolescents: A national perspective. *Children Today, 16,* 10–15.

Kumabe, K. T., Nishida, C., & Hepworth, D. H. (1985). *Bridging ethnocultural diversity in social work and health.* Honolulu: University of Hawaii.

Lynch, E. W., & Stein, R. C. (1987). Parent participation by ethnicity: A comparison of Hispanic, black, and Anglo families. *Exceptional Children, 54*(2), 105–111.

McGoldrick, M., Pearce, J., & Giordano, J. (Eds.). (1982). *Ethnicity and family therapy.* New York: Guilford.

Met, M. (1987). Parent involvement in foreign language learning. *ERIC/CLL News Bulletin, 11*(1), 2–3, 7–8.

Morgan, D. P. (1982). Parent participation in the LEP process: Does it enhance appropriate education? *Exceptional Education Quarterly, 3,* 33–40.

National Coalition of Advocates for Students (NCAS). (1988). *New voices: Immigrant students in U.S. public schools.* Boston, MA: Author.

Nicolau, S., & Valdivieso, R. (1988). The future of the Spanish language in U.S. public schools. *Migration World, 16,* 59–61.

Powell, G. (1983). The psychosocial development of minority group children. New York: Brunner/Mazel.

Sandhu, H. K. (Fall, 1988). *Parent involvement: A resource for the education of limited English proficient students.* Silver Springs, MD: National Clearinghouse for Bilingual Education.

Seligman, M., & Darling, R. (1989). *Ordinary families, special children: A system approach to childhood disability.* New York: Guilford Press.

Spector, R. E. (1979). *Cultural diversity in health and illness.* New York: Appleton-Century-Crofts.

Stern, J., & Chandler, M. (1987). *The condition of education.* Washington, DC: U.S. Department of Education.

Torres, I. (1983). *Hidden messages: Awareness of nonverbal communication of Hispanics.* Gainesville, FL: University of Florida Press.

Turnbull, A. P., & Turnbull, H. R. (1986). *Families, professionals, and exceptionality: A special partnership.* Columbus, OH: Merrill.

Westby, C. E., & Rouse, G. R. (1985). Culture in education and the instruction of language learning-disabled students. *Topics in Language Disorders, 5*(4), 15–28.

Yao, E., & Houng, C. (1987). Teaching English to Asian immigrant children. *Educational Horizons, 66,* 43–45.

6

COMMUNICATING WITH FAMILIES OF CHILDREN WITH DISABILITIES OR CHRONIC ILLNESS

Roberta Krehbiel and Roger L. Kroth

The term *communication,* as it is used in this chapter, refers to the interactions that take place between parents and the professionals who support their adaptation to children who have disabilities or are chronically ill. We will provide an overview of skills necessary for consideration by professionals who want to build and nurture a positive and proactive relationship with these parents. The goal of professional interaction is to maximize family potential so the family can independently meet demands and prevent the occurrence of secondary problems.

We make several assumptions about the families of children with special needs and the professionals who work with them. First, the crisis of diagnosis typically creates high levels of stress for families that may result in a need for intervention. The uprooting of traditional dreams and changes in expectations of parenting may require skilled and sensitive professional support to help parents "replant" and readjust. Next, we assume that the mental health professional (psychiatrist, psychologist, counselor, social worker) views the family as unique and strives to respect each family's perspective throughout the relationship. A professional's recognition of the influence of his or her personal values, beliefs, biases, and viewpoints helps to meet the family on neutral ground. Finally, professionals who work to support families of children with special needs are constantly seeking to expand, refine, and improve their ability to communicate.

Interpersonal communication skills include listening, specialized listening, interviewing, responding, problem solving, and anticipatory guidance. Each skill is an act of enabling (Benjamin, 1974/1981 p. xii) that helps the parent recognize ways of coping and adapting appropriate to their own worldview.

Listening

Hobbs (1975) stated that parents are the true experts on their children and professionals must learn to become consultants to parents. In order to serve as consultants, professionals must be empathic and "take a walk in someone else's shoes." This is partially accomplished through learning and practicing skills of listening. Listening is more than just hearing; it means becoming aware of parental beliefs, values, life-styles, and preferences in child-rearing practices.

Listening Paradigm

We all have definite and diverse ideas about what makes a good listener—and so do parents. It is up to the professional to determine what type of listener the parent needs or wants at any given time. Kroth (1985) conceptualized four types of general listening behavior: passive nonlistening, active nonlistening, passive listening, and active listening. Two types of listening behavior work counterproductively to the parent–professional relationship. The passive nonlistener tends to "hear" but not to listen. If asked, the passive nonlistener could repeat back what is said but does not engage in any verbal or nonverbal feedback that shows interest. The active nonlistener, by talking excessively and not following the thoughts of the speaker, never lets the other person get to the point.

The remaining two quadrants of the listening paradigm describe the passive and active listener and support the parent–professional relationship. Kroth suggested that the passive listener is valuable when a parent needs to discharge frustration, anxiety, worries, and aspirations or even to hear their own solutions. A passive listener uses nonverbal messages of acceptance and few words to encourage this discharge. The following excerpt from "Ginny," in Bombeck's *Motherhood, The Second Oldest Profession* (1983), illustrates the need for a passive listener:

> This is the only house on the block that will never have a swing set or a path across the yard. I'm a mother whose kid will never play in the toilet. Never tug at my leg when I'm on the phone. Never tear up my favorite magazine. Never run away from home stark naked. He'll never play patty-cake. Never pull my hair. He'll never even know my name. (p. 75)

The active listener uses reflective verbal comments to help the parent clarify, understand, and problem solve within the context of the family's beliefs and values. Examples of active listening occur throughout this chapter. The professional should shift between active listening behavior and that of a passive listener following the lead of the parent.

In our enthusiasm to share our advice and knowledge we often forget to listen. We may become distracted from the content because we are busy formulating a response. As Satir (1988) says, "To the degree that you are involved with internal dialogue, you stop listening" (p. 70). When tempted to fall into certain response patterns due to the feeling of having heard it all before, the professional should remember that parents of children with special needs are neither a homogeneous group (Kroth, 1985), nor extremely diverse from families raising children with no life-long involvement. A valuable schematic for the professional is the three-link chain of listening-thinking-responding. The following statement by Benjamin (1981) offers professionals a self-check on their listening skills:

> If during the interview you can state in your own words what the interviewee has said and also convey to him in your own words the feelings he has expressed and he then accepts all this as emanating from him, there is an excellent chance that you have listened and understood him. (p. 47)

Specialized Listening

Professionals who have not spent time working with parents of children with special needs can easily fall prey to old myths and potentially destructive stereotypes such as the tendency to see pathology where none exists. This section includes some areas where specialized listening on the part of the professional will help the family's progress. The professional specifically listens for: family strengths, feelings of power and powerlessness, and dynamics surrounding life cycle stages and transitions, such as normalization, high-risk periods, stigmatized social values, and burden of care.

Family Strengths

Professionals in our society can readily identify dysfunction and what causes families to fail. This knowledge often interferes with recognition of family strengths even though most people function well after experiencing major life crises. Stinnett and Defrain (1985) found that all families share six major strengths that the professional who functions as a specialized listener can recognize and reinforce: commitment, time, communication, appreciation, coping ability, and spiritual wellness.

That "members of strong families are dedicated to promoting each other's welfare and happiness" is a strength labeled as *commitment* by Stinnett and Defrain

(1985, p. 14). This quality can be noted in the following discourse by a parent, "My wife works days and I work the night shift. That's what's best for Kelly and our son, and our family. We have to do this while Kelly is in so much danger and her life is at stake" (Krehbiel & Sheldon, 1986). Stinnett and Defrain reported that strong families spend planned quality *time* with each other. Part of quality time is devoted to *communication* among family members; and part of the communication is devoted to showing *appreciation* for individuals in the family.

Stinnett and Defrain (1985) also found that "strong families are able to view crises as an opportunity to grow" (p. 14). This *coping ability* is reflected in a personal statement by a mom who related, "My family is closer since we have had to try and come together to figure out this strange label of 'learning disability.' Before we were not careful about how we communicated with each other. Now we are careful of how we speak to Danny and to each other." Finally Stinnett and Defrain reported that "strong families have a sense of greater good or power in life" (1985, p. 14), and this spiritual wellness gives them strength and purpose.

Dunst, Trivette, and Deal (1988) summarized other nonmutually exclusive qualities of strong families termed *family functional style:* purpose, congruence, problem solving, flexibility and adaptability, balance, positiveness, and a clear set of rules, values, and beliefs. These authors stated that the combination of qualities is important and not all strong families are characterized by the presence of all qualities.

We believe it is necessary for the professional to listen selectively for the positive attributes and resources of families. Families come for help when they are stuck in situations that require change and when solutions are not seen as available (Minuchin, 1974). Professionals must recognize and help families use their strengths in order to expand their repertoire of behaviors. As parents of children with special needs learn to parent differently and to feel competent, they will mobilize these strengths in unique and culturally appropriate ways.

Power and Powerlessness

Specialized listening requires professionals to hear parental concerns about feelings of power and powerlessness. Basch (cited in Anthony & Benedek, 1975) contends that "throughout life, the feeling of controlling one's destiny to some reasonable extent is the essential psychological component of all aspects of life" (p. 513). Disability or acute illness can cause a sense of powerlessness because of the parent's inability to influence or stop the situation. This sense of powerlessness may result in disorganization, a slowing of family development, and periodic inability to cope. For some parents feeling powerless can be vicious. The disability or illness creates a feeling of having no control, rendering the parents overwhelmed and vulnerable to stress. Unable to pace their lives, the parents experience more failure as the stress piles up and normal coping strategies are not successful. The professional listens for the painful statements of powerlessness and supports the parent in achieving some feeling of control over the situation:

Mom:	He can't talk. He will never tell me he loves me, or even that he hates me! I am his mother, but I might as well be nothing.
Professional:	Mothers need feedback of some kind, and Raymond will never talk to you.
Mom:	Never. Ever. As long as I live. He is trapped in that body with that brain.
Professional:	Do his eyes or his face ever speak to you?
Mom:	Yes. I guess. I know when he hurts and when he is tired and when he needs to eat.
Professional:	Raymond tells you some things, but not others.
Mom:	Yes. Not enough. But maybe I should look for some other signs. Maybe some signs of love.

Life Cycle Stages and Transitions

According to most theorists the stages of the family life cycle include the unattached young adult, marriage, the family with children, the family with adolescents, launching children and moving on, and the family in later life (Carter & McGoldrick, 1980). These stages require new learning and mastery of new roles, and involve change. The transitions from stage to stage are accompanied by varying amounts of stress. Minuchin (1974) believes that professionals must recognize the stress of adapting to change as families make transitions: "With this orientation many more families who enter therapy would be seen and treated as average families in transitional situations, suffering the pains of accommodating to new circumstances" (p. 60).

No better words could be spoken on behalf of families with children who have disabilities or chronic illness. These families must adapt to expected life events, while simultaneously coping with unexpected events, transitions, and stress that accompany a catastrophe (Figley & McCubbin, 1983). The added stressors that occur because of crisis require that parents cope in ways that may appear dysfunctional to others. We will briefly discuss potential life-long stressors: normalization, high-risk periods, stigmatized social values and personal value changes, and prolonged burden of care.

Normalization. For families living with children who have major problems, the need to feel normal is powerful:

> We deal with cardiac specialists, pulmonary specialists, nutritionists, several surgeons, public health nurses, neurologists, occupational therapists, physical therapists, speech therapists, an early intervention program, counselor, case manager from children's medical services and the state legislature. This is not normal but we try to make our family as normal as possible. (G. W., personal communication, January, 1989)

Professionals can explore ways families accomplish feelings of normality by using exploratory questions such as: "How do you find time to be a regular family?" The constant struggle for normality should be viewed as healthy and reinforced appropriately.

Stress is often exacerbated by the service delivery systems that parents rely on to reduce stress (Seligman, 1979). For example, a parental push toward being normal or typical may be viewed by professionals as denial. In addition there may be short periods of time when parents might indeed deny the existence of a problem, thus withholding what each discipline would consider essential intervention. Many families learn to cope by prioritizing therapeutic and educational intervention and limiting the time the child spends with outsiders. They learn to respect their child's right to be a child and family member first, a member of society second, and a consumer of social services last.

High-risk periods. The second area of stress involves high-risk situations typical during the life cycle of families who have children with disabilities or chronic illness. Wikler, Wassow, and Hatfield (1981) identified ten periods when the developmentally disabled child's deviance from normality rekindles parental grief. These periods are: diagnosis, time for walking, time for talking, siblings surpassing the child's growth, alternative placement, entry into school, management crisis, the onset of puberty, 21st birthday, and guardianship. An example of stress related to school entry was related by a parent to the authors:

> "I think I am doing so well. Sophia is in preschool with good teachers and therapists. I believe all is going just fine. But I am nervous and anxious about . . . what? I don't know. Maybe I am trying to make something there that isn't." A parent within earshot of this mother later introduced herself and said she too felt the same, but had identified her worry: In 8 months the children would be going to public school and would have to be "labeled" in order to get services.

Other high-risk periods include repeated hospitalizations and required learning of life-saving equipment; repeated assessment and evaluation of developmental

levels; decisions about placement in the least-restrictive environment; and development of a circle of support and acquaintances where the common link is
disability or chronic illness. In addition parents must interact with specialized
physicians, educators, therapists, and child care people who must be carefully
cultivated so that they fully understand the needs of the child. In each of these
periods there is potential for exposure of personal values and life-style preferences
that may be criticized by others or found wanting by the professional community.

The professional who listens carefully realizes that each high-risk period and
accompanying family tasks involve varying levels of stress. Families must make
quantum leaps in their knowledge and readjust emotionally in short amounts of
time. With each new situation professionals can assist to reactivate coping
mechanisms by asking such questions as: "What did you do in the past when . . . ?"
In addition the professional and family must sort through these coping mechanisms
to be sure they are not in need of revision based on the current stage of family and
child development. The following example illustrates this point:

Parent:	I don't know what is happening. Before we could tell him what to do and he would do it right away. Now nothing we do works.
Professional:	So there seems to be a change now. . . .
Parent:	Yes, a drastic change. Almost overnight.
Professional:	Let's go back and retrace. As you remember, try not to leave out when things worked and why you thought they worked. . . .

The professional can also identify behaviors that interfere with adaptation such as
overwhelming emotional reactions or habitual family problem solvers whose
inflexibility can bring new learning to a halt.

Stigmatized social values. A third area for specialized listening is stigmatized
social values, which can be a recurring nightmare for those families with children
who are different in appearance and behavior. The following story was related to
the first author by a mother of a child with a syndrome that left her arms and part
of her face very deformed:

> We were in line at the grocery store when a woman two baskets back
> yelled, "Why in the world is that child that way?" I said, "We had her
> done that way. What do you think of it?" The woman was speechless.
> The people in the grocery store applauded. . . .

After this incident, the professional had the opportunity to explore this mother's
feelings and the recurrence of grief reactions. When the mother's coping strategies

of humor and assertiveness were brought to her attention she was able to share her feelings of guilt at being flippant and not taking the time to educate the bigoted public about children with special needs. This incident reminds us of the serious harm that is done to families when disabilities are perceived as an indication of personal worth. The professional realizes that stigma may alter a family's range of activity and explores that possibility in this possible interchange:

Professional:	That incident was particularly hard for you. Have there been others?
Parent:	Yes. No. Well, not really. We don't take her with us very much. I guess just for that reason.
Professional:	It's easier not to deal with the comments.
Parent:	Yes. Right now it is.
Professional:	You say "right now." What have you thought of to help you deal with the stigma?

Goldfarb, Brotherson, Summers, and Turnbull (1986) offer some good tips to parents for coping with stigma that include role play, humor, and open discussion.

There will be situations when a parent recognizes the effects of previous personal values about disabilities and illness. In most cases, exposure to children with special needs came when the parents were young and their personal experience and exposure to positive aspects were limited. When this occurs parents may need to talk through feelings of discomfort or guilt about how they used to perceive children with special needs.

Burden of care. As professionals come into contact with families of children with disabilities and chronic illness they become more specialized in listening for evidence of stress due to the prolonged burden of care during the life cycle. Stein and Jessop (1982) developed an index that measures five dimensions of burden of care that can be applied to parenting a child with disabilities or chronic illness. We have supplied a comment to illustrate evidence of each dimension:

- the added dependency of a child who cannot perform age-appropriate activities of daily living independently. (Parent: I finally realized that everything we take for granted is going to take much more time than we ever expected.)
- the psychological burden entailed in the child's prognosis. (Parent: The most difficult part is never knowing what tomorrow is going to bring.)
- a disruption in family routines. (Parent: For the rest of our lives we will never be sure that planned events will work out.)
- the fixed deficits in the child requiring compensatory parental behavior. (Parent: I found myself doing things most fathers don't even think about when their child turns 3.)

• medical/nursing tasks that parents need to perform. (Parent: The fear is always there that you'll do something wrong with all the technical apparatus.)

With such children the burden of care is continuous and parents are often too exhausted and anxious to seek respite. These families have good reason to shelter their children longer than other parents for no one can make definite statements about the future. Sensitive professionals can encourage the family to explore rest and respite sources both informally through the family, or formally through agencies that provide trained caregivers.

Effective listening will provide the professional with information on the disability or the illness; the effects of the crisis on the family; the life-styles, beliefs, and values of the family; the coping styles; and so forth. Effective listening will also provide the parent with a trusted ally. This section also suggested that professionals become specialized in their listening. They must note strengths, feelings of power and powerlessness, and stressors that occur over the lifetime such as efforts toward normalization, added tasks during high-risk periods, stigmatized social values, and experiences of burden of care.

Interviewing

In the course of their work with families, professionals gather large amounts of information about the family. They must collect data in ways that are not influenced by personal experience, training, and knowledge of psychological dynamics before generating hypotheses about family functioning. This section explores techniques of interviewing in which possible themes are not suggested in the early stages of the interview. A major goal is to provide parents with the opportunity to volunteer information spontaneously. The professional notes strong and consistent patterns and themes. We will begin this section by briefly discussing rapport building and the importance of making the parent an informer.

Rapport Building

The professional's responsibility is to begin the relationship with the family through rapport building. Spradley (1979) conceptualized rapport on a continuum because it develops in a patterned manner. An awareness that a continuum of rapport exists helps the professional to exercise patience in the relationship. By realizing that it takes time for the parent to learn skills, the professional does not prematurely define the parameters that the relationship will follow.

According to the continuum, during initial contacts with parents there is a sense of apprehension and uncertainty. This is followed by a brief period of exploration where the parents and professionals observe each other, try to discover what the other person is like, and what they want to hear. Both may be asking, "What does he want me to say?" "Can she be trusted?" (Spradley, 1979, p. 80). The third stage of rapport is cooperation between the professional and parent who have both learned what to expect of each other. During the final stage, termed participation, parents bring new information to the attention of the professional in ways that are reflective of their analysis of the situation. To build rapport the interviewer should continually explain reasons for the information: "I want to ask you some very general questions about life with your son Tommy so that I can get to know and understand your situation better."

As professionals build rapport they assist the parent in adopting the role of informer. Parents may be unaware that the information they possess about their own life-ways and beliefs can be used productively. In addition, many parents may not have been asked to share or to give their opinion during past encounters with professionals and therefore do not recognize the potential value of their contribution. One goal during the early stages of the interview is to get the parents to speak unself-consciously in their own language—the language of parents who have very specialized knowledge.

A roadblock to becoming an informer is that a parent may be unable to generate any sentences to describe the situation (Ivey & Authier, 1978). The following exchange illustrates this type of roadblock:

Professional: Would you like to tell me some of the reasons you came to see me today?

Parent: Yeah, I am having trouble with my husband. He doesn't seem to like Jerry [the child with handicaps].

Professional: Can you tell me more about how you know?

Parent: Not really. I just know.

Professional: How has your husband acted that makes you think he doesn't like Jerry?

Parent: Nothing. I just know.

The professional must interact in ways that support the parent in learning how to respond and in becoming an informer. In this way the professional can profile the family's beliefs, values, and life-style preferences.

Ethnographic Interviewing

Professionals need to provide for families of children with disabilities or chronic illness a framework within which they "can express their own understandings in their own terms" (Patton, 1980, p. 205). We will briefly describe ethnographic interviewing (Spradley, 1979) as a technique for gathering the stories of families in an open-ended manner.* Spradley's particular approach to ethnographic interviewing is easily remembered and is useful to inexperienced interviewers who are not concerned with research or ethnography per se, but are interested in nonbiased descriptions of families (Krehbiel, 1988; Krehbiel & Askew, 1988).

The actual ethnographic interviewing questions are grouped by Spradley (1979) and labeled as grand tour, mini tour, example, experience, native language, and hypothetical. The grand tour question asks for a description of how things usually exist. The mini tour question is used to investigate smaller aspects of the description given during the response to the grand tour question. Example questions ask parents to clarify some description by giving an example. Experience questions ask parents for any experiences they have had in some particular setting. Native-language questions ask the parents, "How would you refer to it?" Hypothetical questions create a hypothetical situation and ask for the parent's response. Krehbiel (1988) has added opinion and feeling questions to Spradley's list.

The following examples, preceded by a rationale for obtaining the information, illustrate the various types of ethnographic interviewing questions. Spradley (1979) reminds us that " . . . expanding the length of the question tends to expand the length of the response" (p. 85). The questions follow the same rules of most interviewing, that is, all should be clear, singular, and neutral or nonjudgmental; and most should be open-ended (Patton, 1980).

Interview Example #1

It is important to gather information about family structure and related life cycle stages in order to get a total profile of the family:

Grand Tour: Tell me about your family members, all those you know or can remember.

A response to this question may yield names and ages of family members over three generations in addition to facts about marriage, divorce, remarriage, illness, death, geographical location, and personal contact.

Interview Example #2

Patterson and McCubbin (1983) discuss a Double ABCX model of family adaptation to stress in families who are subjected to catastrophic situations. This

---

*Use of Spradley's work was first suggested to the first author by Carol Westby (personal communication, 1988).

model looks at family efforts *over time* to adapt to multiple stressors. In the model, *a* (the stressor event)—interacting with *b* (the family's resources)—interacting with *c* (the definition the family makes of the event)—produce *x* (the crisis; or disorganization/imbalance in the family). The next example explores the *c* factor in this model which is the definition the family makes of the event: their appraisal of its impact on the family as a whole as well as on individual members. Consider the following types of ethnographic questions that may provide information about parental perceptions:

Grand Tour: Tell me the diagnosis as you understand it.

Mini Tour: Earlier you said you did not know what this was going to do to your son's grandparents. Would you talk about that some more?

Example: You mentioned that you have all kinds of expectations for Arlene. Please share some examples with me.

Native-Language: I noticed you used the term "learning disabilities." I think that everyone has their own ideas of what that is. Would you take a minute to tell me what this means in your family?

Interview Example #3

The *b* factor on the Patterson and McCubbin model (1983) suggests that stress is mediated by the resources (both internal and external) available to the family. We need to know the family's view of their own social support:

Grand Tour: Who are the people you consider most helpful to you at this time?

Example: Would you tell me some of the specific ways these people contribute their help?

Example: Often people would like to help out but just don't know what parents need. What are some of the ways you have "educated" your friends and family?

Interview Example #4

The staff of Project Ta-kos makes suggestions for interviewing a family regarding their perspectives on health and healing. Several excerpts from Project

Ta-kos are included throughout this example. First, it is necessary to determine the degree of concurrence between expert opinions regarding diagnosis or assessment results and the family's perceptions and concepts of the problem:

Grand Tour: Tell me what you or your family think is going on here with Chan.

With this type of question you may get the family's perceptions of health in a medical sense or in a holistic sense. The professional then establishes the family's *degree of concern* about the child's special needs (the family's major concerns are usually voiced first and more than once as they are sharing information) and finally attempts to arrive at their greatest areas of concern:

Hypothetical: If you had all of these worries written on cards and you had to put them in order, which would you put at the top of the pile?

Next, the professional asks questions to arrive at the family's feelings about the interventions and treatments for the child or about the future:

Opinion: What do you think school [treatment] does for your child? (Or, What are the best things that you are doing?)

Assume that at some point during the parent's discussion the mother expresses fear at being required to do a certain type of intervention with her child at home:

Hypothetical: Imagine yourself doing therapy with Isabel in the tub. What do you see happening?

Please note, if a professional is speaking to a family whose dominant language is not English, and the professional is not fluent in that language, it is wise to ask a knowledgeable colleague whether such phrases as "picture this . . . " or "imagine this . . . " are used in that language.

Hammerschlag (1988) made the following statement in his book titled *The Dancing Healers:* "When we professionals think that we are the only ones doing the healing, we are setting ourselves up for pain and disillusionment" (p. 6). With some cultural groups, it is necessary to inquire about others helping the child and whether we should coordinate with them:

Opinion: You have a lot of people in your family and outside your family who really seem to care about Joseph. Should we talk to any of them before we get going?

During a later interview, the professional determines more exactly the family's expectations about growth or change:

Opinion: As you said, getting Flora to sleep through the night will really help her. We will all work toward that. How long do you think it will take before she sleeps for at least 3 hours straight?

Interview Example #5

Just when families should increase natural social supports, some supports actually shrink. The professional explores this phenomenon with parents in the following example:

Experience: What are you experiencing now with your friends— now that Carla's behavior is getting so out of hand?

In this approach to interviewing, the interviewer's professional or personal agenda is not involved. If after several visits the professional sees the child completely differently than the family sees him or her, that agenda remains in the background until trust is built and the professional can comfortably suggest some other views. We assume that listening and interviewing go hand-in-hand and that the professional weaves the two together as necessary and appropriate. The next section reviews the third strand of the braid, responding.

Responding

From a counseling perspective and inherent in active listening, the purpose of responding is to work with parents to understand their frame of reference and to assist them in resolving problems. Theory and research are translated into practical skills and models in many materials and books. Although each author may offer a slightly different slant to the communication relationship, all are concerned with the "bridge or barrier" responses available to the professional. Due to the vastness of the topic, we will not discuss the various characteristics or types of responding skills, but instead refer to such writers as Rogers (1955), Benjamin (1981), Carkhuff and Anthony (1979), Garrett (1982), Egan (1982), Webster (1977), Haley (1976), Minuchin (1974), Ivey and Authier (1978), Satir (1988), and Goldstein (1980).

There is ample evidence to suggest that some parents of children with developmental disabilities or chronic illness manifest grief reactions at diagnosis

(Fortier & Wanlass, 1984; Kubler-Ross, 1969; Olshansky, 1963; Solnit & Stark, 1961), and periodically throughout the life of the child (Menolascino, 1977; Wikler et al., 1981). Moses (1983) writes that parents cannot grieve alone, and need support through states of shock, denial, anxiety, anger, guilt, and depression. We suggest that professionals listen and respond to parents of children with special needs from the perspective of parental grief and their prolonged burden of care. As the parents tell their story, professionals reflect an understanding of feelings in order to keep the doors of communication open. In the following comments, grief is suggested by the parent and the parent is supported through the response of the professional:

Parent: It might be better if Janey just dies.

Professional: Today your pain for Janey is very strong.

Parent: People will always stop to stare at him, all of his life.

Professional: It seems that people are not always aware of the harm they can do.

Parent: We will never have other children.

Professional: All that you've been through makes you question your future.

Parent: Is this what people call "quality of life"? I don't think so.

Professional: You're taking another look at the meaning of life now.

Parent: Right now, I hate everyone connected with "special children."

Professional: Right now everyone reminds you that there is something not right with Jess.

Parent: I feel like everyone is rejecting me and our family.

Professional: Just when you need support people don't come through for you.

Parent: I am going to kill somebody before this is over.

Professional: You feel on fire thinking about the injustices your daughter suffers.

Parent: I know it is my fault. I am the one who gave birth to this child.

Professional: It's painful when you believe you caused your child to be disabled.

The professional also prepares to explore questions that reflect feelings of prolonged burden of care which seems to be universal for parents of children with special needs:

Parent:	Am I doing the right thing for my child?
Professional:	That question will plague you for the rest of your life. There are ways to analyze the situations to help answer your question. We can go through this together when you are ready.
Parent:	Am I expecting too much or too little?
Professional:	Let's take a look at this question together. We can look at child development in general, at your daughter's feelings about herself, and at your level of comfort.
Parent:	Am I the only person going insane trying to deal with this?
Professional:	Right now you have so many decisions to make it makes you crazy.
Parent:	I know this is my fault.
Professional:	In your mind, you'll go through every moment before the accident, over and over, trying to answer that question.
Parent:	Why me? Why my child? (Some questions just need a passive listener.)

Although we offered a few examples of responses in the above sample questions, we believe a discussion with a parent who has "been through it all" will be invaluable to the professional who wishes to gain a deeper insight of feelings of prolonged burden of care.

There are many ways to strengthen or reinforce the parent's efforts to raise a child with special needs through professional responding. Positive, nonpatronizing comments made at the appropriate moment serve this purpose:

> You've come a long way in learning medical terminology.
>
> You have discovered the roots of Paul's refusal to maintain his diet. Tell me how you did that.
>
> So things are still frustrating and difficult, but you have gotten the routine under control.
>
> There are some new parents that I see who would like to talk with another parent. Would you be ready to talk with them?

Parents also benefit from verbalizing the positive and articulating their own strengths. Two questions used by Affleck, Tennen, and Gershmann (1985) allow parents to redefine or reframe the crisis as beneficial:

> As difficult as this situation has been for you and your family, have there been any benefits, gains, or advantages that come from having a child [with special needs]? Many parents of children [with special needs] asked themselves the question "Why me?" Do you have an answer to this? (p. 654)

Affleck et al. (1985) also caution against taking the parent too far with positive evaluations and purposeful interpretations: "Such communications, however well-intentioned, may be received hostilely by people who have not drawn such conclusions on their own" (p. 656).

Problem Solving

Ivey and Authier (1978) suggest that when parents leave a professional–parent relationship, they should come away with competencies that allow them to view problems from new perspectives. This means finding new solutions to old difficulties and new solutions to new complications that may arise.

Before entering into problem-solving activity with the parent, the professional becomes aware of preferences parents have regarding child-rearing. Sampling a story from Turnbull, Turnbull, Bronicki, Summers, and Roeder-Gordon (1988) illustrates this point: A young man, whose mother hated doing laundry and had it sent out, was being taught to do laundry in school. The teacher considered this part of being able to live independently. To the young man, being independent meant earning enough money to pay someone else to do his laundry and he resisted the task and teacher's attempts to get him to do the task. Armed with appropriate knowledge about life-styles of individual families, professional problem solving will be succinct and offer a better fit with family needs. (See Simeonsson, Bailey, Huntington, & Comfort, 1986.) The objective is to problem solve with parents, not to solve problems for parents.

In order for families to solve problems effectively and gain mastery over their situation they will also need great amounts of information pertaining to everything from the etiology of the disabling problem, to taxes and insurance, to specialized toothbrushes. Endless roadblocks including time-consuming exploration and bureaucracy prevent parents from obtaining needed information. For problem solving to be successful the professional must become aware of the roadblocks that parents face in gaining needed information.

Most problem-solving approaches include problem definition, goal selection, strategy selection and implementation, and evaluation. In the beginning the professional models problem-solving strategy (perhaps by verbalizing these steps) and uses direct questions such as "What have you tried in order to solve this problem?" and "What would you like to try next?" All stages or steps eventually become the responsibility of the parent with the professional providing guidance, sequencing, and reflection.

Several reasons why some parents have difficulty in problem solving were suggested by Dixon and Glover (1984). First, they may never have learned the responses necessary for certain problems. This is especially true for most of the problems facing families of children with special needs and is the reason they turn to "professionals" for advice on the particular disability or illness. In addition, parents may not recognize that they possess effective problem-solving responses that can be generalized to new situations. Finally, effective problem-solving responses may be blocked by excessive anxiety and other emotional states.

As professionals gain experience in working with families of children with special needs, they become more attuned to the potential stressors that may arise. The final section describes the concept of anticipatory guidance and when it might be used in a way that benefits parents.

Anticipatory Guidance

From a medical perspective, the premise of anticipatory guidance suggests that the optimal time for the introduction of information relating to common problems arising during child-rearing is just prior to the age at which such problems are likely to appear. Effective professionals are familiar with the affective, cognitive, and physical development of children and share these developmental patterns within families before they happen. The information helps remove fear, uncertainty, and anxiety and allows parents to make informed decisions.

Anticipatory guidance about development must be given with extreme care to parents of children who have special needs. Even though there is similarity in developmental patterns, by the nature of their disability or illness these children develop differently in many skill areas. Professionals must neither dwell on the child's future because of the potential for free-floating anxiety, nor ignore anticipatory guidance about development. Most parents have built-in time clocks and become anxious when milestones are not being reached. Many parents feel the difference in quality and know intuitively that early disabilities and illness can cause problems in emotional and social development as the child grows older. Only the parents themselves know how much information about the future they need in order to make decisions, and only they know how much information they can handle at any period of time.

There are several ways to approach the delivery of anticipatory guidance. The professional can periodically inquire about the parents' needs by such statements as:

> Some parents are comfortable knowing about what is supposed to come next and some wish to let the professionals keep up with everything. What is best for your family?

Next, through careful listening the professional recognizes a parent's readiness to receive information and reflects that during visits:

> For the last two visits you have made comments about whether Sarah will walk. Can your occupational therapist tell you what he is looking for; the steps he is looking for to let him know about Sarah's progression toward walking?

> I sense your worry about Michael's lying. Let me tell you what I know about lying with children who are his age . . .

According to Golan (1980) the anticipation of a crisis is itself an ameliorating factor. The professional may choose to prepare the family for certain events that may cause excess stress such as younger sibling advancement, developmental progress reviews, behavior management as the child grows older, and the child's 21st birthday. In this way the family can ready themselves for decision making and better understand their emotional reactions. As the following example illustrates, there also will be times when the professional realizes the family has not allowed certain thoughts about future events to surface and must bring that to their attention:

> Now that Linda is entering puberty, I know you are wondering what should be done to educate her about sex. First, let's talk about how you feel about the appropriate behavior for a teenager. Then let's try to remember her 6-year-old mind as we consider what to do.

Krehbiel and Beam (1986) made the following suggestions in a presentation to professionals who work with families of young children with disabilities or chronic illness:

> "Learn" your families. Become skilled in observation. Determine a family's flexibility, adaptability, and readiness levels. Be aware that each family will handle the information you give them in a unique manner.

> Be discreet and couch comments about the future in generic terms. For example a professional might say, "Some families have told me they begin to feel anxious very early even though their child will not change programs until the fall. . . . "

Share anticipatory guidance information only at "teachable moments." For example, when the parent makes comments about the energy it takes to care for S., the interventionist might observe, "You must have to keep healthy yourself to continue to care for all the family."

Anticipate that it is natural for families to dwell on normative developmental milestones and give them other information such as Vygotsky's "zone of proximal development" (1978). Teach parents to attend to and concentrate on behavior other than typical developmental milestones, such as independence, imitation, initiation, and self-regulation.

Use goal attainment scaling (such as suggested by Holroyd & Goldenberg, 1978) to help parents fine-tune their expectations and lessen the discrepancy between expectation and reality.

Up to this point we have discussed the *delivery* of anticipatory guidance. One final point for professionals to consider is the use of anticipatory guidance to offer appropriate support for predictable periods of vulnerability in families. Time is not lost in discovering the cause for various reactions, because it is known that these short-lived states can be triggered by certain transitions, social stigma, and feelings of burden of care as discussed earlier.

In conclusion, the purpose of delivering anticipatory guidance is to educate parents about what the future may hold for their child. It is given with deliberate care and consideration so as not to alarm the family or cause an excess of anxiety. As with delivery of sensitive information (Krehbiel & Sheldon, 1985; Kroth, Olsen, & Kroth, 1986), the professional must consider the readiness of the parents, the type of material to be delivered, the environment, time and timing, and the imprecision of language. The professional also uses anticipatory guidance by being personally prepared for parental emotional upheaval that centers around predictable periods for many families.

Summary

We have explored several interpersonal communication skills from the perspective of families with children who are disabled or chronically ill: passive and active listening, specialized listening, interviewing, responding, problem solving, and anticipatory guidance. We believe we present a perspective that will enhance the well-being of these families and promote the competence needed to raise children with special needs. These skills represent a minute portion of professional demands. The challenge is to learn from the family, to understand the complexity of families and their ecologic reference, to avoid overgeneralization, and to enjoy working with each family in terms of their uniqueness and diversity.

Exercise #1

Ask a colleague or local parent support group to role-play using the situations below. Practice responding in ways that will enable the parent to feel more in control and not as powerless.

Parent: The cardiologist thinks an operation will be useless, that the baby will die soon anyway of heart failure. The surgeon disagrees. To her, cardiac surgery will remedy the situation and prolong life.

Parent: They called me to come to what they call an Education, Appraisal and Review (E.A. & R.) at school. All the paperwork was done when I arrived. They had classified my child as behavior disordered and assigned him to a "D"-level classroom. I was stunned. They even had goals and objectives written out. It was as though I wasn't even there. Wasn't even the father of my child.

Parent: I know occupational therapy will help K. But they say she's performing motorically according to her age level and therefore she can't qualify. We can't afford outside therapy now with all the bills piling up from her last operation. . . .

Parent: I take P. to clinic on Tuesday and again on Thursday. I have to get off work to do this. If I want to see the doctor who ordered all this I have to go on Friday. I am a pinball. . . .

Parent: It's the insurance. They will cover G. at Children's Medical Services if the doctor diagnoses him as multiply handicapped. But the doctor says his hearing loss is not that bad, so he's just (just!) physically handicapped. But we can't afford the specialized hearing aids. . . .

Parent: I knew something was wrong. I know it was his shunt. But the doctors said, "No . . . he just had a revision. It can't be that." But I know my son. I know when he's different and he is different now. We have no money to go for another opinion because we have to go out of state. . . .

Exercise #2:

Assume a parent begins to discuss the meaning of social stigma and asks about the interviewer's personal feelings. The reader should think about his or her own values and how he or she will respond to the parent.

Exercise #3:

The following quote from Brower (1987) illustrates the reality of dealing with social stigma. What response would be made to a parent who relates this information:

> So many people said, "I'm so sorry." We were still excited about Stephanie's birth and people were sending condolences. We even received sympathy cards from people instead of cards of congratulations. (p. 17)

References

Affleck, G., Tennen, H., & Gershman, K. (1985). Cognitive adaptations to high-risk infants: The search for mastery, meaning, and protection from future harm. *American Journal of Mental Deficiency, 89*(6), 653–656.

Anthony, E. J., & Benedek, T. (1975). *Depression and human experience.* Boston: Little, Brown & Co.

Benjamin, A. (1981). *The helping interview* (3rd ed.). Boston: Houghton Mifflin. (Original work published 1974)

Bombeck, E. (1983). *Motherhood, the second oldest profession.* New York: Dell.

Brammer, L. (1973). *The helping relationship: Process and skills.* Englewood Cliffs, NJ: Prentice-Hall.

Brower, D. (1987, July/August). The rubberband syndrome. *The Exceptional Parent Magazine,* pp. 17–20.

Carkhuff, R. R., & Anthony, W. A. (1979). *The skills of helping.* Amherst, MA: Human Resource Development Press.

Carter, E. A., & McGoldrick, M. (1980). *The family life cycle: A framework for family therapy.* New York: Gardner Press.

Dixon, N., & Glover, J. A. (1984). *Counseling: A problem-solving approach.* New York: John Wiley & Sons.

Dunst, C. J., Trivette, C. M., & Deal, A. G. (1988). *Enabling and empowering families: Principles and guidelines for practice.* Cambridge, MA: Brookline.

Egan, G. (1982). *The skilled helper: A model for systematic helping and interpersonal relating* (2nd ed.). Monterey, CA: Brooks/Cole.

Figley, C. R., & McCubbin, H. I. (1983). *Coping with catastrophe.* New York: Brunner/Mazel.

Fortier, L. M., & Wanlass, R. L. (1984). Family crisis following the diagnosis of a handicapped child. *Family Relations, 33,* 13–24.

Garrett, A. (1982). *Interviewing: Its principles and methods.* New York: Family Service Association of America.

Golan, N. (1980). Interventions at times of transition: Sources and forms of help. *Social Casework, 61,* 259–266.

Goldfarb, L. A., Brotherson, M. J., Summers, J. A., & Turnbull, A. P. (1986). *Meeting the challenge of disability or chronic illness: A family guide.* Baltimore: Paul Brookes.

Haley, J. (1976). *Problem-solving therapy.* San Francisco: Jossey-Bass.

Hammerschlag, C. A. (1988). *The dancing healers: A doctor's journey of healing with Native Americans.* San Francisco: Harper & Row.

Hobbs, N. (1975). *Issues in the classification of children.* San Francisco: Jossey-Bass.

Holroyd, J., & Goldenberg, I. (1978). The use of goal attainment scaling to evaluate a ward treatment program for disturbed children. *Journal of Clinical Psychology, 34,* 729–732.

Ivey, A. E., & Authier, J. (1978). *Microcounseling: Innovations in interviewing, counseling, psychotherapy, and psychoeducation* (2nd ed.). Springfield, IL: Charles C. Thomas.

Krehbiel, R. (1988, April). *Developing the IFSP as a process: Interviewing and support skills.* Workshop presented to the Family Service Delivery Training Institute (Sponsored by the Department of Special Education, San Diego State University), San Diego, California.

Krehbiel, R., & Askew, L. (1988, November). *Interviewing techniques for use in developing the individual family service plan.* Paper presented to the Division for Early Childhood, International Early Childhood Conference of Children with Special Needs, Nashville, Tennessee.

Krehbiel, R., & Beam, G. (1987, November). *Anticipatory Guidance: A tool for primary prevention of stress.* Presentation to the Division for Early Childhood, National Conference on Children with Special Needs, Denver, Colorado.

Krehbiel, R., & Sheldon, P. (1985). *Sharing sensitive information with families.* (Videotape; 33 minutes). Available from Alta Mira Specialized Family Services, 3501 Campus Blvd., Albuquerque, New Mexico, 87106.

Kroth, R. L. (1985). *Communicating with parents of exceptional children.* Denver: Love.

Kroth, R. L., Olsen, J., & Kroth, J. (1986). Delivering sensitive information: Or, please don't kill the messenger! *Counseling and Human Development, 18*(9), 1–11.

Kubler-Ross, E. (1969). *On death and dying.* New York: Macmillan.

Menolascino, F. J. (1977). *Challenges in mental retardation: Progressive ideology and services.* New York: Human Sciences Press.

Minuchin, S. (1974). *Families and family therapy.* Cambridge, MA: Harvard University Press.

Moses, K. L. (1983). The impact of initial diagnosis: Mobilizing family resources. In J. A. Mulick & S. M. Pueschel (Eds.), *Parent professional partnerships in developmental disabilities services* (pp. 11–34). Cambridge, MA: Academic Guild.

Olshansky, S. (1962). Chronic sorrow: A response to having a mentally defective child. *Social Casework, 43,* 190–193.

Patterson, J. M., & McCubbin, H. I. (1983). Chronic illness: Family stress and coping. In H. I. McCubbin & C. F. Figley (Eds.), *Stress and the family: Coping with normative transitions* (pp. 5-25). New York: Brunner/Mazel.

Patton, M. Q. (1980). *Qualitative evaluation methods.* Beverly Hills: Sage.

Project Ta-kos. Alta Mira Specialized Family Services, 3501 Campus Blvd., Albuquerque, New Mexico, 87106.

Rogers, C. R. (1975). Empathic: An unappreciated way of being. *Counseling Psychology, 5,* 2–10.

Satir, V. (1988). *The new peoplemaking.* Mountain View, CA: Science and Behavior Books.

Seligman, M. (1979). *Strategies for helping parents of exceptional children.* New York: Free Press.

Simeonsson, R. J., Bailey, D. B., Huntington, G. S., & Comfort, M. (1986). Testing the concept of goodness of fit in early intervention. *Infant Mental Health Journal, 7*(1), 81–94.

Solnit, A. J., & Stark, M. H. (1961). Mourning and the birth of a defective child. *Psychoanalytic Study of the Child, 16,* 523–537.

Spradley, J. P. (1979). *The ethnographic interview.* New York: Holt, Rinehart, & Winston.

Stein, R. E., & Jessop, D. J. (1982). A noncategorical approach to chronic childhood illness. *Public Health Report, 97,* 354–362.

Stinnett, N., & Defrain, J. (1985). *Secrets of strong families.* Boston: Little, Brown and Company.

Turnbull, H. R., Turnbull, A. P., Bronicki, G. J. B., Summers, J. A., & Roeder-Gordon, C. (1988). *Disability and the family: A guide to decisions for adulthood.* Baltimore, Paul H. Brookes.

Webster, E. J. (1977). *Counseling with parents of handicapped children.* New York: Grune & Stratton.

Wikler, L., Wasow, M., & Hatfield, E. (1981). Chronic sorrow revisited: Parent vs. professional depiction of the adjustment of parents of mentally retarded children. *American Journal of Orthopsychiatry, 51,* 63–70.

Supplementary Reading

Bronfenbrenner, U. (1979). *The ecology of human development: Experiments by nature and design.* Cambridge, MA: Harvard University Press.

Cochran, M. M., & Brassard, J. A. (1979). Child development and personal social networks. *Child Development, 50,* 601–616.

Crnic, K. A., Friedrich, W. N., & Greenberg, M. T., (1983). Adaptation of families with mentally retarded children: A model of stress, coping and family ecology. *American Journal of Mental Deficiency, 88*(2), 125–138.

Garbarino, J., & Sherman, D. (1980). High-risk neighborhoods and high-risk families: The human ecology of child maltreatment. *Child Development, 51,* 188–198.

Hobbs, N., Dokecki, P. R., Hoover-Dempsey, K. V., Moroney, R. M., Shayne, M. W., & Weeks, K. H. (1984). *Strengthening families.* San Francisco: Jossey-Bass.

Newbrough, J. R., Simpkins, C. G., & Maurer, H. (1985). A family development approach to studying factors in the management and control of childhood diabetes. *Diabetes Care, 8*(1), 83–92.

Turnbull, A. P., Brotherson, M. J., & Summers, J. A. (1987). The impact of deinstitutionalization on families. In R. H. Bruininks & K. C. Lakin (Eds.), *Living and learning in the least restrictive environment.* Baltimore: Paul H. Brookes.

7

COUNSELING APPROACHES WITH PARENTS AND FAMILIES

Harriet C. Cobb and Ronald E. Reeve

Counseling is an extremely important service that mental health professionals offer to parents and families of handicapped children. Physicians, educators, social service personnel, and other professionals also provide essential services, some of which share common characteristics with counseling. However, counseling is a unique type of service. It involves a special kind of relationship between a person who requests help (the client) and a person trained to provide that help (the counselor or therapist) (Patterson, 1986). Although the term *counselor* sometimes is used to refer only to individuals trained in a graduate program in "counseling," we will use the term in a more generic sense to mean a professional trained to do counseling/therapy regardless of professional title. Included are counselors, psychologists, clinical social workers, psychiatrists, and probably half a dozen other titles.

The approach to counseling that is taken with a particular problem may vary widely, depending upon the following: (1) the nature and severity of the presenting problem, (2) the theoretical model of the counselor, (3) the developmental level of the child, (4) the point at which the family appears to be in their understanding and acceptance of the handicap, (5) the time available, and (6) the economic resources available (if the family is to pay for the service). For example, if the child is mildly handicapped, the counseling issues may revolve primarily around the educational and peer relations needs of the child. The counselor would encourage the parents to communicate closely with the school and recommend ways in which the child could become involved in appropriate peer-related activities. A supportive, consultation role on the part of the therapist would be appropriate. If, however, the child is severely handicapped and difficult to manage at home and school, an intensive multidimensional approach may be necessary that could include direct parent counseling, consultation with the school, and family therapy. Regardless of the particular counseling issue, professionals must realize that handicapped children function within the context of a family system.

Counselors who work primarily from one theoretical model may focus on those aspects of the presenting problem that lend themselves most appropriately to their perspective. For example, the behaviorally oriented counselor may concentrate on teaching parents behavior modification skills and may refer the parents to a family counselor for dealing with emotional issues. A primarily "person-centered" therapist may devote the sessions to assisting the parents in clarifying their feelings about the handicapped child, then refer them to a school psychologist for consultation regarding educational matters.

Parents with a 5-year-old retarded child who is about to enter school have very different issues from parents of a 22-year-old who is about to enter the world of work. The mental health professional, of course, also must deal quite differently with parents who are just learning the extent of their child's handicap, as compared to those who have been to their fourth IEP meeting at the school and are frustrated about the progress their child is making.

Both time available and economic resources play a role in whether the counseling will be more short term and focused on coping with crises versus being long term and providing a resource to which families can return at various points in their lives with the handicapped family member.

The counseling process may be thought of as primarily *educative, facilitative,* or *remedial.* The educative component refers to the provision of basic information with regard to such things as the nature of the handicap, resources available to the family, and specific behavior management techniques. Bibliotherapy can be a useful adjunct to the counseling process, as the use of books can often reinforce the concepts presented to the parents and enable them to absorb information at their own pace. Some parents simply may not be ready to absorb a barrage of information regarding their child's handicapping condition until a later stage; the written information is available when they are ready.

In order to fulfill an educative role with parents of the handicapped, the therapist must be knowledgeable about all issues related to the disability. Counselors who do not possess the information needed should either refer the parents elsewhere or quickly educate themselves, ideally making use of peer supervision in the process. They must know relevant laws regarding rights of the handicapped for financial assistance, education, access to facilities, vocational training, etc. Counselors also must be aware of community resources such as parent support groups, advocacy organizations, and respite care providers. To the extent possible, counselors of families of the handicapped should become part of the "network" of individuals and organizations concerned with the handicapped in their community, e.g., the

ARC, special education groups, independence resource centers, etc. A major goal of educative counseling is assisting parents to become as knowledgeable about the handicap as possible.

Facilitative counseling involves a balance of providing support and information for the parents (the educative function of counseling) while at the same time reinforcing their efforts at independent problem solving. The facilitative component involves assisting the family in identifying its strengths and developing new ways of coping with the inevitable stresses of having a handicapped member. The remedial function of counseling refers to the therapeutic task of targeting dysfunctional patterns and developing strategies for helping parents to correct a problem. This is often the most challenging task for a therapist and involves assessing the interactions among family members and perhaps teaching entirely new patterns of relating to each other. In any counseling relationship, and sometimes within a single counseling session, one or all of the functions of counseling—educative, facilitative, and remedial—may be appropriate.

For example, the Joneses brought their 8-year-old son, Carl, to a counselor for evaluation. Carl was of average intelligence but had a severe attention deficit hyperactivity disorder (ADHD) which was interfering with both schoolwork and his behavior at home. Mrs. Jones expressed concern that Carl was going to be "just like his dad." (Carl's biological father reportedly was a moody, restless man who was difficult to live with. He died of cancer when Carl was 2.) Placement in special education and a prescription of Ritalin played a role in improved classroom performance for Carl. However, he continued to be difficult to manage; and his mother remained in counseling for emotional support and guidance in coping with Carl's behavior. Mr. Jones attended family sessions only sporadically but did attempt to follow through with suggestions for parenting, according to Mrs. Jones. Carl's two siblings attended sessions periodically in an effort to work on Carl's place in the family. Carl had an extremely low self-concept and was prone to compare himself negatively with his brother and sister. Mr. and Mrs. Jones had come to realize the dynamics of "scapegoating" and responded by avoiding blaming all family woes on Carl. It was clear, however, that parenting Carl *was* more challenging than parenting the other two children. Thus, the nature of counseling had been to empathize with the Joneses' situation and provide them with coping skills. The therapy was educative, facilitative, and remedial in nature, with bibliotherapy used as a means of providing information about attention deficit disorder from an external source. It is interesting to note how the Joneses' response to information about ADHD varied, depending on the developmental stage of the family in relating to Carl. Initially, Mrs. Jones was convinced that Carl's misbehavior was deliberate. An insight-oriented focus in the parent counseling seemed to help her acknowledge her "unfinished business" with her first husband. Later, the Joneses tended to perceive Carl's problems as the fault of the school.

At the present stage of counseling, they both have a better understanding of the disorder and appreciation for their role in contributing to effective family functioning.

Theoretical Orientations

A variety of theoretical approaches are potentially appropriate for working with parents and families, including humanistic, behavioral, cognitive, psychodynamic, and family systems orientations.

Originally identified as "client-centered" and now referred to as "person-centered," Carl Rogers' theory of counseling is the best known of the *humanistic* approaches (Rogers, 1961). It is based on the premise that people are basically good and generally capable of solving their own problems. Individuals have a natural, internal motivation to move toward "self-actualization," a stage of intrapersonal adjustment, and autonomy. The best way for the counselor to understand the client's problem is to take the perspective of his or her internal frame of reference, or perception of reality. This empathic focus on the client's reality is one of the essential conditions for success of therapy, according to Rogers. The other conditions are as follows:

1. two people are in psychological contact;
2. the client is in a state of incongruence and is experiencing anxiety;
3. the therapist is integrated in the relationship and is a "congruent" individual;
4. the therapist feels unconditional positive regard for the client;
5. the communication of the therapist's unconditional regard and empathy to the client is achieved.

Clearly, establishing an empathic relationship with parents of the handicapped is a critical element in effective counseling. These parents often experience emotional distance from the many professionals they encounter during the course of initial diagnosis, recurring evaluations, and educational and/or vocational interventions. For example, one parent of a Down's Syndrome child expressed the pain she felt when everyone around her seemed to be emphasizing how "well" she was coping with her handicapped child; no one seemed to be in touch with her deep depression related to her awareness of the chronicity of the situation. In her case, an important step toward healing was the therapist's empathy with the pain first, without an expectation for the parent to come to terms with the handicap and accept it after some prescribed period of time.

The *behavioral* approaches, based on theories of learning, focus on observable behavioral changes that occur as a result of the counseling. Specifically, the behavioral orientation refers to the systematic application of a variety of techniques, including reinforcements and methods to reduce the frequency of behaviors (such as "time out" and response cost), to modify targeted behaviors. (See, Kazdin, 1984, for a clear presentation of these techniques.)

As an example, parents of a moderately retarded 10-year-old wanted help changing their daughter Alice's table manners. They reported that, with no apparent provocation, Alice would spit out her food or throw it across the table. Her parents believed that they had established rules for appropriate behavior at the table with their other children, but Alice just ignored them, and punishing her was ineffective. The counselor suggested that the parents administer a token—a sticker on a chart—along with social praise for every 2 minutes of appropriate eating behavior. The frequency of food throwing and spitting decreased dramatically with the use of stickers and praise, so that the parents soon were able to give Alice only one sticker per meal to maintain good table manners. Furthermore, the success of this behavioral program provided a much needed boost for the parents to use positive reinforcement in other situations as well, such as brushing teeth at bedtime, getting dressed in the morning, etc.

Cognitive approaches operate on the belief that thoughts and emotions are closely intertwined, and that faulty thoughts are at the route of most psychological problems. Cognitive therapists try to help clients identify distortions in their thinking and in their appraisals of situations, and then help them to substitute more correct, or more psychological, functional appraisals and interpretations. Albert Ellis' "rational emotive therapy" (RET) (Ellis, 1979) is an example of a cognitive model that emphasizes changing thoughts so that feelings and behavioral changes can follow.

In recent years most behavioral therapists have come to acknowledge the importance of cognitive variables, and most cognitive therapists now recognize the power of behavioral techniques. This has resulted in a blending of cognitive and behavioral approaches, usually referred to as *cognitive behavioral,* probably best exemplified by the work of Donald Meichenbaum (Meichenbaum, 1977). He has focused on the client's self-statements about stress and especially about his or her perception of the ability to cope with stressors. Meichenbaum assumes that thought influences behavior. Before entering therapy, the client's internal dialogue may consist of negative self-statements and images. In therapy, the therapist attempts to modify the client's conclusions about a specific problem. A "translation" process occurs, in which the therapist offers alternative explanations and interpretations of the client's thoughts and "self-talk." This process enables the client to believe that improvement is truly possible. New coping behaviors are provided, or are taught to the client, for the client to try outside of therapy, and these are discussed in subsequent sessions. Through rehearsal and feedback the client moves toward a more successful mode of coping.

A parent of one handicapped child, for example, entered therapy with depression and chronic anxiety. He could not shake the belief that he and his wife were being punished for something. Through the cognitive-behavior interventions provided by his counselor he was able to reframe his belief by accepting the concept that *most* families are faced with obstacles to overcome, and this was theirs. His feeling of being singled out and his guilt were no longer present. The change clearly was a cognitive one. The difficulties associated with having a handicapped child remained; yet the father was able to let go of the sense of doom that was preventing him from moving forward.

The *psychoanalytic* approach to counseling is based on Freud's principles of personality development, although in practice Freud's original set of assumptions has been extended considerably. This approach emphasizes the importance of the developmental stage of the client and past parental pressures as contributors to personality dynamics. The individual attempts to cope with anxiety-producing unconscious conflicts by using defense mechanisms. It is the task of the therapist to assist the client in recognizing and overcoming the use of these defenses.

This approach is insight oriented as it attempts to provide the client with a "corrective emotional experience." The aspects of emotional abreaction, intellectual insight, and dealing with repressed memories are all interrelated in the therapy process. A necessary part of therapy includes direction of repressed attitudes toward the therapist, which is known as "transference." The working through of the transference to real-life situations is a goal of the therapy. The concept of "countertransference" refers to the therapist's emotional reactions to the client that may impede the process of counseling. For example, if a counselor believes that dealing with a handicapped child truly is an insurmountable difficulty, this clearly will interfere with counseling.

Modern psychodynamic therapies are seen as being of relatively short duration. Although not as readily related to the issues of dealing with a handicapped child as some other perspectives, the psychoanalytic approach's principles of transference, countertransference, defense mechanisms, etc., are useful in understanding the counseling process generally. Any method of assisting the client to grasp the reality of a situation and cope with it is applicable to a variety of psychological issues, certainly including those confronted by parents and families of the handicapped.

Family therapy is an established mode of intervention for working with parents of a handicapped child. Family therapy is a broad term that encompasses a diversity of philosophical orientations that have in common the approach of working with the child in the context of all or part of his or her family. The parent of an exceptional child often enters counseling as part of a couple or family unit. Although the handicapped child may not be the focus of counseling, dealing with the implications of the handicap usually is one of the major life issues the client brings.

A fundamental premise of family therapy/counseling is that families are interactive systems that are organized such that a change in one part of the system is likely to result in changes in other parts. A well-functioning family has a hierarchy, or clear rules with regard to how decisions are made and which family members have authority to make decisions. The nature of communication and the balance of power are often indicators of how a family is adapting to a handicapped member.

Boundaries exist within a healthy family, helping to define individual and subsystem roles. For example, in a healthy system the parents have the authority over the children, and the husband and wife participate in a cooperative subsystem. In the "enmeshed" family, boundaries between subsystems do not exist, thus preventing individual members from developing their own identities. On the other hand, boundaries are so rigid in "disengaged" families that it is difficult for cooperation to develop across boundaries. In these families there is little closeness, which precludes, for example, pulling together during crises such as the birth of a handicapped child. A lack of positive affect among family members is associated with family dysfunction.

One of the authors saw a family with five children, one of whom was profoundly mentally retarded. The mother, a single parent, expressed her concern that she doubted that she and her four nonhandicapped children could cope with the continued needs of the retarded 15-year-old much longer, although she would not consider residential placement. This mother perceived her family as disconnected and "burned out," with few enjoyable times. The four nonhandicapped children were 9, 12, 17, and 19 years old. Each shared in responsibilities for the care of their handicapped sibling, with little differentiation of roles among themselves, or between the mother and the children.

Counseling focused on establishing and clarifying boundaries for the individual members. The mother and the two older siblings were reinforced in their roles as the "parents." The younger children were then freed of the enormous responsibility they felt, for example, for feeding a brother who might choke to death if they made a mistake. Then, with clearer boundaries established, the counselor helped with practical issues such as providing respite time for each of the three "adults" so that they could engage without guilt in activities away from home. The two younger siblings were freed to be children. Over time, the family was able to focus less on the handicapped child as their ever-present "burden." This actually appeared to allow them to have fun in family outings and to accept their handicapped sibling more positively, rather than just as their confining, consuming responsibility.

Issues Commonly Encountered in Counseling

All families progress through developmental life cycles: becoming a couple, child bearing, entering school, adolescence, postparental years, and aging (Olson, et al., 1984). However, the family with a handicapped child may experience these cycles punctuated by events that affect the family system in unique ways. According to Fewell (1986), certain periods may be especially difficult for families with a disabled child: encountering the disability, early childhood, initial schooling, adolescence, and beginning adult life.

Reactions to the Initial Diagnosis

Regardless of whether their child is found to be handicapped at birth or much later, the news precipitates an emotional crisis with which parents must cope. A model commonly cited to help in understanding parents' reactions to the initial diagnosis of their child as handicapped is borrowed from the grief literature (Solnit & Stark, 1961). From this perspective the parents are viewed as having "lost" the idealized, healthy, normal child for whom they had longed and come to expect. With the realization that their child is handicapped, parents experience the "death" of their idealized child. The reactions often are intense, perhaps approximating those associated with the actual loss of a loved one. Stages involved in the grieving process have been identified, including shock, denial, guilt, anger and blaming, and eventual achievement of equilibrium as movement is made toward acceptance. However, greatly complicating the grieving process is the fact that the handicapped child remains, placing constant demands on the parents and serving as an ever-present reminder of their loss. Olshansky (1962) used the term "chronic sorrow" to characterize the ongoing feelings parents experience because they cannot completely work through their grief.

Not all professionals who work with parents of the handicapped accept the grief model as a useful conceptual framework for understanding parents' attempts to cope with the crisis of the initial diagnosis. Although the emotional reactions to the realization that their child is handicapped are undoubtedly intense, it may be just as useful to think of this as the equivalent of trying to cope with any other major family crisis (e.g., loss of a job, divorce, a sudden move, etc.). For one thing, not all parents "work through" the steps delineated in the grieving process; any of the stages may be re-experienced at any time, or a parent may never move beyond the anger/blaming stage. Also, it is important to realize that the two parents do not necessarily move through the stages at the same time. Thus each situation should be evaluated, and each reaction should be considered unique. As Seligman and Darling (1989) point out, several factors may influence the type of reaction a family will have, including socioeconomic status, actual physical appearance of the child, prior information, religiosity, and social support.

The most common mistake professionals make at this point is to be overly optimistic about the severity of the child's problems. A natural human tendency is to want to make the parents feel better. However, making the parents happier by minimizing the child's condition is counterproductive in the long run. At the other extreme, some professionals seem to err by presenting the "worst case scenario." They apparently believe that preparing parents for the worst outcomes will make anything short of that situation easy to accept. Neither extreme is helpful.

Of course, for many parents, this will be their first encounter with this particular handicap. Counselors often can help by steering parents toward clear, accurate, comprehensive information about the child's condition. Factual knowledge is greatly preferable to what the parents may be imagining.

The goals of counseling at this point should include helping the parents to see that their reactions, including their powerful emotions, are *normal*, automatic, perfectly understandable ways of responding. They need to accept that their feelings are part of a coping, healing process which will take time and energy, but which they almost certainly will survive.

As soon as practically possible, parents can benefit greatly from being put in touch with others who have gone through similar experiences. This experience can help the parents feel less alone and "singled out" for the difficult task of raising a handicapped child. The group experience can provide significant credibility to the notion of eventual acceptance of the situation. Universality and installation of hope are two of the most important curative factors that group counseling has to offer parents. Counselors should become personally acquainted with support and advocacy groups to which they can confidently send parents, knowing these groups will help normalize the experience for parents encountering this crisis. However, the counselor must be sensitive to the readiness of the parents to participate in a group.

It is not unusual for parents, particularly those in the early stages of the grief process, to resist the reality that associating with other parents with handicapped children brings to them. One couple reported that attendance at a picnic sponsored by a support group was a depressing experience. Both parents and children were present, which enabled this couple to see how their then 2-year-old child probably would look as he grew older. The stark reality of a malformed physical appearance was disturbing to them, and they terminated their involvement in the group. The couple would have benefited from more extensive preparation before entering the group. At a later time this couple found support and comfort from these same families.

Shopping Behavior

Professionals often encounter parents who bring their child in for assessment in order to get another "second opinion" about the nature and severity of the handicap despite the fact that the child has already been evaluated numerous times. Related to this, in a counseling situation, parents may lodge complaints about the perceived incompetence of the other professionals who have been involved with their child.

This may occur because parents are still at the "anger/blaming" stage of adjusting to having a handicapped child. Usually, however, it can best be understood as a normal reaction of people who are confused and frustrated by what seem to them to be contradictory messages from professionals. It must be acknowledged that some professionals *are* willing to make firm statements without a valid basis for doing so, and that others *are* unwilling to give parents any clear diagnosis or prognosis. Part of the problem, though, is the nature of the disciplines involved. Parents are drawn from the ranks of the normal population, so most do not have backgrounds in medicine, psychology, and education. They tend to think of each of these as much more exact sciences than they actually are.

Counselors can best respond by acknowledging the legitimacy of the parents' frustrations. They then can assess the level of knowledge and understanding the parents have of child development and of the disciplines with which their child is involved. Rather than perform an unnecessary, expensive evaluation (which also may be traumatizing to the child), the counselor may better spend the time educating the parents and interpreting the professional jargon into understandable language so the parents can know exactly what the professionals were trying to say.

Effects on the Marital Relationship

Having a child can alter the nature of any marital relationship. There may be markedly less time and energy to devote to the spouse, and this can place stress on the relationship. Most parents cope with these changes, in part because of the joy and pride the child also brings to them, and perhaps in part because they know the child will only be with them during this time-limited stage of their lives.

The severity of the strain brought on by having a handicapped child can be influenced by a number of factors. The handicapped child is typically not what the parents wanted/expected, requires even more time and energy than other children, and may appear in need of permanent parental care. The financial burden often is great, putting further pressure on the parents. There may be a feeling of embarrassment about having produced a "defective" child, so the self-esteem of one or both parents may suffer, making them less able to function in the relationship with their spouse. One parent might blame the other, citing as evidence some handicapped relative, or some real or imagined action such as a medication taken during pregnancy, a fall, etc.

If the couple involved had a problematic relationship prior to the handicapped child's arrival, the additional stress may be the "final straw." Research regarding marital integration generally presents a mixed picture. On the negative side, in families with a handicapped child the number of desertions and divorces is higher

(Telford & Sawrey, 1981) and the rate of suicide and alcoholism is increased (Block, 1978) compared to control families. Despite these findings, most such parents *do* manage to cope, and in fact it is not uncommon for couples to report that the pressure of the handicapped child actually brought them closer together. In some cases, this appears to be a negative bonding, with parents saying, in effect, "We must stay together at all costs." Clearly, maintaining (or achieving) a satisfactory marital relationship is important if the family is to adapt, and outside professional help can be a key factor in that process.

Fathers tend to be less involved in the day-to-day care of a handicapped child. This can be interpreted as rejection on the father's part, or as an indication of family disengagement. Although these may be accurate perceptions in some cases, counselors will err if they jump to that conclusion. Because of the necessity for *someone* to be home, and given the economic reality that men typically make more money than women, couples may agree that it makes sense monetarily for the husband to work and for the wife to provide the primary care for the child. When that is a shared decision, it actually may indicate a more functional adaptation than equally sharing care but having to survive with fewer economic resources. This is another example of the importance of considering each family as unique and of getting to know their special circumstances prior to acting on assumptions.

Sibling Concerns

While having a handicapped child in the family may greatly affect the parents and their interactions, it also alters the entire family system. Brothers and sisters often report that the presence of a handicapped sibling was the single most important element in their own development. Some of the negative reactions to be expected are the following (Chinn, Winn, & Walters, 1978; Wentworth, 1974): (a) *resentment and jealousy,* because of the parents' extra attention to the handicapped child, the amount of money that goes to treatment, limitations on their own participation in trips and other experiences, requirements for them to baby-sit, etc.; (b) *hostility,* because they may see the handicapped sibling as the source of all their problems. This may be seen in verbal or physical abuse directed toward the sibling, or in disobedience and other acting out behaviors directed toward the parents; (c) *guilt* over having negative feelings toward their sibling, or because of their own good fortune for having been born normal; (d) *fear* of acquiring the disability themselves, or that their own offspring might be handicapped, or that they may one day be left to care for the sibling on their own; (e) *shame and embarrassment* about the handicapped child's presence in the family, including concerns about how to explain their sibling to peers and visitors to the home and embarrassment about being seen in public with the sibling; (f) *rejection,* which may manifest itself in denying the reality of the impairment or, more commonly, in withholding affection or pretending the sibling does not exist; and (g) *pressure* from unrealistically high expectations placed on them by some parents who seem to want them to make up for their sibling's limitations by overachieving.

But there are also reports of siblings responding positively, experiencing an increased family closeness and a positive sense of responsibility. Professionals should not automatically conclude that the sibling is being negatively affected.

The impact of the presence of a handicapped sibling varies greatly in form and intensity depending on the relative ages of the children, the presence of other, normal siblings, the gender of the siblings, the severity of the handicap, the economic status of the family, and a host of other variables. Girls are generally expected to help with the day-to-day care of a handicapped sibling more than boys, so they often will experience the effects more intensely. If the normal sibling is older than the handicapped child, greater expectations for help are likely to be placed on the normal child. Siblings whose families easily can afford to pay for outside help, respite care, special equipment, etc., can be spared many of the unfortunate side effects felt by children in poorer families.

Normal siblings obviously can benefit from the counseling process. Counselors should consider several factors when working with these siblings. They should check to see what factual knowledge base the siblings have about the handicapping condition involved; although the parents may have educated themselves at the time of the initial diagnosis, they may have neglected to provide information continually to their normal children at a level they could understand. If needed, counseling could begin with a major educative component. Contact with other children who have handicapped siblings in a group counseling format can be extremely valuable in normalizing the experience. Children have models for typical behavior and emotions as they go through most other developmental tasks but they commonly never encounter another child with a handicapped sibling who can share how they feel, how they act, etc.

An important goal in counseling siblings is to let them know that it is O.K. to feel hostility, jealousy, etc. toward their handicapped sibling. *All* siblings experience these negative emotions toward each other; this is *normal.* On the other hand, it is also important to help the normal siblings gain perspective on the extent to which their handicapped brother or sister actually is *the* big problem in their lives—it is too easy to blame all one's problems on a scapegoat. Another important counseling goal is to help normal siblings develop appropriate "scripts" that they can use to explain their handicapped sibling's condition to people they encounter. Having something specific in mind to say is greatly preferable to the discomfort children feel if they do not know how they might respond in given circumstances. Role playing is a good way to provide practice with these scripts.

Deciding Whether to Have More Children

Especially in families in which the first child is handicapped, the issue of having additional children will arise in counseling. Parents may hesitate to do so for fear that subsequent children also will be handicapped, or out of concerns about their ability to provide well for other children given the cost of caring for the handicapped child, or because of concerns that the handicapped child will harm a younger sibling. Counselors must help parents clarify the factors so that an appropriate focus can be obtained. If a genetic component was involved in their child's handicap, or if prenatal maternal complications contributed, specialized medical information is essential, and the counselor should either help the parents acquire that information or refer them to persons who can provide it. The other issues involved are much more subjective. The counselor can aid by helping the parents to communicate fears, life goals, etc., to each other. Such decisions can be made more objectively in the context of counseling.

Peer Relations

Most handicapped children have restricted opportunities for interaction with children their own age. Social skill deficits accompany many handicapping conditions, and physical disabilities limit the activities in which many handicapped children can engage. Sports and musical activities often are outside the ability levels of handicapped children, and it is in these settings that much informal interaction occurs for normal children. Parents often find that they cannot simply drop the child off to play with friends. The child may experience social rejection— other children frequently are cruel to children who are different. A counselor should encourage the parents not to shield their child from interaction with the outside world because this will prove detrimental to the child's long-term development. Instead, parents can be encouraged to manufacture friendship opportunities by choosing likely candidates and arranging times and places where the interactions can most likely succeed. Supervision can be provided if needed. In addition, counselors can work directly with the handicapped child, or through the parents, to teach social skills to the child. These might include such topics as looking at people when you talk to them, dealing with anger, sharing toys, etc. Guided practice will be necessary, including role playing and controlled experience with peers. A number of social skills training programs, complete with visual aids and other prompts, are commercially available. Children also should be taught "scripts" for how to deal with questions about the nature of their handicap, because these are sure to come from other children.

Dealing with Sexual Behavior

Sex education is difficult to deal with for many parents, even without the complications of a handicapped child. With many handicapped children, especially those who are mentally retarded, sex is an especially complicated concern. Some people think that the retarded should not be sexually active, and avoid providing sexual information in the naive hope that the child will not show an interest in sex. It *is* difficult to know how much to teach about sexual topics when the likelihood of experiencing a sexual relationship is relatively low, as is the case with some severely handicapped children. Nonetheless, all humans have sexual feelings that they need to understand at whatever level they are capable of handling. Counselors can help parents get in touch with their own concerns about the sexuality of their handicapped child, then enable them to make informed decisions about how and how much to teach. In circumstances where the parents' discomfort is so high that they cannot deal with the topic alone, the counselor may provide the information for the child either in an individual session or, preferably, in the presence of the parents.

Planning for the Child's Future

Entry into adulthood is an important transition stage both for parents and their handicapped child. The issues of the separation process can be difficult for families in that the normal trend toward increasing independence from the family is complicated by the disability. Parents may need assistance in recognizing their child's normal need for individuation from the family psychologically, while simultaneously requiring more emotional and financial support than a non-handicapped child. Many decisions must be made with regard to living arrangements, i.e., will the "adult" child remain at home, or are there other acceptable alternatives such as group homes, supervised apartments, etc.? The extent to which the child can earn money independently plays a significant role in the necessity for continued parental responsibility. Extended vocational training and/or assistance in job placement are factors to be considered in assisting the parents and child in decision making.

The nature of the counseling continues to include educative and facilitative components at this point. Parents may need to be directed toward social service agencies and job training/rehabilitation centers for such things as information about social security benefits related to the disability.

The counselor must be sensitive to the parents' emotional experiences with regard to their child that may have evolved through several stages by this time. Old "crises" may re-emerge, such as feelings of deep disappointment about the unfulfilled dreams of having a "perfect" child to launch into the adult world.

Final Words

Counselors who work with parents and families will be most effective if they view these clients as normal people with a full range of strengths, weaknesses, and life circumstances who, in addition, are attempting to cope with the special challenges involved in having a handicapped child in the family. Thus, although some specialized knowledge base and unique perspectives are important for counselors to obtain, the most basic requirement for effectiveness in this role is that the professional be a perceptive, sensitive, caring human being who can listen empathetically, evaluate the special circumstances of *these* clients, and then apply good counseling skills.

References

Block, J. (1978). Impaired children. *Children Today, 7,* 2–6.

Chinn, P., Winn, J., & Walters, R. (1978). *Two-way talking with parents of special children.* St. Louis: C. V. Mosby.

Ellis, A. (1979). Rational-emotive therapy. In R. J. Corsini (Ed.), *Current psychotherapies* (2nd ed., pp. 185–229) Itasca, IL: F. E. Peacock.

Fewell, R. (1986). A handicapped child in the family. In R. R. Fewell & P. F. Vadasy (Eds.), *Families of handicapped children* (pp. 3–34). Austin, TX: Pro-Ed.

Kazdin, A. E. (1984). *Behavior modification in applied settings* (3rd ed.). Homewood, IL: Dorsey Press.

Meichenbaum, D. (1977). *Cognitive behavior modification: An integrative approach.* New York: Plenum Press.

Olshansky, S. S. (1962). Chronic sorrow: A response to having a mentally defective child. *Social Casework, 43,* 190–193.

Olson, D. H., McCubbin, H. I., Barnes, H., Larsen, A., Muxen, M., & Wilson, M. (1984). *One thousand families: A national survey.* Beverly Hills: Sage.

Patterson, C. H. (1986). *Theories of counseling and psychotherapy* (4th ed.). New York: Harper & Row.

Rogers, C. (1961). *On becoming a person: A therapist's view of psychotherapy.* Boston: Houghton Mifflin.

Seligman, M., & Darling, R. B. (1989). *Ordinary families, special children: A systems approach to childhood disability.* New York: Guilford Press.

Solnit, A., & Stark, M. (1961). Mourning and the birth of a defective child. *Psychoanalytic Study of the Child, 16,* 523–527.

Telford, C., & Sawrey, J. (1981). *The exceptional individual* (4th ed.). Englewood Cliffs, NJ: Prentice-Hall.

Wentworth, E. (1974). *Listen to your heart.* Boston: Houghton Mifflin.

8

INTERVENING
WITH ABUSING PARENTS
OF HANDICAPPED CHILDREN

Marvin J. Fine

Since the focusing of national attention on child abuse over 35 years ago (Kempe, Silverman, Steele, Droegemueller, & Silver, 1962), our awareness of the scope of the problem has grown enormously. Whether there is more abuse or greater public sensitivity to and reporting of the subject is not clear; in either case, the incidence figures are alarming. There are reports of over 1 million children each year suffering some form of abuse (U.S. Dept. of Health and Human Services, 1988). Definitional and compilational problems have plagued researchers in obtaining accurate figures. Data that are reported will usually be labeled by other professionals as an underestimate of what actually may be occurring in American society.

The historical bases of identification of child abuse have been actual physical abuse and/or neglect. The more recent concerns with psychological and even sexual abuse have expanded the numbers of identified abused children (Garbarino, Guttman, & Seeley, 1986; Hart & Brassard, 1987). Children who have been belittled, threatened, or emotionally manipulated can be psychologically damaged in ways that affect their interactions with peers, schooling, and society. Children caught up in parental conflict can easily become psychological casualties, despite both parents' insistence that they love their children and would not knowingly hurt them. And certainly we understand how children sexually molested or exploited can be deeply psychologically impaired.

Although incidence figures and definitional differences can be debated, there is a clearer though still unequivocal picture of the sequelae of abuse. At the least,

This chapter is an expansion of Fine, M. J. (1986). Intervening with abusing parents of handicapped children. *Techniques, 2,* 353–363.

these children are at high risk for a range of personal and social difficulties that can be lasting. Ammerman, Cassisi, Hersen, and Van Hasselt (1986) reviewed the outcome literature in relation to (a) medical and neurological effects, (b) intellectual and cognitive functioning, (c) academic achievement, (d) behavioral disorders and psychopathology, and (e) social development. All of these areas were found to be affected negatively to some extent, with many children showing negative effects across all areas. The development of aggressive patterns, learning difficulties, and lower intellectual functioning suggests the potential for long-term and pervasive repercussions to experiencing abuse.

Abuse and the Handicapped Child

Considering the vulnerability of the handicapped child and the kinds of stresses that this child potentially places on the family, it would seem that a greater incidence of and possibly more severe kinds of child abuse would occur within families of a handicapped child. One review of the literature, however, concluded that

> [t]he evidence reviewed in this paper does not demonstrate the clear causal link between prior handicaps and abuse. Indeed, more recent prospective research suggests that handicapping conditions are unrelated to abuse. (Starr, Dietrich, Fischhoff, Ceresnie, & Zweier, 1984, p. 62)

A more recent review of the literature (Ammerman, Van Hasselt, & Hersen, 1988) argued the increased likelihood of abuse among handicapped child populations but again acknowledged contradictory results and research flaws. These authors considered a number of risk factors for the young handicapped child, including the implications of early separation, disruption of attachment, and parental stress.

Longo and Bond (1984) echoed the findings of many researchers on the inability to depict the family as "pathologically" stressed and experiencing a range of marital and family problems because of the presence of a handicapped individual. Tavormina, Boll, Dunn, Luscomb, and Taylor (1981) have pointed out that researchers and clinicians operating from such a preconception have often stereotyped families of a handicapped individual in dysfunctional ways and in doing so have perpetuated those beliefs within the professional community.

These observations are not meant as a disclaimer that there is abuse of handicapped children. There is ample evidence that handicapped children are being abused and that families with a handicapped individual can be stressed (Beckman, 1983; Farber, 1959; Gallagher, Beckman, & Cross, 1983). The error, if indeed there is one, is the automatic assumption that family stress leads to such pathologies as abuse; we need to recognize that many families have been able to develop useful coping and adaptation strategies around the presence and care of the handicapped individual (Crnic, Friedrich, & Greenberg, 1983; Kazak & Marvin, 1984; Longo & Bond, 1984). It also appears that, at times, writers on the effects of a handicapped child on family dynamics have ignored the full range of potential stresses placed on any family by children. Barsch (1968) discussed how a number of common parent issues could be misinterpreted in relation to families with a handicapped child instead of being understood as problems that any parent might experience. It seems that if one family with a handicapped child does develop appropriate coping and adaptation strategies and yet another family with a similarly handicapped child is unable to respond in an adaptive way, the issue is not the child per se but other family, interpersonal, or ecological considerations.

The intent of this chapter is to consider a broad systems and family ecology orientation toward understanding and intervening with abusive families. Although the examples and discussion relate mainly to families with a handicapped individual, the analysis and observations have a more heuristic application. The viewpoint being presented is not original but brings together an awareness of family dynamics (Jung & Cook, 1985; Minuchin & Fishman, 1981) with an appreciation of the cultural background and the subsystems within which people exist (Bronfenbrenner, 1979). Justice and Justice (1976) presented a psychosocial systems model that is somewhat similar with its view of individual family members interlocking within a family system which in turn is nested within a broader societal or cultural matrix. This view is also complementary with the ideas presented in a paper by Belsky (1980) on child maltreatment from an ecological viewpoint, and with Jung and Cook's (1985) description of a family systems approach to child assault.

Case Example

The following case summary illustrates a number of important considerations relevant to understanding the dynamics of abusive families with a handicapped child and to intervening helpfully with such families.

Mrs. K. had been a teacher prior to her marriage and had a background of experience with early elementary school children where she dealt with children of different ability levels and personality characteristics. She came from a family where people tended to discuss problems and where verbal interchanges were commonplace. Mr. K. came from a family where obedience on the part of children was a very important value. Although corporal punishment was not used extensively or severely, his father exercised a very dominant role in terms of being the disciplinarian and his word was seldom challenged by the children. Mr. K. did very well in mathematics and the sciences and subsequently became an engineer. As he advanced in his company, the nature of his work took him away from home for periods of time, sometimes for weeks.

The marriage was reasonably happy as described by both spouses, with Mrs. K. being the more social and verbal partner and her husband less communicative and intensely involved in his work. There were no conflicts around money or decision making, and in general there seemed to be tacit agreements on their respective marital roles without much discussion.

The birth of their first child, Phillip, was a happy event with positive anticipation on both their parts. The little boy was a full-term baby without any birth complications but his subsequent development proceeded quite slowly. The father was less aware of the slowness with which the child reached various developmental milestones because of his time away from home. The mother, however, did express a growing concern over the child's slowness of development. Feedback from physicians who periodically saw the child was generally on the order of reassuring the mother that Phillip was just a slow developer; they pointed out that because there were no notable medical or physical problems he would eventually catch up to other children his age. The mother's response was to become progressively more concerned and protective. The father's response was to become progressively more impatient and to begin believing that the child was stubborn and somehow holding back from more appropriate behavior. Also of note were the reactions of the extended family. Mrs. K.'s parents were sympathetic and supportive of Phillip's difficulties and of the parental stress. Mr. K.'s parents were fairly communicative but conveyed a sense of discomfort with the situation and actually commented in passing that no one on their side of the family ever had those kinds of problems.

The parents finally did receive a "descriptive" diagnosis from a pediatric clinic of Phillip experiencing a pattern of irregular development with specific, moderate delays. The etiology was unknown, and the prognosis was guarded in that Phillip's future progress was considered unpredictable. The recommendation was for Phillip to attend a developmental preschool program that would emphasize motor and language development activities. The mother assumed responsibility for the logistics of Phillip's attendance, while the father remained skeptical of the medical opinion and the need for a special preschool program.

When Phillip was 3 years old they had a second child whose development proceeded quite normally and whose apparent precosity further set off Phillip as a different child. The father began to use physical punishment with Phillip and developed a habit of holding Phillip tightly by his shoulders, shaking him, and insisting that he shape up and do what he was supposed to do. Spankings became more frequent and severe. Phillip began to act shy and fearful in group situations, preferred to spend time alone, and became even more reluctant to attempt new experiences. The father's belief that Phillip was willfully choosing to be a different and negative child was reinforced by Phillip's behavior. The marital relationship began to suffer, the mother became even more protective of Phillip, and the father's interactions with Phillip became more physically and psychologically abusive as he attempted to correct and modify the child's behavior. During this time the father began spending more time in play with the younger child, who was beginning to present discipline problems for the mother.

Discussion

Much of the writing on child abuse has tended to look at abusive situations in a linear cause–effect fashion. For example, one line of research had to do with examining the relationship between abusive parents and their own experiences as an abused child (Main & Goldwin, 1984). There are studies on the socioeconomic correlates to abusive situations (Pelton, 1981) and on the extent to which the abused child might even be provoking abuse (Johnson & Morse, 1968). It has become increasingly clear, though, that the study of unitary variables has not been highly productive in terms of a comprehensive understanding of the problem and in planning an intervention program. It seems to be potentially more useful toward understanding and ameliorating abusive situations to examine the abusing family as a system. An examination of the family context is vital because that is where all the variables play themselves out and in some kind of systemic pattern (Berger, 1980; Fine & Holt, 1983; Garbarino & Gilliam, 1980; Jung & Cook, 1985).

The family as a microsystem includes the nuclear family, parents, children, and whoever else is in the home. The structure of the family reveals patterns of communication, affection, and authority. Subsystems and boundaries within the nuclear family are often expressed as the parent and child subsystems. The nuclear family is nested within and interconnects to broader systems, including extended family and cultural, educational, and socioeconomic systems. Individuals influence and are influenced reciprocally by these different systems. Family values, historic parenting patterns, and members defining their roles in relation to other family members all influence current functioning.

Some families are relatively open to change and evidence a good capacity to adapt successfully to new events. Members "close ranks" and work together supportively. Other families resist change and are threatened by new events that challenge rigidly adhered to patterns and beliefs.

Although no one case can disclose or reflect all that we know about abusing families and the presence of a handicapped child, there are a number of observations that one can make about Phillip's situation that have generalizability. First, the abuse of Phillip may appear as fairly mild when considered against the background of dramatic accounts of almost sadistic behavior by parents. Yet the majority of reported cases are not the highly dramatic variety but instead are approximations of Phillip's situation. Second, the psychologically abusive impact of the father's behavior needs to be considered in its seriousness. We can only speculate as to the effects on Phillip's self-esteem and the anxiety he might experience in new learning situations. Historically, psychological abuse has existed in the shadows of the more obvious examples of physical abuse.

Another way in which Phillip's case reflects research findings is that as a "normal appearing" but mildly impaired child his behavior was more easily attributable by the father to a willful act rather than being viewed as somehow a function of a disability (Martin, 1982). The ambiguity of diagnosis and prognosis is not only frustrating to parents who want clear answers but encourages projections and "wishful thinking." The view of Phillip as somehow choosing to act "different" put the father in the position of believing that his wife was being manipulated by the child and that it was up to him to intervene. The father's beliefs about parental responsibilities were learned from his experiences with his own father and required him to be in charge of his family and its well-being. The child's developmental problems struck at the core of the father's sense of adequacy as a parent. These feelings were exacerbated by his own parents' discomfort with Phillip and their defensiveness about possible genetic influences.

The mother's background within her own family and in terms of her professional training as a teacher prompted her to seek help and advice from appropriate professionals. Her work with children in the public schools helped her to be aware that problem situations can involve ambiguity and that one needs to work over time with a child experiencing a problem. The father's more black and white view of the world and his sense of exactness led him into a discounting process with the various professionals from whom they attempted to obtain help.

The father progressively became less willing to discuss the child's difficulties with his wife, and both parents felt more alienated within the family. The parent conflict, the anger and blaming, and, in particular, the father's denial tended to block either parent from seeking community assistance such as a parent support group, thereby exacerbating their respective feelings of alienation. The father was even reluctant to discuss the situation with friends, while the mother was more able to use friends for emotional support. The sense of aloneness and alienation on the part of family members has been identified as a significant contributing factor toward incidents of child abuse in normal as well as handicapped families (Polansky, Chalmers, Buttenweiser, & Williams, 1979).

The father was apparently more comfortable clinging tenaciously to the belief that Phillip was a willfully disobedient child than dealing with the awareness that his child was "defective." Helping the father to better understand and accept some of the realities and ambiguities of Phillip's subtle disabilities would be a very important albeit challenging task for the professional worker. This will require a "letting go" by the father of the need for a normal functioning child and probably a related grieving process by him for the loss of the child that never was.

There is evidence that the sorrow parents may experience around the handicapped child is likely to recur at different points in the child's development. As the child fails to meet certain developmental milestones, the realities of the child's condition are again revealed and can trigger a recurrence of the mourning process. This finding argues for a continuum of services over the life of the handicapped person (Wikler, Wasow, & Hatfield, 1981). We can only speculate as to how the father's closeness to the younger child and accompanying distancing from his wife and Phillip have influenced the mother's management problems with the younger child. The side-taking and triangulating of relationships is reflective of the growing dysfunctionality of the family.

The case of Phillip illustrates how a handicapped individual can have a great many repercussions within the family depending on what the parents and family bring to the situation in terms of stability, communication and coping skills, availability of support systems, and even religious beliefs (Kazak & Marvin, 1984). What other kinds of stress is the family under and what other transitions are occurring in the family? How does the focus of the parental conflict around Phillip reflect some unresolved issues between the parents and serve to detract the parents from facing each other over those issues? The case also illustrates that child abuse occurs across all socioeconomic strata even though there is greater incidence within the lower socioeconomic range (Pelton, 1981).

Intervention

Intervention in cases of abuse can mean different things. The removal of the child from an abusing situation always needs to be considered if it is believed that the child remains in imminent danger. But even in such cases, the eventual return of the child to the family should be a goal. This would require preparatory work with the parents to ensure the viability of the child's re-entry.

There is a range of options that could be available or developed within any community. Individual or group therapy, family therapy, parent education and training, and some form of direct home supervision are possibilities. Although some parents will voluntarily seek assistance through therapy or parent training, many are directed to "treatment" by some agency, usually the court or welfare system. There is seldom a comprehensive plan; available services in a community are often used even if only marginally appropriate.

One common intervention is to require the parents to attend parenting sessions such as STEP (Dinkmeyer & McKay, 1977), PET (Gordon, 1970), or Active Parenting (Popkin, 1983). These programs as offered in a community are usually open to any interested persons and might therefore include already competent parents as well as parents with minimal skills, destructive attitudes, and a history of abusive behavior. Parent education programs tend to be informational and skill-building oriented and can be helpful to parents. However, personal accountability is low, and the programs are time-limited, usually running several sessions.

This writer had the experience of offering general parenting programs and at termination having some parents request written documentation that they had attended. I was unaware that they had been required to attend because of reported child abuse, found them to be passive participants, and had no real sense of what they had gained or how they might be parenting differently. However, they did satisfy the court's directive.

I am also aware of cases where parents were required to participate in therapy until the therapist recommended termination. This can create the potentially bizarre scenario of parents having to continue indefinitely, with a therapist unwilling to release them because some potential for abuse still exists (as if it did not exist in all of us).

Home visitor programs operated through social welfare services have become another alternative. These may be particularly beneficial where the parent(s) feel overwhelmed by the day-to-day demands of home management and child care. A "visitor," often a paraprofessional with evidence of successful home and child management skills, can prove helpful by being on-site to demonstrate, coach, and teach parents more effective skills.

Perhaps more so with a handicapped versus normal child, educational intervention is of major importance; that is, helping parents to understand the nature of the child's condition, the course of development, and, in an educative way, to make them aware of the kinds of frustrations and problems that will emerge along the way. It is not uncommon to find abusing parents experiencing unrealistic developmental expectations of their children.

The alienation factor, as indicated, has been identified as a contributor toward abuse. Parents of handicapped children may not be aware of community resources, parent networks, and other kinds of support processes that are available in their community. Tied in with this is respite care. In cases where the child's handicapping condition requires fairly constant attention, the stress on parents can become enormous as they almost become captives of the child's condition. For single parents and even couples with a severely handicapped and needy child, the "trapped" experience can be overwhelming with potential for growing resentment toward the child. Many communities are developing forms of respite care and this is an important avenue for reducing parental pressures.

The availability of a trained professional to hold a series of group meetings with parents of young handicapped children to process their experiences, their successes and failures, etc., becomes another valuable direction of intervention. This can serve as a reality feedback procedure and one that can help parents to understand that what they are experiencing is in a sense normal. There are a growing number of "parents supporting parents" types of groups that can help parents learn about the handicaps, how family members can work together, and, most important, that others have had and survived similar experiences.

Attitudinal Considerations

Regardless of the kinds of programs being implemented, the required participation of parents can create an impression of the program being punitive. One of the first tasks of the involved professional, regardless of program format, is to encourage a positive perception of the experience in terms of its potential helpfulness and in the way that the parents are identified as concerned and loving, but probably frustrated. Because the parents might believe that others (e.g., social welfare agencies or the courts) have not understood them and have been punitive toward them, the parents may be understandably defensive.

Unquestionably the abusive behavior on the part of parents must terminate; it is argued, though, that in many instances the most helpful intervention by professionals will come from a sympathetic view of the plight of the family and family members as opposed to viewing the abuser as a "mad dog" or "deranged" individual. The pattern of abusing behavior is frequently symptomatic of problems in the family and usually of the frustration and unhappiness of a number of family members (Brassard & Appelaniz, in press; Fine & Holt, 1983).

For any involved professional it is important to maintain a sympathetic view of the parents as struggling to adapt and cope with the effects of the child on the family. A professional should have the insight and compassion to see through the abusive behavior to the kinds of deep-seated parental concerns and scares that often characterize the abusing parent. Such a posture can be quite difficult to maintain given the professional's aversive reaction to parents who have harmed a handicapped child. Minuchin and Fishman described this issue in a family therapy situation:

> The therapist is forcing himself to act against his own inclinations. It would give the therapist great pleasure at this point to tell the mother exactly what he thinks of people who mistreat children. But if this child is not be removed from his parents—which is always a chancy solution—then family change is his best hope. In order to achieve that change, the therapist must keep the family in therapy. This can be done only by creating a therapeutic system in which the parents feel supported and understood before there is any challenge. (p. 41)

A Multidimensional View of Intervention

There is a homeostatic dynamic in families that encourages the maintenance of the status quo; relationship patterns once established have ways of reinforcing themselves. Some changes that occur in dysfunctional families are mainly cosmetic, with fundamental patterns of behavior and beliefs remaining intact. The data on the effects of intervention with abusing families are not highly encouraging, with predicted success rates of only 40% to 50% (Starr, 1979).

The reported difficulties with precipitating change in abusing families may be related to the relatively superficial level of intervention, the use of narrow bands of intervention, or the time-limited nature of the intervention. A several-pronged approach that operates on an (a) education-information level, (b) skill acquisition level, (c) belief-insight level, and (d) behavioral change level may have greater potential for success. As shown in Figure 8.1, those four areas of emphasis overlap and in doing so can effectively reinforce each other. Together they constitute a potentially effective and comprehensive intervention program.

Programs may be offered through community agencies, schools, or even within the context of a private psychotherapy practice. Although formats are likely to differ—for example, a time-limited versus open-ended group—the four areas seem important elements of a comprehensive program. Insight alone is unlikely to lead to major changes. New information, a different understanding of self, new or enhanced skills, and monitored practice all together are more likely to move the person into different and potentially lasting belief, attitudinal, and behavior patterns.

A group experience can have added benefits to individual contacts. The opportunities to feel less singled out and to share information and experiences can be very supportive. The group is also a more efficient structure for reaching a greater number of persons under conditions of limited professional resources.

Ideally, within one agency there might exist several tracts or programs that parents and families can move through. An example could be where the parents might be counseled as a couple and also participate in a discussion group with other parents; subsequently they might join a time-limited parent education group. The abused child could even receive individual counseling, as needed, and might in time join the parents for a family therapy experience. Some specific educational and community resource components might also be built into the overall program.

More usual circumstances would have one location identified as the primary source of intervention such as a community mental health clinic. The involved professionals can still conceptualize a broader, systemic, and ecological framework that allows for connecting the parents selectively to other programs and resources within the community. In the case of Phillip's parents, couple's therapy would seem indicated to help them work out the anger and hurt that is now pushing them apart. Some family-of-origin focus would assist them in seeing what they brought to the relationship and the way that current extended family relationships are influencing how they are dealing with Phillip.

Their involvement in a parent support group that included educational components would also be helpful. The father could benefit from specific information on developmental delays in children and hearing from other parents who, like him, are struggling with feelings of frustration and anger over the ambiguities of their

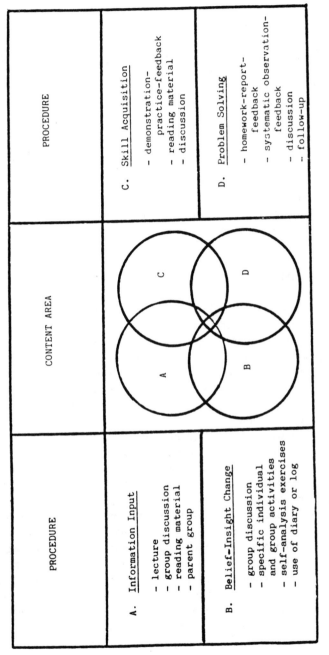

PROCEDURE

C. Skill Acquisition

- demonstration-practice-feedback
- reading material
- discussion

D. Problem Solving

- homework-report-feedback
- systematic observation-feedback
- discussion
- follow-up

CONTENT AREA

PROCEDURE

A. Information Input

- lecture
- group discussion
- reading material
- parent group

B. Belief-Insight Change

- group discussion
- specific individual and group activities
- self-analysis exercises
- use of diary or log

Figure 8.1. Program Emphasis

child's behavior. To hear others share how they tried to force more appropriate behavior from the child, lost control, were hurtful with the child, then remorseful, then angry, then withdrawing, etc., would assist the father in realizing that he was not alone nor was he a terrible person.

Through either the couple's therapy group or some other program vehicle, the father could be taught some anger control techniques. It is hoped that the parents would learn how to be more supportive of each other as they adapt to the recognition that Phillip will need their support, understanding, and guidance for the years ahead. Both parents, working together, could gradually help Phillip to feel better about himself, to believe that he can please his parents, and to approach new learning situations with less anxiety. These last happy scenarios may be some time in coming but are achievable to a reasonable degree.

The following discussion elaborates on the four areas of focus, but each professional is encouraged to develop a comprehensive framework appropriate for his or her professional context. The specifics of program and community resources will vary, requiring initiative and creativity on the part of professionals.

The Education-Information Level

Books, pamphlets, lectures, and films are ready vehicles for conveying important factual information regarding the handicapping condition, its course of development, and how families can productively respond. Information on normal development and appropriate expectations should also be included. Some parents have incorrect expectations for their children, project a negative intent to the child when he or she does not perform, and then feel justified in punishing the child. It is important for parents to appreciate the normal variances of child development and to learn to see each child as an individual. Especially in the case of different handicapping conditions with ambiguous prognoses, parents can benefit from developmental information to help them sort out the medical picture.

Information on families in general, descriptions of problem-solving styles, and discussion of the impact of the handicapped child on all family members, especially siblings, can also be very helpful.

Typical educational formats are usually nonthreatening because there can be a minimum of personal involvement by the participants. Even where discussion and personal sharing follows a film, many parents often sit passively, listening to the few who get actively engaged in discussion. Each parent involved in a treatment program is going to respond differently. Some will need time to acclimate and to learn how to respond and think through family situations. The parent who sits passively at first, if emotionally supported, may subsequently open up and become a more active participant. If parents are pushed too hard at first to participate, their defensiveness may increase along with progressively less cooperative involvement.

The education-information level is also where information on organizations dealing with certain handicaps as well as information on community support services such as a respite care program can be shared.

The Belief-Insight Level

This level can also involve a combination of educational inputs, but should represent calculated occasions for the parents to personalize their experiences. Parent or whole family counseling sessions can more easily surface the feelings of different family members and reveal dysfunctional patterns that maintain tension and abusive behavior. Parent education programs that utilize some family therapy techniques encouraging exploration of family patterns and the family history can also be a valuable input at this level (Fine & Jennings, 1985).

The goals at the belief-insight level would be to increase family members' awareness of destructive family patterns, their own feelings and needs in both the contemporary scene and from a family-of-origin perspective, and to help family members achieve a healthier view of themselves and other family members.

A cognitive behavioral framework can also be helpful in encouraging parents to examine their thoughts, and how feelings and behavior can follow. Cognitive strategies can assist parents in overriding an emotional overaction with appropriate behavior. A simple example is a parent who learned that he could still think and choose appropriate interventions with the child, *even though* he was becoming angry. In another case, the parent became aware of a sequence of thinking that she went through that encouraged angry reactions, then learned a series of positive self-statements she could make that supported a positive response to the child.

Helping parents access social support systems of either a community or extended family nature may require changes in their beliefs about the child and their own needs. An examination of their resistance to reaching out and accepting community support will probably reveal specific thoughts and feelings about the handicapped child, personal responsibility, and the anticipated reactions of others. This is an important area to explore with the family because of the positive mediating influences of social support (Dunst, Trivette, & Cross, 1986).

It is hypothesized that without changes at the belief-insight level, generalizability and permanence of behavior changes by the parents will be limited.

Skill Acquisition and Behavior Change Levels

These two levels can be conceptualized separately but in operation should interface. Within a clinic or training group setting, the parents can be advised on techniques around such topics as child care, discipline, managing anger, and how to use each other for support. Specific relaxation and stress reduction techniques can also be demonstrated and practiced. Modeling, role playing, and behavioral rehearsal are potentially effective, action-oriented ways of training parents.

The professional worker may also be able to observe the parents and child interact in a playroom or even through home visits. This allows for coaching and immediate feedback to the parents. The feedback is extremely important in positively reinforcing gains, but also in heading off parent frustration. For example, parents can be taught that even if they started to react angrily they can still shift to a more positive response. For some parents, once they "goof up," they feel frustrated and then continue the angry, abusive response, as if they had no control. This is similar to someone on a diet who takes a cookie and then thinks that if they took one, they may as well have ten, and feels unable to stop.

The cognitive analyses mentioned earlier can be taught as a set of skills to be implemented by the parents at stress times. The importance of the cognitive components is that they can support the parents' developing a view of self as "being in control" and "able to think clearly." These views counteract the historical self-view of some parents as becoming "out of control" or "losing it" as soon as they experience anger or get into some trigger situations.

Once certain skill areas have been identified and demonstrated with opportunities for practice within the session, then the parents will be expected to try out the new skills at home. Some record of specific incidents, data collection, or vignettes can be brought back to regular sessions for processing and, most important, for feedback. Positive reinforcement is crucial at this point. The parents need to see themselves changing and succeeding. The important changes are not only in terms of specific parent–child behaviors but also in parent–parent behaviors of a collaborative, mutually supportive nature and in overall healthier family interaction patterns.

The Family Emphasis

The professional worker needs to be cognizant at all times that the family is the focus of treatment even though the steps of intervention may seem at times to focus more narrowly on information or specific skills. For example, in a processing discussion around some new behavior the parents have attempted, the inquiry should include who else was involved, how others in the family are responding, whether the grandparents (or whoever else is an important extended member) are aware of what is happening and what they are saying or doing.

The feedback given to the parents should reinforce what seem to be changes in their thinking and attitudes, and in family behavior patterns. As stated, the parents need to begin seeing themselves as changing, as more competent in parenting and as more supportive of each other. In essence, a positive, family adaptation process has been initiated that should lead to success outcomes which, in a cyclical fashion, become reinforcing of the new behavior patterns. If this described phenomenon occurs, then the likelihood of successful, enduring, and generalizable changes in family functioning should increase with the most important consequence of resolving the child abuse issue.

Summary

Child abuse, whether with a handicapped or normal child, can be conceptualized as an expression of a dysfunctionality in the family. This argues for a broad family orientation to intervention. Although a handicapped child can represent a stressful event to a family, there is evidence that many families do adapt and cope adequately with the child.

The efficacy literature on intervention with abusing families has not been encouraging. The multilevel intervention model being proposed may increase the likelihood of the family changing and maintaining positive changes. Each of the focuses—information, belief, skill, and behavior change—interfaces with the others. This framework can serve as a blueprint for persons developing intervention programs with abusing parents.

The example presented of a mildly handicapped child and of fairly mild abuse, although not very dramatic, does illustrate a number of considerations in understanding the dynamics of abuse with a handicapped individual. The professional worker needs to assume a sympathetic posture with the family struggling to cope, albeit not very effectively, rather than viewing the abusing parent as a horrible person. Strengthening of the family's positive adaptation and coping skills and elimination of negative reciprocal behavior patterns between parents and the abused child are reasonable goals of intervention. Ongoing support and teaching the parents to be help seekers and acceptors are also important.

References

Ammerman, R. T., Cassisi, J. E., Hersen, M., & Van Hasselt, V. B. (1986). Consequences of physical abuse and neglect in children. *Clinical Psychology Review, 6,* 291–310.

Ammerman, R. T., Van Hasselt, V. B., & Hersen, M. (1988). Maltreatment of handicapped children: A critical review. *Journal of Family Violence, 3,* 53–72.

Barsch, R. H. (1968). *The parent of the handicapped child: A study of childrearing practices.* Springfield, IL: Charles C. Thomas.

Beckman, P. (1983). Influences of selected child characteristics on stress in families of handicapped infants. *American Journal of Mental Deficiency, 80,* 150–156.

Belsky, J. (1980). Child maltreatment: An ecological integration. *American Psychologist, 35,* 320–335.

Berger, A. M. (1980). The child abusing family: Part I. Methodological issues and parent-related characteristics of abusing families. *The American Journal of Family Therapy, 8,* 52–68.

Brassard, M. R., & Apellaniz, I. (in press). The abusive family: Theory and intervention. In M. J. Fine & C. Carlson (Eds.), *The handbook of home-school intervention: A family systems orientation.* Boston: Allyn & Bacon.

Bronfenbrenner, U. (1979). *The ecology of human development.* Cambridge, MA: Harvard University Press.

Crnic, K. A., Friedrich, W. N., & Greenberg, M. T. (1983). Adaptation of families with mentally retarded children: A model of stress, coping, and family ecology. *American Journal of Mental Deficiency, 88,* 125–138.

Dinkmeyer, D., & McKay, G. (1977). *Systematic Training for Effective Parenting.* Circle Pines, MN: American Guidance Service.

Dunst, C. J., Trivette, C., & Cross, A. H. (1986). Mediating influences of social support: Personal, family, and child outcomes. *American Journal of Mental Deficiency, 90,* 403–417.

Farber, B. (1959). Effects of a severely mentally retarded child on family integration. *Monographs of the Society for Research in Child Development, 24*(Whole no. 71).

Fine, M. J., & Holt, P. (1983). Corporal punishment in the family: A systems perspective. *Psychology in the Schools, 20,* 85–92.

Fine, M. J., & Jennings, J. (1985). What parent education can learn from family therapy. *Social Work in Education, 8,* 14–31.

Gallagher, J. J., Beckman, P., & Cross, A. H. (1983). Families of handicapped children: Sources of stress and its amelioration. *Exceptional Children, 50,* 10–19.

Garbarino, J., & Gilliam, G. (1980). *Understanding abusive families.* Lexington, MA: Lexington Books.

Garbarino, J., Guttman, E., & Seeley, J. (1986). *The psychologically battered child: Strategies for identification, assessment, and intervention.* San Francisco: Jossey-Bass.

Gordon, T. (1970). *Parent effectiveness training.* New York: David McKay.

Hart, S. N., & Brassard, M. R. (1987). A major threat to children's mental health: Psychological maltreatment. *American Psychologist, 42,* 160–165.

Johnson, B., & Morse, H. A. (1968). Injured children and their parents. *Children, 15,*147–152.

Jung, M., & Cook, P. (1985). A family systems approach to child assault. In J. Meier (Ed.), *Assault against children: Why it happens and how to stop it.* San Diego, CA: College Hill Press.

Justice, B., & Justice, R. (1976). *The abusing family.* New York: Human Sciences Press.

Kazak, A. E., & Marvin, R. S. (1984). Differences, difficulties, and adaptation: Stress and social networks in families with a handicapped child. *Family Relations, 33,* 67–76.

Kempe, C. H., Silverman, F. N., Steele, B. F., Droegemueller, W., & Silver, H. K. (1962). The battered child syndrome. *Journal of the American Medical Association, 181,* 17–24.

Longo, D. C., & Bond, L. (1984). Families of the handicapped child: Research and practice. *Family Relations, 33,* 57–65.

Main, M., & Goldwin, R. (1984). Predicting rejection of her infant from mother's representation of her own experience: Implications for the abused-abusing intergenerational cycle. *Child Abuse and Neglect, 8,* 203–217.

Martin, H. P. (1982). The clinical relevance of prediction and prevention. In R. H. Starr, Jr. (Ed.), *Child abuse prediction: Policy implications.* Cambridge, MA: Ballinger.

Minuchin, S., & Fishman, H. C. (1981). *Family therapy techniques.* Cambridge, MA: Harvard University Press.

Pelton, L. H. (Ed.). (1981). *The social context of child abuse and neglect.* New York: Human Service Press.

Polansky, N., Chalmers, M., Buttenweiser, R., & Williams, P. (1979). Isolation of the neglectful family. *American Journal of Orthopsychiatry, 49,* 149–152.

Popkin, M. H. (1983). *Active parenting.* Atlanta: Active Parenting.

Starr, R. H. (1979). Child abuse. *American Psychologist, 34,* 872–878.

Starr, R. H., Dietrich, K. N., Fischoff, J., Ceresnie, S., & Zweier, D. (1984). The contribution of handicapping conditions to child abuse. *Topics in Early Childhood Special Education, 4,* 55–69.

Tavormina, J. B., Boll, T. J., Dunn, N. J., Luscomb, R. L., & Taylor, J. R. (1981). Psychosocial effects on parents of raising a physically handicapped child. *Journal of Abnormal Child Psychology, 9,* 121–131.

U.S. Department of Health and Human Services. (1988). *Study findings: Study of national incidence and prevalence of child abuse and neglect: 1988.* Washington, DC: National Clearinghouse on Child Abuse and Neglect.

Wikler, L., Wasow, M., & Hatfield, E. (1981). Chronic sorrow revisited: Parent vs. professional depiction of the adjustment of parents of mentally retarded children. *American Journal of Orthopsychiatry, 51,* 63–70.

SECTION

Focus on Exceptionality

9

THE FAMILY WITH A MENTALLY RETARDED CHILD

H. Thompson Prout
and
Susan M. Prout

The identification and recognition of intellectual handicaps, i.e., mental retardation, has been an issue in the human service, medical, and education professions for many years. Most of the research and concern has been focused on the mentally retarded individual and his or her characteristics, care, education, and adaptation. Although the impact on the families of mentally retarded persons has long been recognized by practitioners, it has been only within the last decade that the family has been emphasized at a research and policy level (e.g., see Gallagher & Vietze, 1986). It is now widely accepted that the presence of a mentally retarded person within a family system has significant impact on that system and its members.

The purpose of this chapter will be to review relevant research on mentally retarded individuals and their families and to discuss professional collaborative roles with the parents. Our discussion will focus on potential collaborative roles, the impact on families, and social-emotional problems of mentally retarded persons. We will conclude the chapter with a historical case study focusing on a mentally retarded child at different ages and developmental levels, with the concomitant effects on the parents and family.

Collaborative Roles with Parents

The collaborations and interventions with parents of mentally retarded children can take many forms. The professional must also assume that parents will be dealing with professionals around their child's well-being throughout the child's life, and thus the collaborative roles should be viewed within a developmental framework that considers family life cycle issues.

Tymchuk (1983) has delineated several models of interventions with parents of mentally retarded persons. The *dynamic* model is more a counseling or therapeutic model that assumes parental behavior is directly related to how the parents internally or psychologically react or deal with their child's disability. This model places more importance on the attitudes and feelings of the parents than on actual management strategies for dealing with the child. Laborde and Seligman (1983) call a similar approach that deals largely with parental adjustment "facilitative counseling." The marital relationship of the parents may also receive some attention in this model. Difficulty or inability in dealing with the child and the disability are viewed as a psychological reaction or conflict of the parents. In order to facilitate the parents' adjustment, these reactions and conflicts must be explored, examined, and resolved. The resolution of these conflicts will allow the parents to be more effective in their parenting role.

The *behavioral* model, in contrast, is more concerned with helping parents improve their parenting skills and deal directly with behaviors presented by their mentally retarded children. Most of the work in this area involves teaching parents how to conduct operantly based behavior modification programs in the home, e.g., how to target and appropriately reinforce specified or desired behaviors. This model is more of a training model than a counseling or therapeutic model.

The *family therapy* model assumes that the family structure or system are affected by the presence of a mentally retarded family member. The family is dealt with as an interacting system and may involve all the family members meeting in a group. This model goes beyond the others by including siblings of the mentally retarded child. A more functional family system will facilitate the adjustment of the mentally retarded child as well as other family members.

Early intervention approaches or *educational approaches* focus on the parents' role in collaborating with educational or developmental programming for their child. Similar to the behavioral model, these focus on training parents to work with their children to maximize their child's cognitive, adaptive, and educational development.

We would add two somewhat related models to Tymchuk's (1983) discussion—the role of collaborative assessment and the resource role of providing information for parents. The *assessment* role is an important collaborative function on a number of levels. Accurate and thorough assessment is vital to planning for the child, helping parents accept the disability of their child, and understanding the extent of the child's problems and their limitations. Assessment conducted in a collaborative style—showing parents the nature of the assessment, perhaps allowing some observation, use of parental information through structured interviews, checklists, and rating scales, etc.—will facilitate the parents' willingness to collaborate and cooperate with the professionals involved with their child. The assessment role, in addition to cognitive, adaptive, and educational areas, should include a thorough assessment of social-emotional functioning of the child. This area, often overlooked, is vital to the child's adjustment. Issues related to this are discussed later in this chapter.

Last, the *resource* role involves the provision of accurate information about the child's disability and programs to assist the child. In effect, it is an educational role. It may involve providing parents with reading materials, directing them to various community resources, and generally providing case management services at various transition points for the child. Explaining appropriate developmental expectations, without setting expectations too low, is a key part of this role.

The Impact of a Mentally Retarded Child on the Family

The Initial Diagnosis and Recognition

Although many parents may suspect that something is "wrong" or "different" with their child, the first official confirmation of developmental delay is traumatic. Depending on the degree and nature of the mental retardation, this confirmation of a diagnosis may occur at different times in the child's development. With advances in genetics and medical screening technology, the diagnosis can occur prenatally. With more severe or obvious mental retardation, the diagnosis is often made at or shortly after birth, or at least within the first 6 months to 1 year of life. Children in the mildly mentally or educable retarded range may not be identified until school entrance. Thus, parents may deal emotionally with the diagnosis at different points in the family development.

Drew, Logan, and Hunter (1988) have described a range of parental reactions and adaptations to the diagnosis of mental retardation of the child. These reactions are mediated and influenced by the degree of retardation (discussed below), general family dynamics, specific characteristics of the family unit (e.g., single-parent, blended family, etc.), presence or absence and adjustment of other children, marital dynamics, socioeconomic level and resources, intelligence of parents, and emotional adjustment coping skills of the parents. Across these parental reactions, there is a general theme of the retarded child being a threat to the parents' self-esteem and self-acceptance. These reactions and adaptations to the diagnosis include the following:

Denial. This is a common reaction, particularly after the initial identification of retardation. Parents may deny that any problem exists or, to a lesser degree, minimize the extent of the problem. At later stages of development, they may attribute the child's limitations to other factors such as poor motivation, laziness, or lack of effort.

Projection of blame. Projecting blame helps protect the parents' self-esteem with regard to causative factors in the retardation. If developmental problems are apparent at birth, parents may initially blame the medical professionals involved in the prenatal early care of their child. They may fabricate or exaggerate what they perceive as improper care for their child. Overt hostility may be present toward the health care professionals. As mentally retarded children grow older and are involved in educational and rehabilitative programs, professionals in these settings may be the target of blame. The parents may blame these professionals for their child's lack of development and even the failure to overcome the handicap. Overzealous parental advocacy and constant challenging of programming may be the vehicles for this projection.

Fear. What is not known about mental retardation in general and their child's condition, specifically, may be very scary to the parents. Often, the term "mental retardation" brings to mind the stereotype of the institutionalized, helpless, and inappropriately behaving individual. The parents may have little notion of what to expect behaviorally and developmentally from their child. There may be fears about causative factors and the potential for other children being handicapped. The parents may have many questions/fears about care for their child, schooling, the future, available resources, etc. Further, there may be considerable fear about reactions from friends, relatives, and the community in general.

Guilt. Guilt is similar to projection of blame except that the blame is directed toward oneself. Parents, and mothers in particular, may search for their causative role in their child's handicap. Obsessing on some event or behavior that the parent feels may have contributed to the retardation may be present. There may be exaggeration of these events or behavior, or self-blame for known causative factors (i.e., an infection) over which they had no control.

Mourning or grief. Some have compared the realization that a child is retarded to mourning or grieving for someone who has died. In anticipation of the birth and in early development, parents have dreams about what their child will be like at future developmental levels. For example, it might take the form of parents buying infant sweatshirts for "XYZ University." Upon the diagnosis of mental retardation, these dreams and hopes for the future are negated and drastically altered. It is as if the child they had dreamed of had died. The acceptance and adjustment of mental retardation may parallel a grieving/mourning pattern for some parents. Unlike the dead child, however, the retarded child remains in the family and may be a constant reminder of the "child that never was."

Withdrawal. The resultant effect of the emotional reaction to their child being mentally retarded may be withdrawal. Although in some cases, this may initially be helpful to "sort out" issues related to their child's retardation, prolonged withdrawal is maladaptive. Continued isolation from friends, relatives, co-workers, etc.; the avoidance of social and community outings; and staying away from public places may be present.

Rejection. Similar to withdrawal, the concomitant emotional reactions may lead to rejecting behaviors toward the child. These may be direct, overt behavior, or may take the form of more subtle psychological rejection. The rejection may be seen as devaluing the child by ignoring or minimizing positive attributes of the child, by setting unrealistic goals for the child, or by leaving or escaping from the family situation.

Acceptance. The final step toward adjustment for the parent is acceptance. If achieved, this may be a long process. It involves the acceptance of the child and his or her handicap and, additionally, self-acceptance. Accepting parents will value the child for who he or she is. Obsessing about causes, blaming others, and other negative emotional reactions will decrease significantly. These parents will find joy in their retarded children, will be forward looking and realistically positive about their children, and engage in behaviors to normalize their lives and their children's lives.

This acceptance may not be complete throughout the life of the child even after the parents have seemingly adjusted to the disability. Wikler, Wasow, and Hatfield (1981) discussed "chronic sorrow" in parents of handicapped children. As the child develops and grows older, each new stage or point of "normal" developmental transition may serve as a reminder of the child's handicaps, limitations, and deficits. This may result in varying degrees of "acceptance" throughout the child's and family's development. What initially seemed to be a positive and accepting parental attitude about the child's handicap may be somewhat less positive as the child grows older.

Degree of Retardation

Many people unfamiliar with mental retardation view these individuals as homogeneous and similarly functioning. This a common assumption made by parents when first hearing the term in reference to their child, and, in many cases, parents may assume a worst case scenario—i.e., their child will be severely handicapped. The degree of retardation and its concomitant behaviors vary tremendously as does the mentally retarded child's role in the family. The levels of retardation—mild, moderate, severe, and profound, according to the American Association on Mental Retardation standards, or educable or trainable mentally retarded for schooling purposes—describe very different types of individuals.

Inherent in these differences are different impacts and types of stressors within the family (Seligman & Darling, 1989).

Consider the contrasting cases of two "well-behaved" mentally retarded adolescent boys, one mildly mentally retarded and one severely/profoundly retarded. The mildly retarded adolescent has a mental or developmental age of approximately 10 years. Although somewhat behind his age-mates, he has acquired most of the basic developmental skills, albeit at later times in his development. He has most of his self-care skills (feeding, bathing, dressing, etc.), has some basic academic skills, can go about the community independently, does chores at home, participates in some school and community activities, is partially mainstreamed at school, is taking vocational training for a postschool job, and his parents can go out at night and leave him alone in the house. He has begun to become quite interested in dating and sexual matters.

The severely/profoundly retarded adolescent has a mental age of approximately 3 to 4 years. He still lacks most of his basic self-care skills—he can messily feed himself, only recently became completely toilet trained, and needs assistance with dressing and bathing. He needs to be monitored at home and in the community and often gets stared at when his parents take him out in the community. His academic skills are limited to color recognition and partial number and letter naming. He attends a self-contained special class and is generally isolated from the rest of his age-mates at school. He can never be left alone at home, and the parents have had a very difficult time finding baby-sitters.

Although neither may present significant behavioral concerns for their parents, these two young men present very different current problems for their families— one is relatively independent, nearer the "norm" for his age, and requires less direct time and effort from his parents, who, however, find themselves dealing with prolonged adolescent identity issues; the other is very dependent, very different from his age-mates, and still requires a great deal of direct care from his parents. Further, there are fewer developmental changes for the severely/profoundly retarded boy, and the parental role has remained constant and demanding. Obviously, the experiences of these parents and families are quite different. The degree of mental retardation of the child clearly presents different types of concerns and stressors for a family and should be considered as a variable in assessing the family dynamics and adaptation.

Several exploratory studies (Mink, 1986; Mink, Blacher, & Nihira, 1988; Mink, Meyers, & Nihira, 1984; Mink, Nihira, & Meyers, 1983) have examined the differences in families with children of different levels of mental retardation. Across these studies, Mink and her colleagues studied family typologies in families of slow learning, trainable, and severely mentally retarded children. Using a clustering procedure, these investigators found that many similar typology patterns existed across these families. However, there also existed a few distinctive patterns among the families of severely retarded children within family types. The details of these typologies are beyond the scope of this chapter and are detailed in

Mink (1986). These studies would seem to suggest that the presence of a mentally retarded child in a family tends to interact with family dynamics to yield typologies that are relatively similar across levels of retardation—there are more similarities than differences. This would suggest that the professional may need to pay considerable attention to the general family typology and not overly focus on the level of retardation. It should be noted that much of the research by Mink's group was done with younger retarded children and their families, and that Mink, Blacher, and Nihira (1988) emphasize the empirical/research nature of their classification system. The clinical significance of the typologies across the family life cycle remains to be demonstrated.

Developmental Impact on Parents and Families

The family life cycle theoretical viewpoint suggests that the development of both the family and its individual members is interactive; individual development affects the stages of family development and vice versa (see Turnbull, Summers, & Brotherson, 1986, for a discussion of family life cycle theory and its implications for families with mentally retarded members). Wikler (1986) found that developmental transition (e.g., adolescence and young adulthood, in particular) were particularly stressful for families. We feel that there are four points in the development of the mentally retarded person that are critical stressor, transition, or adjustment periods for the parents and family. Any of the collaborative roles delineated previously may be utilized at any of these points, but some of the roles may be more prominent at different points. The following are four points in the development of the mentally retarded child that present some of the collaborative issues.

Identification and early childhood. The parental reactions detailed earlier in this chapter are particularly relevant here. The reaction to the diagnosis of mental retardation is often dominated by affective and emotional responding. As noted above, the point at which the diagnosis is made and the conclusiveness of the diagnosis may vary with the obviousness or the degree of the retardation. Parents of a severely retarded child or a child with a clearly identifiable syndrome may be made aware of their child's handicap very early in the child's development. Further, the obviousness of the handicap may be more difficult to deny. The mildly retarded child may not be identified until as late as after school entrance. Parents of mildly retarded children are likely to have developed a different type of emotional attachment to what they may presume to be a "normal" child. Because their child did not seem strikingly different from other children, the diagnosis may be more difficult to accept, i.e., a greater probability of denial. Regardless of when the diagnosis is made, the parents are likely to have individual emotional reactions requiring support.

The professional at this identification point needs to assess the child carefully and be able to explain the implications of the assessment to the parents. This explanation should be probabilistic, yet realistic. It should offer the parents prognostic information that neither paints an overly "gloomy" picture of the child's future and thus limits expectations, nor should it prevent the parents from dealing with the reality of the child's handicap. This, indeed, may be a fine line in communicating diagnostic information to the parents. Assessment information should also orient the parents for the current appropriate developmental expectations for their child. Because of the emotional response of the parents, the dynamic or therapeutic role may be an important professional role in helping the parents "work through" or adjust to their child's handicap. Assisting the parents with both home-based and school or agency early intervention programming is important, as is serving as a resource in providing information for the parents.

School entrance. Assuming that the child has been identified prior to reaching school age, most parents will have reached some level of adjustment to their child's mental retardation. However, their child's "differentness" starts to become more obvious at this stage. The parents begin to deal with special education and its concomitant assessment, placement, and educational planning meetings, different class arrangements, etc. Because of the nature of public education, the developmental delay of their child thus becomes "public." Further, while other children progress in the basic academics, the parents of mentally retarded children see their children working on more basic skills. Parents see other children the same age as their child progressing, while their child obviously lags behind—the fact that their child is mentally retarded and different may be painfully reinforced by the early school experience.

The professional may continue in the dynamic role by providing support for the parents as they continue to deal with their child's retardation, which is made more realistic by school entrance. Some of the emotional reactions often observed at the initial diagnosis may recur in somewhat different form. The resource role in understanding the various processes, procedures, and parental rights related to involvement with special education may be prominent at this stage. Further, involvement with collaborative planning of the child's education will continue.

Adolescence. As many parents will attest, the adolescent period is a difficult one from a social-emotional standpoint. The "normal" adolescent experiences physical and hormonal changes that also produce concomitant social-emotional reactions. For the most part, mentally retarded adolescents are subject to the same physical changes and sexual development, yet they remain cognitively delayed. The child may not easily understand these changes, and the parents may not be prepared to view their child as a sexual being. Both the parents and the child may need assistance in dealing with human sexuality issues. Further, the appearance of social-emotional problems may be more prominent at this stage of development.

Studies (discussed later in this chapter) support a higher incidence of problems in mentally retarded adolescents when compared to nonretarded adolescents. Mildly retarded adolescents, in particular, also become more aware of their "differentness" from their age-mates and their limitations at a critical point in identity development.

At this stage, the professional may be most helpful to parents in helping them deal with the social-emotional development of their child. The dynamic, family therapy, and behavioral roles may be useful in facilitating emotional and social skill development. The resource function may lead parents to materials about both normal and atypical adolescent development with particular reference to human sexuality issues.

Community and vocational transition. This stage involves helping the parents prepare for their child to leave home. Again, the parents are reminded of their child's limitations. Rather than an independent or competitive job or further education, their child may be transitioning to a supervised job, sheltered workshop, or day treatment program. Instead of moving out on his or her own, their child may be moving to a supervised setting with other mentally retarded persons. The mentally retarded young adult may have relatively few residential and vocational options, some of which the parents may find less than desirable. The process of "letting go" and fostering independence of their child may be difficult for some parents.

In addition to the supportive role, two further roles may be helpful to parents at this stage. The first is thorough assessment of adaptive, community living, social, and vocational skills. The issue of diagnosis has long been resolved, but more criterion-based assessment to determine basic daily living and survival skills will facilitate a successful and developmentally appropriate transition. Second, the resource role again becomes important. Similar to helping parents understand special education at school entrance, the parents are now entering a situation where they encounter a wide variety of social service agencies who provide services for handicapped adults. Dealing with vocational rehabilitation, day programs, social security, health programs, group homes, supervised apartments, etc., may be very confusing. The professional should assist the parents in helping them select the most normalizing and least restrictive vocational and residential situations for their child.

Mental Retardation and Social-Emotional Functioning

In recent years, there has been increased interest in the emotional problems of mentally retarded persons. Prior to this recent interest, many of the problematic behaviors and symptoms displayed by mentally retarded persons were thought simply to be a characteristic of mental retardation and not representative of genuine and separate psychopathology. In fact, social-emotional functioning among mentally retarded persons received little attention from both researchers and practitioners. Perhaps an indication of more contemporary thinking lies in the fact that the *Diagnostic and Statistical Manual of Mental Disorders* (Third Edition-Revised) of the American Psychiatric Association (1987) now notes that "the prevalence of other mental disorders is at least three to four times greater among people with Mental Retardation than in the general population" (p. 29).

The prevalence of such problems with mentally retarded children is typified in a study by Cullinan, Epstein, Matson, and Rosemier (1984). In this study, educable mentally retarded adolescents (13–18 years of age) were rated by their teachers on the Behavior Problem Checklist (Quay & Peterson, 1979). A similar group of nonretarded age peers were also rated by their teachers. The mildly retarded adolescents showed significantly higher scores on the Conduct Disorder dimension, which reflects aggressive and disruptive behavior patterns, and on the Personality Problem dimension, which reflects difficulties with anxiety and withdrawal. The Conduct and Personality dimensions are the two major factors on the Behavior Problem Checklist and account for the majority of the variance in behavioral deviance. In a similar study, Epstein, Cullinan, and Polloway (1986) compared elementary *and* secondary educable mentally retarded and nonretarded students on the Behavior Problem Checklist. Factor analysis was completed on the combined sample and yielded factors they labeled Aggression, Attention Disorder, Anxiety-Inferiority, and Social Incompetence. For three of the factors—Aggression, Attention Disorder, and Anxiety-Inferiority—the educable mentally retarded students showed significantly more problems than their nonretarded peers at all age levels and for both sexes. Some differences were found on the social competence factor but not as consistently as with the other factors. It was noted that this factor did not overlap to a great degree with the notion of adaptive behavior. In general, it appears that many mentally retarded children would be considered to have significant behavior problems in a variety of areas. Obviously, this higher prevalence would present problems for their families.

Prout, Marcal, and Marcal (1989) used a meta-analysis procedure to analyze self-reported patterns of social-emotional adjustment among mentally retarded persons. They looked at studies in which mentally retarded persons (predominantly children and adolescents) had completed self-report inventories of major personality variables. The bulk of the measures assessed depression, self-esteem or self-concept, and/or anxiety. Across these studies, they found a consistent pattern for mentally retarded persons to report concerns that were in the more pathological or problematic direction when compared to nonretarded groups. That is, they tended to self-report relatively more depression, higher anxiety, lower self-esteem, etc.

These studies, among others, highlight the social-emotional problems presented by mentally retarded children and adolescents. There appears to be a higher prevalence of problems both in the observable behavioral areas as well as in the more affectively and emotionally related areas. It is now well accepted that mentally retarded persons are susceptible to psychopathology and emotional problems and disorders. A few generalizations can be made about this area:

• Mentally retarded persons are susceptible to the full range of emotional and psychological problems as are the "normal" or nonretarded population.
• Lowered intelligence places an individual "at risk" for the development of emotional problems and may be seen as a related predisposing factor.
• The incidence and prevalence rates for emotional disorders among mentally retarded persons appear to be significantly above those in the general population.
• Many problems in adjustment and adaptation of mentally retarded persons that are thought to be related to retardation may be more related to problems in social-emotional functioning. For example, the failure of a mentally retarded person in a job placement may be more related to a social-emotional problem than a lack of job skills related to lowered intelligence. In addition to vocational situations, this may be seen in family and residential settings and other life transition situations.

Three other issues are important to consider in this context. First, is the concept of "dual diagnosis." In general, dual diagnosis refers to the coexistence of two (or more) significant, identifiable, and "separate" disorders, problems, or conditions. It is different from the "multiple diagnosis" concept in that the disorders represent major diagnostic classifications or systems. With respect to mental retardation, dual diagnosis refers to the coexistence of mental retardation *and* emotional or psychiatric disorders. There has been much debate about causative issues and the necessity to establish primary and secondary diagnosis. Many of these distinctions (i.e., primary vs. secondary), we feel, are semantic. Both cognitive and social-emotional functioning are important areas to be addressed.

The second issue relates to the problems in diagnosing emotional disorders in the mentally retarded population. Many of the instruments and assessment techniques utilized with the general population are either inappropriate for or not normed on cognitively lower functioning individuals. Some of the adaptive behavior scales include measures of maladaptive behavior, but many of the areas assessed seem to focus on problems more often seen in individuals functioning at or below the Moderate Mental Retardation range. Thus, there are few measures appropriate for persons in the mentally retarded ranges.

The third issue involves the concept of "diagnostic overshadowing" (Levitan & Reiss, 1983; Reiss, Levitan, & Syszko, 1982; Reiss & Syszko, 1983). Diagnostic overshadowing refers to a tendency for clinicians and professionals to downplay or ignore mental health problems when they also are aware that the person functions in the mentally retarded range. In a series of analogue studies, Reiss and his colleagues presented professionals with case studies that were identical with the exception that in one case the individual was described as having an IQ in the mentally retarded range, and in the other, the person's functioning was described in the average range. When the subject of the case study was described as retarded, the clinicians were less likely to diagnose an emotional disorder and recommend appropriate therapeutic interventions. This may translate to actual underdiagnosing of emotional problems in lower functioning persons and difficulty in obtaining mental health services for these individuals. The diagnostic overshadowing concept is relevant to both dual diagnosis and the lack of appropriate assessment instrumentation.

Collaborative Issues

The greater incidence of emotional and behavioral problems among mentally retarded persons strongly suggests that professional collaboration should include the option of providing mental health services to the mentally retarded person and his or her family. Assessment should not just focus on the developmental delays of the individual—social-emotional assessment should be included as a significant component of assessment at all levels of development. Collaborative assessment will include the collection of informant data from the parents. If a mental health problem is identified, a variety of mental health services might be provided that have elements of dynamic, family therapy, or behavioral roles. In fact, Tymchuk (1983) supports a combined model of intervention when working with parents.

Case Study

The following provides a chronology of events that a set of parents, Robert and Martha R., encountered as they raised their daughter Katie. These events occurred around the stressor points of identification and early childhood, school entrance, adolescence, and transition. As will be seen, these stressor points also involved collaboration with a variety of professionals throughout Katie's development. The case example demonstrates both positive and moderately conflictual collaborations that are likely to occur.

Identification and Early Childhood. Katie was born at 30 weeks' gestation with a birth weight of 4 pounds, 1 ounce, and an Apgar Score of 4 at 1 minute and a subsequent score of 6. Oxygen was administered immediately following birth due to anoxia. She was delivered vaginally following a labor of 8 hours during which no medication was administered to the mother. However, Martha, Katie's mother, received medication to delay labor following premature contractions 36 hours prior to her birth. The pregnancy, which occurred when Martha was 33 years old, was uncomplicated, as were her three previous pregnancies. There was no history of any genetic or medical problems among family members, and no cause for the premature birth was identified.

Following the delivery, Katie was moved to a neonatal intensive care unit where her condition stabilized after 24 hours. Postnatal testing revealed no identifiable complications or problems. Katie was breastfed during her month-long hospital stay until she was discharged at 5 weeks of age with a weight of 5 pounds, 8 ounces. Robert and Martha were informed by the neonatalogist and pediatrician that Katie had approximately a 10% chance of later developmental problems. However, her developmental milestones appeared within normal limits in all areas and no significant medical problems occurred except ear infections, which began at 6 months of age and continued periodically until age 3½. Following a routine pediatric examination at age 2, Katie was referred for a speech and language evaluation at a local clinic due to possible delays in both receptive and expressive language. The concerns about possible delays were on the parents' observations and reports to their pediatrician. Although this referral was stressful for the parents, Mr. and Mrs. R. hoped that the language delays were related to the frequent ear infections. The R.'s also rationalized that since Katie was the youngest of three children, she really had no reason to speak more than a few words in their busy household.

The results of the speech and language evaluation indicated that articulation skills were within normal limits with only developmental errors noted. Oral mechanism was adequate for speech production. However, the language evaluation indicated a receptive delay of approximately 9 months and an expressive delay of 1 year. Katie and her parents were referred to a preschool program for language impaired children. No reason for the delays was given, but the parents were reassured that early intervention was critical and would hopefully remediate the language deficits. Mr. and Mrs. R. remained hopeful that the delays were limited to the language area.

An area of difficulty for the parents, besides accepting the fact that their young daughter had language delays and required special services so early, was explaining the situation to other family members and friends. It was difficult for them to explain the delays clearly to others who frequently gave unsolicited advice such as "She's fine—she's just spoiled being the little one." Martha R. also felt responsible for the problem, feeling that she must have done something "wrong" during the pregnancy to have "caused" the prematurity. She also was afraid that her husband blamed her even though he professed to have no concerns about Katie's development and expressed confidence that she would be fine.

Katie's progress in the language program was minimal. Although she acquired new skills and vocabulary, her rate of progress continued to be at roughly 6 months per year. At the end of 18 months in the program (Katie's chronological age now

3 years, 6 months), she was again referred for comprehensive developmental, psychological, and medical evaluation to help more clearly identify her developmental status and educational needs. Her parents, although overtly cooperating with the referral, responded defensively and questioned the necessity of a further evaluation. The results of the evaluation indicated generally normal physical development, but with delays of approximately 8 months in fine motor skills; receptive language and cognitive skills were at the 2½-year level, and expressive language at the 2-year level. Additional reports from the parents indicated delays in adaptive skills, particularly in self-help, communication, and socialization areas. A diagnosis of mild mental retardation was explained to the parents.

The parents' response was initially one of confusion about the diagnosis and developmental information that they had been given and how it translated to their view of Katie. Mental retardation, from their perspective, meant having obvious physical and cognitive problems—this was not their Katie. They felt a great deal of anger and hostility toward the psychologist, physician, and speech and language clinician who conducted the evaluation, as well as toward the preschool program staff for failing to provide an adequate program for Katie.

The process of understanding Katie's developmental delays was prolonged for both parents. Both reported an adjustment period that included increased moodiness and irritability, and periodic depression, and questioning the causes of the problem and the validity of the diagnosis. They often felt frustrated with Katie when she was unable to perform certain tasks, yet they tended to overestimate her progress when she acquired a new skill. Observation of other children Katie's age facilitated their awareness of her delays, but their acceptance of the diagnosis was not complete.

School entrance. Upon Katie's entrance into kindergarten, her parents began their role as child advocates by rejecting the public school district's recommendation that Katie be placed in a self-contained class for children with developmental delays. In order to obtain full-day educational programming, Mr. and Mrs. R. agreed to a half-day special class placement in a program for language impaired children and the other half-day in a regular kindergarten class. This placement was generally successful for Katie, although socially and academically her skills were well below her regular classmates'.

Her subsequent elementary school program involved regular class placements with support services of special education and language therapy. Katie had progressively more difficulty understanding the material in the regular classes and utilized the special education services to facilitate her understanding of class material as well as to foster basic skill acquisition. Social problems began to arise in the third grade when she refused to do classwork and became resistant to attending school. Peer relationships also became more problematic as her interests and social maturity became increasingly different from her classmates', often resulting in Katie being teased or ignored by her schoolmates. Her parents responded to her behavioral changes with frustration and anger, which was directed primarily at the school. They did not accept the educational staff's repeated recommendation for a self-contained class placement, but did agree to a second opinion evaluation by professionals outside of the school district. In addition to the educational concerns, Mr. and Mrs. R. were faced with the need to balance Katie's needs with those of her siblings, who were also at times confused about Katie, somewhat resentful about the amount of attention she received from the parents, and occasionally embarrassed by her behavior. Katie's elementary school years were marked by considerable family conflict, a well as ongoing disagreements with school personnel. Gradually, the parents became more aware of her educational and developmental deficits as her progress became more noticeably less rapid and different from those of her age-mates. This gradual awareness seemed to decrease the tendency to blame and disagree with school personnel and led to a degree of resolve within the family.

Adolescence. Following a second opinion evaluation, which confirmed the findings of previous evaluations by the school personnel and other clinicians, Mr. and Mrs. R. had fewer questions about the diagnosis and began to focus more on the implications of the diagnosis for themselves and Katie. A special class placement was agreed upon that included individual and group social skills training as a support service. Peer interaction difficulties became a dominant concern, particularly as Katie became more interested in boys. Because she was attractive and friendly, her parents and school personnel were concerned about her ability to make appropriate social judgments, especially with respect to sexual relationships.

Katie began to question her parents more persistently about "what's wrong with me." She began to ask this question during middle school, but now the questioning was both more emotional and frequent. Katie began resisting her parents' requests with angry outbursts and periods of crying. The stress level in the family continued to increase as Katie progressed in high school because Katie was not involved in social activities to which she aspired. She wanted to be involved in sports and cheerleading, but did not make the teams at tryouts, and she hoped to go to school dances and proms.

A positive aspect of the school experience was Katie's success in a child care vocational training program. Despite this, Mr. and Mrs. R. began to acknowledge their disappointment in their plans for Katie when their friends' children, many of whom were Katie's age, were preparing for college and involved in extracurricular activities. Private counseling for the family was begun during Katie's high school years as a means of dealing with Katie's depression, low self-esteem, and socialization problems. However, the counseling also provided a mechanism for the family to express their concerns, disappointments, and feelings of guilt.

Although these feelings were not as intense or as frequent as in the earlier years for the parents, they still continued to appear intermittently.

A plan for guardianship was also developed upon Katie's reaching age 18. The issues around sibling responsibility in the event of parental death or disability were particularly difficult for the family to consider and resolve.

Transition. As many of the members of Katie's graduating class embarked on college or vocational careers, Katie enrolled in a job training program in child care sponsored by the Office of Vocational Rehabilitation and conducted at a local rehabilitation center. Following a year of on-site training at the center, for which Katie was paid a small sub-minimum wage, she was able to gain employment in a day care setting as an aide.

At the same time, Katie moved into a supervised living apartment with two other mildly mentally retarded young women. Initially, both Katie and her parents had difficulty adjusting to their life-style changes. These changes, particularly in the areas of control and independence, forced Katie to become more independent and to make her own decisions, responsibilities with which she had little experience. Her parents also had to allow her more freedom to make her own decisions. For the parents, this highlighted their dependence on Katie and the impact that she had on their lives. The absence of Katie from their home and their daily supervision resulted in a major readjustment for the R.'s. They hadn't realized how much of their lives revolved around caring for Katie.

Katie continued to receive counseling through the residential agency around dating, sexuality, possible marriage, discrimination/normalization issues, self-advocacy, and employment issues. At times, the parents had difficulty accepting the agency's push for Katie's extensive community involvement and independence. Katie's parents remained involved with some decision making and input around Katie's employment and living arrangements. However, each progression to more independent levels was viewed by the parents with both happiness and cautious concern. These changes invariably were stressful for the parents.

Summary

The presence of a mentally retarded person in a family has significant impact on the parents and the dynamics of the family. The reactions of the parents range from the emotional area to the need for information. A variety of professional roles are required to deal with the many issues that face mentally retarded individuals and their families. The acceptance of the disability by the parents, the level of the disability, and the social-emotional concerns often presented by mentally retarded persons are key factors in collaborative work. Further, the professional must view the collaboration across the life span of the mentally retarded person and the concomitant family life cycle.

References

American Psychiatric Association. (1987). *DSM-III-R: Diagnostic and statistical manual of mental disorders* (3rd ed., rev.). Washington, DC: American Psychiatric Association.

Cullinan, D., Epstein, M. H., Matson, J. L., & Rosemier, R. A. (1984). Behavior problems of mentally retarded and nonretarded adolescent pupils. *School Psychology Review, 13*, 381–384.

Drew, L. J., Logan, P. R., & Hunter, M. L. (1988). *Mental retardation: A life cycle approach* (4th ed.). Columbus, OH: Merrill.

Epstein, M. H., Cullinan, D., & Polloway, E. A. (1986). Patterns of maladjustment among mentally retarded children and youth. *American Journal of Mental Deficiency, 91*, 127–134.

Gallagher, J. J., & Vietz, P. M. (Eds.). (1986). *Families of handicapped persons: Research, programs, and policy issues.* Baltimore: Brookes.

Laborde, P. R., & Seligman, M. (1983). Individual counseling with parents of handicapped children: Rationale and strategies. In M. Seligman (Ed.), *The family with a handicapped child: Understanding and treatment* (pp. 261–284). Orlando, FL: Grune & Stratton.

Levitan, G. W., & Reiss, S. (1983). Generality of diagnostic overshadowing across disciplines. *Applied Research in Mental Retardation, 4*, 59–64.

Mink, I. T. (1986). Classification of families with mentally retarded children. In J. J. Gallagher & P. M. Vietz (Eds.), *Families of handicapped persons: Research, programs, and policy issues* (pp. 25–44). Baltimore: Brookes.

Mink, I. T., Blacher, J., & Nihira, K. (1988). Taxonomy of family life styles: III. Replication with families with severely mentally retarded children. *American Journal of Mental Retardation, 93*, 250–264.

Mink, I. T., Meyers, C. E., & Nihira, K. (1984). Taxonomy of family life styles: II. Homes with slow learning children. *American Journal of Mental Deficiency, 89*, 111–123.

Mink, I. T., Nihira, K., & Meyers, C. E. (1983). Taxonomy of family life styles: I. Homes with TMR children. *American Journal of Mental Deficiency, 87*, 484–497.

Prout, H. T., Marcal, S., & Marcal, D. (1989). *A meta-analysis of self-reported personality characteristics of developmentally and learning disabled persons.* Manuscript submitted for publication.

Quay, H. C., & Peterson, D. R. (1979). *Manual for the Behavior Problem Checklist.* Highland Park, NJ: Authors.

Reiss, S., Levitan, G. W., & Syszko, J. (1982). Emotional disturbance and mental retardation: Diagnostic overshadowing. *American Journal of Mental Deficiency, 86*, 567–574.

Reiss, S., & Syszko, J. (1983). Diagnostic overshadowing and professional experience with mentally retarded persons. *American Journal of Mental Deficiency, 87*, 396–402.

Seligman, M., & Darling, R. B. (1989). *Ordinary families, special children: A systems approach to childhood disability.* New York: Guilford Press.

Turnbull, A. P., Summers, J. A., & Brotherson, M. J. (1986). Family life cycle: Theoretical and empirical implications and future directions for families with mentally retarded members. In J. J. Gallagher & P. M. Vietze (Eds.), *Families of handicapped persons: Research, programs, and policy issues* (pp. 45–66). Baltimore: Brookes.

Tymchuk, A. J. (1983). Interventions with parents of the mentally retarded. In J. L. Matson & J. A. Mulick (Eds.), *Handbook of mental retardation* (pp. 369–380). New York: Pergamon.

Wikler, L. M. (1986). Family stress theory and research on families of children with mental retardation. In J. J. Gallagher & P. M. Vietze (Eds.), *Families of handicapped persons: Research, programs, and policy issues* (pp. 167–195). Baltimore: Brookes.

Wikler, L. M., Wasow, M., & Hatfield, E. (1981). Chronic sorrow revisited: Parent vs. professional depiction of the adjustment of parents of mentally retarded children. *American Journal of Orthopsychiatry, 51,* 63–70.

10

THE FAMILY WITH A YOUNG DEVELOPMENTALLY DISABLED CHILD

Beth Doll and Mary Wysopal Bolger

Collaborative models of service to handicapped children are those in which parents and professionals work in unison to meet developmental needs of a child. Making parents partners in the education of young handicapped children has become the most respected approach for early intervention programs. One benefit of this partnership is that it maximizes the effects of early intervention; the impact of professional intervention can be broader and more practical when parents extend the intervention into the home and family environment. More important, collaborative early childhood interventions reflect a deep respect for the parent–child relationship. Because collaboration values the competence of the parent as much as that of the professional, engaging in collaboration can reaffirm the parents' skills and knowledge, and the importance of their interaction with the child. As such, collaboration can provide parents with the confidence and experience to become powerful advocates for their child.

Collaborative interventions are especially appropriate to serve the needs of young handicapped children whose dependence on parental care is more marked and whose interaction with parents is more intense and more frequent than that of older children (Peterson, 1987). Gains demonstrated by children in early intervention programs have been shown to be influenced by home environment, the social support available to the family, and family characteristics (Dunst & Leet, 1987). Family involvement is clearly necessary if the young child is to make optimal progress. The collaborative approach to early intervention programming has been reinforced by the enactment of the Education of the Handicapped Amendments of 1986, federal legislation that identifies families of young handicapped children as legitimate participants in intervention. This orientation toward early intervention requires that educational programs be developed and evaluated that address familial adaptation to the handicapped child as well as child progress.

Full partnership requires considerably more effort on the part of the professional than may initially be apparent. To act as true partners, parents must be allowed to participate in the decision making and brainstorming that plan a child's intervention, as well as the implementation of already formed plans. Parental goals and parent-directed activities must be incorporated into a child's plan. To support full parental participation, professionals must be prepared to provide parents with detailed information about the child, his or her progress, and the program; to reinforce learning that occurs at home in the same way that parents reinforce what occurs at school; to offer parents training in unfamiliar information or procedures; to include the parent as a participant in teaching; and to adjust their teaching and service in ways that parents advise (Peterson, 1987). Parent–professional contacts occur frequently and in an informal, ongoing way when both are partners in serving the child's needs.

Effective collaboration also demands a realistic understanding of the competence and knowledge of the parents. When the parents' competence is insufficient for the demands imposed on them by collaboration, intervention efforts can overwhelm the family and become a failure experience. When parental participation in intervention is constricted, the experience may underwhelm the family and serve as one more example of professionals patronizing the family. Thus collaboration with parents of young handicapped children requires a special sensitivity to the needs and experience of the family so that a match can be achieved between parental competence and collaborative demands.

This chapter will review the special characteristics of families of young handicapped children and the implications these hold for implementing collaborative models of intervention. In particular, attention will be paid to those professional practices that involve parents in decision making and encourage parents to discover and exercise their own expertise in parenting their handicapped child. Collaborative interventions will need to be individualized to different families, and ways to assess and adjust to these familial differences will be discussed.

Characteristics of Families of Young Handicapped Children

Parents of young developmentally disabled children are often relatively new to the role of raising a handicapped child and may still be unsure of how to assume it. Until recently, they were part of the uninformed masses that rarely interact with disabled persons, and they may still hold some stereotypic views of their child's handicap and its implications. In many cases, the nature and implications of their child's developmental condition are as yet uncertain, and the parents are frequently required to tolerate a fair amount of ambiguity about their child's needs or future development. Moreover, their grief over the child's handicapping condition is likely to be fresh, and consequently more painful, and may exert a stronger influence over their ability to interact effectively with the nonhandicapped world. The family of a young, developmentally disabled child is more likely to be a young family, facing the financial and social adjustments that all young families face but that are exacerbated by the special problems presented by their handicapped child. The experience of each family will be unique, and the realities of these parental resources must be carefully balanced if collaborative efforts are to be successful. It is unfortunate, then, that characterizations of these families are all too frequently cliché-ridden and shallow. Families require precise, individual evaluation if their needs and resources are to be assessed accurately.

Familial Stress

Professional, financial, social, and marital pressures are frequently more intense for young families while parents work to establish their careers, acquire resources, and adjust to their marriage. Professionals who work with families of disabled infants and preschoolers are keenly aware that all of these adjustment difficulties can be intensified by the presence of a handicapped child. Career responsibilities may intrude into the time needed to care for a handicapped child, and the medical needs of the child may place a strain on family finances. Indeed, studies that compare families with and without handicapped children do show that stress is understandably higher among parents raising handicapped children (Beckman-Bell, 1981; McKinney & Peterson, 1987). Surveys suggest that families of the handicapped experience a divorce rate double that of the general population (Tew, Payne, & Lawrence, 1974) and report increases in marital tension (Gath, 1978), suicide (Love, 1973), and desertion (Reed & Reed, 1965).

Those studies that examine the particular sources of this stress demonstrate that it is directly and pragmatically tied to the increased demands of parenting a handicapped child (Kazak & Marvin, 1984). Stress levels are generally found to be higher in families of physically handicapped children whose handicap, in reality, places more caregiving demands upon the family (McKinney & Peterson, 1987). For example, mothers of spina bifida children ascribe their stress to their children being less adaptable to change and more demanding of day-to-day care (Kazak & Marvin, 1984). Parents report that their activities as a family become restricted with the birth of their handicapped child (Blackard & Barsh, 1982) and that time has become a treasured rarity (Dunlap & Hollingsworth, 1977). Providing care for the handicapped child will be even more difficult in situations where both parents have employment outside of the home. Parents report that it is nearly impossible in many cases to find day care providers willing and able to assume the demanding task of caring for a handicapped child. In many cases, one parent (usually the mother) must give up a career to stay home with the child. Some of the stresses that these parents face are likely to be chronic as their handicapped child will acquire self-care skills slowly and with great effort. As an example, one mother living in a rural community described 3 years of driving her developmentally delayed son to daily classes at an early childhood center 25 miles away. Some caregiving may extend indefinitely into the future, as new events produce another cycle of demands. In the face of such demands, family resources can become strained or even exhausted.

It would be a mistake, however, to assume that these are always dysfunctional families. Although it is certain that the birth of a handicapped child alters the course of life for both the parents and the siblings, these changes are not always detrimental. Sophisticated questioning will reveal strengths as well as vulnerability in the handicapped child's family system. A less flexible but functional division of duties among parents frequently develops with the birth of the child, with mothers assuming a rather heavy caregiving role and fathers taking responsibility for additional financial burdens (Howard, 1978; Kazak & Marvin, 1984). While both parents may feel constrained by this division, they also become important and inseparable partners in parenting. Parents also report that maternal fatigue and concerns about having another handicapped child interfere with comfortable sexual intimacy (DeMyer, 1979; Kazak & Marvin, 1984). However, general marital satisfaction remains as high as in other families (Dunlap & Hollingsworth, 1977) and may in fact improve due to an increased respect, affection, and consensus shared between parents (Kazak & Marvin, 1984).

Collaborative intervention with these families was inconceivable under the traditional assumption that the birth of a developmentally disabled child was a traumatic event that created pathological response in the family system (Cummings, 1976; Cummings, Bayley, & Rie, 1966; Farber, 1959). When families were thought to be traumatized, they were not seen as capable of making important contributions to the child's developmental program. Effective collaborators have adopted a coping model in which families of handicapped children are considered by evaluating the resources they use to adapt to the demands. Families that are characterized as coping are seen as functional and capable partners in the child's intervention. When parents are viewed as victims of trauma, professionals feel bound to lighten their burden by assuming some of the responsibility for the handicapped child's care. When parents are seen as adaptable and coping, professionals are more likely to recognize the commonalities they share with the parents and are obliged to supplement rather than supplant the parental care of the child. Professionals who search for and recognize the families' strengths and effectiveness are more likely to leave the essential responsibility for the child with the parents and family.

While acknowledging that early intervention efforts should be collaborative, many professionals continue to find it difficult to devise roles for parents that truly share with them responsibility for the child's program. Too often, involving parents as partners has not acknowledged the breadth of parental competence and potential for parental contribution. Instead, these efforts focus narrowly on training parents to be teachers of their handicapped child. This is a cost-effective approach because parents typically spend more time with their child than a professional. However, it may have an unintended effect upon family functioning if needs of the individual family members are not recognized. Involving the parent as a teacher may disrupt other family roles and create unintended additional burdens on family members. The role of teacher may decrease the enjoyment the parent derives from interacting with their child. Effective collaboration demands that parental suggestions for goals and activities be accepted as well as parental participation in the implementation of these; with parent input, it is more likely that parental services to the child will enhance the parent–child relationship and incorporate goals that parents identify as easing the child's adaptation to family life. As examples, some parent-identified goals for young handicapped children have included being able to eat at McDonalds without standing out as different, being able to play independently for 15 minutes with a toy, or being able to ask for a drink when thirsty or a snack when hungry.

It is important to ensure that families are not so stressed by the increased demands of collaboration that the family system becomes dysfunctional. Effective collaboration must respect the reality of the family's caregiving burden and the value of their time. Services that infringe upon the time of the handicapped child's family should be carefully evaluated to see that they are truly necessary. For example, repeated diagnostic evaluations may not improve the child's services measurably and could occupy entire days out of the family's summer. Services should be offered at times that are not in conflict with the caretaking duties of the family, and in ways that allow parents to retain control over the family schedule. Early evening can be a difficult time for parents to meet if a child's range of movement exercises must be completed after the meeting has adjourned. It is especially important that each professional working with the family be fully aware of the time demands imposed by other professionals, so that the totality of family responsibility is realistic.

Even parents who stridently and effectively advocate for the needs of their child may be less vocal in protecting their personal needs. In some cases, parents may feel a need to become super parents, juggling the needs of their handicapped and nonhandicapped children and meeting all of the expectations that are imposed upon them. They may depend on professionals to suggest moderating the child's program in a way that is knowledgeable about and sensitive to the family needs. If the family is to remain the most desirable and optimal environment for the child, it is important that the family's needs as well as child's needs be appropriately addressed in early intervention programs.

Emotional Status of the Family

The intense and unpredictable emotions that punctuate the parenting of a developmentally delayed child also contribute to familial distress. The sense of loss that accompanies the birth of a handicapped child has been compared repeatedly to the grief that accompanies death and dying (Lamb, 1983; Legeay & Keogh, 1966; Ryckman & Henderson, 1965). Parents of the developmentally delayed experience cycles of anger, denial, guilt, sadness, and acceptance as they attempt to reconcile the child they have been given to the child they were expecting to raise. Parents of a young handicapped child have only recently lost the "expected child" and so their grief is likely to be more pronounced. Moreover, the contrasts between the handicapped child and the "expected child" are more stark when they observe the frequent and striking milestones that normal children are achieving in the preschool years; other children born at the same time are acquiring the independence of talking, walking, exploring, and achieving more rapidly and more convincingly than their own child.

Parents often draw strength from the intense emotional bond that they develop with their child; Peterson (1987) provides an excellent discussion of how this bonding can be disrupted when a child is handicapped. Emotional attachment is a reciprocal process, affected by the child's responses to the parent as these elicit the parent's responses to the child. A child's handicap may prevent him or her from seeking out the contact and interaction of the parents in the same ways that other children do. A hearing-impaired child may be unresponsive to the mother's cooing. A visually impaired child may not face the father as he enters the room. Autistic children may resist cuddling during feeding. Thus parents may not receive the emotional support from their handicapped children that facilitates bonding and attachment.

Parents' emotional adjustment to having a handicapped child will have an impact upon their involvement as partners in the collaborative process. Ross (1964) identified parental resistance to training as part of the mourning process. Being part of special training programs and involved with special educators and therapists is a constant reminder that their child is different. Feelings of anger and resentment over having a handicapped child may be directed at the professionals working with the parents. The parents may also feel incompetent in responding to their child's needs, particularly if typical child-rearing skills are ineffective in securing a response from the child. Loss of self-esteem and feelings of insecurity as a parent may result. Professionals need to be sensitive to these emotional responses. At a time when parents are less prepared to assume the role of advocate, less expert in their child's needs, and less comfortable in their social role, life events have propelled them into the time-intensive and emotionally draining chore of parenting their young handicapped child.

If an effective collaborative relationship is to develop between parents of the handicapped preschooler and the professionals that serve their child, each must value the competence and expertise of the other. This collaboration can be undermined when professionals, overwhelmed by the tragedy and stress they witness, begin to protect and shelter the family. A professional's sympathy can diminish the perceived competence of the family he or she intends to serve. As an example, parents are sometimes "allowed" to be uninvolved in a handicapped child's program because the constant reminders of the handicap are thought to be so difficult. In one family where this continued for several years, the child's mother finally explained that she felt unnecessary and uninvited when program planning meetings were scheduled with little effort to secure her assistance. Instead of sympathizing and protecting, professionals should express their concern by respecting the integrity and capability of the family system.

Most professionals successfully allow the parent to be somewhat unpredictable, ambivalent, angry, and sad without feeling personally responsible or blamed for the family's distress. All too often, however, the grieving process is considered to be maladaptive or even pathological. It is useful instead to regard the cycles of grieving as a normal process families live through when accommodating to the birth of a handicapped child. Successful grieving allows the family to work simultaneously to meet the child's immediate needs without giving up hope for the beneficial future of the child or confidence in themselves as persons. Nor are parents of the handicapped child caught in a perpetual cycle of grief and anger; feelings of loss wax and wane and are interspersed with frequent periods of joy while parents discover and enjoy their handicapped child. Professionals who work closely with the child experience a similar albeit less intense grief and can become similarly unrealistic in their vision of the child and his or her gifts. Sensitivity to one's own feelings of sadness and enjoyment can enhance recognition of the parents' experience. Empathy with that experience is important, as parents frequently complain of being stereotyped as tragic characters, and patronized by pity. They notice, with disappointment, that others rarely acknowledge their family's joy. As a father explained, "I know Chris can't talk, but I want people to know how much fun he is to be with."

Social Support

The adequacy of the social support provided by neighbors, friends, and the extended family has traditionally been presumed critical in the adjustment of the handicapped child's family. One researcher was even led to suggest that, because of this, early intervention programs would be more effective when conducted in groups (McKinney & Peterson, 1987). Parents agree and frequently describe the group interaction as one of the most appreciated factors in early intervention programs (McKinney & Peterson, 1987). Although not socially isolated, families of the handicapped do report having slightly fewer friends and describe a family and friendship network that is highly interconnected (Kazak & Marvin, 1984). However, the adequacy of this support network outside of the family does not appear to be the most critical variable in determining whether the family is under excessive strain. Instead, it is the degree to which the other spouse is perceived to be sharing in the parenting burden that predicts parental stress (Kazak & Marvin, 1984; McKinney & Peterson, 1987).

Thus, it is critically important for professionals to respect the spousal relationship when collaborating with parents of handicapped preschoolers and infants. In many cases professionals must be satisfied to meet with one parent, while the other cares for the child. The lack of suitable child care or an intractable home care routine can make it impossible for both parents to leave the home simultaneously. Child care can be provided at meeting sites, but does not always resolve the conflict if the child is hypersensitive to changes in daily routine or requires special care during that time. Programs that provide training to one parent can and should be made available to the other via tape recordings or extra copies of handouts. The division of responsibility that parents choose to assume within their marriage must be acknowledged by the professionals who work with them.

The Family in the Community

At the same time as they cope with their own grief, parents may be faced with the disappointment of the extended family and community and may be assuming the weighty role of "comforter" for each other and for people outside the family. The loved ones who provide the family's social support may be awkward in the face of the birth and unskilled at greeting the family or child with the same ease and familiarity as before. Parents frequently mention this need to blend child, family, and community as the primary goal of early childhood intervention—one that may be overlooked by professional members of the collaborative team.

Parent organizations have been stressed as important means to address social dissonance experienced by families of the handicapped. Parent-organized activities may address the needs of families of the handicapped more directly than those organized by professionals. As an example, a group of parents at a local early childhood program established very different goals for their group than the professional staff had anticipated: Rather than talk about behavior management, they wanted to develop ways to deal with their children's anger and sadness and to find ways to interact more normally with parents of nonhandicapped children. At the same time, parent organizations may in fact be less accessible to parents of young handicapped children because of the serious time constraints, the demands of other young children, and the perceptions parents may have that their child isn't like the other handicapped children in the group. Moreover, parents will be seeking a social niche for themselves within their community that incorporates both handicapped and nonhandicapped children; parent organizations can prevent them from resuming participation in networks of social support that existed before the birth of their handicapped child. As an alternative, some parents may require a less organized form of interaction with other parents of handicapped children. A personal contact with one other parent may substitute for attendance at group meetings or conferences.

Parents of young handicapped children are also very aware and appropriately concerned that their children are at risk for failure to develop effective social behaviors. Their children are more likely to be engaged in solitary play, to ignore attempts other children make to initiate play, and to spend more time watching and less time talking than nonhandicapped preschoolers (Strain, 1983, 1985). As one father of a Down's Syndrome 4-year-old poignantly explained, he depends on the altruism of nonhandicapped children to pull his son into normal play interactions. As a result, families in this group were constantly seeking ways to explain the handicapping condition to nonhandicapped siblings and neighborhood children, as well as ways to blend their handicapped children into the community of childhood.

The parents' community is the child's community, and parents are the logical agents to mainstream their child into the world of everyday events. However, young parents are frequently new to the world of childhood and need assistance learning how to communicate in child-compatible words, to view the handicap from the child's eye, and to adapt to the brief and unpredictable conversations that children offer. Parents in one parent group frequently used opportunities to meet with other parents to talk about this concern. During these group discussions parents shared their expertise, anticipated the questions that children ask about the handicapped child, and planned effective answers together. Discussions among families allowed them to clarify in their own minds what they wanted other children to know about their handicapped child and how to handle the conversation with sensitivity when their child was present. Parents frequently used these opportunities to describe confusing or surprising conversations they had already had with other children and helped each other understand what was meant.

Parents frequently request instruction in explaining handicaps to young children through their natural communication systems: through stories and in play. Reading a well-written story about a handicap can make a child more available to conversation by raising his or her interest, posing innumerable questions for parents to react to, and allowing the child to enter more fully the world of the handicapped child. Professionals can support parents in these attempts by locating books that include handicapped models and, with parents, by evaluating whether these present handicaps with sensitivity. Reading lists are included in many of the published programs that support mainstreaming handicapped preschoolers (i.e., Closer Look, 1981; Chapel Hill Training Outreach Project, 1983).

Handicapped dolls are another effective strategy for introducing the non-handicapped preschooler to the world of the handicapped (Chapel Hill Training Outreach Project, 1983). Cloth dolls can be made by parents or church or community groups and, with props, can be given handicaps similar to those of a child in a play group or preschool. Children can be introduced to the handicapped role through adult-directed play, and the dolls can then be left in neighborhood play areas to be available for free play. By assuming in play the role of a handicapped doll, a preschooler can be prompted to experience the handicap, in a limited way, to discuss it in familiar words, and to explain some of their feelings about handicaps to an available adult.

Siblings of a Handicapped Preschooler

Parents of a young handicapped child are also likely to have other young children at home; it is often difficult for them to resolve conflicts between the needs of their handicapped child and the nonhandicapped siblings. Siblings of handicapped children are frequently given less parental time and share fewer family activities than children without handicapped siblings (Dunlap & Hollingsworth, 1977). Parents frequently need assistance having fun with the handicapped child and incorporating the child into family activities that are enjoyable to their nonhandicapped children as well as to the handicapped child. These are difficult roles to juggle successfully. In one family, a second grader complained that he was given a swimming pool for his birthday because then his handicapped younger brother could play in it too.

Few resources address this need as well as the *Let's Play to Grow* program sponsored by the John P. Kennedy, Jr. Foundation (1977). *Let's Play to Grow* materials describe adaptations of such familiar recreational activities as volleyball, soccer, kite flying, dance, and jumping rope that allow handicapped children to participate and enjoy. The foundation facilitates the integration of the handicapped child into play activities with nonhandicapped friends and relatives (both children and adults) by sponsoring the formation of *Let's Play to Grow* groups in communities and neighborhoods. It endorses the collaborative model by establishing parents as directors of the community play groups, and providing technical assistance with mainstreaming and administration of programs through staff in Washington, DC.

The Family and the Professional World

Because early intervention programs involve multiple professional disciplines, parents of a young handicapped child are typically involved with educators, nurses, physicians, social workers, nutritionists, psychologists, and other parents. Interacting with multiple professionals from various disciplines can, in and of itself, be an overwhelming task for parents who are already struggling to understand their child's disability. Many parents sit at multidisciplinary meetings in silence and confusion. An inability to decode complicated professional jargon or to negotiate the protocol that governs professional meetings may convince parents that they are indeed ignorant of their child's needs. In fact, professional protocol should be the least important detail in planning a child's program. Professionals can help parents by collaborating effectively and efficiently with each other: developing treatment programs that coordinate as opposed to fragmenting services; designating a case manager who can interpret meetings to parents; interrupting ongoing discussions to request parent input, and, if necessary, interrupting professionals to reiterate parental comments; informing the parent about available community resources; and assuming responsibility for effectively working with one another. Most important, professionals need to seek out opportunities for informal, social interactions with parents if they are to be truly accessible to families of handicapped children (Peterson, 1987). It is the responsibility of the professional members of collaborative teams to break down any artificial barriers that professional jargon or etiquette may present to parental participation.

To become full partners in planning their child's program, parents need accurate information about their child and the handicapping condition. Many parents eventually become expert consumers of the technical literature describing the nature and treatment of their condition. Parents of the young handicapped child are not yet expert in their child's condition: They frequently haven't read widely about the child's handicap, are unfamiliar with the vocabulary the professionals use to describe the child, and may be unsure of what changes to expect from the child in the future. Thus parents will request carefully selected reading material and repeated conversations with expert parents or other professionals in order to develop an understanding of what is known and what is not known about the child's condition.

In some cases, parents themselves, seeking diagnoses and advice, take a child to a multitude of professionals. This is sometimes dismissed as "Doctor shopping." In fact, seeking second or even third opinions is a parent's prerogative and can be conceptualized as a reasonable solution to parents' needs for more information and more definitive descriptions of the child's condition and needs. Parents may need "permission" and even assistance to obtain second opinions from other professionals and encouragement to keep each person informed of the other's work so that steps aren't repeated unnecessarily or overlooked.

One reason that information has been withheld from parents is that it lacks certainty. Assessment procedures are not as reliable for young children as they will be once the child reaches the age of 10 or 12 (Ulrey & Schnell, 1982). Diagnoses are frequently ambiguous because of this lack of reliability and because there is limited information about how the child will change over time. Powerful risk factors associated with early childhood disabilities have been identified, but clearly these factors do not adequately predict how well the child will be able to adapt to the handicap (Werner, 1986). For example, although it is clear that children are more likely to be disabled if they experience birth complications, the impact of these health trauma on eventual child disability varies tremendously. Much of the variability in child progress is explainable by family variables such as the quality of the parent–child interaction, parental attitudes toward their child's learning, and the amount of social support given the family (Peterson, 1987).

As a result of the uncertainty, professionals are likely to make ambiguous and difficult to understand statements about the child's abilities or prognosis, because so much remains unknown while the child is still young. Different, noncategorical diagnoses are applied to young handicapped children; children who are autistic, aphasic, or severely retarded may all be called "developmentally delayed." The use of such generic descriptions may be appropriate when a more precise description of the child's condition is truly unavailable. In some situations, however, noncategorical labels may mask information about the child that professionals know but are uncomfortable sharing with the parent. For example, one mother had not been told 2 years after her child's automobile accident that the injury had caused permanent paralysis and profound retardation. She had been carefully saving the child's first bicycle, bought a few days before the accident. Withholding critical information from parents can only make the family's adjustment to the child more difficult.

Uncertainty can be emotionally draining as well as difficult to understand. While the extent of a child's handicap remains uncertain, both parents and professionals can hope that the disability will be minimal. Professionals have sometimes sought to protect the handicapped child and his or her parents from a disturbing diagnosis by withholding information about the possibilities until a certain diagnosis was available. This was done with the best of intentions; parents could draw more hope from the description that their child was developmentally delayed than from the diagnosis of moderate mental retardation. Still, that hope is almost always accompanied by an underlying and pervasive worry that the delay would continue or worsen.

Adjustment to a child's handicap takes time. Parents need an opportunity to learn about the diagnosis given their child, to observe the child to see if the diagnosis fits, and to decide whether they can accept that label for their child's condition. When diagnosis is deferred because of the child's young age or uncertain condition, this process of acceptance is also delayed. If alternative diagnoses are not discussed by the time the child enters the public school system, then the definitive categorical labels used in public special education programs can be unexpected and alarming for parents. Their dismay is understandable; they have not been given the time they need to accommodate to the labels and the future implications these hold for the child.

Parents will be most successful in adapting to their child's handicap if given a very complete description of all information available about the child, and the alternative explanations that can be made given that information. In some cases, this may require discussion of some disturbing diagnostic possibilities such as retardation or pervasive developmental disorders. Parents, by becoming partners in the diagnostic process, may be able to resolve some of the diagnostic dilemmas by providing informed observations of the nuances of their child's behavior and skills. Thus collaborative approaches to diagnostic decisions are in the best interest of the child as well as the parent.

Individual Plans for Family Involvement

Just as individuals differ from one another in their values, goals, desires, and needs, so do families. Finding a match between family characteristics and program goals is key to serving families with handicapped children effectively. A family struggling to provide adequate medical care for their medically fragile child may view educational programming as lower on a list of priorities that need to be met. Or parents' feelings of anger over having a handicapped child may interfere with their implementation of a program plan. One parent, although pleased with the large-motor exercise program developed for her child, confessed that she valued most the fact that the equipment used in the program attracted other children to play with her son. Selecting goals or implementing strategies that do not take into consideration family needs, wants, and capabilities may result in resistance to intervention, guilt on the part of parents who are unable to fulfill the goals, and possible resentment toward the handicapped child. Intervention programs that offer a match between family characteristics and program goals have a greater likelihood of enhancing family adaptation to the handicapped child as well as increasing family involvement in the treatment program (Peterson, 1987).

Parents who are intensely committed to providing their handicapped child with the best chance are not always able to place limits on how much they're willing to give up for their child. Thus, a comprehensive analysis of the family's resources, goals, values, vulnerabilities, coping styles, parent–child interactive styles, and needs should precede the development of early intervention treatment goals. Assessment protocols that allow parents to describe appropriate family needs and goals are more likely to foster treatment goals that are compatible with the family and that encourage and sustain parent involvement. Resulting programs focus on providing resources to the parents in addition to the child and foster more parental involvement, less stress, and more successful interactions with their children (Griest, Forehand, Rogers, Breiner, & Williams, 1982; Wahler & Dumas, 1984).

Implementation of a family assessment model will not be easily accomplished. Families change over time, and information about family needs and resources must be updated constantly. Most educators have not received training in conducting family assessments and developing family-centered goals and many feel unqualified or uncomfortable performing this task. Moreover, there are a limited number of clinically sound and educationally relevant assessment tools to assess family systems in this manner (Bailey & Simeonsson, 1984; Walsh & Wood, 1983). Two instruments, the Family Resource Scale (Dunst & Leet, 1987) and the Parenting Stress Index (Abidin, 1986) have been used extensively with young handicapped children and their families and could be used to support a family systems assessment.

The Family Resource Scale (Dunst & Leet, 1987) is an instrument that assesses household resources in families with a handicapped child. The 30-item rating scale assesses components of interpersonal and intrapersonal support within the family. The components evaluated include financial resources, child care, health care, food, shelter, and social supports. The Family Resource Scale aids parents in describing their family's daily living needs and incorporating these needs into individual treatment plans.

The Parenting Stress Index (PSI; Abidin, 1986) provides a useful evaluation of the emotional resources that parents draw upon in their daily interactions with their young handicapped child. The PSI is a 120-item parent-report checklist that assesses the degree of stress parents are experiencing in their child care role. The scale yields a total parenting stress score and separate domain scores that represent the portion of parental stress attributable to child characteristics, the portion attributable to parent characteristics, and the portion attributable to situational life events. The scale is helpful in allowing parents to clarify the degree to which the parent–child interaction has been affected by difficult child characteristics, as well as the emotional resources they can draw on to support that interaction.

An assessment of family needs only becomes useful once results are integrated into a plan for family services. A family plan is now required under the Education of the Handicapped Amendments of 1986. Family plans will be most useful if they are co-constructed with the parent and include goals for the child, for the family, and for their interaction that reflect the concerns and expertise of family members and professionals. The plan should recommend activities that have potential for meeting the goals and, in assigning responsibility for these activities, should clarify the contributions to be made by family members and professionals. Strategies for periodic review and revision of the plan will provide opportunities for family and professional to continue to collaborate in their efforts to serve the child.

Summary

Having a handicapped child is an event that creates change in the family unit. In many ways, these families respond like many other families faced with a crisis or sudden change. However, there are some factors that are unique responses to having a handicapped child. These, then, are essential for effective collaboration with families of young handicapped children—that the professional be sensitive to the unique challenges facing families of handicapped children and aware of the coping strategies they use; that the professional also continue to acknowledge the commonalities these families hold with all other families of young children, handicapped and nonhandicapped; that this sensitivity continue to be reflected in the daily practices of professionals that serve young handicapped children; that the professional remain sensitive to changes in the unique strengths and needs that each family brings to its child-rearing task and directly assess the resources and requirements of each individual family; that programs developed for each child and family are planned individually to reflect the special needs and strengths they possess; and that the family be permitted to exercise its resources and judgment by sharing in the responsibility for planning and implementing their child's intervention. The collaborative approach to early childhood intervention is more difficult to plan, to implement, and to evaluate than traditional professional-dominated early intervention models. Its challenge is made worthwhile by its sensitivity to children as family members. The family is the handicapped child's most valuable resource; the family systems approach allows professionals to nurture and protect this resource for the child.

References

Abidin, R. R. (1986). *Parenting Stress Index* (2nd ed.). Charlottesville, VA: Pediatric Psychology Press.

Bailey, D. B., & Simeonsson, R. J. (1984). Critical issues underlying research and intervention with families of young handicapped children. *Journal of the Division of Early Childhood, 9,* 38–48.

Beckman-Bell, P. (1981). Child-related stress in families of handicapped children. *Topics in Early Childhood Special Education, 1,* 45–53.

Blackard, M. K., & Barsh, E. T. (1982). Parents' and professionals' perceptions of the handicapped child's impact on the family. *The Journal of the Association for the Severely Handicapped, 7,* 62–70.

Chapel Hill Training Outreach Project. (1983). *New friends: Mainstreaming activities to help young children understand and accept individual differences.* Chapel Hill, NC: Author.

Closer Look. (1981). *Getting to know each other: A reading list to help you learn more about children and handicaps.* Washington DC: Author.

Cummings, S. T. (1976). The impact of the child's deficiency on the father: A study of fathers of mentally retarded and of chronically ill children. *American Journal of Orthopsychiatry, 46,* 246–255.

Cummings, S. T., Bayley, H., & Rie, H. (1966). Effects of the child's deficiency on the mother: A study of mothers of mentally retarded, chronically ill and neurotic children. *American Journal of Orthopsychiatry, 56,* 595–608.

DeMyer, M. K. (1979). *Parents and children in autism.* New York: Wiley.

Dunlap, W. R., & Hollingsworth, S. J. (1977). How does a handicapped child affect the family: Implications for practitioners. *Family Coordinator, 26,* 3–17.

Dunst, C. J., & Leet, H. E. (1987). Measuring the adequacy of resources in households with young children. *Child: Care, Health, and Development, 13,* 111–125.

Education of the Handicapped Amendments of 1986, 20 U. S. C. 1400–1485 (1987).

Farber, B. (1959). Effects of a severely mentally retarded child on family integration. *Monographs of the Society for Research in Child Development, 24*(Whole no. 71).

Gath, A. (1978). *Down's syndrome and the family: The early years.* London: Academic Press.

Greist, D. L., Forehand, R., Rogers, T., Breiner, J., & Williams, C. (1982). Effects of parent enhancement therapy on the treatment outcome and generalization of a parent training program. *Behavior Research and Therapy, 20,* 429–436.

Howard, J. (1978). The influence of children's developmental dysfunction on marital quality and family interaction. In R. Lerner & G. Spanier (Eds.), *Child influences on marital and family interaction* (pp. 275–295). New York: Academic Press.

John P. Kennedy, Jr. Foundation. (1977). *Let's Play to Grow: For families, for schools, for communities.* Washington, DC: Author.

Kazak, A. E., & Marvin, R. S. (1984). Differences, difficulties, and adaptation: Stress and social networks in families with a handicapped child. *Family Relations, 33,* 67–77.

Lamb, M. E. (1983). Fathers of exceptional children. In M. Seligman (Ed.), *The family with a handicapped child* (pp. 125–146). New York: Grune & Stratton.

Legeay, C., & Keogh, B. (1966). Impact of mental retardation on family life. *American Journal of Nursing, 66,* 1062–1065.

Love, H. (1973). *The mentally retarded child and his family.* Springfield, IL: Charles C. Thomas.

McKinney, B., & Peterson, R. A. (1987). Predictors of stress in parents of developmentally delayed children. *Journal of Pediatric Psychology, 12,* 133–150.

Peterson, N. L. (1987). *Early intervention for handicapped and at-risk children: An introduction to early childhood special education.* Denver, CO: Love.

Reed, E. W., & Reed, S. C. (1965). *Mental retardation: A family study.* Philadelphia: W. B. Saunders.

Ross, A. O. (1964). *The exceptional child in the family.* New York: Grune & Stratton.

Ryckman, D. B., & Henderson, R. A. (1965). The meaning of a retarded child for his parents: A focus for counselors. *Mental Retardation, 3,* 4–7.

Strain, P. S. (1983). Identification of social skill curriculum targets for severely handicapped children in mainstream preschools. *Applied Research in Mental Retardation, 4,* 369–382.

Strain, P. S. (1985). Programmic research on peers as intervention agents for socially isolated classmates. *The Pointer, 29,* 22–29.

Strom, R., Daniels, S., Wurster, S., Rees, R., & Goldman, R. (1984). A comparison of childrearing attitudes of parents of handicapped and nonhandicapped children. *Journal of Instructional Psychology, 11,* 89–103.

Tew, B., Payne, H., & Lawrence, K. (1974). Must a family with a handicapped child be a handicapped family? *Developmental Medicine and Child Neurology, 16,* 95–104.

Ulrey, G., & Schnell, R. R. (1982). Introduction to assessing young children. In G. Ulrey & S. J. Rogers (Eds.), *Psychological assessment of handicapped infants and young children* (pp. 1–11). New York: Thieme-Stratton.

Wahler, R., & Dumas, J. (1984). Changing the observational coding styles of insular and noninsular mothers: A step towards maintenance of parent training effects. In R. Dangel & R. Polster (Eds.), *Parent training: Foundations of research and practice* (pp. 379–416). New York: Guilford Press.

Walsh, W. M., & Wood, J. I. (1983). Family assessment: Bridging the gap between theory, research and practice. *American Mental Health Counselors Association Journal, 23,* 111–120.

Werner, E. E. (1986). A longitudinal study of perinatal risk. In D. C. Farran & J. D. McKinney (Eds.), *Risk in intellectual and psychosocial development* (pp. 3–27). New York: Academic Press.

11

THE FAMILY WITH A CHRONICALLY ILL CHILD

Steven W. Lee

Historically, parents who tried to act as collaborators with medical and other human service providers in the care of their children were often met with contempt and a lack of cooperation. In fact, parents often were barred in their attempts to be close to their hospitalized child because hospital personnel believed that the parent being with the child constituted spoiling the child, overprotectiveness, or a neurotic symbiosis (Azarnoff & Hardgrove, 1981). It was also often felt that better child care was afforded by nursing staff during a child's stay in the hospital. Azarnoff and Hardgrove (1981) add that "Parents took great care not to offend the staff by questioning these policies, by appearing to be too close to their child, or by knowing too much. They feared that if they displeased the staff in whose hands their child's well-being rested, revenge on the child might result or care might be withheld" (p. 5). Physician collaboration with parents has historically been circumscribed as physicians have accepted a superior role to their patients, as noted in the 1847 AMA Code of Ethics which indicates that the physicians' role is to "unite tenderness with firmness and condescension with authority, so as to inspire the minds of their patients with gratitude, respect and confidence" (Gallessich, 1982, p. 20).

Parents have also been criticized by professionals in other fields as being the cause of behavior problems in their children (Kozloff, 1979). It was felt that therapeutic treatment for the parents was every bit as necessary as that for the child if the child was to function adequately.

The view of parents as second-rate caregivers who should be treated with condescension and as the likely primary cause of their child's problems is clearly one that would prohibit true and co-equal collaboration between the professional and the parent. However, research over the last 40 years on the positive effects of parental intervention with children, along with studies that demonstrate the negative effects of parent–child separations and the strength of the parent–child bond on the emotional well-being of family members, has done much to change the medical and educational communities' views on the value of parental involvement. In addition, the federal government, recognizing the need to provide parents' rights in the educational arena, passed P.L. 93-380 and P.L. 94-142. Both of these laws provide a number of procedural safeguards against the misuse of information about children or assessment of children without parental permission and involvement in the process. However, the archaic views mentioned above still linger as they have been ingrained over time and are likely resistant to change. The need for a book of this sort points out that professional collaboration with parents is still a relatively new and evolving mind-set.

The damage done by a negative view of parents reduces the probability of effective treatment for the child from both medical and educational standpoints. From a collaborative standpoint, a number of authors have pointed out that disproportionate power relationships tend to restrict the communication flow between members (Alpert, 1977; Kramer & Nagle, 1980; Kurpius, 1978; Pryzwansky, 1974). The view that parents are not equals in the collaborative process may therefore unduly restrict communication and not allow the professional to work as an ally with parents. However, when parents are involved in the medical care of their child, children seem to recuperate faster, parents express greater satisfaction with their child's hospital care, and the child seems to be more cooperative with medical procedures (Wolfer & Visitainer, 1975). Collaborative involvement with parents in some medical settings serves to normalize the environment and thereby reduce stress, provides security for the child, and helps support the growth and development of the child within the family (Hardgrove, 1980). Parental involvement as equal partners in the process of serving their child serves important physical and emotional needs of the child and parent and seems to hasten recovery and improvement in the ill child. The professional who fails to view the parent as a co-equal agent in the care and treatment of the child may jeopardize the quality of care to the child and diminish the probability of an optimal treatment outcome.

The Chronically Ill Child and Family Problems

The problems associated with having a chronically ill child appear to be qualitatively different for the child and family from those of having children with other handicaps. These qualitative differences seem to revolve around the identification (diagnosis) of the child, the nature of the disability, and an unclear involvement with the educational system.

Identification or diagnosis of a medical disorder in children involves ongoing interaction with the medical community and medical personnel, unlike diagnosis of educational handicaps, which may require only intermittent involvement with the medical community and more intense involvement with the educational system. As noted above, the authoritarian stance taken by medical personnel toward parents can be a problem (Azarnoff & Hardgrove, 1981) that serves to invite conflict and creates interpersonal and role difficulties that compound the distress already encountered through having a chronically ill child.

The chronic illness of a child may be life threatening, terminal, or may worsen and remit over the short term. The family and the child must deal not only with the profound implications of the illness but also with the cyclical nature of chronic illness, from acute needs to remission. If the acute needs are combined with life threat, a huge stressor is placed upon the family in each acute phase. In contrast, families of children with other handicaps (i.e., educational handicaps) do not as frequently experience life threats to their child or the short-term cyclical nature of acute phases with remission.

Chronically ill children often have special needs that the educational system is not equipped to handle. As a result, identification of these children as educationally handicapped and their type of placement may vary greatly. Within the educational system, children with other exceptionalities have somewhat clearer identification criteria and somewhat more uniform educational deficits that result in more homogeneous educational placements.

The above-mentioned issues serve to distinguish some of the problems that are qualitatively different between chronically ill children and their families and those families of children with other handicaps. Professionals working with the families of chronically ill children should be aware of these qualitative differences and not assume that experience in serving parents and children with other handicaps is sufficient for understanding and consulting with these families.

Family Problems

Many authors (Friedrich, 1977; Hannah & Midlarsky, 1985; Sargent, 1983) assert that families must adjust to change when their child becomes chronically ill and must learn to cope with a variety of life-style and interpersonal changes within the family. Frequently families and their chronically ill children do adjust to change without an increased need for professional consultation. However, these parents rarely come to the attention of helping professionals.

Because of the associated stress, families having a chronically ill child are considered to be "at risk" for psychopathology among individual members (McCollum & Gibson, 1970; Meyerwitz & Kaplan, 1967) and in jeopardy of family interaction problems (Minuchin, Baker, & Rosman, 1978; Sargent, 1983).

Difficulties that are often noticed with parents and families of chronically ill children have been identified by several authors and will be outlined here. It should be remembered that these problems are not present in all families with chronically ill children, and their presence likely depends on various premorbid family interaction patterns as well as a variety of other variables.

Sargent (1983) has noted that problems within families of chronically ill children may include issues of enmeshment, overprotectiveness, and rigidity. Enmeshment refers to a high involvement or overresponsiveness among family members. Furthermore, in an enmeshed family, there is a high degree of sensitivity between family members and minor upsets are responded to with closeness. Individuals within the family lack their own identity and have difficulty differentiating themselves from the family unit. Overprotectiveness (Sargent, 1983) refers to a tendency to shelter other family members from psychological or physical harm. When this extends to the major areas of family life, "individual competence and autonomy are retarded, and personal control and problem solving are inhibited" (Sargent, 1983, p. 53). Rigidity refers to a tendency to maintain stability within the family unit. Sargent (1983) argues that this tendency exists even when traditional methods of family interactions become dysfunctional. The inability to communicate then further compounds the family's problems. Because of these problems Sargent (1983) argues that such families have a low tolerance for conflict, resulting in the family viewing small conflicts as disproportionately threatening and intolerable.

Friedrich (1977) described the analogy between the grief reaction in the death of a loved one to that experienced by the parents who grieve the loss of the normal child they had expected. The cyclical nature of chronic illness features acute phases and remission, and in the acute phases the parent may re-experience the same grief reaction as with the initial diagnosis. As a result, it may be onerous to work through the grief stages to conclusion.

Lawler, Nakielny, and Wright (1966) noted a much higher degree of psychopathology and marital discord in parents of dying children. Emotional problems such as anxiety, depression, denial, hostility, and an inability to care for the sick child were noted in studies by McCollum and Gibson (1970) and Meyerwitz and Kaplan (1967). Depression in the sick child and the parents (Tropauer, Franz, & Dilgard, 1970), as well as communication difficulties among immediate family members and between the family and relatives, has been noted by Turk (1964). Problems of this sort serve to isolate the family with the ill child and reduce the effect of familial support systems. McCubbin et al. (1983) observed that parents of chronically ill children have an inadequate amount of leisure time either with their families or by themselves. Furthermore, leisure activities, including involvement in social activities with friends, were often endorsed by parents as important supportive functions in coping with having a chronically ill child.

Specific issues with the siblings of handicapped children have been examined by Hannah and Midlarsky (1985). These issues cover problems of increased responsibilities for the nonhandicapped siblings including caretaking of the sick child and additional chores around the home. More time is often provided to the sick child, resulting in feelings of neglect and isolation in the siblings. Parents may increase their expectations for the nonhandicapped siblings in the educational and/or athletic arenas in compensation for the lost expectations of the sick child. Finally, Hannah and Midlarsky (1985) point out that family size seems to have a bearing on problems with the siblings because in a larger family, caretaking responsibilities can be shared and the sick child is less conspicuous and therefore "an atmosphere of normality prevails" (p. 514). Smaller families seem more likely to experience dysfunction (Trevino, 1979).

Due to these problems families of chronically ill children are more "at risk" for dysfunction. Major adjustment problems, when present within a family, seem to affect everyone including the sick child.

The School

School is often of great importance in the lives of chronically ill children as it is their link with the mainstream of the child and adolescent culture. School adjustment in chronically ill children has not been well studied (Drotar, 1981). We do know that chronically ill children often have excessive and intermittent absences. They may have limitations in their ability to participate fully in school, and they may require special tutoring or homebound instruction. Richman and Harper (1978) found that mildly handicapped children with cleft lip and palate and cerebral palsy significantly underachieved academically when compared with their normal peers. The underachievement was attributed to "the general characteristic of personality inhibition" (Richman & Harper, 1978, p. 16), as chronically ill children may be reluctant to draw attention to themselves. This inhibition may limit competitiveness and drive which are often necessary for academic achievement.

Despite these limitations, school adjustment of chronically ill children seems to be quite good (Drotar et al., 1981). However, school adjustment appears to be related to the type of condition. For example, Harper, Richman, and Snider (1980) found that children with a cleft lip and palate showed a higher degree of impulse inhibition in school than a matched sample of children with cerebral palsy. Limitations on sample size in this study as well as other considerations make these results difficult to generalize.

School intervention for chronically ill children is an area in which little research has been forthcoming. However, psychologists in the schools attempting to intervene in the interest of the chronically ill child have a variety of intervention modes to choose from. Among them are the following:

1. *School System Consultation.* Intervention at this level may include advocacy programs for chronically ill children or developing parent support groups. System-level programs highlight this level of intervention.

2. *Principal/Teacher Consultation.* This involves indirect intervention that is *case* specific by consulting with the teacher or principal. There is no direct intervention from the psychologist (consultant) to the ill child.

3. *Counseling the Ill Child.* A very familiar approach is individual psychotherapy with the ill child. Services of this sort may also include counseling with a group of chronically ill children.

4. *Counseling with the Siblings of the Ill Child.* This approach features traditional individual or group counseling with siblings of the ill child. This is a unique strategy to promote family stability through the brothers and sisters of the ill child.

5. *Parent Consultation.* This is an indirect approach to helping the child by working with the parents. This technique is the focus of the remainder of this chapter.

Parent Consultation

Why parent consultation? A number of factors point to consultation as an important and needed human service intervention. The psychologist working within a consultative framework may serve more children in a shorter time by imparting psychological techniques to parents who can work with their child. From a preventive standpoint, the parents may gain skills that will enable them to work with their ill child (or the siblings) in more effective ways in the future.

When a child is diagnosed as chronically ill, the family's involvement with medical and educational personnel increases. As a result, parents may experience consultative relationships with both medical and educational personnel. The contrast between these two models may leave the parents confused about their role, and perhaps without the ability to participate collaboratively in the consultative process. The following is a critical look at the medical service delivery model in comparison with the collaborative-consultative model.

Medical Service Delivery Model

Figure 11.1 shows the medical service delivery model. This traditional approach is characterized by the focus on the ill child only. As noted in Figure 11.1, daily interaction takes place between the parent(s) and the ill child as well as the neighbors, relatives, and siblings. The referral (arrow #1) comes from the parent to the physician who then assesses/examines the ill child (arrow #2). The physician then reports his or her findings to the parents and describes the treatment plan that the physician or his or her operatives (i.e., nurses, physician's assistant) will carry out (arrow #3). The treatment emanates from the physician (arrow #4) and is directed toward the ill child.

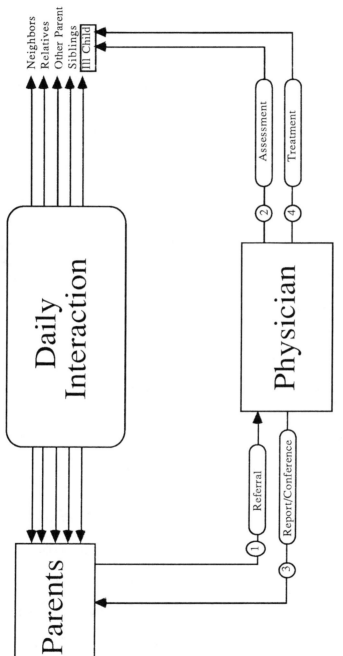

Figure 11.1. Medical Service Delivery Model.

Note. From T. B. Gutkin (personal communication, October, 1982). Adapted by permission.

Collaborative-Consultative Service Delivery Model

Figure 11.2 shows the collaborative-consultative service delivery model. This model focuses primarily on the parent and the daily interaction of the parent with the child and other important persons within the child's life. Secondarily, the model may focus on the ill child as the target of assessment and treatment. Within the collaborative-consultative service delivery model, the referral may come from the parent requesting help from the psychologist/consultant (or other education professionals) as shown in Figure 11.2 (arrow #1). The consultant's assessment in this model would include an interview with the parent relative to the problem at hand (arrow #2a) and an evaluation of the daily interaction between the parent and the ill child (arrow #2b). This evaluation may include direct observation of the parent–child interaction or information collected through parent- or child-completed behavior rating scales. Occasionally, the consultant may evaluate the ill child directly (dashed arrow #2c), but this is rarely necessary. After the assessment phase is completed, collaborative consultation is initiated between the parent and the consultant (arrow #3) using a problem-solving format as well as a variety of other consultation skills on the part of the consultant that will be discussed later. Finally, treatment is initiated by the parent within the daily interaction with the child (arrow #4). In the collaborative-consultative model the parent/consultee is responsible for carrying out the treatment.

Model Comparisons

Although both of the above-mentioned models have utility within their respective systems, the aspects of each model have such sharp contrast that it is helpful for the professional to be fully aware of these differences when attempting to work effectively with parents of chronically ill children. Within the medical service delivery model, the focus is on the ill child only and other aspects of the child's life are often ignored. The medical model approach in working with parents is often prescriptive as the physician *tells* the parent(s) what the medical people will do and what the parent will do for the ill child. The treatment emphasis in the medical model is on the ill child and not on the daily interaction and may therefore disregard the relationship between the parent and child which undoubtedly plays a large part in treatment effectiveness. Medical model treatments largely ignore the family and how they may be coping with chronic illness. Even when family issues are addressed, the process in the medical model is often prescriptive (i.e., "You do this and you'll get better"). Because the focus is on the ill child only, little or no change for the child results in little altering of the stress surrounding the illness. The medical model for service delivery features one-way communications (note arrows in Figure 11.1) and very little serious collaboration. Last, the medical orientation

Figure 11.2. Collaborative-Consultative Service Delivery Model.

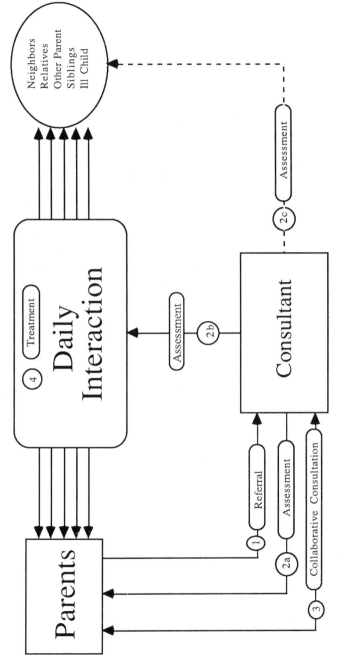

Note. From T. B. Gutkin (personal communication, October, 1982). Adapted by permission.

uses terminology that is unfamiliar to the parent and breeds anxiety due to fear of the unknown.

In the collaborative-consultative service delivery model, the focus is on the daily interaction of the parents with the ill child and with significant others in the child's life. The process is collaborative, featuring mutually agreed upon goals and interventions that maximize parent ownership for the goals and interventions and increase the likelihood that they will be carried out. The collaborative process includes the family, relatives, and neighbors by examining their role in enhancing the environment for the ill child, the parents, and siblings. There is open and ongoing communication between the consultant and the parent(s), which allows for evolving positions or views of the problems of the child and family that may be incorporated in the consultation process. The collaborative-consultative process uses a problem-solving orientation in which both the parent(s) and the consultant play an important role in examining the problems of the child and family and devising intervention plans. The collaborative-consultative process takes a different posture toward the parent, viewing the parent as competent, and the relationship as encompassing joint responsibility for intervention or change and mutually working together. Finally, the collaborative-consultative model uses familiar terminology in that the problems as depicted by the parent are the focus of the consultative effort.

Consultants attempting to work with parents of chronically ill children should be aware that these parents are likely getting a vastly different view of working with professionals from the medical community. Parents may have difficulty understanding or adjusting to the collaborative or more participative role. A description of collaboration (i.e., mutual working together, joint responsibility) during the initial consultative session would be quite helpful to the parents of chronically ill children so they may fully participate.

Collaborative Consultation with Parents of Chronically Ill Children

As previously noted in collaborative consultation, both the parent and the consultant have input into the problem-solving process. The consultant should have both *process* and *content* expertise. Process expertise refers to skills of engaging and interacting with the parent/consultee. It includes methods of solving problems and communication skills with the parent/consultee. Process skills can be used with any type of consultee with any type of problem. Content expertise refers to the body of knowledge and skills with reference to the problem at hand, in this case dealing with problems of ill children and coping with a chronically ill child. A consultant with a high degree of content expertise is familiar with the relevant research in the content area and the effectiveness of various intervention approaches.

General approaches to process consultation have been outlined elsewhere (Conoley & Conoley, 1982; Gutkin & Curtis, 1982), therefore this discussion will focus predominantly on issues of content expertise. Process expertise will be discussed only with reference to important process issues in consulting with the parents of chronically ill children.

Process expertise. As previously noted, process expertise involves the methods or techniques used in working with a parent/consultee. In this vein, a problem-solving approach, using a sequence similar to that shown in Table 11.1, may help the parent not only to solve current problems, but also to function preventively. This approach is designed to help prevent future problems, depending upon the degree to which the consultant passes along the problem-solving skills to the parent (Gutkin & Curtis, 1982).

In using the problem-solving sequence in a collaborative way with parents of chronically ill children, there are a variety of technical and communication skills that will likely enhance the relationship and make the consultation more fruitful. For example, it should be communicated to the parent that the relationship is *co-equal* in terms of power. It is not a supervisory relationship, but one of equality. The parent brings a vast body of knowledge about the child, and the consultant brings knowledge of education and/or psychology to the relationship.

Table 11.1
Problem Solving Sequence

---

1. Establish a calm and rational atmosphere.
2. Define and clarify the problem(s).
   a. Identify and prioritize all the problems and determine which will be worked with first.
   b. State the problem in concrete, behavioral terms. Be specific.
   c. When appropriate, divide the problem into its component parts and determine which component or combination of components should be dealt with first.
   d. Identify the terminal goals.
3. Analyze the forces impinging on the problem.
   a. Identify forces that impede the solution of the problem.
   b. Identify forces that contribute to the solution of the problem.
   c. Identify forces that may be neutral and must be taken into account in solving the problem.
4. Brainstorm multiple alternatives (solutions) for the problem.
5. Evaluate and choose among alternatives.
6. Specify consultant and consultee responsibilities.
7. Implement the solution(s).
8. Evaluate the effectiveness of the action and recycle if necessary.

Responsibility is important to communicate to the parent. The consultant is responsible for regulating the problem-solving process and contributing some content expertise. The consultant should also be available mentally and physically, model effective problem solving, and be patient. The responsibilities of the parent include contributing content expertise (knowledge of the child), being involved in the problem-solving process, and taking action on the plan that results from consultation. Last, the parent is responsible for initiating, maintaining, and terminating the consultative relationship. The responsibility for success or failure lies jointly with the consultant and the parent.

The relationship between the consultant and the parent should be viewed as voluntary, and the parent should have the freedom to reject any solutions generated. These aspects of the relationship serve to empower the parents to have control over the relationship and ownership for interventions for their child that are generated from the consultative endeavor.

An array of effective communication skills help the consultant to gain and maintain rapport as well as to achieve clarity of communication with the parent. Skills such as paraphrasing, providing accurate empathy, restatements, use of time, and styles of opening and closing interviews as well as many other communication skills are all critical to effective consultation. The reader is directed toward Benjamin (1969), Gutkin and Curtis (1982), Beier (1966), and Rogers (1951) for a full discussion of relevant communication techniques.

Content expertise. Content expertise in working with parents of chronically ill children involves knowledge of intervention strategies that are helpful to parents, siblings and the ill child. The following is a literature review of findings and techniques that seem to be effective for families with chronically ill children.

McCubbin et al. (1983) studied 100 families having one or more children with cystic fibrosis. A questionnaire was administered to the parents to identify coping behaviors of the mothers and fathers. Three substantive factors or behavior sets were found that were significant in helping parents to cope. These included (1) maintaining family integration, cooperation, and an optimistic view of the situation; (2) maintaining social support, self-esteem, and psychological stability; and (3) understanding the medical situation. Factor #1 included behaviors such as the parent believing things will work out, believing in the medical care, believing in God, and building closer relationships with family members. Factor #2 contained behaviors such as continued involvement with friends, eating, sleeping, getting away, working, and hobbies. Factor #3 included talking with other parents in the same situation, talking with the medical staff, and reading about how others handled these problems. McCubbin et al. (1983) also noted that positive changes in the child's health were associated with coping Factor #2 for both the fathers and the mothers.

Hall and Richmond (1984) discussed guidelines for consulting with parents of handicapped children, some of which are applicable to the parents of chronically ill children. These authors noted that parents need time on their own and time together to relieve the stress and strain of the situation. Groups of parents with similar problems seem to offer support and help parents to feel that they are not alone. The financial burden of a long-standing illness can cause significant stress for the family. The consultant should be knowledgeable about financial help for the family. The consultant should help parents learn to trust their decisions with reference to their ill child. Although the parent(s) may seek advice that may be helpful, they must ultimately live with decisions they make about their sick son or daughter.

Sargent (1983) summarized some guidelines designed for psychotherapists that may be applicable for consultants in working with parents of chronically ill children. Sargent (1983) believes that parents should be in charge of managing the illness, and that the less-involved parent should be included as much as possible. Parents should agree in planning for their children and should cooperate to maintain maturity and responsibility of the sick child.

Friedrich (1977) outlined the value of support groups for parents, that may allow them to "publicly mourn" for their child as well as gain strength from other group members. Friedrich (1977) also noted that a strictly medical approach toward the ill child is anxiety provoking and confusing. As a result, parents and other human service professionals should attend to the psychosocial needs of the child.

Cobb and Medway (1978) summarized the literature in general parent consultation and concluded that general parent consultation is more effective with groups with higher income and education. In addition, Cobb and Medway (1977) assert that modeling techniques with parents and intensity of the training are related to successful outcomes.

Potter (1988) states that parents should help children to be responsible for as much of their own care as possible as this provides them with a feeling of control versus dependence. Parents should be encouraged to ask questions about their child's care from medical personnel.

With reference to the siblings, Potter (1988) suggests that parents should help the well siblings to develop their own identity and to understand distinctions between themselves and the ill brother or sister. Furthermore, siblings should be informed about the nature and progression of the illness of their brother or sister. McKeever (1983) asserts that siblings may feel responsible for the ill child's condition, therefore a clear and rational explanation of the cause of the illness may be particularly therapeutic for the well sibling. The effects of an ill child are often far reaching; therefore, when consulting with parents of a chronically ill child, collecting information on the academic achievement, sleeping, eating, and mood of the siblings is often quite important.

If the ill child's school progress is hindered by the illness, then the child may be eligible for special services. These services may include homebound instruction, special counseling, physical or occupational therapy, or in-school special help

(Potter, 1988). The parent should maintain a contact person within the school who can coordinate homework, lessons, and classmate contact with the ill child.

Guidelines for Working with Parents of Chronically Ill Children

The following summary of guidelines is extracted from the above-mentioned review and should be considered by consultants.

1. Use a collaborative (mutual working together) approach in working with parents.
2. Optimism about their child's situation seems to help parents to cope; help parents to develop an optimistic but realistic view of their child's illness.
3. Encourage religious beliefs, as these seem to assist parents in coping.
4. Encourage parents to maintain involvement with relatives and neighbors as well as immediate family.
5. Discuss the importance of supporting the spouse and allowing oneself to be supported.
6. Help parents to encourage independence in the ill child. This may include having the child responsible for his or her own medication.
7. Encourage parents to get time alone.
8. Help parents to maintain adequate eating and sleeping behavior.
9. Parents who continue working and/or maintaining hobbies seem to cope better.
10. Discuss the value of keeping in shape physically and being well groomed.
11. Help parents to meet with groups of parents who have similar problems.
12. Know the financial services that are available to parents of chronically ill children.
13. Encourage parents to get input from others but ultimately make their own decisions regarding their child.
14. Encourage parents to be in charge of illness management, especially the less-involved parent.
15. Help parents to ask questions and continue communication with the medical staff treating their child.
16. Know of bibliographic references that a parent may read relative to their child's illness and other parents' reaction to it.
17. Help parents to explore support groups of parents who also have children who are chronically ill. Groups of this sort seem to have a beneficial effect for parents.
18. Parents should be encouraged to inform the well siblings about the nature and progression of the illness in their brother or sister.
19. The consultant should help the parents to understand the special services for which their child may be eligible at school and specify a school contact person to coordinate homework, lessons, and classmate contact with their ill child.

Research

Little research in this area of collaborative involvement with parents of chronically ill children has been done. Research directions in this area may fruitfully focus on the variables within the collaborative process (i.e., ongoing communication, joint responsibility, mutual decision making, problem-solving process). In addition, further research on approaches to helping parents, siblings, and relatives cope with the devastating effects of having a chronically ill or dying child are needed. Finally, strategies that link the educational and mental health communities with parents of chronically ill children in an effort to humanize the care of the child and coping in the family should be empirically evaluated.

Summary

This chapter discussed the fundamental differences between the medical and collaborative problem-solving models, both of which parents with chronically ill children will confront in attempting to work with helpers using these two differing orientations. Aspects of these two models were discussed within the context of the specific problems that affect the families of chronically ill children.

Aspects of process and content expertise that are needed to assist the collaborative consultant in working with families of chronically ill children were gleaned from the literature. This information was provided as a summary of guidelines that may aid the consultant in reducing the stress associated with having a chronically ill child.

References

Alpert, J. L. (1977). Some guidelines for school consultants. *Journal of School Psychology, 15,* 308–317.

Azarnoff, P., & Hardgrove, C. (1981). *The family in child health care.* New York: Wiley.

Beier, E. (1966). *The silent language of psychotherapy.* Chicago: Aldine.

Benjamin, A. (1969). *The helping interview.* Boston: Houghton Mifflin.

Cobb, D. E., & Medway, F. J. (1978). Determinants of effectiveness in parent consultation. *Journal of Community Psychology, 6,* 229–240.

Conoley, J. C., & Conoley, C. W. (1982). *School consultation: A guide to practice and training.* New York: Pergamon.

Drotar, D. (1981). Psychological perspectives in chronic childhood illness. *Journal of Pediatric Psychology, 6,* 211–228.

Drotar, D., Doershuk, C. F., Boat, T. F., Stern, R. C., Matthews, L., & Boyer, W. (1981). Psychosocial functioning of children with cystic fibrosis. *Pediatrics, 67,* 338–343.

Friedrich, W. N. (1977). Ameliorating the psychological impact of chronic disease on the child and family. *Journal of Pediatric Psychology, 2,* 26–31.

Gallessich, J. (1982). *The profession and practice of consultation.* San Francisco: Jossey-Bass.

Gutkin, T. B., & Curtis, M. J. (1982). School-based consultation: Theory and technique. In C. R. Reynolds & T. B. Gutkin (Eds.), *The handbook of school psychology* (pp. 796–828). New York: Wiley.

Hall, C. W., & Richmond, B. O. (1984). Consultation with parents of handicapped children. *The Exceptional Child, 31,* 185–191.

Hannah, M. E., & Midlarsky, E. (1985). Siblings of the handicapped: A literature review for school psychologists. *School Psychology Review, 14,* 510–520.

Hardgrove, C. (1980). Helping parents on the pediatric ward. A report on a survey of hospitals with "Living-In" programs. *Paediatrician, 9,* 220–223.

Harper, D. C., Richman, L. C., & Snider, B. C. (1980). School adjustment and degree of physical impairment. *Journal of Pediatric Psychology, 5,* 377–383.

Kozloff, M. A. (1979). *A program for families of children with learning and behavior problems.* New York: Wiley.

Kramer, J. J., & Nagle, R. J. (1980). Suggestions for the delivery of psychological services in secondary schools. *Psychology in the Schools, 17,* 53–59.

Kurpius, D. J. (1978). Defining and implementing a consultation program in the schools.*School Psychology Digest, 7,* 4–17.

Lawler, R. H., Nakielny, W., & Wright, N. A. (1966). Psychological implications of cystic fibrosis. *Canadian Medical Association Journal, 94,* 1043–1046.

McCollum, A. T., & Gibson, L. E. (1970). Family adaptation to the child with cystic fibrosis. *Journal of Pediatrics, 77,* 571–578.

McCubbin, H. I., McCubbin, M. A., Patterson, J. A., Cauble, A. E., Wilson, L. R., & Warwick, W. (1983, May). CHIP—Coping Health Inventory for Parents: An assessment of parental coping patterns in the care of the chronically ill child. *Journal of Marriage and the Family,* 359–370.

McKeever, P. (1983). Siblings of chronically ill children: A literature review with implications for research and practice. *American Journal of Orthopsychiatry, 53,* 209–217.

Meyerwitz, J., & Kaplan, H. (1967). Familial responses to stress: The case of cystic fibrosis. *Social Science and Medicine, 1,* 249–266.

Minuchin, S., Baker, L., & Rosman, B. L. (1978). A conceptual model of psychosomatic illness in childhood. *Archives of General Psychiatry, 32,* 1031–1038.

Potter, M. L. (1988, March). Children and chronic illness. *Communique,* p. 26.

Pryzwansky, W. A. (1974). A reconsideration of the consultation model for delivery of school-based psychological services. *American Journal of Orthopsychiatry, 44,* 579–583.

Public Law 93-380, Family Educational Rights and Privacy Act, 1974.

Public Law 94-142, Education of All Handicapped Children Act of 1975.

Richman, L. C., & Harper, D. C. (1978). School adjustment of children with observable difficulties. *Journal of Abnormal Child Psychology, 6,* 11–18.

Rogers, C. R. (1951). *Client-centered therapy: Its current practice, implications and theory.* Boston: Houghton Mifflin.

Sargent, J. (1983). The sick child: Family complications. *Developmental and Behavioral Pediatrics, 4,* 50–56.

Trevino, F. (1979). Siblings of handicapped children: Identifying those at risk. *Social Casework, 60,* 488–493.

Tropauer, A., Franz, M. N., & Dilgard, V. W. (1970). Psychological aspects of the care of children with cystic fibrosis. *American Journal of Diseases of Children, 199,* 424–432.

Turk, J. (1964). Impact of cystic fibrosis on family functioning. *Pediatrics, 34,* 67–71.

Wolfer, J., & Visitainer, M. (1975). Pediatric surgical patients and parents: Stress responses and adjustment. *Nursing Research, 24,* 244–255.

12

A PROGRAM FOR FAMILIES WITH CHILDREN WITH LEARNING DISABILITIES

Chriss Walther-Thomas, J. Stephen Hazel,
Jean Bragg Schumaker, Sue Vernon,
and Donald D. Deshler

The challenges of raising a family in today's world are great. Economic pressures, the changing roles of mothers and fathers within the family constellation, and the demands of helping children cope with pressure from their peers (e.g., to take drugs and skip school) all contribute to stress on the family unit. This stress can be significantly magnified when a family has a child or children with learning disabilities. Some of this stress can result from the elusive nature of learning disabilities. Indeed, the term "learning disabilities" has often been referred to as the "hidden handicap" (Anderson, 1970). That is, to the casual observer, the youth with a learning disability appears to be perfectly normal. Because of the "hidden" nature of the disability, initial acknowledgment of its existence may be difficult for families (Kronick, 1976; Vigilante, 1983; Willner & Crane, 1979). Often a full diagnosis of the disability does not occur until the child has been in school for an extended period of time. Such "late" diagnosis of a disability can lead to further problems. On the one hand, parents may be frustrated and confused by the discovery of a disability in a child who seems capable in many ways. On the other hand, some parents may be relieved finally to learn there are reasons for the problems they have observed; however, these parents may experience guilt that the disability was not identified earlier.

Also because of the "hidden" nature of learning disabilities, parents of children with mild to moderate disabilities may take longer to accept the presence of the disability than parents of children with more clearly defined problems (Willner & Crane, 1979). Children with severe disabilities generally demonstrate consistently delayed patterns of development that are quickly observed. Consequently, parents of children with severe disabilities are forced to acknowledge the discrepancies that exist between their own children at an early age and peers of their children who do not have disabilities (Rappaport, 1965). The problems of children with mild to moderate disabilities may not be as easily defined. They often experience wide swings with regard to meeting developmental milestones. These inconsistencies in their performance can make understanding and acceptance of their problems more difficult (Willner & Crane, 1979).

Although there are often no obvious signs of a learning disability, compared to the signs readily observed in individuals with physical disabilities or severe developmental disabilities, the effects of a learning disability are very real and can touch every aspect of a growing child's life. Despite the fact that learning disabilities are typically thought to be conditions that affect how children and youth perform in school, the same cognitive deficits that often lead to school failure can lead to failure in other areas. As Silver (1983) noted, a learning disability is " ... not just a school disability; it is a total life disability" (p. 58). Thus, the presence of a learning disability can impinge on a child's learning of many things: how to interact with peers, how to interact with adults, how to play sports, how to do chores, and how to complete tasks on time. As a result, the child's self-image and relationships with others suffer.

To be sure, the subtle and complex difficulties associated with a learning disability can involve virtually all aspects of a child's and a family's life (Vigilante, 1983). Pfeiffer, Gerber, and Reiff (1985) noted that the presence of a learning disability can result in dysfunction in three interrelated domains: (a) the child's learning and emotional growth at school; (b) the child's learning and emotional growth at home; and (c) the psychological health of the entire family system. Parents are often confused about how to deal with these dysfunctions. For example, in relation to school failure, parents of children with learning disabilities continually face the dilemma of trying to decide how much is realistic to expect (Caplan, 1976). If parents push, they worry that the pressure is too great. Often, performance problems of a child in school can become more complicated if the expectations of the parents are not reasonable given the child's condition (e.g., Berman, 1979; Giannotti & Doyle, 1982). Perhaps because of this possibility, mothers of children with learning disabilities tend to have lower expectations for their children's future achievement than mothers of normally achieving children. In fact, the expectations of such mothers are generally lower than the children's own personal expectations for themselves (Chapman & Boersma, 1979).

Despite these lower expectations, a child's failure in school often leads to parent–child conflicts. Indeed, problems in school have been noted to be a primary source of conflict between parents and children (Berman, 1979; Caplan, 1976; Giannotti & Doyle, 1982). The parent who does not clearly understand the nature of the disability may conclude that the child's failure is a result of factors such as a general lack of ability (Chapman & Boersma, 1979), stubbornness, willfulness (Meier, 1976), or a lack of effort (Siegel, 1976). Parents who are frustrated and confused about their child's performance may develop maladaptive parenting behaviors such as inappropriate expectations, overprotection, indulgence, and denial (Doleys, Cartelli, & Doster, 1976).

A child's failure within the home and community setting can be similarly problematic. Because children with learning disabilities "look normal" to their brothers, sisters, other relatives, and neighbors, the source of their errors, omissions, and blunders is often misunderstood. The child may be viewed as a burden or source of embarrassment for some members of the family (Osman, 1982). Siblings may view the child with learning disabilities as "failing on purpose" to gain preferential treatment from parents (Kronick, 1976).

As with school problems, parents are often baffled with regard to dealing with the dysfunctions that their children exhibit in home and community settings and the reactions of those around them. Because children with mild to moderate disabilities may remain peripherally in the mainstream of community life, they continue to encounter difficulties in these settings as they mature. Their inconsistent performance makes anticipating the outcomes of challenges they face at each new stage of development difficult for parents. Hopeful parents are often tempted into believing that new demands will be easier for their children than they usually prove to be. Murphy (1982) noted that watching children struggling with challenges and encountering frequent failure is painful and disappointing to parents. Willner and Crane (1979) concluded that parents of children with mild to moderate disabilities experience chronic disappointment.

Such developments are unfortunate in that they may have a profound effect on the psychological health of the whole family system (Blacher-Dixon, 1981). Other factors related to helping the child with learning disabilities can adversely affect the equilibrium of the family as well. For example, Kaslow and Cooper (1978) noted that parents may feel that they need to allocate inordinate amounts of family resources to help the child who has a learning disability. This can adversely affect family functioning by creating negative feelings among family members. Siblings, for example, may feel less important and less loved than the child with the learning disability (Kronick, 1976) because they receive less attention than the child with the disability. Margalit (1982) has suggested that pressures due to the costs of special services, fatigue from daily management of difficult child behaviors and needs, and the self-doubt that parents experience regarding the appropriateness of their child-bearing practices can disrupt family equilibrium. Kozloff (1979) agreed that families of children with learning disabilities experience an energy drain due to the amount of time needed to cope with factors related to the disability while trying to maintain normal family routines. Such pressures may also result in a less organized family life. Owen, Adams, Forrest, Stolz, and Fisher (1971), for example, found that the homes of children with learning disabilities were less organized than those of nondisabled children with regard to structured activities, assigned responsibilities, and schedules. Additionally, Philage and Kuna (1975) noted that feelings of fatigue and other pressures on family resources may result in decreased interactions with others outside the immediate family. Parents may choose to maintain relationships primarily with those facing similar problems. Such choices can result in feelings of isolation and the creation of "the LD-focused family." The ongoing difficulties the child experiences coupled with the parents' ongoing frustration, disappointment, and feelings of isolation can lead to a situation where the child inadvertently becomes a target for other family and parent frustrations (Silver, 1974).

Thus, the presence of a learning disability not only can profoundly affect the child's growth at school and within the home and community; it can adversely affect the psychological well-being of the family as a whole. Clearly, the ability of family members to understand and cope effectively with the demands associated with the condition is a major factor related to the happiness of the family and the successful development of the child (Bryan & Bryan, 1981). Unfortunately, families often lack the knowledge and skills needed to cope with these demands. Few programs are available to help family members develop the skills needed to respond to the unique demands of these children. Although various authors (e.g., Kroth & Otteni, 1983; Roth & Weller, 1985) have proposed models to guide professionals interested in helping these families and a few specific skill development programs do exist (e.g., Dinkmeyer & McKay, 1976; Patterson & Forgatch, 1987), there are no comprehensive programs that have been empirically validated for parents of children with learning disabilities.

Given this need for a validated program, staff members of the University of Kansas Institute for Research in Learning Disabilities (KU-IRLD) began working to develop and evaluate a program that will enable parents to help a child with learning disabilities successfully, while coping with the associated demands and pressures on the family as a whole. This work has spanned several phases: the Survey Phase, the Development Phase, the Field-test Phase, and the Revision Phase. A description of each phase and the results of that phase follow.

Survey Phase

An initial goal associated with the KU-IRLD Families Project was to gather information from parents of children with learning disabilities about the kinds of skills they wanted to learn, the kinds of skills they wanted to teach their children, and the format of training that they would prefer. As an initial step to reach this goal, 10 couples whose children had learning disabilities were interviewed for 2 hours each. They were asked questions about their concerns and needs with regard to their child with learning disabilities. Based on the results of these interviews and a literature review, a survey instrument was developed. It had six major sections within which parents could respond. In the first section, parents were asked to rate the importance of learning each of 26 skills, identified from the interview and literature review, using a 7-point Likert-type scale (with 1 representing "Not important to learn" and 7 representing "Very important to learn"). For example, parents were asked to rate (within separate items) the importance of learning a skill for "solving family problems" and a skill for "communicating effectively with our child with learning disabilities." The 26 items focused on six domains of family life: (a) the development of interpersonal relationships within the family, (b) the preparation of children for independent living and careers, (c) the teaching of social skills to children, (d) the development of self-confidence in children, (e) the teaching of coping strategies (e.g., organizing time, stress management) to children, and (f) the development of a home academic support system.

In the second section of the survey, parents were asked to rank each of these six domains with regard to its importance for families with a child with learning disabilities. In the third section of the survey, parents were asked to rank the top three sources of support for their child. The options provided in this section included parents, teachers, employers, extended family members, therapists/counselors, significant adults in the community (coaches, clergy, youth group leaders), and friends. These sources of support were identified from the initial interviews. In the fourth section, parents were asked to identify and rank the three best formats for them to learn new skills. Parents could choose among options such as weeknight classes, weekend workshops, and Saturday morning classes. In the fifth section, parents were asked to provide information regarding family earnings, number of children, and age at which their child was diagnosed as having a learning disability. In the last section, parents were asked, in an open-ended format, to identify the skill that they would most like to teach to their child with learning disabilities.

The survey was distributed through the auspices of the International Association of Children and Adults with Learning Disabilities (ACLD) to parent members across the nation. One hundred and seven surveys out of 185 were returned. Twenty additional surveys were received from one ACLD chapter where a few members copied the survey and distributed it to the other members. Ninety-four percent of the respondents were mothers. Nine percent of the families earned less than $24,900, 19% earned between $24,900 and $35,000, and 72% reported incomes at $35,000 and above. The average number of children per family was 2.8.

The parent responses to items in the first section of the survey indicated that all 26 listed skills were important or very important to learn. The lowest mean rating of a skill was 5.58, and the highest mean rating was 6.56 on the 7-point scale. The five most highly rated skills were: communicating effectively with children (mean = 6.56); teaching children and youth how to make important decisions (mean = 6.52); teaching children and youth how to make friends (mean = 6.50); developing confidence in children (mean = 6.48); and building positive family relationships (mean = 6.33). When respondents ranked the six domains by importance, they ranked them in the following order:

1. fostering children's self-confidence,
2. developing children's social skills,
3. teaching coping skills,
4. building family relationships,
5. developing independent living/career planning skills, and
6. providing home academic support.

The preferred training format selected by the parents was weeknight classes scheduled over a period of time. Second and third choices were low-cost audio or video home-learning programs and weekend workshops, respectively. Parents indicated that they viewed themselves as the greatest source of support for their children.

When the parents were asked to describe the skill they would most like to teach their children, the majority made one or more responses. Of the 156 responses in this section, 51 (33%) were related to social skills (e.g., conversation, getting along with others, making friends, maintaining friendships, asking for and accepting help), 35 (22%) were related to teaching their children to have confidence in themselves, and 29 (19%) were related to academic skills (e.g., reading, writing, note-taking, studying for tests, and taking tests). The remaining responses were related to such skill areas as independent living, organization, goal setting/self-motivation, coping skills, and problem solving.

The Development Phase

These survey results indicated that parents were interested in learning a variety of skills for helping their children with learning disabilities. Parents especially indicated an interest in learning skills that related to improving family relationships by rating two items in this area among the top five rated items. They also indicated a strong interest in teaching their children social skills, academic skills, and decision-making skills and in fostering self-confidence.

Based on these findings, a parent education program, called the "Families Program," was developed by the KU-IRLD staff to focus on teaching parents the skills they desired to learn that would help them cope with the demands they face as parents of children with learning disabilities. The first step in the Development Phase of the program was to specify the philosophical foundation for the program. Five major assumptions were identified. First, within the philosophy of the program, the presence of a disability is not necessarily equated with problems. As

Goldfarb, Brotherson, Summers, and Turnbull (1986) stated, "Disabilities are not problems; they are conditions. Conditions are not problems in themselves, but they may bring problems, or they may make other problems more difficult to solve" (p. 3). Thus, learning disabilities are not necessarily defined as problems; instead, they are seen as conditions that may create problems that need to be addressed by families. This perspective is important, for a program that will be maximally effective must focus on the problems that are associated with the disability that have an impact on the family and not on the disability itself.

The second philosophical underpinning adopted for the program was based on work by researchers at the KU-IRLD (Seabaugh & Schumaker, 1980) who found that children with learning disabilities must have a real stake in their lives and their futures if they are to be motivated to learn new skills. That is, if they are to become successful, they must be given responsibility for their lives and feel a measure of control in the decision-making process. Thus, one philosophical assumption associated with the Families Program is that children and their parents must form a partnership and must relate openly and effectively with each other while working toward successful outcomes together. This foundation for the program requires that parents give up their traditional role of "I am the parent, and you will do what I say" and adopt the posture of facilitating their child's work toward success and eventual independence.

The third assumption associated with the program, that all family members must be involved in the program in some way, was based on the dynamic nature of families and the notion that any family intervention planned to help a child with learning disabilities must also consider the effects on other family members (Amerikaner & Omizo, 1984). That is, a decision was made to do everything possible to involve all members of the family in a collaborative process to improve the situation of the family as a whole.

Fourth, a basic assumption underlying the Families Program is the notion that each family has unique needs. Thus, each family requires an individual approach because of the diversity arising from differing types of learning disabilities manifested by the child in the family, family sizes and forms, cultural backgrounds, socioeconomic factors, and individual characteristics (e.g., coping styles, intellectual capacity). The multitude of ways in which these factors can be combined underscores the need to design a program that is responsive and flexible to meet the unique needs of each family (Turnbull & Turnbull, 1986).

Fifth, the program is founded on the concept that a program for parents must be skill-based. That is, in addition to providing parents with information, the program must also ensure that parents master specific skills for more effective communication with their children, for teaching new social and academic skills, and for facilitating their children's problem solving, decision making, goal setting, and goal attainment, if they are to have an effect on their children's lives and their children's self-esteem. Parents must master skills for helping their children become successful so that the children can directly experience success and feel more capable.

Based on these premises, the literature review, the national survey results, and the experience of KU-IRLD staff members, four parent skills were designed for the program. The first skill, the Relationship-Building Skill, was designed to enable parents to develop rapport with their children by encouraging their children to talk to them while refraining from negative judgmental statements, using attentive listening skills, and expressing their empathy, concern, and love. This skill was targeted as the initial skill to be taught to parents because it serves as the foundation upon which parents can build stronger relationships with their children. That is, parents need a method for understanding their children's feelings, worries, ideas, and goals in order to know in what areas their partnership needs to be activated. Clearly, if the child is to be positively drawn into the partnership, its focus must be related to the child's concerns.

Besides the Relationship-Building Skill, three other parent skills were designed for inclusion in the program. These skills were designed to be generic so that parents could learn a basic routine that could be applied to a wide variety of situations. The generic nature of the skills allowed for an individualized approach for all participating families because each family could apply the skills to whatever demands and problems they were facing. Because parents indicated that they wanted to teach their children a variety of skills, a Teaching Skill was designed such that it could be generatively used to address a wide variety of needs (e.g., social, academic, independent living, and time-management/organizational skills). Its design was based on an instructional methodology (Deshler, Alley, Warner, & Schumaker, 1981) which was founded on empirically sound learning principles and which has been shown to be effective in teaching new skills to children with learning disabilities (e.g., Hazel, Schumaker, Sherman, & Sheldon-Wildgen, 1982; Schumaker, Deshler, Alley, Warner, Clark, & Nolan, 1982; Schumaker, Deshler, Denton, Alley, Clark, & Warner, 1982).

Because parents had also indicated that they wanted to teach their children decision-making skills and because research has indicated that children with learning disabilities have difficulty reaching decisions through problem-solving processes and also have difficulty learning how to problem solve (e.g., Hazel et al., 1982; Schumaker, Hazel, Sheldon, & Sherman, 1982), a skill was designed for parents to use in *facilitating* their children's problem solving and decision making. This Problem-Solving Skill involves helping the child define the problem, identify solutions to the problem, evaluate those solutions, decide on the best solution, and make a plan for carrying out the solution. Emphasis within the skill is placed on the child's role in deciding which solution should be chosen because experience has shown that children will be more likely to carry out solutions of their own choosing rather than those that have been chosen for them.

Because parents had also indicated that they wanted to enhance their children's self-esteem, and self-esteem may be based, in part, on previous success, the Goal-Achievement Skill was designed to enable parents to help their children set goals and achieve those goals. The skill involves helping the child identify an area within which he or she wants to work or improve, set a goal within that area, identify the tasks to be accomplished to reach the goal, accomplish those tasks, and reward him- or herself for accomplishments. Emphasized within the Goal-Achievement Skill is the parent's and the youth's role with regard to accepting responsibility for completing particular tasks and helping each other complete tasks.

Each of the four skills (Relationship Building, Teaching, Problem Solving, and Goal Achievement) was carefully defined, and the components of the skill were specified during the Development Phase of the project.

For example, the component steps of the Teaching Skill are shown in Table 12.1. These steps are to be used by a parent after preparing for the teaching interaction (e.g., deciding what to teach, how to teach it, and specifying rationales for why the child/youth should want to learn it) and initiating the interaction in a positive way using components of the Relationship-Building Skill.

The first step in the Teaching Skill, which involves describing the skill to be taught, includes naming and defining the skill for the child. For example, a parent might name and describe the skill of "Asking for Help" to the child in words the child would understand by saying something like, " 'Asking for Help' is a skill for getting people to explain something to you or to help you get something done."

The second step in the Teaching Skill is to provide rationales for using the skill. Here, the parent focuses on the advantages of using the skill and the disadvantages of not using it by asking the child why the skill is important and providing additional explanations about the importance of the skill. For example, the parent might ask the child, "What are the good things that can happen if you ask for help and get the help you need?" or "What are the bad things that can happen if you don't know how to do something and you don't ask for help on it?" If the youth cannot answer, the parent might say to the youth, "If you use the 'Asking for Help Skill,' you will get the help you need, and you'll get your work done correctly. That way, you'll avoid having to do it over, and you'll save time. If you don't know how to ask for help, you're likely to have to do the work again, and you will miss out on activities you enjoy like playing soccer and going out with your friends."

The third step in the Teaching Skill is to discuss example situations in which the skill can be used. In this step, the parent and child discuss the general characteristics of situations in which the skill can be used (e.g., "Whenever you're not sure what to do or how to do it . . .") and discuss example situations of when the skill can be used (e.g., "When the teacher has given you an assignment and you don't know how to start . . .").

Table 12.1
Component Steps of the Teaching Skill

Describe the skill to be taught
  —Name the skill.
  —Provide an explicit definition of the skill.

Provide rationales for using this skill.
  —Discuss why this skill is important to your child.
  —Be specific about the benefits.
  —Talk about the short-term advantages of the skill.
  —Personalize the reasons to your child's situation.
  —Make sure your rationales are believable.

Help your child think of situations where the skill can be used.
  —Discuss general characteristics of situations in which use of the skill is appropriate.
  —Help the youth think of situations in different settings.

Discuss the steps of the skill.
  —Discuss each step with your child and why it is important.

Provide a model of the skill.
  —Model the skill for the youth by using all the steps.

Verbally rehearse the steps in the skill.
  —Involve your child in verbal rehearsal of the steps.

Practice the skill in role-play situations.
  —Ask your child to practice the skill in a role-play situation.
  —Provide feedback after each role-play attempt that is positive, corrective, personal, and
    specific.
  —Require a criterion level of performance.

Plan practices in which your child can use the skill.
  —Determine situations when the skill can be used.
  —Plan a time to check on skill use.

Thank your child for cooperation and effort.
  —Make a personal, encouraging statement of thanks, or compliment, praise, or show
    affection.

Discuss the benefits of learning the skill.
  —Discuss specific benefits of using the skill.

The fourth step of the Teaching Skill is to discuss the steps in the skill. This step involves breaking the skill into its component steps and discussing each step with the child. The steps in the skill of "Asking for Help" might include: say the person's name, explain the problem, ask for help, listen, ask for clarification, and thank the person. As each step is discussed, examples and reasons for the steps are provided by the parent or elicited from the child.

The fifth step of the Teaching Skill is to provide a model of the skill. Here, the parent demonstrates the use of the skill in a role-play situation so the child can see how the steps of the skill are translated into words and actions in a smoothly flowing interaction. The sixth step is to facilitate the child's verbal rehearsal of the steps of the skill until the child can repeat the steps from memory. This is important if the child is to be able to instruct him- or herself as he or she performs the skill.

The seventh step of the Teaching Skill is to practice the skill in role-play situations. Here, the parent prompts the youth to identify practice situations in such diverse environments as home, school, and work. Once the situations have been identified, the parent uses the identified situations as the context for skill practice using role-play activities. The parent provides constructive feedback after each practice attempt and requires additional practice as needed. Practice continues until the youth can meet a criterion level of performance in a role-play situation that ensures mastery of the skill. In the eighth step of the Teaching Skill, the parent arranges a time to check on skill use by having the child report on the success of his or her efforts.

The last two steps involve thanking the youth for his or her efforts and cooperation and discussing the benefits of learning the skill. These steps serve to reinforce the child's efforts and help motivate the child to use the skill.

Once the skills had been specified as described above, a "family meeting" procedure was designed to be used to enhance family organization and family fun. Because the results of the literature search and family interviews had indicated that families with children with learning disabilities were poorly organized, had few routines to follow, and rarely planned activities together, the agenda for the "family meeting" was designed such that a variety of issues (e.g., family rules, schedules, goals, routines, outings, vacations) could be openly discussed and settled. The agenda also included time for participating in fun activities together as a family. The family meeting format allowed for the participation of all family members in a collaborative approach to meeting family needs.

After the skills and the family meeting agenda had been designed, training materials (i.e., presentation outlines, handouts, role-playing materials, overhead transparencies, and homework activities) were developed for use in the parent training sessions.

The Field Test Phase

Four families with children with learning disabilities volunteered to participate in the initial field test of the Families Program. For all four families, both parents participated. The ages of the youths with learning disabilities ranged from 12 to

15 years, and the ages of the parents ranged from 35 to 41 years. Family size ranged from four to six members.

The four skills (Relationship Building, Problem Solving, Teaching, and Goal Achievement) plus the family meeting procedures were taught to the parents within a series of eight weekly training sessions. The first session, a half-day Saturday workshop, covered information about learning disabilities and their potential effects on children. Specifically, the condition of learning disabilities was defined; the ramifications of the condition for learning at home, in school, in extracurricular activities, and within social interactions were discussed; and the role of parents with regard to helping a child learn was described. The program goals and philosophy associated with the program also were discussed. In addition, the Relationship-Building Skill was taught. In subsequent evening sessions, the remaining skills and family meeting procedures were covered. The final two sessions each focused on a skill area that the parents wanted to teach their children. One session related to the teaching of social skills. The other related to teaching youths how to prepare for tests in school.

Instruction provided in each session followed a standard format. An overview of the skill was presented that included a definition, rationales, example situations, and steps in the skill. Next, a model of the skill was presented followed by small group practice using the skill. Feedback was provided to the parents regarding their individual performance of the skills, and additional practice was conducted when needed and as time allowed. A homework assignment was given at the end of each session that required the parents to use the new skill with their child and to audiotape the interaction. During each subsequent session, homework assignments and previously learned skills were reviewed, and problems and successes were reported and discussed.

Two types of instruments were used to assess the effectiveness of the program: (a) role-play assessment instruments that were used to assess the parents' performance of skills and (b) social validity questionnaires for measuring consumer satisfaction with the program. A multiple baseline across skills design was used to assess the parents' acquisition of the four skills. The parents participated in individual role-play sessions at the beginning and end of each training session. Some, but not all, skills were tested in each role-playing session. The trainer read aloud a description of a parent–child scenario, played the role of the child, and scored the parents' performance on a checklist listing the components of the given skill. Each role-play session was audiotaped for later reliability checks. Interscorer agreement on individual role-play situations ranged from 65% to 100% with a mean of 85%.

The results of the field test are encouraging. The mean scores for the parents' pre- and posttraining performance of each of the four skills are shown in Figure 12.1. Across all skills, mean baseline performance was stable. During baseline, the parents performed an average of 38% of the skill steps in the Relationship-Building

Figure 12.1

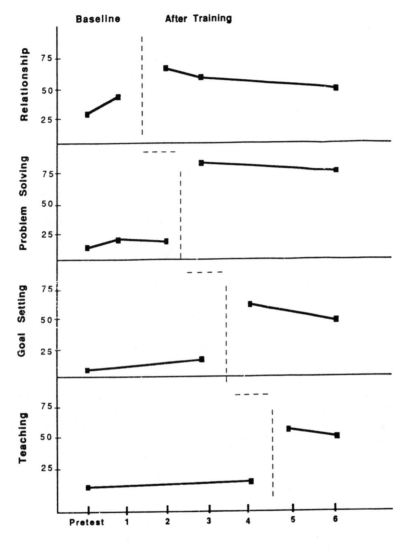

Skill. After training, they performed an average of 69% of the steps. For the Problem-Solving Skill, parents performed an average of 15% of the skill steps during baseline and 81% of the steps after training. For the Goal-Achievement Skill, the parents performed an average of 9% of the skill components during baseline. Their performance of this skill increased to an average of 59% after training. They performed an average of 6% of the components of the Teaching Skill during baseline and an average of 59% of the components after training.

Thus, overall, the participants made substantial gains with regard to their performance of the skills. These improvements in skill level only occurred after training was implemented. Several parents mastered each skill above the 75% level (an arbitrarily chosen criterion for mastery); however, for the majority of the group, mastery was not attained. For example, only 25% of the trainees attained mastery on the Relationship-Building Skill and the Goal-Achievement Skill, and 38% of the parents mastered the Teaching Skill. The parents' performance scores on the Problem-Solving Skill were higher; 75% of the parents met mastery on this skill.

Although the percentage of parents mastering each skill appears small, there were significant changes in the parents' behavior as a group. Before training, in role-play situations with the trainer, the "typical" parent in the group conversed with his or her "child" by asking a series of "yes/no" questions and by dominating the conversation with advice or a lecture. The parent sometimes used a harsh voice tone or derogatory name for the child, usually guessed at the cause of the child's problems, chose solutions to the problems with little input from the child, and often expounded on how well he or she was able to deal with a similar problematic situation when he or she was the youth's age. After training, the "typical" parent greeted his or her child by name or an affectionate nickname; asked open-ended questions; listened attentively; responded to the child nonjudgmentally; made statements of empathy, praise, caring, or encouragement; and ended the conversation pleasantly. Also after training, the parent was more likely to facilitate the child's identification and solution of problems, help the child identify and choose goals, and develop a realistic time frame for completing tasks to reach these goals. The parent often offered his or her assistance to the child, took time to teach skills, and set up specific times to discuss outcomes of previous conversations. After training, the typical parent made more statements showing that he or she cared about the child.

All of the parents reported that the use of the learned skills had enabled them to help their children. For example, one couple reported the successful use of the Teaching Skill with their 13-year-old son. The family had moved recently from Chicago, and their son, Jeff, was having difficulty adjusting to 7th grade in the new community. He had told his parents that it was very hard for him to talk to kids in his classes. He reported that, in one of his classes, he had heard some girls call him "stuck-up." Jeff's parents decided that he needed to learn to talk to peers. Using the Teaching Skill, they worked with Jeff at home on the skills needed to initiate and maintain a conversation. They helped Jeff to understand the importance of the skill, provided models of the skill, and practiced the skill in role-play situations. They gave him encouragement and feedback on his practice efforts. He made a commitment to try the skills at school at least once a day for a month. Each day, he would select possible situations at school where he could use the skill and then he attempted to initiate and maintain a conversation. Together, he and his parents monitored his progress. Every night after dinner, he discussed his conversation attempts with one or both parents. Quickly, he became skillful at critiquing his own performances. By the end of the month, he reported that he was talking to a number of students every day. He reported that he now believed that he could make new friends and was feeling happier.

In addition to parents noticing changes in their children's behavior, the children reported changes in their parents' behavior when they were asked to complete a consumer satisfaction questionnaire about the changes they noticed in ways their parents were behaving or in routines around the house. Sixty percent of the youths reported that there were positive changes in the way their parents helped them with homework. One youth mentioned that his father had changed because " . . . now he makes me study harder." With regard to the changes that youths liked best, their comments included: "[I liked] learning how to set goals," "They [parents] are not as strict, and they are more trusting," "Dad controls his temper," "Mom does goal setting, step-by-step, and talks more," and "Mom doesn't rush through home-work—I do it by myself, but she sits and makes sure I do it right." Only one youth commented that he did not like the changes that had been made in his family. His comment was, "They don't give me answers to homework anymore." When asked whether the Families Program had been useful for their family, 100% of the youths reported that it was useful. The youths made comments such as, "It [the program] helps with communication," "They [parents] trust me more," "We get along better and get more help from our parents," "Dad talks more," and "My grades have risen."

The results of the parent consumer satisfaction questionnaire were also positive. Overall, parents reported that the training was beneficial to them and their families. On a 7-point Likert-type scale (with 7 being completely satisfied and 1 being completely dissatisfied), parents were very satisfied with the usefulness of the program (mean = 6.6), instructional methods (mean = 6.4), clarity of information presented (mean = 6.4), professionalism of trainers (mean = 6.9), opportunities to ask questions (mean = 6.3), opportunities to get questions answered completely (mean = 6.6), the training environment (mean = 7.0), and the training materials (mean = 7.0). The only areas that were rated in the "slightly satisfied" range were the organization of the workshop (mean = 5.7) and the amount of time spent for training (mean = 5.7). For both of these areas, parents indicated that they wanted a longer training program. General positive comments made by parents regarding the program included: "The best thing about the training was coming to a better understanding of my kids and what they're going through with this disability," "The training really helped me as a person to relate with others better, not just my child," "The problem solving and skill teaching have helped more than anything, but the relationship building was also very valuable," and "The most valuable thing about the training was learning how to help my child learn different skills academically and socially." Negative comments focused on the short nature of the training and the role-play activities. The negative comments were: "Not enough time," "Would have liked more sessions," "Role plays were not my thing," and "More feedback needed during role plays."

Conclusion

The data gathered during the Field Test Phase have been useful in the identification of areas in which the Families Program is effective and where refinement is needed. The content delivered and the training methods used during the workshop sessions seem to be appropriate for and accepted by parents. Parents attended the workshops regularly with few absences. They indicated that they wanted more training sessions, probably because they felt they had not mastered the skills and because they wanted additional support. Refinements or revisions seem to be needed in several areas. First, the skills taught in the current program, although described as useful by the parents, contained many steps and appeared to be difficult to learn. Future revisions of the program will include skills that have been simplified and for which mnemonic devices have been developed to facilitate parent acquisition. Second, in the initial field test, several staff members were involved as instructors, especially during role-play activities. Such staff ratios will not be practical in most training situations across the nation. Thus, in future field tests, skilled parent graduates of the program may serve as instructors, co-leading groups with each other or with school professionals. Additionally, methods of conducting role-play practice with fewer staff members will be explored. Third, parents appear to need some form of ongoing support to continue the use of their newly acquired skills. Support groups for parents may be implemented for those who have completed the program. Other forms of support (e.g., individualized planning sessions for families) will also be explored. Finally, measures of childrens' and parents' interactions in the home need to be collected to determine the extent of generalized use of the skills by the parents. If generalized use of the skills is not apparent, methods for promoting generalization must be developed.

Refinements in the program have been made to address each of these concerns, and additional field tests are currently underway. These changes should enhance the effectiveness of the program in meeting the needs of families with children with learning disabilities who are faced with many challenges. The Families Program was designed to help families meet these challenges. Built on a foundation of information gathered from parents and the existing research literature, the program includes instruction on parenting skills related to developing strong relationships with children, teaching new skills to children and problem solving, and setting and attaining goals with children. All of the skills are taught in the context of a partnership between the parents and their children so that parents can enlist their children's personal involvement in effectively coping with the many problems and difficulties that confront them. Only by working collaboratively with families in the development, implementation, and evaluation of programs can effective strategies be developed to improve the happiness and success of families. Such an approach utilizes the talent and knowledge that exist within families to help them grow and develop.

References

Amerikaner, M., & Omizo, M. (1984). Family interaction and learning disabilities. *Journal of Learning Disabilities, 11,* 540–543.

Anderson, L. E. (1970). *Helping the adolescent with the hidden handicap.* Belmont, CA: Fearon/Laer Siegler.

Berman, A. (1979). Parenting learning-disabled children. *Journal of Clinical Child Psychology, 8*(3), 245–249.

Blacher-Dixon, J. (1981). Socialization influences on preschool handicapped children. In B. K. Keogh (Ed.), *Advances in special education.* Greenwich, CT: JAI Press.

Bryan, T. H., & Bryan, J. H. (1981). Some personal and social experiences of learning disabled children. In B. K. Keogh (Ed.), *Advances in special education.* Greenwich, CT: JAI Press.

Caplan, P. J. (1976). Helping parents help their children. *Bulletin of the Orton Society, 26,* 108–123.

Chapman, J. W., & Boersma, F. J. (1979). Learning disabilities, loss of control, and mother attitudes. *Journal of Educational Psychology, 71*(2), 250–258.

Deshler, D. D., Alley, G. R., Warner, M. M., & Schumaker, J. B. (1981). Instructional practices for promoting skill acquisition and generalization in severely learning disabled adolescents. *Learning Disabilities Quarterly, 4*(4), 415–421.

Dinkmeyer, D., & McKay, G. D. (1976). *Systematic Training for Effective Parenting (STEP).* Circle Pines, MN: American Guidance Service.

Doleys, D., Cartelli, L., & Doster, J. (1976). Comparison of patterns of mother-child interaction. *Journal of Learning Disabilities, 14,* 420–423.

Giannotti, T. J., & Doyle, R. R. (1982). The effectiveness of parental training on learning disabled children and their parents. *Elementary School Guidance and Counseling, 17,* 131–134.

Goldfarb, L. A., Brotherson, M. J., Summers, J. A., & Turnbull, A. P. (1986). *Meeting the challenge of disability or chronic illness: A family guide.* Hillsdale, NJ: Lawrence Erlbaum.

Hazel, J. S., Schumaker, J. B., Sherman, J. A., & Sheldon-Wildgen, J. (1982). Application of a group training program in social skills and problem-solving to learning disabled and non-learning disabled adolescents. *Learning Disability Quarterly, 5,* 398–408.

Kaslow, F. W., & Cooper, B. (1978). Family therapy with the learning disabled child and his/her family. *Journal of Marriage and Family Counseling, 4*(1), 41–49.

Kozloff, M. A. (1979). *A program for families of children with learning and behavior problems.* New York: Wiley.

Kronick, D. (1976). *Three families: The effect of family dynamics on social and conceptual learning.* San Rafael: Academic Therapy Publications.

Kroth, R., & Otteni, H. (1983). Parent education programs that work: A model. *Focus on Exceptional Children, 15*(8), 1–16.

Margalit, M. (1982). Learning disabled children and their families: Strategies of extension and adaption of family therapy. *Journal of Learning Disabilities, 15,* 594–595.

Meier, J. H. (1976). *Developmental and learning disabilities: Evaluation, management, and prevention in children.* Baltimore: University Park Press.

Murphy, M. (1982). The family with a handicapped child: A review of the literature. *Developmental and Behavioral Pediatrics, 3*(2), 73–82.

Osman, B. (1982). *No one to play with: The social side of learning disabilities.* New York: Random House.

Owen, F. W., Adams, A. A., Forrest, T. F., Stolz, L. M., & Fisher, S. (1971). Learning disorders in children: Sibling studies. *Monographs of the Society for Research in Child Development, 36*(Serial no. 144).

Patterson, G., & Forgatch, M. (1987). *Parent and adolescents living together.* Eugene, OR: Castalia.

Pfeiffer, S. I., Gerber, P. J., & Reiff, H. B. (1985). Family-oriented intervention with the learning disabled child. *Journal of Reading, Writing, and Learning Disabilities International, 1*(4), 63–69.

Philage, M., & Kuna, D. (1975). The therapeutic contract and LD families. *Academic Therapy, 10,* 407–411.

Rappaport, L. (1965). The state of crisis: Theoretical considerations. In H. Parad (Ed.), *Crisis intervention: Selected readings* (pp. 22–31). New York: Family Service Association of America.

Roth, L., & Weller, C. (1985). Education/counseling models for parents of learning disabled children. *Academic Therapy, 20*(4), 487–495.

Schumaker, J. B., Deshler, D. D., Alley, G. R., Warner, M. M., Clark, F. L., & Nolan, S. (1982). Error monitoring: A learning strategy for improving adolescents' academic performance. In W. M. Cruickshank & J. W. Lerner (Eds.), *Best of ACLD, Vol. 3* (pp. 170–183). New York: Syracuse University Press.

Schumaker, J. B., Deshler, D. D., Denton, P. H., Alley, G. R., Clark, F. L., & Warner, M. M. (1982). Multipass: A learning strategy for improving reading comprehension. *Learning Disability Quarterly, 5,* 295–304.

Schumaker, J. B., Hazel, J. S., Sherman, J. A., & Sheldon, J. (1982). Social skills performances of learning disabled, non-learning disabled, and delinquent adolescents. *Learning Disability Quarterly, 5,* 388–397.

Seabaugh, G. O., & Schumaker, J. B. (1981). *The effect of self-regulation training on the academic productivity of LD and NLD adolescents.* (Research Report #37). Lawrence, KS: University of Kansas Institute for Research in Learning Disabilities.

Siegel, E. (1974). *The exceptional child grows up.* New York: Dutton.

Silver, L. (1974). Emotional and social problems of a family with a child who has developmental disabilities. In R. E. Weber (Ed.), *Handbook on learning disabilities: A prognosis for the child, the adolescent, the adult.* Englewood Cliffs, NJ: Prentice Hall.

Silver, L. (1983). Therapeutic interventions with learning disabled students and their families. *Topics in Learning and Learning Disabilities, 3*(2), 48–58.

Turnbull, A. P., & Turnbull, H. R. (1986). *Families, professionals, and exceptionality: A special partnership.* Columbus, OH: Merrill.

Vigilante, F. W. (1983). Working with families of learning disabled children. *Child Welfare, 62*(5), 429–436.

Willner, S., & Crane, R. (1979). A parental dilemma: The child with a marginal handicap. *Social Casework: The Journal of Contemporary Social Work, 1,* 30–35.

13

PARENTS AND FAMILIES OF CHILDREN WITH AUTISM

Richard L. Simpson and Jo Webber

Autism and Its Characteristics

Living with an autistic child is difficult. Although children with autism may demonstrate characteristics found in other disabled children, the combination and severity of their behavioral and communication deficits often prevent any semblance of a typical parent–child relationship. These characteristics, as first described in 1943 by Leo Kanner, include:

1. inability to relate to others in an ordinary manner;
2. extreme autistic aloneness that seemingly isolates the child from the outside world;
3. resistance to being picked up or held by parents;
4. language deficits, including mutism and echolalia;
5. in some cases, an excellent rote memory;
6. early specific food preferences;
7. extreme fear of loud noises;
8. obsessive desire for repetition and sameness;
9. few spontaneous activities such as typical play behavior;
10. bizarre and repetitive physical movements, such as spinning or rocking;
11. normal physical appearance.

Others have condensed and reworked the definition of autism (Creak, 1961; Ritvo & Freeman, 1981; Wing, 1972); however, Kanner's original case study is still regarded as descriptive. Thus, it is generally accepted that autistic children show some combination of the following:

1. inability to relate to other people, including an absence of social smiling, an apparent preference for interaction with objects rather than people, and failure to show distress when a parent leaves the room;
2. language deficits, including mutism, echolalia, noncommunicative speech, pronoun reversals, and immature grammar;
3. sensory impairment characterized by over- or underresponding to noise, touch, and visual stimuli;
4. abnormal affect, including extreme or no fear reactions, tantrums, and uncontrolled giggling and crying;
5. self-stimulation, including spinning self and objects, repetitive hand movements, rocking, humming, etc;
6. inappropriate play, including self-stimulation;
7. extreme resistance to environmental changes, food, everyday schedule, familiar routes, etc. (Koegel, Rincover, & Egel, 1982).

Furthermore, children with autism show abnormalities from an early age, most are mentally retarded, and some acquire epilepsy in adolescence.

In addition to listing characteristics, Kanner (1943) speculated that the cause for these children's disturbance may stem from the fact that the parents "were strongly preoccupied with abstractions of a scientific, literary, or artistic nature, and limited in genuine interest in people" (p. 250). Thus, the parents of the original 11 autistic children seen by Kanner were intelligent, achieving, seemingly "cold," and of upper socioeconomic status (Wing, 1972). Others have supported this notion of parent responsibility, including Bettelheim (1950), who went so far as to advocate "parentectomy," that is, institutionalizing children with autism so that parents could be replaced with institutional staff and professionals considered more caring and competent. Due to these early views of autism and its causes, parents not only had to live with a very difficult child, they were also blamed for causing the disorder.

It is currently accepted that parents are not the cause of their child's autism. Many children come from neglectful environments, yet show no autistic characteristics. Furthermore, parents of autistic children do not fit a particular pattern in terms of SES, personality type, or profession (Rimland, 1964). Rather, evidence seems to point to neurological dysfunction as the cause of autism (Blackstock, 1978; Damasio & Maurer, 1978; Hier, LeMay, & Rosenberber, 1979; Ritvo & Freeman, 1978; Rutter, 1970), a disorder that affects about 4.5 people in 10,000 (Lotter, 1966; Wing, 1981).

The parents of an autistic child face many difficult practical and emotional problems (Wing, 1972). Emotionally, they may contend with the guilt that often accompanies the birth of a handicapped child and the placement of their child in a residential facility. Even with evidence to the contrary, many parents believe that somehow they are responsible for their child's disorder. Thwarted expectations arise as parents and family members see nondisabled children achieve childhood and adolescent milestones. A child's dependency may cause parents and family members to worry about what will happen to the member with autism subsequent to parental death. Will he or she be able to live independently and be employed? Will other children in the family be responsible for the handicapped child? Is an institution the only answer?

Due to retardation in cognitive development, prolonged infant and toddler stages create practical problems related to teaching self-help functions, dealing with general health factors, and managing difficult behavior. Historically, few services (e.g., preschool, day care, respite services, health care, leisure-time options) have been available to children with autism because these youngsters typically have little functional communication and may be difficult to manage. As a result, social activities for the family may be severely curtailed, and financial burdens may be great.

Because children with autism typically appear normal, the general public may not realize a child with autism is handicapped and may blame parents when the child publicly displays aggressive and bizarre behavior. Additionally, parents and family members, perhaps seeing some precocity in memory, artistic tendencies, or mathematical skills, may hold unrealistic expectations for their child and, therefore, will continue to be disappointed or blame themselves for a child's lack of progress. An autistic child typically shows little affection, in fact appears aloof, so that parents are infrequently reinforced by their children.

Finally, autism is a rare disorder, and support systems of people who understand the syndrome are not readily available. For all these reasons, parents of autistic children often must deal with their difficult child virtually alone, leading to great stress and strain.

Effects of Autism on Parents and Families

Children with autism present unique and significant challenges to parents and families. The multiple and severe disabilities of these children are such that families with autistic members typically present a variety of needs requiring support and understanding. Accordingly, collaborative involvement between professionals and families, as well as mutual support, is essential.

The underpinnings of effective professional, parent, and family member collaboration include trust, understanding, confidence, and a willingness to allow the other party to develop a meaningful partnership. Additionally, awareness of the impact of autism on parents and families is significant. According to Buscaglia (1975), "a disability is not a desirable thing and there is no reason to believe otherwise. It will, in most cases, cause pain, discomfort, embarrassment, tears, confusion and the expenditure of a great deal of time and money" (p. 11). Thus, almost without exception, parents of handicapped children have reported difficulties directly associated with their children's condition (Fewell, 1986; Turnbull & Turnbull, 1978). Gorham (1975) identified a variety of problems and obstacles she and her family experienced when adjusting to and attempting to accommodate her handicapped child. Thus it was only after "accumulating some scars which clearly mark us as parents as members of the 'lost generation' " (p. 522) that they were able to survive the ordeal. It should come as no surprise, then, that the presence of a child with autism often poses significant challenges for parents and families (Breslau, Staruch, & Mortimer, 1982; Wright, Matlock, & Matlock, 1985). In this regard, Handleman and Harris (1986) pointed to several major transitional issues parents and families with handicapped children, including those with autism, experience across the life span. These issues, from the time of the parents' marriage until their offspring's adulthood, are shown in Table 13.1.

From a family systems perspective (Fiedler, 1986; Turnbull, Summers, & Brotherson, 1984), an autistic child affects and in turn is affected by the family's structure, interactions, functions, and life cycles. An understanding of these variables will assist professionals in assessing the impact of a child with autism on a family, and subsequently in identifying and implementing appropriate support and strategies.

Within a family systems model, *family structure* refers to various familial elements, including socioeconomic status (e.g., the family may be required to spend limited resources for medical and therapeutic services for their autistic child), cultural background, composition (e.g., single-parent families can be easily overwhelmed by the demands of an autistic child), human and nonhuman resources (e.g., respite services and peer support are often unavailable to parents of autistic children), attitudes, and values. Children with autism may have a significant impact on (as well as be impacted by) their family structure in instances where they consume an inequitable share of resources and when a family's structure fails to match the needs of an autistic child. Additionally, coping strategies and styles may influence the degree to which families are able to accommodate children with autism effectively as well as influence their behavior and development.

Family interactions refer to family members' relationships, including marital, sibling, parental, and extrafamilial relationships. According to Olson, Russell, and Sprenkle (1980), interactions within these subsystems are based on cohesion—the force by which family members are held together (i.e., family members may be overly involved or more or less disengaged from an autistic family member); adaptability (i.e., a family's ability to respond to circumstances associated with accommodating a child with autism); and communication (i.e., family members' ability to send and receive clear messages, provide feedback, reveal their needs and feelings). A child with autism poses significant demands and thereby places great stress on the family's capacity to function effectively (Zionts & Simpson, 1988). However, family members' ability to engage in positive and effective interactions bodes well for their capacity to accommodate children with autism effectively.

Table 13.1
Families of the Developmentally Disabled—Transitional Challenges

Phase	Normative	Added or Different
Marriage	Adaptation to spouse's routines, values, etc. Development of negotiation skills Separation from family of origin Pursuit of vocational goals	None
Birth and infancy	Adjustment of routine to include child Adaptation to changes in marital relationship Negotiation on philosophy of child care with spouse Negotiation on extended family involvement with child	Acceptance of diagnosis Meeting medical needs Resolving issues of blame, anger Dealing with sorrow
Kindergarten	Child's increased independence Separation between parent and child Increased influence of other people	Continued dependence Acceptance of special school placement Use of special child management methods
School years	Growing independence Personal development of parents Development of sibling relationships	Continued dependence Constraints on parents' growth Extra burdens on siblings Growing gap with peers
Adolescence	Intensive separation, individuation struggle Increased marital stress Need of aging grandparents for attention from parents	Continued dependence, must encourage separation Increase in emotional and physical fatigue
Adulthood	Child's transition to own nuclear family Renewal of marital relationship Acceptance of life achievements Illness of self or spouse Death of spouse	Continued dependence Renewal of marriage more difficult Risk of burnout Need to plan for child's care after parents' death

Note. From *Educating the Developmentally Disabled: Meeting the Needs of Children and Families* (pp. 154, 159, 161) by J. S. Handleman and S. L. Harris, 1986, San Diego: College-Hill Press. Copyright 1986 by College-Hill Press. Reprinted by permission.

Family functions are the various unique need areas families must consider: economic, educational, vocational, physical, rest/recuperative, affection, socialization, self-definition, and guidance. Each of these functions is significant, and only by responding to each can families function optimally. Thus, overemphasis on any individual function (e.g., excessive emphasis on home training for a child with autism) may decrease the family's capacity to respond effectively to other equally important needs. It should come as no surprise that the autistic child's unique and demanding nature frequently strains the family's ability to maintain a balance of functions.

The *family life cycle* refers to the sequence of developmental and non-developmental changes all families experience. Goldenberg and Goldenberg (1980) described the cycle as "successive patterns within the continuity of family living over the years of its existence—with members aging and passing through a succession of family roles" (p. 14). Families of children with autism can be expected to experience disruptions in this typical cycle (Fewell, 1986). For example, autistic family members will rarely achieve the social and economic independence of nondisabled members, and may increase family stress by failing to progress in a manner typical of others. Attempts to compensate for family cycle delays and disruptions, including institutionalization, and factors associated with the ability of the family to care for members with autism over the life cycle (e.g., death, infirmity of parents) may also increase stress and erode a family's functioning capacity.

Although children with autism will inevitably have a significant effect on their families (Kozloff, 1975; Simpson & Regan, 1986), the nature and extent of this influence can be guided by awareness and sensitivity to family issues on the part of the professionals who come into contact with the autistic child and his or her family.

Meeting the Needs of Parents and Families of Children with Autism

A basic and dominant need among parents and families of children with autism is to secure appropriate direct services for family members with autism. The significance of other parent and family needs cannot be underestimated; however, in most instances these are secondary to finding suitable educational, residential, and treatment programs. Thus, a number of parents have observed that until they identified an appropriate school or program for their disabled child they were unable to consider other needs (Simpson, 1982). The need for and importance of direct service resources for children with autism are often overlooked when considering parent and family needs; however, this basic need will typically override all other parent and family considerations.

Levels of Parent/Family Participation

Except for identifying appropriate direct services, needs of parents and families of children with autism are heterogeneous. Thus, several authors have presented strong arguments for individualized parent and family service and support programs (Fiedler, 1986; Kroth, 1985; Simpson & Fiedler, 1989). In accordance with the emphasis on individualization, professionals must permit parents and families to choose the degree and type of involvement that is commensurate with their personal needs and preferences. Involvement may take place at one of five levels: awareness, open communication, advocacy and participation, problem solving and procedural application, and partnership. At any given time, parents and families may be at more than one level of involvement (e.g., parents may demonstrate a desire for both open communication, and advocacy and participation). Additionally, involvement levels may vary across time (e.g., a family may move from awareness to partnership).

Among the five levels of parental involvement, *awareness* is a parent/family baseline condition. Parents and families choosing this level of involvement should receive information about autism, including its characteristics and patterns; school-related procedures and strategies employed with students with autism; and resources (e.g., counseling, respite care) available to the child and family. Awareness implies a low level of parent and family involvement; however, it nonetheless requires that professionals apprise parents and families of basic facts pertaining to children with autism and parent/family services and programs.

Open communication refers to a level of involvement characterized by effective information sharing and communication between parents, family members, and professionals. This stage should be the desired participation level for all parents and families (i.e., in spite of other involvement, all parents and families should engage in ongoing communication with professionals).

Advocacy and participation involvement characterizes parents and family members who desire to be involved actively in promoting services and programs for their children. Examples of such participation include membership on autism advocacy boards and agencies; volunteer service to organizations serving children and youth with autism; and participation in training programs for parents and families wishing to be involved actively in making educational and treatment decisions (e.g., selecting IEP goals and objectives).

Problem solving and procedural application is an option for parents and families who are able and motivated to implement programs and procedures for autistic individuals in natural environments. Examples of this level of engagement include application of management programs in home settings, home-based tutoring programs, and training program implementation (e.g., toileting and eating programs).

Partnership refers to parent/family involvement wherein families participate on an equal basis with professionals in identifying, implementing, and evaluating programs for children and youth with autism. At this level of involvement, parents may independently identify goals and objectives for their child; develop training procedures for achieving the goal, and evaluate generalization of the skill in other settings.

In most instances, increased parent and family involvement and participation does not necessarily mean "better involvement." For example, parents who choose to participate at an open communication level may function more effectively and thus better satisfy family needs than parents who participate at a partnership level. Accordingly, professionals must accommodate various levels of parent and family involvement. To this end, individualizing parent and family participation is the first step to satisfying parent and family needs.

Parent and Family Programs

Families and parents have varied and inconstant needs subsequent to direct education and treatment services for children with autism. They need information, knowledge and skills to deal with their child and they need support from outside the family to assist with coping and problem solving. Programs and services that address these needs can generally be classified into five categories: (a) information sharing; (b) partnership and consumer-advocacy training; (c) natural environment training programs; (d) counseling, therapy, and support services; and (e) school and community participation programs. An understanding of these elements by parents and family members, and the professionals with whom they interact, will assist in identifying and satisfying specific family needs.

Information sharing is an essential, underlying component of effective professional services. Nearly all parents and families of children with autism want and need information about autism, such as definitions (e.g., *autism, autistic-like, pervasive developmental disorder*), prevalence, characteristics of the syndrome, etiology, and prognosis. Additionally, many want to discuss why professionals have such difficulty in agreeing on the precise nature and course of autism.

Professionals must also disseminate and discuss with parents and family members any findings and recommendations that relate to individual children, including diagnostic information (e.g., cognitive abilities, speech and language skills and deficits, behavioral and social strengths and weaknesses, educational and vocational abilities, neurological deficits). Most parents and family members also wish to discuss and possibly observe educational, vocational, and treatment programs recommended or being considered for their children. Specifically, educational programs should be discussed (and demonstrated) in terms of their philosophy, opportunities for integration with nonhandicapped children, manage-ment procedures, curricula, ancillary services and support programs (e.g., OT, speech), and evaluation methods. Special attention must be directed to the unique nature of programs for children with autism even with parents who may be knowledgeable of educational and treatment methods for other types of disabled children.

Beyond the basics discussed above, ongoing and informational information exchange is a basic element of a collaborative relationship between parents and professionals. This collaboration can keep parents involved with their child's development and provide a source of comfort to families. Thus, professionals must regularly discuss with parents and family members any progress and program changes.

A collaborative partnership is two-sided—it also requires that parents share appropriate information with professionals. Such information should include family history, parent expectations, school history, and regular updates on significant developments occurring outside school.

Their specific information needs vary from family to family. For instance, some parents may be concerned about guardianship and legal issues affecting their autistic child. Thus, professionals must be able to provide assistance in these areas, relying, for example, on information such as that provided by Apolloni (1984) and Frolik (1983). Similarly, parents may require information on how to obtain medical and dental services for children with autism, because some practitioners are either unprepared or unwilling to accept as patients children who have autism.

Partnership and consumer-advocacy training refers to training parents and family members to advocate more effectively for their autistic children and to be more efficient participants and consumers of educational and professional services. The Education for All Handicapped Children Act (P.L. 94-142) ensures parental involvement in educational planning, decision making, and implementation; however, parents receive few training opportunities to enable them to carry out these functions. Only a small percentage of parents may actually request advocacy and participation training; however, this does not necessarily mean an absence of interest or need. Rather, they may be unaware that such training is appropriate or available. Hence it is the professional's responsibility to remind them of their rights and be prepared to offer the necessary services.

Training within the partnership and consumer-advocacy domain may include: (a) information about school and community resources (e.g., mental health services, medical care programs); (b) workshops and other training programs regarding parents' rights and responsibilities, particularly as related to the Educa-tion for All Handicapped Children Act; (c) training programs and information that addresses participation in Individualized Education Program (IEP) conferences; and (d) techniques of information sharing and professional–parent conferencing. Not every parent and family member will require or want training in this area;

however, a collaborative partnership between families and professionals is facilitated when such training opportunities are made available.

Natural environment training programs include opportunities for parents and other family members to acquire behavior management, tutoring, and program implementation skills appropriate for use with autistic children in home and community settings. The extensive needs of children with autism and the proven effectiveness of parents and family members as change agents in natural environments (Atkeson & Forehand, 1978; Simpson & Swenson, 1980) make training in this domain logical for parents and families wishing involvement at the problem solving and procedural application level.

Most behaviorally based parent training programs proceed from the assumption that autistic children's school progress is enhanced when parents are trained to use behavior therapy. Behavior therapy has clearly been found to be effective in the treatment of children with autism (Donnellan, 1980; Lovaas, 1977; Lovaas & Newsome, 1976; Risley, 1968; Schreibman & Koegel, 1981). Moreover, research has shown that parents are potentially effective behavioral intervention agents (Freeman & Ritvo, 1976; Koegel, Egel, & Dunlap, 1980; Koegel & Rincover, 1974; Kozloff, 1975; Schopler & Reichler, 1971; Wing, 1972). In a study of the maintenance effects of behavioral training with autistic children, Lovaas and Koegel (1973) concluded that clinic treatment without parent training failed to promote lasting gains.

Koegel, Schreibman, Britten, Burke, and O'Neill (1987) conducted a comprehensive study of the effects of behavioral training with autistic children. One group of children received treatment from clinicians without family involvement, while the second group was trained exclusively by their parents, who had previously been trained to use behavioral techniques. The authors measured treatment effects on the children as well as effects on the family. Results showed more initial improvement in the children and more durable treatment gains as a result of 25 to 50 hours of parent training than 225 hours of clinic training. In addition, the parent training group resulted in significant increases in the frequency of recreational/leisure activities. Finally, psychological and marital adjustment measures did not indicate abnormality in either group, implying that parent training did not adversely affect family dynamics.

A variety of behaviorally based parent training programs have been developed for use with disabled children, including those with autism. Table 13.2 lists several such programs and their major elements.

Even though some parents and family members of children with autism will not make use of them, *counseling, therapy, and support programs* should be available. Specifically, these programs may offer (a) support groups for parents, siblings, and family members, including those sponsored by the Autism Society of America; (b) individual and group therapy resources; (c) crisis intervention services; and (d)

Table 13.2
Parent Training Programs and Major Components

Program title	Components	Reference
Responsive Parenting	• applied behavioral analysis • 8 two-hour weekly meetings • uses role playing • requires certified group leaders	Hall, 1981
Winning!	• parents of 3 to 12 yr.-olds • basic behavioral techniques • training modules include written material and videotapes • movement based on mastery of previous skill • uses role plays and homework • deductive approach	Dangel & Polster, 1984
CBTU Program	• goal setting, differential attention, positive reinforcement, precision requests, problem solving • 6- to 8-week two-hour sessions • written material, role plays, modeling, home projects • problem-solving booster sessions	Jensen, 1985
RETEACH	• 10-week, data-based training • behavior modification & language training • specific lesson design format • homework, pretest, posttest • ongoing consultation	Handleman & Harris, 1986
TEACHING MAKES A DIFFERENCE	• behavior management techniques • information sharing • 6- to 8-week two-hour sessions • related to individual needs • home intervention programs • encourages parent volunteers in classroom	Donnellan-Walsh et al., 1977

counseling and support programs, including respite care. Parents of children with autism are no longer viewed as the cause of their children's disability, thus they do not necessarily require therapy. Such an exoneration, however, does not imply that many parents will not experience stress, depression, and other emotional responses directly associated with living day to day with an autistic child. Hence, appropriate support resources should be made available.

The various services for families of autistic children may be delivered in several formats. For instance, Auerbach (1968) delineated group formats appropriate for aiding parents and families in meeting their informational, support, advocacy, and counseling needs: (a) formal academic training (to increase understanding of child development, family relations, advocacy techniques, legislation, research, etc.); (b) group dynamics (to facilitate individual growth and self-validation); (c) group counseling (to assist in problem solving); and (d) group psychotherapy (to remove "pathological blocks that stand in the way of the continuing acquisition of knowledge and understanding needed to enable the growth process to continue" [p. 37]). Auerbach noted that although teachers, psychologists, social workers, and psychiatrists could lead these groups, professional training should be matched with group objectives (e.g., use of psychologists or psychiatrists to conduct group psychotherapy sessions).

Additionally, Handleman and Harris (1986) described a consultation strategy for assisting parents and families deal with issues associated with having a disabled child. Their program (CONSULTED) does not focus on direct training but on how to facilitate family problem solving. The nine basic elements of the strategy are identified below.

1. Confer—assess what problems the family perceives and what kind of help they would like.
2. Observe—observe in the home or the community to document pertinent information about the perceived problem.
3. Name problems—define the problem in specific terms.
4. Set priorities—be sensitive to the needs of the parent; set priorities for solutions.
5. Utilize resources—analyze what resources are available (e.g., space, respite care, materials, time).
6. Label obstacles—analyze obstacles to success. For example, resistant family members, cognitive level of the child, lack of parental skills, emotional needs of parents may promote failure. Refer for additional services if necessary.
7. Try intervention—consultant steps aside so that family can proceed with own problem solution. Stay in touch for reinforcement and resources.
8. Evaluate outcome—once a week evaluate intervention progress with the parents.
9. Determine next step—continue intervention, modify the plan, or proceed to another perceived problem.

Two areas are particularly germane to this model of home consultation: language and adaptive behavior development for the handicapped child.

An additional area of family support may involve siblings. Any brothers and sisters of the autistic child, as part of the ecosystem, may require information, assurance, and other forms of emotional support (Berg, 1973; Grossman, 1972; Kaplan, 1969; Klein, 1972). These needs are intensified by the fact that parents often focus inordinate attention on handicapped children, sometimes ignoring the needs of the nonhandicapped siblings. When informed and aware of their role, nonhandicapped siblings can often facilitate growth and development of handicapped children by serving as positive role models and behavior-change agents (Colletti & Harris, 197; Schreibman, O'Neill, & Koegel, 1983).

Knoblock (1982) described a sibling support group working toward the goal of (a) increasing children's awareness of handicaps, (b) providing a forum for children to share experiences, (c) encouraging group problem solving, (d) imparting information about educating handicapped children, and (e) providing specific skill training. Several activities, including simulations, trust walks, communication through drawings, interviews, and information sharing over snacks, were used to facilitate involvement between autistic and nonhandicapped siblings.

Respite care may also be sought by many parents and families. These programs can take the form of in-home baby-sitting, center day care (after school and weekends), or placement of the autistic child in foster families, group homes, or institutions for 24 hours or longer. Respite care provides the family with time for social activities, vacations, or just a rest period away from a handicapped child (Joyce, Singer, & Isralowitz, 1983).

In response to a legislative recommendation that "families of autistic persons have significant need for support services, such as respite care, counseling, and training programs" (Joint Committee on Autism Report to the Texas Legislature, 1982, p. 4), the Texas Department of Mental Health and Mental Retardation provided funding for several pilot programs serving autistic children. One of these programs was developed by the Austin-Travis County Mental Health and Mental Retardation Center (ATCMHMR) to provide various forms of respite to families with autistic children in the area. The services included (a) after-school care, (b) Saturday programs, (c) in-home baby-sitting, (d) parent training, and (e) summer school. Participating mental health workers and teachers were trained in behavior modification techniques and consultation skills. Parents could participate in the services for the length of time they chose. A parent advisory board provided the project staff with feedback on family needs and program effectiveness. Community agencies such as the Austin Parks and Recreation Department and the Austin Community Schools provided additional recreational programming for the children.

To support these efforts further the local parent advocacy group (Capital Area—Autism Society of America) organized informal and formal activities for the families in conjunction with the ATCMHMR project. These activities provided training and support for families. Siblings were often included in the respite and recreational activities. In addition, parents formed a volunteer group to disseminate information about services for autistic adults. This group has also attempted to affect legislation pertaining to developmentally disabled adults in Texas. Only one of the 20 children participating in the program was subsequently placed in an institution, suggesting that respite care services can provide the time necessary for families to develop resources and to feel empowered to deal with their autistic child.

Parents and families of children with autism should also have the opportunity to serve the general needs of persons with autism and related disabilities through participation in *school and community participation programs*. Such opportunities may take the form of serving on advocacy and advisory boards; disseminating information about autism; advocating for autism-related legislation, services, and resources; serving as volunteers in classroom, agency, and/or other programs; or working as support and advocacy agents. Parents and family members with needs and interests in this area often work through and in conjunction with the Autism Society of America, a particularly effective and active organization.

Summary

Children with autism can be expected to present unique and significant challenges for parents and family members. The role of professionals who assist families in accommodating and adjusting to children with autism will be facilitated by (a) developing an individualized plan for various parent/family participation levels (awareness, open communication, advocacy and participation, problem solving and procedural application, and partnership) and (b) understanding potential parent/family needs. Assistance may be offered in the form of information sharing, partnership and consumer-advocacy training, natural environment training programs, counseling, therapy and support services, and school and community participation programs.

References

Apolloni, T. (1984). Who'll help my disabled child when I'm gone? *Academic Therapy, 20,* 109-114.

Atkeson, B., & Forehand, R. (1978). Parents as behavior change agents with school-related problems. *Education and Urban Society, 10,* 521-540.

Auerbach, A. B. (1968). *Parents learn through discussion: Principles and practices of parent group education.* New York: John Wiley.

Berg, K. (1973). Christina loves Katherine. *Exceptional Parent, 3*(1), 35-36.

Bettelheim, B. (1950). *Love is not enough.* Glencoe, NY: Free Press.

Blackstock, E. (1978). Cerebral asymmetry and the development of early infantile autism. *Journal of Autism and Childhood Schizophrenia, 8,* 339-353.

Breslau, N., Staruch, K., & Mortimer, E. (1982). Psychological distress in mothers of disabled children. *American Journal of Disabled Children, 136,* 682-686.

Buscaglia, L. (1975). *The disabled and their parents: A counseling challenge.* Thorofare, NJ: Slack.

Colletti, G., & Harris, S. L. (1977). Behavior modification in the home: Siblings as behavior modifiers, parents as observers. *Journal of Abnormal Child Psychology, 1,* 21-30.

Creak, M. (1961). Schizophrenic syndrome in childhood: Progress of a working party. *Cerebral Palsy Bulletin, 3,* 501-504.

Damasio, A., & Mauer, R. (1978). A neurological model for childhood autism. *Archives of Neurology, 35,* 777-786.

Dangel, R. F., & Polster, R. A. (1984). WINNING! A systematic, empirical approach to parent training. In R. F. Dangel & R. A. Polster (Eds.), *Parent training: Foundations of research and practice* (pp. 166-174). New York: Guilford Press.

Donnellan, A. M. (1981). An educational perspective on autism: Implications for curriculum development and personal development. In B. Welcor & A. Thompson (Eds.), *Critical issues in educating autistic children and youth* (pp. 53-88). Washington, DC: U.S. Dept. of Education, Department of Special Education.

Donnellan-Walsh, A., Gossage, L. D., LaVigna, G. W., Schuler, A., & Traphagen, J. D. (1977). *Teaching makes a difference: Teachers manual.* Santa Barbara, CA: Santa Barbara County Superintendent of Schools.

Fewell, R. (1986). A handicapped child in the family. In R. R. Fewell & P. F. Vadasy (Eds.), *Families of handicapped children* (pp. 3-34). Austin, TX: Pro-Ed.

Fiedler, C. R. (1986) Enhancing parent-school personnel partnerships. *Focus on Autistic Behavior, 1*(4), 1-8.

Freeman, B. J., & Ritvo, E. R. (1976). Parents as paraprofessionals. In E. R. Ritvo (Ed.), *Autism: Diagnosis, current research and management* (pp. 61-92). New York: Spectrum.

Frolik, L. A. (1983). Legal needs. In E. Schopler & G. B. Mesibov (Eds.), *Autism in adolescents and adults* (pp. 319-334). New York: Plenum Press.

Goldenberg, I., & Goldenberg, H. (1980). *Family therapy: An overview.* Monterey, CA: Brooks/Cole.

Gorham, K. A. (1975). A lost generation of parents. *Exceptional Children, 41*(8), 521-525.

Grossman, F. K. (1972). *Brothers and sisters of retarded children: An exploratory study.* Syracuse, NY: Syracuse University Press.

Hall, M. C. (1981). *Responsive parenting.* Shawnee Mission, KS: Responsive Management.

Handleman, J. S., & Harris, S. L. (1986). *Educating the developmentally disabled: Meeting the needs of children and families.* San Diego, CA: College-Hill Press.

Hier, D., LeMay, M., & Rosenberber, P. (1979). Autism and unfavorable left-right asymmetries of the brain. *Journal of Autism and Developmental Disorders, 9,* 153-159.

Jenson, W. R. (1980). *Children's behavior therapy unit's parenting group.* Unpublished manuscript, University of Utah, Salt Lake City, UT.

Jenson, W. R. (1985). Skills preference in two different types of parenting groups. *Small Group Behavior, 16,* 549-555.

Joint Committee on Autism Report to the Texas Legislature. (1982). *Autism: An intricate dilemma.* Austin, TX: Author.

Joyce, K., Singer, M., & Isralowitz, R. (1983). Impact of respite care on parents' perceptions of quality of life. *Mental Retardation, 21,* 153-156.

Kanner, L. (1943). Autistic disturbances of affective contact. *Nervous Child, 3,* 217-250.

Kaplan, F. (1969). Siblings of retarded. In S. B. Sarason & D. J. Sarason (Eds.), *Psychological problems in mental deficiency (4th ed.)* (pp. 186-208). New York: Harper & Row.

Klein, S. (1972). Brother to sister, sister to brother. *Exceptional Parent, 2*(1-3), 10-28.

Knoblock, P. (1982) *Teaching and mainstreaming autistic children.* Denver: Love.

Koegel, R. L., Egel, A. L., & Dunlap, G. (1980). Learning characteristics of autistic children. In W. S. Sailor, B. Wilcox, & L. J. Brown (Eds.), *Methods of instruction with severely handicapped students* (pp. 101-134). Baltimore: Brookes.

Koegel, R. L., & Rincover, A. (1974). Treatment of psychotic children in a classroom environment. Learning in a large group. *Journal of Applied Behavior Analysis, 7,* 45-59.

Koegel, R. L., Rincover, A., & Egel, A. L. (1982). *Educating and understanding autistic children.* Boston: College-Hill.

Koegel, R. L., Schreibman, L., Britten, K. R., Burke, J. C., & O'Neill, R. E. (1987). A comparison of parent training to direct child treatment. In R. L. Koegel, A. Rincover, & A. L. Egel (Eds.), *Educating and understanding autistic children* (pp. 260-280). Boston: College-Hill Press.

Kozloff, M. A. (1975). *Reaching the autistic child: A parent training program.* Champaign, IL: Research Press.

Kozloff, M. A. (1981). Systems of structured change: Changing families of severely deviant children. In J. E. Gilliam (Ed.), *Autism: Diagnosis, instruction, management, and research* (pp. 177-199). Springfield, IL: Charles C. Thomas.

Kroth, R. L. (1985). *Communicating with parents of exceptional children.* Denver: Love.

Lotter, V. (1966). Epidemiology of autistic conditions in young children. *Social Psychiatry, 1,* 124-137.

Lovaas, O. I. (1977). *The autistic child.* New York: Lovington.

Lovaas, O. I., & Doegel, R. L. (1973). *Behavior modification in education, NSSE Yearbook.* Chicago: University of Chicago Press.

Lovaas, O. I., & Newsome, C. D. (1976). Behavior modification with psychotic children. In H. Leitenberg (Ed.), *Handbook of behavior modification and behavior therapy* (pp. 160-184). Englewood Cliffs, NJ: Prentice-Hall.

Morgan, D. P., & Jenson, W. R. (1988). *Teaching behaviorally disordered students: Preferred practices.* Columbus, OH: Merrill.

Olson, D. H., Russell, C. S., & Sprenkle, D. (1980). Marital and family therapy: A decade review. *Journal of Marriage and the Family, 42*(4), 973-993.

Public Law 94-142, The Education of All Handicapped Children Act of 1975.

Rimland, B. P. (1964). *Infantile autism.* New York: Appleton-Century-Crofts.

Risley, T. R. (1968). The effects and side effects of punishing the autistic behaviors of a deviant child. *Journal of Applied Behavioral Analysis, 1,* 21-34.

Ritvo, E. J., & Freeman, B. J. (1978). National Society for Autistic Children definition of the syndrome of autism. *Journal of Autism and Childhood Schizophrenia, 8,* 162-167.

Ritvo, E. J., & Freeman, B. J. (1981). Definition of the syndrome of autism. In B. Wilcox & A. Thompson (Eds.), *Critical issues in educating autistic children and youth* (pp. 316-332). Washington, DC: National Society for Children and Adults with Autism.

Rutter, M. (1970). Autistic children: Infancy to childhood. *Seminars in Psychiatry, 2,* 435-450.

Schopler, E., & Reichler, R. J. (1971). Parents as co-therapists in the treatment of psychotic children. *Journal of Autism and Childhood Schizophrenia, 1,* 87-102.

Schreibman, L., & Koegel, R. L. (1981). A guideline for planning behavior modification programs for autistic children. In S. M. Turner, K. S. Calhoun, & H. E. Adams (Eds.), *Handbook of clinical behavior therapy* (pp. 54-73). New York: John Wiley and Sons.

Schreibman, L., O'Neill, R. E., & Koegel, R. L. (1983). Behavioral training for siblings of autistic children. *Journal of Applied Behavior Analysis, 16,* 129-138.

Simpson, R. L. (1982). *Conferencing parents of exceptional children.* Rockville, MD: Aspen.

Simpson, R. L., & Fiedler, C. R. (1989). Parental participation in individualized education program (IEP) conferences: A case for individualization. In M. Fine (Ed.), *The second handbook on parent education: Contemporary perspectives* (pp. 145-171). New York: Academic Press.

Simpson, R., & Regan, M. (1986). *Management of autistic behavior.* Rockville, MD: Aspen.

Simpson, R., & Swenson, R. (1980). The effects and side-effects of an overcorrection procedure applied by parents of severely emotionally disturbed children in a home environment. *Behavioral Disorders, 5*(2), 79-85.

Turnbull, A., Summers, J., & Brotherson, M. J. (1984). *Working with families with disabled members: A family systems approach.* Lawrence: University of Kansas, University Affiliated Facility.

Turnbull, A., & Turnbull, R. (1978). *The other side of the two-way mirror.* Columbus, OH: Merrill.

Wing, L. (1972). *Autistic children: A guide for parents and professionals.* New York: Brunner/Mazel.

Wing, L. (1981). Sex ratios in early childhood autism and related conditions. *Psychiatry Research, 5,* 129-137.

Wright, L. S., Matlock, K., & Matlock, D. (1985). Parents of handicapped children: Their self-ratings, life satisfaction and parental adequacy. *Exceptional Children, 32,* 37-40.

Zionts, P., & Simpson, R. (1988). *Understanding children and youth with emotional and behavioral problems.* Austin, TX: Pro-Ed.

14

THE FAMILY WITH A GIFTED CHILD

Reva C. Friedman (Jenkins)
and Thomas J. Gallagher

"Oh, to have a gifted child!" begins an advertisement for a newsletter oriented toward parents of bright youngsters, as if selling a "hot" product to prospective subscribers. "Somewhere to turn" proclaims another, offering sustenance through games, toys, activities, and advice for gifted children and their (seemingly) beleaguered parents.

The numbers of organizations, conferences, publications, and products aimed toward gifted children, their parents, and teachers have increased dramatically within just the past decade. These increases are very visible indicators of the widespread popularity of public policies designed to protect the rights of this special population. However, the explosion of publicity and publications does not offer clear diagnostic guidelines and intervention alternatives for meeting the needs of gifted children. If anything, more questions are raised than are answered. How should professionals in school settings support identified children? their unlabeled siblings? their parents?

Building an effective, collaborative relationship with parents of gifted children needs to be grounded in an understanding of the phenomenon of exceptional ability within social and familial contexts. Although gifted individuals have been noted throughout recorded history, systematic support and education in public schools are relatively recent developments, beginning in the early part of this century.

In this chapter, we integrate key research findings into a framework for understanding giftedness in a familial context. Issues particular to parents of gifted students are highlighted. Principles for encouraging more collaborative relationships are offered.

257

Understanding Exceptional Ability

Characteristics of Giftedness

Over the past 4,000 years, tremendous changes have occurred in the ways in which giftedness has been conceptualized, identified, and supported: from divinity to contiguous with ordinary behavior, from neurotic to normal, from inexplicable to highly understandable and quantifiable. Every new development in understanding and measuring intelligence has had a salutary effect on the field of gifted child education (Grinder, 1985).[1]

Despite these advances, it is not generally recognized that gifted youngsters can experience problems in school, simply as a result of possessing exceptional abilities. Characteristics associated with giftedness and creativity can be manifested in destructive as well as positive ways. For example, Seagoe (1974) points out that commonly accepted indicators of giftedness such as persistence can be manifested as stubbornness or rebelliousness, a high degree of retentiveness can result in acting out against routine and drill, and critical thinking ability can be interpreted as skepticism and negativity.

Building on this theme, Kaplan, Madsen, Gould, Platow, and Renzulli (1979) emphasize that high potential can be a disadvantage rather than an advantage. They add that one's expectations for a gifted child can act as an obstacle to interpreting the child's behavior as gifted. The writers conclude that giftedness can be "heaven" as well as "hell," and that effective diagnostic procedures are rooted in a thorough knowledge of the ways in which giftedness may be demonstrated.

Research on the impact of being labeled as gifted confirms that exceptional ability is not necessarily enviable. For example, several researchers have focused on self-perceptions of bright students. Janos, Fung, and Robinson (1985) found that gifted children who report feeling "different" from their average peers are more likely to manifest a diminished self-concept. In a series of studies, Coleman and Fults (1982, 1985) confirmed that gifted students experience significant drops in self-concept when receiving special education services. Jenkins-Friedman and Murphy (1988) discovered that maladjustment to gifted education services is reflected in unrealistic self-perceptions. Clearly, public acknowledgment of exceptional potential carries costs as well as benefits and thus might require services extending beyond the referral, assessment, and instructional planning process.

---

[1]For a more complete discussion of the history of the field, the reader is referred to *The Gifted and Talented: Developmental Perspectives* (Horowitz & O'Brien, 1985) and the *Seventy-eighth Yearbook of the National Society for the Study of Education* (Passow, 1979).

Features of "Gifted" Families

In study after study, the profile of typical "gifted" families is the epitome of a self-actualizing family system (Frey & Wendorf, 1985). Mutually supportive relationships, appropriate degrees of closeness, flexibility, and open expression of thoughts and feelings characterize the family with at least one child participating in a gifted education program (Cornell, 1983a, 1983b). This pattern is strongly associated with higher overall child adjustment, self-esteem, and academic self-concept, as well as fewer discipline, self-control, and anxiety issues (using data from child self-reports and teacher observations). When compared to families with no identified children, "gifted" families more highly value recreational, intellectual, and cultural pursuits, although not in the context of an achievement or competitive framework (Cornell & Grossberg, 1987).

These findings become important when comparing parental perceptions of their child as gifted to the child's personality adjustment. Positive labeling on the part of parents has been found to be associated with taking pride in the child's accomplishments, healthier child personality adjustment, better communication, and more intimacy in parent–child relationships, whether or not the child is formally identified (Cornell, 1983a; Cornell & Grossberg, 1988).

Issues Facing "Gifted" Families

The presence of a gifted child can also have an impact on the family in negative ways. For instance, making the gifted child the focal point of the family can lead to inappropriate comparisons among siblings (Peterson, 1977).

Because bright children often act and sound like adults, parents can find themselves blurring role distinctions. For example, in the recent case histories of 120 young eminent persons (Bloom, 1985) and case studies of six prodigies (Feldman & Goldsmith, 1986), the researchers note that these extraordinarily bright children were often called on to act as adults regarding decisions affecting their talent development. They regularly engaged in "adult" activities such as setting performance standards, deciding to move away from home at young ages to pursue advanced training, evaluating the quality of their instruction—even choosing their teachers. Some "spillover" to family interactions is natural, but can lead to an imbalance of power in the family, particularly when there is only one labeled child. Cornell (1983b) found a tendency among the latter families for parents to relinquish control of family interactions, and instead to process to the child's direction, ideas, and decisions.

In the early years following identification, parents report an overpowering sense of responsibility to "do right by" their gifted child (Hackney, 1981). This might include fears regarding their adequacy to raise the youngster or feelings of guilt that they are neglecting the child's growth. To the degree that parents feel inadequate, family interactions can be adversely affected. Conflict resolution is hampered, and one parent often becomes more peripheral with regard to discipline and/or school issues (Frey & Wendorf, 1985). Parents may compensate for their feelings by placing excessive performance demands on themselves and their children. These additional pressures can negatively affect the identified child's performance in school and stimulate psychological problems for the entire family system.

Summary

Identifying a child as gifted can be partly a function of the ways in which the child's behavior is perceived. At its most positive, identification is an organizing force, shaping the family's corporate personality and structuring family relations to actualize the potential of every family member. Issues can emerge for these families when only one sibling is identified as gifted, especially if the parents do not actively value the unlabeled sibling. Adultizing the gifted child and maintaining parental role boundaries are additional challenges parents face.

Building a Partnership with Parents of Gifted Children

Differing philosophical orientations plus sets of accepted assumptions and choices of operating principles will necessarily shape each relationship between a school psychologist and the parents of gifted children. Given the profiles, challenges, and needs of gifted youngsters and their families reviewed earlier in this chapter, we advocate relationships that empower families of gifted students.

In this section, we describe the barriers to creating a collaborative relationship, and we present a rationale for employing an empowerment approach for working with gifted students and their families. The section concludes with examples of ways to promote empowerment.

Challenges to a Collaborative Relationship

Several factors combine to distance "gifted" parents from schools. Economic pressures can mean that increased time and energy needed for occupational and life-sustaining activities diminish parental accessibility to school and devalue the importance of school involvement (Blanchard, 1981). A lack of appropriate information, expertise, skills, and experience in working with other adults and the perceived threat of the school system (particularly for low-income parents) makes parents seem diffident or antagonistic when dealing with school professionals (Blanchard, 1981; Dettmann & Colangelo, 1980).

Parents who feel intimidated by the knowledge that their child is gifted may develop inaccurate expectations and choose inappropriate goals for their child (Hackney, 1981). The belief that "everything is all right" if the child's grades are acceptable and the child is not complaining about school helps parents rationalize a de facto policy of minimal involvement in the child's educational program (Callahan, 1982). A cycle of alienation, defensiveness, and mistrust often results.

Friedman (1978) points out that school personnel have much to learn from families, because the "family school" is the child's first source of learning and may be an important link to understanding and treating a student's unique learning issues. However, schools, too, might contribute to a lack of collaboration. Blanchard (1981) credits two damaging beliefs for the failure to use parental input fully. First, when school personnel discount parental abilities, they are far less likely to involve parents actively in developing and implementing educational plans for a bright child. Second, a sense of threat that (untrained) parents might be more effective in working with a bright child than the professional can lead to territoriality and defensiveness, driving a wedge between parents and the school staff.

School traditions of extremely limited educational programs (cf. Wolf & Stephens, 1984) can further alienate families of gifted students. Likewise, well-meaning but inadequate accommodations made for parents, such as limiting acceptable parental roles to field trip organizer, lobbyist, or classroom aide (cf. Cassidy, 1981), can contribute to separating the "family school" from the public school.

Four Examples

Scenario #1: The referral process. In mid-September, the Brents[2] receive their first contact from the district's gifted program. A form letter explains that the Brents' 9-year-old daughter has been referred for gifted education testing. An information packet about the gifted program and a standardized "permission to test" form are enclosed. The Brents complete and return the form. They anxiously await the results.

Understanding parents. To meet parents' needs, we must realize what it is like for a parent to be asked to consent to special testing to determine if their child is

---

[2]All situations are based on actual events. Names and identifiers have been changed to protect families' identities.

gifted. Even if they initiated the referral, they may still be apprehensive. Ross (1964) points out that parents who are told that their child is gifted often react in a way that is similar to parents who are informed that their child has a learning disability. There is a public recognition that the child is different—often equated to adjustment problems and remedial learning needs. Many parents react to this cognitive and emotional dissonance with doubts about their own abilities and adequacies and fear of making a mistake that will irreparably damage the child's budding abilities (Hackney, 1981).

Scenario #2: My child is gifted. When the Brents are next contacted by the school psychologist, it is with a brief letter. "We are happy to inform you that your child has qualified for gifted education services. Please read through the enclosed information and then either schedule an appointment or simply sign the enclosed permission form and return it to this office."

Understanding parents. Identifying a child may well have more of an impact on the family system than on the newly labeled youngster (Dirks, 1979). When the assessment process indicates giftedness, children tend to react favorably to the process, particularly in fully functional families (Colangelo & Dettmann, 1983; Frey & Wendorf, 1985). In contrast, many parents often express confusion about what they should do and what changes they need to make in order to serve their child's special needs (Cornell, 1983a, 1983b; Hackney, 1981; Peterson, 1977; Rimm, 1986).

Mathews (1981) observes that staffing conferences, traditionally forums for airing and alleviating concerns, frequently dissolve into a monologue with little or no real input from the gifted child or his or her parents. "The procurement of a parental signature on the individual educational plan . . . [is] frequently the only outstanding feature of these sessions. These experiences can be frustrating to parents and do little to enhance their knowledge or attitudes about various dimensions of the program" (p. 208).

Unless parents receive assistance to understand giftedness and to set appropriate expectations, their early reaction of pride and delight can give way to distress, dissatisfaction with the school program, and disruption of the family system (Friedman, in press; Mathews, 1981).

Scenario #3: My child is not gifted. The Carters also received a letter: "Thank you for allowing your child to be assessed for the gifted education program. At this time we have found no need for special services. We are confident that continued enrollment in the regular program is in your child's best interest. Feel free to schedule a conference if you would like additional information about the testing process and/or results."

Understanding parents. Research on children who have been evaluated for gifted education programs but not placed (and their parents) is regrettably nonexistent. However, the confusion, frustration, and dissonance these parents experience is easy to imagine. Not only does the child fail to be identified as bright, but the youngster is labeled as not gifted. It is important to keep in mind that these parents and their children are unlike families whose child is identified as not needing other types of special education services. In the latter situation a negative judgment affirms a child's abilities. In the case of a youngster identified as not possessing special talents, the verdict can be devastating.

How can helping professionals assist parents and students to work through their feelings of inadequacy and even anger? How can we prevent the child from a profound loss of esteem in the eyes of self, parents, peers, and teachers?

Scenario #4: Life after identification. The Brents' daughter has been receiving gifted education services for about a month. Her daily schedule has been adjusted so that she can attend the weekly gifted class. Jennifer seems to enjoy her new teacher and the program's activities. However, Jennifer's parents feel excluded from the gifted program and frustrated about their inability to support her in their usual ways.

Understanding parents. Beyond lists of "do's" and "don'ts" and "how-to" manuals on parenting, little information is typically shared with parents of gifted children (Colangelo & Dettman, 1983). The most popular format for parent educational programs is a "one-shot" evening presentation by the gifted program staff (cf. Wolf & Stephens, 1984), rather than sustained efforts that blend parents' expertise with the gifted program, or educational programs based on an assessment of parents' issues and needs.

Aside from the incompleteness of the above information, its content is often overly simplistic. Mathews (1981) questions the validity and objectivity of presentations such as the "I Know What You Are Going Through Because I Have A Gifted Child, Too" or the "I Understand Your Child Because I Was/Am Gifted, Too" approaches. He asserts that these perspectives are limited by their subjective examination of the issues. As the speakers in these categories insist on supporting their egos from a single case study, the audience begins to question the credibility of the presentation; thus, its potential usefulness is limited.

In our work with "gifted" parent support groups, we have found that their concerns focus on topics such as setting appropriate standards, supporting affective growth, promoting positive peer and sibling relationships, and enhancing communication (Jenkins-Friedman, 1982). Others have identified information concerning educational alternatives (Debinski & Mauser, 1978), learning styles and interpreting educational placement and programming (Malone, 1975). Of most importance to parents is the freedom and opportunity to ask questions of educators (Callahan, 1982; Debinski & Mauser, 1978; Mathews, 1981).

Summary

Parents play a pivotal role in facilitating their child's continued affective and intellectual growth (Bloom, 1985; Feldman & Goldsmith, 1986; Fine, 1977; Hackney, 1981). Concomitantly, they can contribute to problems such as under-achievement (Fine & Pitts, 1980; Rimm, 1986) and disabling perfectionism (Friedman, in press; Jenkins-Friedman, Bransky, & Murphy, 1987). If parents are to make responsible decisions concerning their gifted children, they need to be well informed and involved appropriately in their child's program (Kroth, 1980).

A Plan for Empowering Parents of Gifted Students

Fine (personal communication, March 1988) identifies four objectives for a collaborative model of parent involvement: (1) educating and (2) subsequently including parents in decision making regarding their exceptional child; (3) assisting parents therapeutically as needed so they will be able to cope more effectively with specific issues regarding their exceptional child; and (4) empowering and enabling parents to work actively on behalf of their exceptional child.

According to Dunst and Trivette (1987), different types of support and assistance, and the manner in which they are offered, either usurp or promote self-sustaining and adaptive behavior. In helping relationships, an empowerment framework adopts a proactive stance; it assumes that help seekers are already competent or that they have the capacity to become competent. Second, the empowerment perspective assumes that any failure to demonstrate competence comes from the failure of social systems to provide relevant opportunities rather than deficits within the person. Third, it assumes that the criterion for empowerment is met when the help seeker attributes change to his or her actions; i.e., demonstrating a sense of control.

In our work with school personnel and parents of gifted children, we have found that the most enduring school–parent partnerships combine three elements: (1) active application of principles of empowerment; (2) flexible role definition for the school psychologist; and (3) a systemic framework for assessment and intervention.

Empowerment Guidelines

Dunst and Trivette (1987) propose 12 principles for empowering and enabling families. We have selected five that have particular relevance for school psychologists working with parents of gifted students.

1. *Offer assistance that is reciprocal.* Accepting aid necessarily places the help seeker in a "one-down" position. "Reciprocity is likely to be the preferred mode of reducing indebtedness to the extent that recipients are made aware of this option and they perceive that the opportunity to reciprocate exists" (Greenberg & Wescott, 1983, p. 95). This principle especially fits parents of gifted children, who tend to act in a "take charge" manner and thus would likely be uncomfortable with the help seeker role.

Example: The Martinis' unfamiliarity with special education procedures makes them seem negative and critical at their daughter's IEP conference. Correctly assessing the situation, the school psychologist is careful to avoid technical jargon and to check for understanding. The psychologist makes a point of soliciting the Martinis' insights about their daughter's abilities and interests. He then includes parent-generated goals on the IEP. At the conclusion of the conference, Mrs. Martini shyly volunteers that she is the president of the state fossil society and would be happy to share some of their work with the gifted program. The gifted teacher makes a date with Mrs. Martini to conduct a lesson during their upcoming archeology unit.

2. *Promote parents' natural resources and support networks.* Enhancing a sense of community and promoting the competence and well-being of the family's social network are empowing rather than dependency-producing activities (Hobbs, 1975). It is important to avoid replacing resources and networks with professional services (Dunst & Trivette, 1987). This principle is important to consider when working with parents of newly identified gifted children, given their tendency to reexamine parenting practices and even to question their competence to raise bright children.

Example: The Gibson family lives in a child-filled and warmly community-oriented neighborhood. However, the parents tell the school psychologist that they are considering moving to the far side of the city so that their gifted daughter will have better access to the public library. They question whether her old friends who are not in the gifted program will the right influences for their child. The school psychologist arranges a meeting of parents, daughter, and gifted and general education teachers. Together the group brainstorms alternatives for nurturing the youngster's intellectual growth while remaining in the context of a supportive and familiar community.

3. *Convey a sense of cooperation and joint responsibility for meeting needs and solving problems.* Participatory decision making characterizes this principle. Involving "gifted" parents as partners with an equal stake in developing, evaluating, and selecting choices for their child will help parents feel valued and a key part of their child's education (Dettmann & Colangelo, 1980).

Example: Rusty, a high school sophomore who has taken part in the gifted program since 3rd grade, is also a highly talented cellist. He recently won a well-deserved scholarship to study with a renowned musician at an area conservatory of music, but lessons, concerts, and travel time conflict with high school classes. The school psychologist and gifted education facilitator work with Rusty and his entire family to determine what is best for Rusty. They work together to resolve issues relative to meeting graduation requirements, scheduling classes, and transportation problems. Thus, the school becomes a partner with Rusty and his family rather than an obstacle to an appropriate education for this bright young man.

4. *Promote parents acquiring behavior that reduces their need for help.* As help seekers become more capable and competent, they also display greater independence and better problem-solving abilities (Skinner, 1978). Encouraging parents' self-directness will help them become more self-sustaining, and thus less likely to need help in the future (Colangelo, 1988; Friedman, 1980; Treffinger & Fine, 1979).

Example: When their twins were first identified as gifted, the Sarnoffs became extremely uncertain about their abilities to generate or judge educational choices. They relied heavily on the school psychologist to propose educational decisions. They also refused to act on any possibility until the psychologist proved her case through documentation and other evidence. The result of this was that the Sarnoffs and the school psychologist were often at odds.

Recognizing the Sarnoffs' pattern as one common to parents of newly identified gifted students, the school psychologist worked with them on reviewing and modifying expectations for their children's work. She subsequently encouraged them to join a support group for parents of gifted children in their district. As they became acquainted with the other parents, read the popular literature, and joined the state organization, their fears dissipated. Hesitation was replaced with collaborative decision making.

5. *Help increase parents' beliefs in themselves as causal agents in producing and maintaining desired changes.* This principle seems to be the prime determinant

of the empowerment model's success. In sum, if help-seeking and help-giving exchanges are to be effective, two conditions must be met. First, recipients of assistance must see themselves as no longer in need of support. Second, these individuals need to see themselves as both responsible for producing the observed changes and maintaining changes (Bandura, 1977). Again, this principle is appropriate for bright individuals and their parents, who tend to be more internally oriented (Hackney, 1981; Jenkins-Friedman, 1982).

Example: The Sarnoffs ultimately became a resource for the school psychologist and did much in their community to assure that the gifted education program received sufficient support and resources. Mrs. Sarnoff joined the political action committee of the state gifted organization. Mr. Sarnoff helped to set up and manage a parent resource network. At the close of their children's annual conference, the school psychologist asked them how the year had gone for them. They each affirmed that they now felt like full partners in their twins' special education programs. The Sarnoffs asserted that their involvement made a significant difference in the quality of their children's education.

The School Psychologist's Role

We support a contingency model for developing an effective partnership with parents of gifted children. A contingency approach assumes that there is no one best way to work with parents; rather, the school psychologist needs to be able to function in many different roles to help families become more competent in mobilizing resources, having needs met, and achieving desired objectives. The notion of tailoring an approach to meet the needs of the learner and to capitalize on his or her strengths is foundational to the field of gifted child education (Kaplan et al., 1979); it is a logical extension to working with their parents.

Researchers outline a vast array of functions applicable to the school psychologist working with parents of gifted children; however, several common themes emerge and can be grouped into a rough hierarchy of increasing involvement (cf. Callahan, 1982; Colangelo, 1988; Dettmann & Colangelo, 1980; Fine, 1984; Hackney, 1981; Loven, 1978; Schatz & Sandborn, 1980). The first role, collaborative diagnostician, emphasizes an information exchange between school and family for purposes of joint program planning. It assumes that all individuals have unique insights and information regarding the bright child, and that the most effective program will result from open sharing of these data. In the case described earlier, the school psychologist actively involved the Martinis in constructing their daughter's educational program by soliciting information about nonschool interests, peer relationships, and learning patterns. The school psychologist ensured that school personnel openly shared their insights into the child's functioning. The IEP that the group constructed was thus the result of teamwork and collaboration.

The second role, communication facilitator, emphasizes promoting school–family interaction, for example, to avoid catching the child in competing system loyalties. The school psychologist, being a member of one system and having insights into the other, can thus serve as a mediator between the two and stimulate collaborative problem solving. When the Gibsons were considering moving, the school psychologist focused on helping them communicate their concerns to their child's teachers and work together to achieve a mutually agreeable solution rather than entrapping their daughter between the goals of the family and school systems.

Building on these functions, the consultant works with family and/or school personnel on specific child-related issues. This role assumes that parents, child, and school share responsibility for solving problems. The school psychologist supports the involved parties in understanding the dynamics of an issue and in generating and implementing solutions. For instance, the school psychologist worked together with Rusty, his parents, and teachers to reach a mutually agreeable solution for scheduling and transportation issues. Both the school and family systems "owned" the problem; each was committed to reaching a solution that affirmed their support to each other and to Rusty.

The most intensive involvement is reflected in the counselor role, combining educator and therapist. In contrast to the consultant role, in this instance the school psychologist works directly with gifted children, their parents, and/or teachers to improve interaction patterns or other specific issues. This role is most clearly reflected in the case of the Sarnoffs. The school psychologist worked with them to understand the nature of their twins' abilities, to restructure family communication patterns to nurture their children's growth, and to seek relevant resources and support.

An empowerment orientation to working with parents would also adopt an attitude of "less is better." That is, as the family system appears more empowered, the school psychologist would focus on surface-level involvement and support. Only more dependent and/or dysfunctional families would need deeper levels of intervention.

A Systemic Orientation

A key quality of an empowerment model is its systemic focus on assessment and intervention. A systemic orientation is far more dynamic than the linear medical model of diagnosis, prescription, and treatment (Fine & Holt, 1983). The child's problems are regarded as ongoing, interactional, and interdependent between the self and the environment (Wendt & Zake, 1984).

Fine and Holt (1983) assert that viewing children's behavior from a systems perspective expands the school-based consultant's view of the contextual function of a particular behavior. This approach is especially suited to working with gifted children, whose complex cognitive and affective functioning and often insightful systemic meta-processing can undermine needed interventions (Fine & Pitts, 1980). The approach can provide a more holistic view of the child and allow for greater family involvement and collaborative problem solving (Dunst & Trivette, 1987; Treffinger & Fine, 1979).

Assessment. A family systems approach begins by evaluating the role the child's giftedness plays in the family, then moving to a broader consideration of family roles and patterns of interactions, e.g., sensitivity of family members to the child and each other (Fine, 1984; Jenkins-Friedman & Fine, 1984; Rimm, 1986). Determining the flexibility of the educational and family systems, particularly sources of stress and support, provides insights into the degree to which the parents feel empowered (Wendt & Zake, 1984).

The following two groups of questions are drawn from the literature described earlier (also cf. Fine, 1984; Rimm, 1986). They are designed to alert school psychologists to problematic patterns that can emerge among bright students, their parents, and school personnel. For example, do the parents use some degree of participatory decision making, or do they adultize their gifted child and process to his or her direction? Do parents maintain appropriate boundaries between themselves and their children? Is every member of the family valued? What are the parents' predominant ego states? Do parents refer to the abilities of their nonidentified children? Do the parents function as a team, or do the mother and gifted child seem to occupy a central position, edging out the father? Is the gifted child the central figure in the family? In what ways are parents encouraging their children's independence? conformity?

How are the children perceived and labeled by their teachers? How well do teachers' expectations correlate with the children's abilities? How well is the child matched to the educational setting? Are there dysfunctional alliances? Do parents encourage an adversarial relationship between their child and the teacher?

Intervention. A systems perspective would apply assessment data in an approach that blends structural and strategic methods. Fine (1984) points out that the most lasting changes transform the way in which systems are structured and operate; i.e., second order change. Strategic interventions, although initially yielding more visible results, tend to be more external, cosmetic, and fleeting. Thus, effective interventions with families of gifted children would incorporate both elements.

Detailed approaches to intervention are covered elsewhere in this book; however, we would like to offer some suggestions for structuring collaborative interventions with parents of gifted children (cf. Callahan, 1982; Culross & Jenkins-Friedman, 1988; Fine & Pitts, 1980; Friedman, 1980; Schatz & Sandborn, 1980).

1. Involve students in conferences whenever possible;
2. arrange a series of meetings with clear agendas and outcomes;
3. reframe problem statements as goal statements;
4. involve all parties in developing alternatives;
5. be prepared for some intitial resistance or sabotage in making deeper level changes;
6. identify resources parents may consult in carrying out their part of a contract; and
7. be early and preventive. Emphasize knowledge, relevancy of information, and empowerment in dealings with parents, teachers, and students.

Summary and Conclusions

In this chapter, we reviewed briefly salient characteristics of gifted youngsters and their families, emphasizing that giftedness is a complex phenomenon carrying adjustment issues for bright children and their families. Challenges to a collaborative relationship were discussed, and principles for enhancing a school–home partnership were presented.

We believe that an empowerment orientation meshes well with the previously described literature profiling families of bright children. Our experiences confirm that well-functioning families of gifted children are virtually models of empowerment. For them, labeling a child as "gifted" is confirmatory rather than reorganizing. Often the parents are bright and/or creative in their own rights. They expect all of their children to be interested, active, and involved with life. They are eager to learn about their child's "special condition" and know how to access relevant institutional, media, and human resources. They apply the information they learn to their own lives as well as to their children's. These parents become informed consumers of educational services and focus on complementing the school program rather than competing with it.

Many more parents of gifted children, however, find the labeling experience and accompanying school contacts dependency forming rather than empowering. We have found that the traditional school-centered orientation toward working with parents of gifted children described earlier actually undermines empowerment. In one fairly typical incident described earlier, parents are treated as passive recipients of information, not as teachers or facilitators of their child's growth. These parents are confused and resentful of reassurances that their gifted child's needs can best be met through expertly trained school personnel. Their contacts with school counselors and psychologists leave them feeling excluded from responsibility for selecting educational alternatives for their gifted child, defensive about their parenting abilities, and distanced from the school program.

In contrast, a partnership paradigm recognizes that all parties have knowledge and expertise that can be beneficial to the child's growth at home and school

(Dettmann & Colangelo, 1980; Fine, 1977; Fine & Pitts, 1980). It is a solid foundation upon which to build collaboration with well-functioning or dependent "gifted" families.

References

Bandura, A. (1977). Self-efficacy: Toward a unifying theory of behavioral change. *Psychological Review, 84*, 191-215.

Blanchard, Y. L. (1981). Exponential alliances—home, school and community: A referent for triadic relationships. In W. L. Marks & N. L. Nostrand (Eds.), *Strategies for educational change: Recognizing the gifts and talents of all children.* New York: Macmillan.

Bloom, B. S. (Ed.). (1985). *Developing talent in young people.* New York: Ballantine.

Callahan, C. M. (1982). Parents of the gifted and talented child. *Journal for the Education of the Gifted, 4*(4), 247-258.

Cassidy, J. (1981). Parental involvement in gifted programs. *Journal for the Education of the Gifted, 4*(4), 284-287.

Colangelo, N. (1988). Families of gifted children: The next ten years. *Roeper Review, 11*(1), 16-18.

Colangelo, N., & Dettmann, D. F. (1983). A review of research on parents and families of gifted children. *Exceptional Children, 50*(1), 20-27.

Coleman, J. M., & Fults, B. A. (1982). Self-concept and the gifted classroom: The role of social comparisons. *Gifted Child Quarterly, 26*, 116-120.

Coleman, J. M., & Fults, B. A. (1985). Special-class placement, level of intelligence, and the self-concept of gifted children: A social comparison perspective. *Remedial and Special Education, 6*, 7-12.

Cornell, D. G. (1983a). The family's view of the gifted child. In B. M. Shore, F. Gagné, S. Larivee, R. H. Tali, & R. E. Tremblay (Eds.), *Proceedings of the Fourth World Conference on Gifted Education: Face to face with giftedness* (pp. 39-50). New York: Trillium Press.

Cornell, D. G. (1983b). Gifted children: The impact of positive labeling on the family system. *American Journal of Orthopsychiatry, 53*(2), 322-334.

Cornell, D. G., & Grossberg, I. N. (1987). Family environment and personality adjustment in gifted program children. *Gifted Child Quarterly, 31*(2), 59-64.

Cornell, D. G., & Grossberg, I. N. (1988). *Parent use of the term "gifted": Correlates with family environment and child adjustment.* Paper presented at the Council for Exceptional Children, Washington, DC.

Culross, R. R., & Jenkins-Friedman, R. (1988). On coping and defending: Applying Burner's personal growth principles to working with gifted/talented students. *Gifted Child Quarterly, 32*(2), 261-266.

Debinski, R. J., & Mauser, A. J. (1978). Parents of the gifted: Perceptions of psychologists and teachers. *Journal for the Education of the Gifted, 1*(2), 5-14.

Dettmann, D. F., & Colangelo, N. (1980). A functional model for counseling parents of gifted students. *Gifted Child Quarterly, 24*(4), 158-161.

Dirks, J. (1979). Parents' reaction to identification of the gifted. *Roeper Review, 2*, 9-11.

Dunst, C. J., & Trivette, C. M. (1987). Enabling and empowering families: Conceptual and intervention issues. *School Psychology Review, 16,* 443-456.

Feldman, D. H., & Goldsmith, L. T. (1986). *Nature's gambit.* New York: Basic Books.

Fine, M. J. (1984). Integrating structural and strategic components in school-based intervention: Some cautions for consultants. *Techniques: A Journal for Remedial Education and Counseling, 1,* 44-51.

Fine, M. J. (1977). Facilitating parent-child relationships for creativity. *Gifted Child Quarterly, 21*(4), 487-500.

Fine, M. J., & Holt, P. (1983). Intervening with school problems: A family systems perspective. *Psychology in the Schools, 20,* 59-66.

Fine, M. J., & Pitts, R. (1980). Intervention with underachieving gifted children: Rationale and strategies. *Gifted Child Quarterly, 24*(2), 51-55.

Friedman, P. G. (1980). *Communicating in conferences: Parent-teacher-student interaction.* Urbana, IL: ERIC Clearinghouse on Reading and Communication Skills.

Friedman, R. (1978). Using the family school in the treatment of learning disabilities. *Journal of Learning Disabilities, 11,* 378-382.

Friedman, R. C. (in press). Families of gifted children and youth. In M. J. Fine & C. Carlson (Eds.), *Handbook of family-school intervention: A systems perspective.* New York: Grune & Stratton.

Frey, J., & Wendorf, D. J. (1985). Families of gifted children. In L. L'Abate (Ed.), *The handbook of family psychology and therapy* (pp. 781-809). Homewood, IL: The Dorsey Press.

Greenberg, M. S., & Westcott, D. R. (1983). Indebtedness as a mediator of reactions to aid. In J. D. Fisher, A. Nadler, & B. M. DePaulo (Eds.), *New directions in helping: Vol. 1. Recipient reactions to aid* (pp. 85-112). New York: Academic Press.

Grinder, R. E. (1985). The gifted in our midst: By their divine deeds, neuroses and test scores we have known them. In F. D. Horowitz & M. O'Brien (Eds.) *The gifted and talented: Developmental perspectives* (pp. 5-35). Washington, DC: The American Psychological Association.

Hackney, H. (1981). The gifted child, the family, and the school. *Gifted Child Quarterly, 25*(2), 51-62.

Hobbs, N. (1975). *The future of children: Categories, labels, and their consequences.* San Francisco: Jossey-Bass.

Hurley, J. R. (1965). Parental acceptance-rejection and children's intelligence. *Merrill-Palmer Quarterly, 11,* 19-31.

Janos, P. M., Fung, H. C. & Robinson, N. M. (1985). Self-concept, self-esteem, and peer relations among gifted children who feel "different" *Gifted Child Quarterly, 29,* 78-81.

Jenkins-Friedman, R. (August, 1982). *Concepts and strategies for working with parents of gifted children.* Paper presented at the meeting of The American Psychological Association, Washington, DC.

Jenkins-Friedman, R., Bransky, T. S., & Murphy, D. L. (August, 1987). *The school psychologist as Prometheus: Identifying and working therapeutically with gifted students "at risk" for disabling perfectionism.* Paper presented at the meeting of The American Psychological Association, New York.

Jenkins-Friedman, R., & Fine, M. J. (1984). A useful framework for parent-teacher contacts. *Roeper Review, 6*(3), 6-10.

Jenkins-Friedman, R., & Murphy, D. L. (1988). The Mary Poppins effect: Relationships between gifted students' self-concept and adjustment. *Roeper Review, 11*(1), 26-30.

Kaplan, S. N., Madsen, S., Gould, B., Platow, J. A., & Renzulli, J. S. (1979). *Inservice training manual: Activities for identification/program planning for the gifted and talented.* Ventura, CA: National/State Leadership Institute on the Gifted and the Talented.

Kroth, R. (1980). The mirror of parental involvement. *The Pointer, 25,* 18-22.

Loven, M. D. (1978). Four alternative approaches to the family/school liaison role. *Psychology in the Schools, 15*(4), 553-559.

Malone, C. (1975). Education for parents of the gifted. *Gifted Child Quarterly, 19*(3), 223-225.

Mathews, F. N. (1981). Effective communication with parents of the gifted and talented: Some suggestions for improvement. *Journal for the Education for the Gifted, 4*(3), 207-210.

Peterson, D. C. (1977). The heterogeneously gifted family. *Gifted Child Quarterly, 21*(3), 396-411.

Rimm, S. B. (1986). *Underachievment syndrome: Causes and cures.* Watertown, WI: Apple.

Ross, A. O. (1964). *The exceptional child in the family.* New York: Grune & Stratton.

Schatz, E. M., & Sandborn, M. P. (1980). Some pragmatics of parent consultation. *Roeper Review, 3*(1), 40-43.

Seagoe, M. (1974). Some learning characteristics of gifted children. In R. A. Martinson (Ed.), *The identification of the gifted and talented* (pp. 20-21). Ventura, CA: National/State Leadership Institute on the Gifted and the Talented.

Skinner, B. F. (1978). The ethics of helping people. In L. Wispe (Ed.), *Sympathy, altruism and helping behavior* (pp. 249-262). New York: Academic Press.

Treffinger, D. J., & Fine, M. J. (1979). When there's a problem in school. *G/C/T,* (10), 3-6.

Wendt, R. N., & Zake, J. (1984). Family systems theory and school psychology: Implications for training and practice. *Psychology in the Schools, 21,* 204-210.

Wolf, J. S., & Stephens, T. M. (1984). Training models for parents of the gifted. *Journal for the Education of the Gifted, 7*(2), 120-129.

SECTION **IV**

Sexuality, Transitions, and Advocacy

15

ISSUES IN SOCIAL-SEXUALITY FOR HANDICAPPED PERSONS, THEIR FAMILIES, AND PROFESSIONALS

Peggy Jo Wallis

Everyone, regardless of the nature or extent of their ability or disability, is a sexual being. Frequently those with handicapping conditions have been denied this recognition by professionals, parents, and society. The disabled are too often viewed as asexual, hyper-sexual, eternal children or too severely handicapped to be concerned with issues of sexuality. Although the historical treatment of the disabled has finally led to setting priorities based upon normalization, focus is most frequently aimed at cognitive issues and daily living or vocational skills.

The issues that arise when addressing social-sexuality are difficult for both parents and professionals. It is a topic in which few are trained and one in which conflicting societal messages provide explicit images while simultaneously implying that it is not something to be talked about openly. Yet the inherent nature and right of the handicapped to have their sexuality recognized makes it necessary that these issues no longer be ignored. Means must be identified to make all parties comfortable—parents, professionals, and the handicapped themselves.

The professionals' role is a pivotal one as they learn from both parents and the handicapped individual during the process of discussion and collaboration. Sensitive issues and concerns must be recognized and dealt with in a straightforward yet sympathetic manner. Frequently the professional becomes the initiator of an awareness that education, intervention, or support might be warranted. For the parent and the handicapped individual alike, professional interaction might involve guidance in understanding and accepting the developmental process and assistance in making the decisions that are inherent in this process.

To provide objective assistance, it is crucial that the professional become aware of the development and variation of values and emotionality connected with this subject, including the recognition of the professional's own feelings and attitudes. He or she must also understand the concept of "sexuality," the "normal" process of social sexual development, the possible impact of disabilities (for purposes of this chapter, disabilities will be considered generically unless otherwise specifically noted) upon this process, and the response of the parent to the maturation of the child. Only from this vantage point will the professional be prepared to begin considering appropriate intervention strategies.

Sexuality

Human sexuality encompasses the totality of who we are biologically, psychologically, and sociologically from birth until death. It is an ongoing, lifetime process that must be seen in its entirety, not as something to be dealt with at adolescence as a singularly biological issue with discussion of "plumbing" and "disaster prevention." Although significant physiological events and transitions occur, sexuality as a process is composed of the basic elements of self-esteem, communication, and decision-making skills and the interaction of these three elements. How people feel about their bodies and the pleasures they can derive, the way in which they express those feelings, and the determination of when, how, and with whom this should occur become key elements (Dixon & Mullinar, 1985).

The varying perceptions of exactly what sexuality (and the related terms of *sex* and *sexuality*) means can cause significant difficulties. Although some view it as a physical act, others define it through the visible physical characteristics of change that come with maturation. For most people, the initial identification is of the physiological aspects (i.e., body changes, intercourse, and reproduction). This limited focus frequently creates a barrier to the consideration of the other elements of sexuality, such as social and psychological aspects, with the result being a delay in dealing with issues in these areas or in their not being addressed at all. This becomes especially pertinent when addressing the needs of people with disabilities, for whom self-esteem, problem solving, communication, decision making, gaining information, and gathering experience in learning the social side of sexuality may be problematic. A broadened perspective is essential in encompassing all psychosocial-sexual issues.

Attitudes and Values

Given the variety of perceptions that occur, it is important for professionals to be sensitive to and aware of the values and attitudes that people, including themselves, have toward social-sexual issues. Both parents and professionals may themselves be "handicapped" by views which, by being narrow in perspective or oppositional to certain behaviors, prove to be restrictive. As the purveyors of information and values, both purposely through education and counseling and inadvertently through behavior, tone of voice, and body language, their perspectives will be conveyed. Professionals and parents must therefore be particularly clear about their own attitudes and the messages they are conveying.

Sexuality is a topic of extreme emotionality in which each individual has his or her own particular feelings and biases. We come to these beliefs through a lifetime of events that become a product of our discretely individual experiences. We each exist within certain parameters that define our value systems and perceptions. These influences include cultural beliefs and customs, the family, economics, peers, the law, the media, science, religion, and the school (Dixon & Mullinar, 1985).

Each generation has unique perspectives of each of these factors and the way in which individuals are expected to behave. The way in which society views sexuality is constantly changing, from Victorian rigidness through the sixties' openness to the present preoccupation with issues of AIDS and sexual abuse. Our value systems, while continuously being influenced by current trends, have had a constant thread; although we recognize that sexuality exists, it is not something to be talked about openly and naturally. When dealing with families, it becomes important for the professional to keep this sense of generation, and the accompanying value structure, in mind.

Parents, many lacking appropriate models themselves, have frequently ignored the topic with their children or approached it "red faced." As bearers of society's values, educational institutions and professionals have reflected this reticence to address the topic wholeheartedly, being fearful yet cognizant of the difficulty of melding all of the community and familial value systems into a whole. Students have received information, if at all, in a piecemeal fashion and usually after the time when the knowledge was necessary. This is particularly true for the handicapped.

The Handicapped

Children and adolescents who are physically or mentally disabled have very much the same concerns about sexuality as do other children. They must learn to cope with generally the same biological changes as other children, as well as the new sexual feelings and desires that come in early adolescence. However, individual disabilities can complicate these tasks of growing up (Thorton, 1981).

The tendency exists to view someone first as handicapped and then as a person. In truth it is society that frequently creates handicaps. Although most disabilities are products of birth and accident, the debilitating impact on a person's life often results not so much from the "disability" as from the manner in which others define or treat that person (Gordon, 1974). It is therefore not surprising that the sexual aspects of disability are unrecognized by some people, denied by others, and, for still others, a matter of distaste. Such attitudes will persist until the public at large becomes more aware of handicapped people as fellow human beings of equal merit and value to others. At present, wholeness in form and function makes up part of the sexual ideal, and the individual tends to become less acceptable as a sexual being, let alone as a sexual partner, according to the extent to which he or she falls short of that ideal (Stewart, 1979).

Historically, the handicapped have been "desexualized" due to disbelief, fear, and the inability to see them as sexual beings. Active suppression resulting from fear of and for the handicapped led to the control of their sexuality through mass institutionalization and passage of compulsory sterilization laws (Bregman & Castles, 1988) in order to "protect society." Inconsistent views of the disabled ranging from their having no sexual needs to the other extreme of viewing males as sexually aggressive and females as sexually promiscuous have resulted in avoidance of the topic and the withholding of necessary information. Equally believed are the misconceptions that "disability breeds disability" and that the disabled should stay with and marry their "own kind," the implication being that the disabled are "defective" and that their most important characteristic is their disability (Cornelius, Chipouras, Makas, & Daniels, 1982).

The handicapped, in not being recognized as sexual, are not encouraged or often permitted to express themselves in this way. That they are viewed as asexual, oversexed, or forever childlike encourages suppression and dependency and perpetuates the view that if they are disabled in one way they are disabled in all ways, including their sexuality. These perspectives have led to segregation, punishment, the denial of the exploration by the disabled of their own sexual expression, and the lack of provision of social-sexual education and training. The result has been inappropriate behaviors, social inadequacy, and isolation.

Many of these attitudes have left the disabled susceptible to various misconceptions. The depiction of the disabled as innocent and vulnerable gives foundation to the myth that if knowledge about sexuality is withheld, it will deter them from engaging in certain behaviors. Likewise the perception is held that if information is presented about sexuality, "putting things in their heads," the disabled will become overstimulated and involved in activities they otherwise would not have chosen or even given thought to. In truth, however, talking or not talking about social-sexual issues will have no influence over the reaching of puberty with the resulting physical and psychological changes occurring.

Not providing information results in actions that are in response to curiosity and ignorance with inappropriate and frequently dangerous behaviors as common outcomes. For many people with disabilities, gaining information independently or developing healthy attitudes toward their own sexuality and sexual responsibility is difficult. Cognitive levels may limit reasoning, decision-making, and problem-solving capabilities, resulting in impulsive behaviors and the lack of comprehension of the consequences of actions. Deficits in reading levels may restrict their ability to access information. Verbal difficulties may preclude their asking questions, as may their lack of knowledge of where, how, or whom to ask.

The inability to utilize and integrate observed social cues (either due to processing, visual impairment, or cognitive functioning) may deprive some people with disabilities of important social learning information. For others, their perceptivity may have given them the message that others do not think they are sexual, so they are uncomfortable asking. Lack of social concepts or access, or overprotection, keeps them from partaking in social opportunities that would provide information. They are therefore on their own to gain information. Some will never seek it. Others may go about it by actions that are really questioning behaviors (touching, grabbing, etc.) in an attempt to seek information. Providing information can lead to a decrease in these inappropriate question-asking and exploratory behaviors.

It is sometimes assumed that there is a specific time schedule by which information should be provided and that to provide information too soon will be detrimental. In fact there are no ill effects from providing information about sex at appropriate stages or ages. Harm, however, can result by withholding informa-tion until after the individual has a particular sexual experience. For the disabled who may not have garnered information through observation, reading, or ques-tioning, natural occurrences of maturity (i.e., menstruation) can be upsetting and perhaps frightening if they have not been prepared for them. An understanding on the part of both parent and professional of the expected physical and social developmental milestones, as well as the impact that disabilities may have upon this growth, becomes important in order to prepare and assist everyone involved through each transition.

Development

From the moment we are born we are affected by the forces around us that will influence our sexual development. One of the strongest and earliest impacts is that of "parent–infant bonding," which develops through touch, eye contact, and soothing talk. Once the relationship is established it usually becomes reciprocal, with the parent (typically the mother) and the child drawing responses from each other (Grantham & Russell, 1985). The initial warmth and nurturing that takes place gives a sense to both the infant and parent of acceptance, creating the foundation for the establishment of security and self-esteem.

This bonding, however, can be disrupted by a variety of factors. For babies born with a disability, parents may be confronted with the emotional loss of the "perfect" child which may result in a degree of difficulty in acceptance of the infant. If parental grief and/or rejection were to be continuous, then socialization and affective development of the child would be influenced (Schuster, 1987). The family itself has to come to terms with the diagnosis, working through a range of their own feelings and reactions as well as dealing with the possible altered behaviors of relatives and friends.

The child, due to medical or psychological difficulties, may not evoke a caring response from the parent or give a rewarding response in return (Grantham & Russell, 1985). The spasticity experienced by a child born with cerebral palsy may result in the infant's lack of "snuggling." A blind baby's lack of eye contact, resulting in greater difficulty in evoking smiles, may prove to be distressing to parents (Lewis, 1987). Additional factors, such as critical medical care for which substantial separation occurs and prolonged institutionalization, may result in the infant not receiving this initial nurturing or providing feedback to the parents. This may delay the development of trust and emotional security.

From the time a child is born it is learning: learning in the first place to recognize its own body and the fact that the body has needs; learning, little by little, of the primary relationship between self and nonself (Stewart, 1979). As children continue through infancy (ages 0–1), this learning begins to take the form of exploration. Initially this is of the immediate environment: the crib, toys, the baby's fingers and toes. The infant will also explore its genitals, which may provoke dismay in those placing adult sexual connotations upon an infant's actions. The response that this behavior elicits can have an impact on the child's future ability to view his or her body in a positive manner.

Although this is a natural stage, for some infants with disabilities there will be a delay in reaching it. This may cause difficulty for the parents as they gradually become aware that the child is not developing as expected, nor functioning in the same way as a child of the same age (Grantham & Russell, 1985). Further concern results if the child, due to developmental delays, engages in this behavior later in the process when it is no longer age appropriate.

Self-image, independence, and gender identity begin to develop as children become aware (ages 1–2) of their own bodily functions and their ability to control them. Toilet training and the connotations that are often made between genitals and negative bodily wastes can have an impact on the child's sense of body image and sexuality. For many children with handicaps, the delay or difficulty in proceeding through this stage results in postponing skills of independence, socialization, and an understanding of privacy. The sometimes necessary continued reliance on a parent or caretaker for dealing with bodily functions may result in a level of dependence. Learned helplessness from infancy and toddler years can continue to affect the quality of interpersonal relationships seriously during the adolescent and young adult years (Schuster, 1987).

In many children with disabilities of a congenital nature, eliminatory and "toilet" considerations become a problem or need more attention than in the able-bodied child (Stewart, 1979). The necessity for a great deal of attention and assistance may result in a significant lack of privacy. Yet, children and adolescents need to have their bodily integrity respected (Miezio, 1983) in order to develop. A delay in establishing or confusion of gender may also result, due to physical or developmental causes.

Frequently, due to the nature of the handicap or the overprotectiveness on the part of the parents or caregivers, the child is unable to have any privacy or independent free time. He or she is not able to engage in natural developmental exploration and experimentation. If children do attempt to do so, they can only do it with other people around because they are never alone, and the other people may tell them that their behavior is not socially acceptable (Fairbrother, 1983). They may practice these behaviors in inappropriate places where opportunity is possible (i.e., back of the bus, coat room) or at a later age when the conduct is inappropriate. The result of these behaviors quite possibly is an inability to progress through the succeeding developmental stages of exploration, sex play, and social interactions. The impact of this may be the inability to develop independent adult characteristics, engagement in appropriate behaviors, or failure to establish a sense of self-worth. If the child cannot play easily with other children when the stage of interactional play arrives, the rehearsal for life that is implied by such play may be impeded (Stewart, 1979).

As children become less egocentric and more aware of others around them (ages 3–5), natural curiosity arises about their similarities and differences. A great deal of questioning about sexual behavior begins to take place as does sex rehearsal play which is a natural way to confirm any kind of important knowledge, not once but many times in many ways (Calderone & Johnson, 1981). Children utilize this practice play to develop conscience and the beginnings of body image and to entrench more firmly their gender identity. At this stage, as the child reaches school age, the next real teachers of the "facts of life" become peers, as they are all agents that modify the child's self-opinion (Symonds & Wickware, 1978).

Although disabilities may result in social isolation at a later age, in terms of people in their network and the frequency of daily contact, the handicapped typically have larger networks than their nonhandicapped peers, though they do not have daily contact with those members as compared to their nonhandicapped age-mates. Handicapped children appear not to be isolated but instead have a large network composed of relatives, adults, and, to a lesser extent, peers. The nonhandicapped, however, show a developmental shift, in terms of an increase in proportion of peers to adults, from 3–6 years, whereas handicapped children do not show this change. It may then be concluded that insufficient peer contact may restrict the handicapped child's opportunity to learn important social skills (Lewis, Feiring, & Brooks-Gunn, 1988) and independence and to develop an accurate body image.

Puberty is a "biological" process that cannot be halted. It is heralded by the physical changes the body undergoes resulting in appearance visibly altered from childhood. This is a heightened time of concern for body image, a judgment that began in the early childhood stage when children first became curious about others' bodies. For the handicapped this can be a continuous difficulty in accepting obvious differences (Craft & Craft, 1983).

This period (ages 6–12) becomes especially difficult for many youngsters with disabilities as they are confronted by society's increased expectations while frequently exhibiting a low tolerance for frustration and failure. Limited access to social activities and lack of acceptance or minimal peer group interaction may delay or inhibit their social skill development. Once again, overprotectiveness directly impedes the disabled child's growth. Physical maturity cannot be stopped (though some will deny its eventuality). Often, however, with the best of intentions, their social-sexual development is curtailed or even halted. The result is persons who are physically adults but who have the social status of children (Craft & Craft, 1983).

Adolescence is the state or process of growing up, the time of transition between childhood and adulthood. It is a "social" process, in which the individual develops his or her understanding of his or her own social and sexual identity (Craft & Craft, 1983). During this time the expectations of others, especially peers, become important. The frustrations and failures of meeting those expectations also must be dealt with. Some of the tasks of adolescence include developing identity and independence, assuming responsibilities, preparing for relationships, and developing values and ethical systems. Disabilities can complicate the completion of these tasks (Thorton, 1981).

In developing one's identity, feedback from others is generally utilized. In many respects, if the feedback is incomplete, unrealistic, or if the person is isolated, the feedback may not be realistic or sufficient. Adolescence is a time when differences are negatively viewed by peers, and self-image and self-esteem can suffer (Thorton, 1981). Body image becomes a central issue in this identity development as young adults come to terms with the ways in which their bodies are different from the popularized ideals (Miezio, 1983). For many adolescents with disabilities, accessing information and feedback may be difficult. For some, such as the blind or the visually impaired, information is difficult to access through the normal communication channels (vision and hearing). For these adolescents, with their growing awareness of sexuality often accompanied by taboos on touching other people's bodies, there may be a period of great confusion and anxiety about their own and other people's bodies and about their feelings (Lewis, 1987).

For the handicapped child and parents alike, adolescence (ages 12 and above) can be a very difficult time as the child struggles to adjust to bodily changes. Frequently, body growth occurs with greater speed than does the child's emotional or conceptual ability to comprehend it. How well children adjust depends to a large extent on cognitive level, coping skills, how they are told about sexuality, and what support they receive from their families and from professional people (Fairbrother, 1983). As the sex drive intensifies and new emotions are felt, attitudes and values established at an earlier age may be examined and challenged. This time has been typified as a generally difficult period for both child and parent as the need to establish independence generates strains and stresses in family relationships. This is especially true concerning sexual matters (Calderone & Johnson, 1981). However, as noted earlier, this movement toward independence may be delayed or difficult for many adolescents with disabilities, resulting in both frustration and concern on the part of the parent. Some handicapped youngsters, however, may be satisfied with their limited freedom, a result of an inability to separate personal values from those of their parents. This suggests that autonomy should be understood as relative to the needs and abilities of each individual (Lewis, Feiring, & Brooks-Gunn, 1988).

For parents, the conflict between caretaking and letting go can be a particularly difficult one. Up until this period their child has been a child, in both years and level of dependency, but for those who will continue to need varying degrees of care and some protection, it is very easy to go on and on treating the growing person as a child. For many parents, seeing their son or daughter as a perpetual child is the only way that they can accept or cope with the handicap (Fairbrother, 1983).

Adult issues create tremendous stress for the disabled and their families. The needs for intimacy and private time become formidable obstacles for the handicapped to surmount as they confront the attitudes of society and the difficulty due to social isolation, parental overprotectiveness, and, in some cases institutionalization, in finding either appropriate partners or opportunity (Bregman & Castles, 1988). The inability for some handicapped persons to conceptualize the abstract components of social-sexuality and their lack of independence training and experience bring doubt to their decision-making abilities and the capacity to give informed consent to activities.

Parents are confronted with the determination of how involved they should become in making social arrangements for their young adult with disabilities. This dilemma is faced by parents when the disability severely limits the young person's ability to move about or tend to his or her own body. In this case, sexual expression may mean that help is required (Miezio, 1983). For many parents, dealing with a young adult who still needs caretaking at a point when independence is the norm creates a hardship. For these parents the lack of opportunities readily available in the community, the time to arrange for social opportunities and the lack of social skills create stress (Brotherson et al. 1988).

Planning for the transition into adulthood can be particularly difficult for the parents of the disabled. They may be approaching this transition unprepared, with little planning regarding the adult needs of their young adult with disabilities. They may also be uncertain as to what their son's or daughter's adult roles and needs will be and unsure of how to prepare them for the transition (Zetlin & Turner, 1985). The recognition of their child's increasing chronological maturity also increases concerns about what the future will hold for them as they cope with their own issues of aging and mortality.

Decision Making and Intervention

The societal expectation exists that as adulthood is reached, independence and separation from parents will occur. It is anticipated that adults will assume appropriate roles of responsibility, making their own decisions and being responsible for the consequences of those choices.

Adulthood requires a constantness of choices. Decision making necessitates the recognition that there is a desire or selection to be made. Specific identification of the decision to make requires a delineation of options and alternatives. Consequences for each of these options must be understood and willingly accepted with the decision.

For the disabled, independence may be impeded by physical and developmental disabilities or by the overprotectiveness of parents and professionals. Opportunity for self-determination may be limited by caretaking needs, mobility, and living situations. For some, self-esteem, which provides the individual with the notion that he or she has the right to make a decision, may have been sorely impaired, and cognitive levels may preclude the recognition and comprehension of the decisions to be made or even the perception that choices are available. The generation of alternatives may be restricted for some people with disabilities so only things that are presented to them or that are stimulated by impulse are seen as possibilities. Likewise, lack of experience and opportunity may limit their perceived and true choices. Some may be unable to formulate an understanding of the consequences ensuing to the action they have chosen, resulting in difficulty for parents and professionals when determining if informed consent has actually been provided.

A balance exists between the ability of the individual to make a decision and the necessity for others to intervene in that process. The greater the ability of handicapped persons to understand fully the decision to be made and to see the alternatives available as well as the resulting consequences, the less need will exist for others to intervene in their decisions. Conversely, in the case of an individual for whom recognition of decisions, available options, and outcomes is difficult, it is more likely that others will be involved in decision making for or with that person.

For parents, the determination of when and how to make decisions and which decisions to make is difficult. They must confront their own feelings about sexuality and their attitudes about their son or daughter engaging in such behaviors as masturbation, dating, intercourse, and entering marriage (Bregman & Castles, 1988). Decision making for parents may involve giving permission for the adult offspring to be sexual. For agency personnel and professionals, legal, moral, and safety issues must be addressed as they attempt to deal with their own sexual attitudes, and reach a consensus with other staff members while at the same time incorporating parental value systems.

One way in which to further this decision-making process is through the provision of education to all parties involved. By working with clients (students) in the provision of information, discussing choices and consequences, and talking with parents about decisions to be made, the possibility exists that more independent or planned decisions might be forthcoming.

Education

It seems logical once we accept the premise that all people have sexual needs to conclude that all people can cope better with those needs if they understand how the needs manifest themselves physically and emotionally. People need to know that they share these needs and feelings with everyone else. They need to know they are not alone in their strange new emotions, their happiness, and their misery (Fairbrother, 1983). However, because of myths, misconceptions, and fear, the disabled have typically received little or no formalized sex education (Craft & Craft, 1978). Yet it is only with accurate information and the opportunity to come to grips with their own sexuality that people with disabilities will be able to express that sexuality in ways that are not harmful to themselves or others (Miezio, 1983).

For this population, for whom barriers (physical, social, emotional, and cognitive) have existed in the understanding of their own sexuality, appropriate education must be provided. Determined by what their futures hold, this information concerning biological, sociological, and psychological issues must be presented using methods and strategies that will provide access and understanding. For some this might mean remaining behavioral and concrete in nature; for others, abstract concepts of relating may be explored.

Because sexuality is a life-long process filled with a multitude of transitions, the provision of knowledge must begin at an early age, not just at the onset of puberty, especially with those for whom learning may be a slow process. The foundation of learning must start early with an opportunity to learn basic biological information and what "normal" behaviors are. For some, such as the visually impaired child who lacks a major tool for learning the explicit and subtle behavior associated with gender expressions and social relationships, it behooves adults—professionals and parents—to start early to help the child feel at home with his or her body and emotions, and to express these in ways that will enhance personal development and social relationships (Schuster, 1987).

Parents and Family

Every child has an impact when it enters a family, but those with disabilities can have a particularly profound effect. As a social unit, there are expectations of family members—how they will interact, the responsibilities that will be assumed, the development of independence (including bringing others into the family unit), and eventual leaving for marriage, education, or employment. However, these social milestones may be arrived at or expressed in significantly different ways when the child has a disability.

Dealing with a son's or daughter's sexuality is difficult for all parents. To think about it too early is to connect thoughts of "sex" with children, something that is viewed as socially and morally inappropriate for adults to consider. Time also plays a role as parents feel issues of sexuality are things they will have to deal with in a distant future. If the topic is addressed, it is usually done in a red-faced, brusque manner providing little information and a message that sexuality is not something to talk about or at the very best something that makes one extremely uncomfortable. More typical, however, is the natural tendency to ignore it for as long as possible, usually until secondary sex characteristics (i.e., facial hair) make the inevitable approach of adulthood impossible to ignore. For parents of some handicapped children, this development may be delayed, thereby further deferring discussion of the issues associated with it.

By far the most significant factor affecting an individual's sex life in the fullest meaning of the term is the impression he or she receives from his or her parents (Symonds & Wickware, 1978). Parents are their child's primary sex educators whether they talk about it or not or if it is presented comfortably or not. Everything that a parent does contributes to being a social-sexual educator of their child, from the way in which the family interacts physically to the way in which they talk to each other. Parents of children with disabilities can be the first and foremost providers of permission and limited information, if they can become comfortable with their child's sexuality. They can be the foundation for a disabled person's positive self-image, sexual independence, and comfort. Most important, parents need to realize that ignoring sexuality does not cause it to go away. Parents have a responsibility to provide effective and relevant information about sexuality to all their children, disabled or not (Cornelius et al., 1982).

How the parents handle the social-sexuality of their handicapped child will be derived initially from their own values and attitudes, not only toward their own sexuality but toward whether they feel that it was in any way connected to their child's disability. For those whose children were handicapped at birth, there may be lingering feelings about the role that the process of conception (sexual intercourse) played in the results. Parents may feel responsible, guilty, or ashamed. Some may see it as a negative reflection of their sexuality.

Any of these perspectives may make it difficult for parents to acknowledge the sexuality of their child—the very action that they may feel caused the disability to occur in the first place. Parents will need to get beyond these feelings in order to nurture their child's own social-sexuality. It is certainly not suggested, however, that parents would feel they must choke down or deny their own feelings. The feelings, values, and attitudes of parents are entitled to as much respect as anyone else's. Parents may, however, want to spend some time thinking about their values and attitudes (Miezio, 1983). To do so means that parents must openly face their own sexuality, as well as acknowledge the sexuality of their child. This is often difficult enough for parents of nondisabled children. For parents of children with disabilities, it is often very painful.

Disabilities bring into focus deep attitudes and values concerning physical attractiveness and sexual behavior. They may trigger parents' fear about their children's future when the time comes that parents can no longer care for them and protect them (Miezio, 1983). Other concerns include:

1. How to talk about sexuality with their children, when to begin, what to say, and how to say it so that it can be understood.
2. How to help their children deal with and understand their sexual feelings.
3. Protecting their children from being abused and teaching them not to exploit others.
4. Determining whether their children should utilize birth control, what method should be used, when would sterilization be appropriate, and who should make these decisions.
5. Dealing with homosexual and masturbatory activities.
6. Determining their child's ability to make judgments and the ability to be independent and sexually responsible.
7. Determining if their children will marry or reproduce. Talking to their children about other options.
8. Understanding how their child's disability may affect their physical development and sexuality.
9. Helping their child to develop a feeling of positive self-esteem, confident body image, and comfort with his or her sexuality. Helping to give children a feeling that they have a right to be sexual but assisting them to make wise choices in the expression of sexuality.
10. Determining how to encourage and provide social opportunities for their children. Deciding who their friends will be. Do they know how to make friends? Can they discriminate between different types of relationships?

Professionals

Professionals are no less subject to the myths and misconceptions of social-sexuality than anyone else. The same attitudes and values have had an impact on their lives as well. As has already been expressed, it is important that the professional first explore his or her own feelings prior to beginning work with the disabled or their families, thereby eliminating the possibility of engendering values that are not in keeping with those of the family and overcoming the possibility of conflict arising.

Professionals are expected to have all the information and be aware of all resources. For many there have been no courses available or taken with the result that they may feel inadequate or overwhelmed when working with disabled youngsters and their families concerning this issue.

In a 1981 study conducted by the Sex and Disability Project, disabled people reported that they were not receiving as many sexuality-related services as they needed and/or wanted, chief among these being sex and disability courses (48.9%). Yet when rehabilitation counselors were polled, 72% said that they did not provide sexuality-related services to clients predominantly because "Clients don't ask for this service" (70%), followed by "Lack of appropriate training" (51%) (Chipouras, 1981). The discomfort of both the disabled and the provider acts in collusion with strongly held societal myths to prevent provision of knowledge.

It is clear that many service providers need and want training about sexuality and disability. It is also obvious that disabled people are interested in receiving sex education/counseling services. To meet these needs, the provision of sexuality-related services must be considered a higher priority than it has been in the past. Policy makers and service providers need to view sexuality as an integral part of every person's well-being, and services addressing sexual issues should be included (if appropriate) in a client's overall plan (Chipouras, 1981).

Yet beyond the basics of information and knowledge provision are a number of value-laden issues that professionals need to approach when dealing with this topic:

1. How to respond in a professional manner and provide appropriate professional recommendations, support, and feedback when the topic may be directly opposed to one's personal value system thereby causing a great deal of discomfort.
2. How to access a client/student's knowledge prior to beginning an educational or counseling program.
3. How to determine a client/student's ability to understand his or her actions or someone else's and to make responsible decisions (informed consent).
4. How to facilitate the provision of information without overstepping boundaries or be in conflict with parental values.
5. How to work with parents so that they are more accepting and positive of their child's sexuality.
6. How to determine when a disabled student/client's behavior is a result of sexual abuse and not their disability. How to determine their ability to understand the consequences and therefore to counsel them.
7. How to deal with clients who exhibit aggressive behaviors perhaps as a result of sexual frustration (i.e., inability to masturbate).
8. How to proceed with educating or counseling students and clients without clear policies in place.

Issues to Be Addressed

There are a great number of issues that parents must confront and address in cooperation with professionals. Parents and professionals, although first embracing the understanding that the disabled are sexual, must also treat them in such a way that knowledge is understood while providing education and information. There is also a need to provide experiences and opportunities for the disabled to not only practice socialization but, to the extent appropriate, to engage in adult relationships. The present lack of social experience may leave youngsters emotionally unprepared for the intimacy and involvement of adult sexual relationships (Bregman & Castles, 1988). Regardless of the extent to which this takes place, the notion that all human beings require an intimacy of touch and caring makes it imperative that this issue be addressed. At present, because of their social isolation, many disabled individuals suffer from a deprivation of touching (Bregman & Castles, 1988).

Interventions

Clearly the most critical intervention is the recognition and acknowledgment of the existence of and right to the expression of sexuality for all people. This simple acknowledgment is as meaningful for the professional as it is for the parent and the person with the disability. Without this basic acceptance, people will forever be denied this most basic of human rights.

If this topic is to be dealt with effectively (and affectively), the professional will need greater information and training to feel comfortable with an increasingly active role. As conversations are begun and a climate developed that encourages openness, parents and people with disabilities will have questions not only about their own sexuality but how to deal with others'. Educational programs for everyone should be encouraged and incorporated into any plan. These programs, of course, should be provided at the appropriate level and utilize accessible information. Comfort level is an extremely important element in addressing this topic, and having a good knowledge base is chief to feeling more competent.

It is important that the professional work with the family on a process rather than focus solely on the content of sexuality at any one period of time. Sexuality needs to be seen as a natural progression in life and life as a series of transitions. In viewing development in such a way, parents and the disabled can not only be assisted through these stages, but transitions can be predicted and prepared for, lessening the emotional trauma of surprise at the occurrence of the inevitable. Assisting families in planning for the future is a promising intervention that may improve the quality of life for the young adult and other family members (Zetlin & Turner, 1985).

There are those who would deal with the issue of sexuality and the disabled by denying them their rights through lack of access. These "segregationists" vary from the extremists, who want to keep males and females completely apart, to the more frequently encountered people who panic when they see a loving relationship developing between two handicapped people. They assume that it must lead to either sexual intercourse or to frustration if the pair do not have the opportunity or perhaps the know-how to consummate their desires. Very often the "segregationists'" views and beliefs are based on the false assumption, which is all too common in our modern world, that only sexual intercourse can satisfy sexual need (Fairbrother, 1983). Parents and professionals in partnership must endeavor to find ways to ensure that a social continuum is available and to seek out ways that enable the disabled to be sexually responsible together, rather than keeping them apart.

Professionals must use their knowledge and assessment criteria to assist parents and the disabled in determining their future capabilities and goals so that appropriate decisions can be made. Parents need support through this stage as with all others. It is imperative that at the important and oftentimes stressful point of transition into adulthood, the few contacts parents do have with professionals be particularly supportive and positive (Zetlin & Turner, 1985). Professionals can use this supportive environment to help parents work through a number of difficult decisions for or with their child.

What are the parents frightened of?

What do they believe sex means to the handicapped people they know?

What signs of sexual awareness and need have they noticed?

What sort of relationships are formed and do the parents allow them to develop freely?

Do they offer the child an alternative, a place where a relationship is socially acceptable?

If the need is to make love and handicapped individuals do not know how, should they be guided?

Should the handicapped be encouraged to marry?

What should be the acceptable criteria before they encourage marriage?

Have the disabled the right to bear children?

What if there is no capability of independent loving? Does that exclude them from marriage? (Fairbrother 1983)

Opportunities should be encouraged and created so that the disabled have an occasion to practice their skills and develop them along with a full realm of choice in their lives. To do so early in a child's life makes each developmental transition easier. There is therefore a positive relationship between planning for adult needs and family functioning (Zetlin & Turner, 1985).

Conclusion

Because the right to appropriate and responsible sexual expression is one of the most basic aspects of adult functioning, normalization theory holds that persons with disabilities have a fundamental right to responsible sexual gratification (Bregman & Castles, 1988). Yet, it is still a common misconception among the public, professionals, the parents, and the disabled themselves that this is not inherently true. It is therefore first and foremost a priority that people begin to work toward providing everyone their humanity regardless of what moral or physical discomfort it creates. To do less than this creates a great deal more damage and pain for someone whose basic rights to simple closeness and touch are often denied. Many barriers are being eliminated. The first was limited access to even more limited information. That is now changing. The second and the most desperate problem is lack of opportunities to form partnerships and loving relationships (Daniels, 1981).

The disabled and those who love them and work with them must labor to develop a world in which their need for social-sexual relationships is respected and their pleasure in being sexual persons is encouraged. The conclusion must be reached that the sexual problems of the disabled are really the problems of parents and professionals and all who come in contact with them. Others' problems, attitudes, beliefs, prejudices, fulfillment, or lack of it are imposed upon those with disabilities. Because the balance of power frequently creates an ability to determine the destiny of these persons, they are intruded upon and their adult rights shaped by others' needs. They are directed and constantly observed in their every move. They are never allowed to be alone. They are not given opportunities to explore relationships independently, to make mistakes, and to find fulfillment. "They" do not need to change; all they need is loving guidance and the opportunity to fulfill themselves (Fairbrother, 1983).

References

Bregman, S., & Castles, E. (1988). Insights and interventions into sexual needs of the disabled adolescent. In A. Dell Orto & M. Blechar Gibbons (Eds.), *Family interventions throughout chronic illness and disability* (pp. 184-191). New York: Springer.

Brotherson, M. J., Houghton, J., Turnbull, A., Bronicki, G. J., Roeder-Gordon, C., Summers, J. A., & Turnbull III, H. R. (1988). Parental planning for sons and daughters with disabilities. *Transitions Into Adulthood, 23,* 165-172.

Calderone, M., & Johnson, E. (1981). *The family book about sexuality.* New York: Bantam.

Chipouras, S. (1981). Sexuality-related services for disabled people. In D. Bullard & S. Knight (Eds.), *Sexuality and physical disability personal perspectives.* St. Louis: C. W. Mosby.

Cornelius, D., Chipouras, S., Makas, E., & Daniels, S. (1982). *Who cares? A handbook in sex education and counseling services for disabled people* (2nd ed.). Baltimore: University Park Press.

Craft, A., & Craft, M. (1978). *Sex and the mentally handicapped.* London: Routledge and Kegan Paul.

Craft, A., & Craft, M. (1982). Implications for the future. In A. Craft & M. Craft (Eds.), *Sex education and counseling for mentally handicapped people* (pp. 299-300). London: Costello.

Daniels, S. (1981). Critical issues in sexuality and disability. In D. Bullard & S. Knight (Eds.), *Sexuality and physical disability personal perspectives.* St. Louis: C. W. Mosby.

Dixon, H., & Mullinar, G. (Eds.). (1985). *Taught not caught: Strategies for sex education.* London: Learning Development Aids.

Fairbrother, P. (1983). The parents' viewpoint. In A. Craft & M. Craft (Eds.), *Sex education and counseling for mentally handicapped people* (pp. 95-108). London: Costello.

Gordon, S. (1974). *Sexual rights for the people who happen to be handicapped.* Syracuse: Center on Human Policy.

Grantham, E., & Russell, P. (1985). Parents as partners. In M. Griffiths & P. Russell (Eds.), *Working together with handicapped children: Guidelines for parents and professionals* (pp. 38-45). London: Souvenir Press and National Children's Bureau.

Lewis, M., Feiring, C., & Brooks-Gunn, J. (1988). Young children's social network as a function of age and dysfunction. *Infant Mental Health Journal, 9,* 142-157.

Lewis, V. (1987). *Development and handicaps.* Oxford: Basil Blackwell.

Miezio, P. M. (1983). *Parenting children with disabilities: A professional source for physicians and guide for parents.* New York: Marcel Dekker.

Schuster, C. S. (1987). Sex education of the visually impaired child: The role of parents. *Journal of Visual Impairment and Blindness, 81,* 98-99.

Stewart, W. F. R. (1979). *The sexual side of handicap: A guide for the caring professions.* Cambridge: Woodhead-Faulkner.

Symonds, M. E., & Wickware, L. (1978). Sex education of children with disabilities. In A. Comfort (Ed.), *Sexual consequences of disability* (pp. 243-245). Philadelphia: George F. Stickly.

Thorton, C. (1981). Sex education for disabled children and adolescents. In D. Bullard & S. Knight (Eds.), *Sexuality and physical disability personal perspectives* (pp. 229-234). St. Louis: C. W. Mosby.

Zetlin, A. G., & Turner, J. L. (1985). Transition from adolescence to adulthood: Perspectives of mentally retarded individuals and their families. *Journal of Mental Deficiency, 89,* 570-579.

16

THE EXCEPTIONAL CHILD GROWS UP: TRANSITIONS

Edward M. Levinson and Lynne M. McKee

Parents of adolescents frequently face emotional turmoil when the time comes for their children to make personal and vocational decisions regarding their future. Adolescent decisions regarding living arrangements, higher education, vocational pursuits, and marriage often cause parents to wonder if they have done their best in providing their children with the skills they need to make realistic and informed decisions, and to become contented, responsible, and self-sufficient adults.

For a variety of reasons, the parents of handicapped adolescents face even greater challenges when the time for such decision making is reached. Many parents continue to feel guilt and personal responsibility for their child's handicap and have difficulty "letting go" when the time comes. Parents of handicapped children are all too often faced with the knowledge that, in the past, the vocational and subsequent life-style options for the handicapped have been quite limited compared to those available for the nonhandicapped population.

Fortunately, society's views toward the handicapped have been changing. Although the right to work is not viewed as an entitlement, efforts are being made to extend the opportunity for meaningful employment to a greater number of handicapped persons. The purpose of this chapter is to explore the issues involved in the transition of handicapped individuals from school to adult society. In so doing, the chapter will review relevant literature on transitioning, including the legislation that facilitated transitioning efforts and transitioning "models." Finally, it will discuss the critically important role of parent–professional collaboration in the transition process.

Overview

The life and employment adjustment concerns expressed by parents of handicapped children alluded to earlier are well founded. A number of sources have explored the adjustment of handicapped persons into the community from the standpoints of employment, living arrangements, and general satisfaction with life. The President's Committee on the Employment of the Handicapped reports that only 21% of handicapped persons will become fully employed, 40% will be underemployed and at the poverty level, and 26% will be on welfare (Pennsylvania Transition from School to the Workplace, 1986). Similarly, Rusch and Phelps (1987) have reported that 67% of handicapped Americans between the ages of 16 and 64 are not working. Of those handicapped persons who are working, 75% are employed on a part-time basis, and of those not employed, 67% indicated that they would like to be employed.

Numerous statewide surveys have also been undertaken in an effort to determine the status of handicapped young people who are no longer in school. Studies in Florida (Fardig, Algozzine, Schwartz, Hensel, & Westling, 1985), Washington (Edgar, 1987), Colorado (Mithaug, Horiuchi, & Fanning, 1985), Vermont (Hasazi, Gordon, & Roe, 1985; Hasazi et al., 1985), and Nebraska (Schalock & Lilley, 1986; Schalock et al., 1986) have indicated that the employment rate for handicapped individuals is generally higher for females than for males and ranges between 45% and 70% depending upon the severity of disability and geographical location (rural, urban, metropolitan). There is also evidence that a large number of those who are employed are employed on a part-time basis, and some studies indicate that many of those employed are earning minimum wage or less. Between 64% and 82% of those contacted reported living at home with their parent/guardian.

There also appears to be an elevated high school attrition rate among handicapped students. Edgar (1987) reports that 42% of learning disabled and behaviorally disturbed students leave school before graduating and that 18% of mentally retarded students do the same. Rusch and Phelps (1987) cite a survey done by Owing and Stocking in 1985 in which 30,000 sophomores and 28,000 seniors including those self-identified as handicapped were studied on a longitudinal basis. Their findings indicate that those students with mild handicaps fared poorly regardless of whether they were receiving regular or special education. They reported that 22% of the 1980 sophomores had dropped out of school between the sophomore and senior year as compared with 12% of the nonhandicapped students. Additionally, 45% of these students were in the lowest quartile on combined vocabulary, reading, math, and science tests, and only 29% of them were enrolled in vocational education classes.

In terms of more severely impaired individuals, there is evidence that of those placed in sheltered workshop situations, very few will ever move into competitive employment. Likewise, a very small percentage of those placed into adult day activity programs will have the opportunity of moving into sheltered or competitive employment opportunities.

There is little doubt that given the high unemployment rate, the high percentage of handicapped individuals continuing to live at home, and the elevated high school dropout rate for the handicapped, efforts in the area of special education have not resulted in integrating these individuals successfully into society.

The economic cost to society of supporting the high unemployment and underemployment rates among the handicapped population is staggering. Poplin (1981) estimated the cost of such dependency to exceed $114 billion per year, and she believed that this figure was increasing yearly. Batsche (1982) offered similar statistics and estimated that the cost of maintaining an unemployed handicapped individual in an institution in Illinois exceeded the cost of educating a person at Harvard! In 1984, the U.S. Department of Education, Office of Special Education and Rehabilitative Services, reported that of the 16 million noninstitutionalized disabled persons of working age, as many as 15 million are potentially employable at an approximate cost savings of $114 billion per year. It should be noted that currently most of the money going to handicapped persons is going into programs that support dependence rather than into programs that attempt to facilitate independence (Pennsylvania Departments of Education & Labor and Industry, 1986).

However, the social, physical, and emotional benefits to be derived by handicapped individuals from successful work and community adjustment are not to be slighted by the economic benefits to be derived by society. When one considers that during the course of a lifetime, 94,000 hours are spent at work (Anderson, 1982), and that the average American spends approximately half of his or her waking hours at work, 5 out of 7 days a week, for all but 2 weeks of the year, the importance of work in people's lives becomes clear. Research has indicated that an individual's self-worth is intimately related to work performance and satisfaction (Dore & Meachum, 1973; Greenhaus, 1971; Kalanidi & Deivasenapathy, 1980; Snyder & Ferguson, 1976; Super, 1957); and that one's overall adjustment to work is associated with both physical and mental health (Kornhauser, 1965; O'Toole, 1973; Portigal, 1976) and overall life satisfaction (Bedeian & Marbert, 1979; Haavio-Mannila, 1971; Iris & Barrett, 1972; Orphen, 1978; Schmitt & Mellon, 1980). Obviously, then, the overall quality of life experienced by a handicapped individual will, to some extent, be influenced by the degree to which that individual successfully obtains and maintains employment.

Despite what many believe, the unemployment and underemployment rates among the handicapped population do not appear to be a function of a lack of available job opportunities. A review of occupational trends and predictions between now and the year 2000 indicates that in the future jobs will be available for individuals who do not possess high skill levels, including handicapped individuals who have been appropriately trained. Projections indicate a significant increase in the number of jobs for health service workers, cleaning and building service workers, food preparation workers, food service workers, and personal service workers (Silvestri & Lukasiewicz, 1987). With appropriate special education and transition services, many handicapped individuals can successfully enter and maintain employment in these and other employment fields.

In an effort to facilitate transition from school to work, federal and state governments are now making the issue of transition a priority for all handicapped citizens. Efforts are being made to integrate and coordinate special education, vocational education, vocational rehabilitation, and other adult services and to provide handicapped individuals with a more functionally oriented curriculum that will better prepare them for adulthood. Many of these efforts have been spurred by federal legislation.

Legislative Background

Legislation designed to assist handicapped individuals in acquiring and maintaining employment can be found in the fields of special education, vocational rehabilitation, and vocational education. A landmark piece of special education legislation is The Education for All Handicapped Children Act of 1975 (P.L. 94-142) which mandated free, appropriate public education for all handicapped children between the ages of 3 and 22. The bill specifically calls for ". . . organized educational programs which are directly related to the preparation of individuals for paid or unpaid employment, or for additional preparation for a career requiring other than a baccalaureate or advanced degree." In 1983, P.L. 94-142 was amended by P.L. 98-199. This amendment gives even greater emphasis to the importance of vocational education for handicapped students by calling for state demonstration grants that would improve secondary special education programs, create incentives for employers to hire the handicapped, increase educational opportunities at the postsecondary level, increase supported work opportunities, and make better use of job-training placement services for the disabled.

In vocational rehabilitation, the Rehabilitation Act of 1973 (P.L. 93-112) provided federal support for the training of both physically and mentally impaired individuals. The law authorized grants to vocational rehabilitation agencies for counseling, training, referral, and other services and mandated that priority be given to those who are the most severely handicapped. This legislation requires that the counselor, handicapped individual, and parent/guardian participate in developing an Individualized Written Rehabilitation Plan that describes the services to be provided to the handicapped individual and indicates what agency is to be responsible for providing the identified services. In 1978, P.L. 93-112 was amended by P.L. 95-602. This amendment emphasizes the provision of services to the severely handicapped, including services related to independent living arrangements. This amendment also calls for cooperative relationships between special education, vocational education, and vocational rehabilitation.

Section 504 of the Rehabilitation Act is sometimes referred to as the "bill of rights" for handicapped persons as it prohibits discrimination on the basis of handicap in any program that receives federal monies. This Act also calls for the mainstreaming of handicapped schoolchildren and for the provision of vocational counseling, guidance, and placement on a nondiscriminatory basis.

The Vocational Education Act of 1963 (P.L. 88-210) authorizes federal grants to assist states in maintaining and improving vocational education, in development of new vocational education programs, and in providing part-time employment to allow individuals to continue vocational training. The aim is to allow all individuals the opportunity of participating in quality, realistic vocational training opportunities. This act also allows federal funds to be used for occupational training with handicapped individuals but it does not mandate that any portion of the funds be utilized in this manner.

The Vocational Education Act of 1963 was amended in 1968 (P.L. 90-576) and again in 1976 (P.L. 94-482) to provide federal support for handicapped persons who had not been given equal access to publically supported vocational education programs. This legislation calls for state plans that provide for the interfacing of special education and vocational education, the use of procedural safeguards from 94-142 to assure that secondary school participants get necessary services, and the mainstreaming of the handicapped with their nonhandicapped peers wherever possible.

In 1984, the Carl D. Perkins Vocational Education Act (P.L. 98-524) amended the Vocational Education Act of 1963. This far-reaching piece of legislation mandates increased services for both handicapped and disadvantaged citizens. Mandates of the legislation include that information be provided to parents and students concerning vocational education opportunities no later than the beginning of 9th grade and at least 1 year before the student enters the grade level at which vocational education is offered. Information must also be given to students and parents regarding the eligibility requirements for enrolling in these vocational programs. Once enrolled, students must receive: an assessment of interests, abilities and special needs; special services including adaptation of curriculum, instruction, equipment, and facilities; guidance, counseling, and career development activities conducted by a professionally trained counselor; and special counseling services designed to facilitate transition from school to postschool employment or training.

Transitional Models

As mentioned in the previous section, P.L. 98-199 is designed to improve the quality of the transition experience for handicapped youth. As such, the bill authorized the Office of Special Education and Rehabilitative Services (OSERS) to spend $6.6 million in grants and contracts for the purpose of enhancing education and related services to improve the transition of handicapped youth into postsecondary education, employment, or other adult services. The major objectives of the bill are to stimulate the development of secondary special education programs and to coordinate services that are involved in the transition process (Rusch & Phelps, 1987).

Office of Special Education and Rehabilitation Services Model (OSERS)

"OSERS Programming for the Transition of Youth with Disabilities: Bridges from School to Working Life" was published in 1984 and became the "generic" roots from which many other transition models grew. In this document (Will, 1984), transition is defined in the following manner:

> The transition from school to working life is an outcome oriented process encompassing a broad array of services and experiences that lead to employment. Transition is a period that includes high school, the point of graduation, additional postsecondary education or adult services, and the initial years in employment. Transition is a bridge between the security and structure offered by the school and the opportunities and risks of adult life. Any bridge requires both a solid span and a secure foundation at either end. The transition from school to work and adult life requires sound preparation in the secondary school, adequate support at the point of school leaving, and secure opportunities and services, if needed, in adult situations. (pp. 9-24)

There are three underlying assumptions inherent in the OSERS model: (1) the individual who is leaving the school system is leaving a somewhat organized system and entering a more complex and confusing system that is not well understood by professionals, let alone by parents and consumers; (2) transition plans should address all persons with disabilities and it is the professional's responsibility to identify the services needed to assist in the transition of each individual; (3) paid employment is the goal of the transition plan. This model calls for a firm high school foundation in which the curricula in both special and vocational education are adequate in terms of allowing students to leave school with job skills appropriate for the local community. Whenever possible, it is suggested that potential employers have an opportunity to observe students' performance within community jobs.

The OSERS model provides for three "bridges" from high school to employment: (1) transition without special services—individuals using their own resources or those used by all citizens to find gainful employment or to continue their education at the postsecondary level; (2) transition with time-limited services—

individuals using such services as vocational rehabilitation and job-training programs to assist in gaining employment; once employment is secured, the individual is able to function independently; (3) transition with ongoing services— individuals using continuing adult services to obtain and maintain employment as an alternative to custodial or sheltered employment. The final outcome of the transition plan is employment.

The Virginia Commonwealth University Model

Paul Wehman (1986) of Virginia Commonwealth University has developed a plan that expands and enhances many of the concepts outlined in the OSERS model. His transition plan suggests that the transition from school to the workplace is a three-stage process that includes the following: (1) input and foundation— school instruction; (2) process—planning for the transition process; and (3) employment outcome—placement into meaningful employment.

The school instruction portion of this plan emphasizes the importance of a functional curriculum within which activities are specifically designed to prepare students for vocational placement. It calls for integrated school services, including exposure to natural work settings with training taking place within the community whenever possible. Finally, it calls for community-based instruction in which students over the age of 12 spend decreasing amounts of time in the classroom and increasing amounts of time at job sites learning job skills, interpersonal skills, and other skills that will directly benefit them when they leave the school environment.

The process of planning for vocational transition includes the development of an individualized transition plan that lists the competencies to be achieved by the student and the transition services to be provided both during and following the school years. The plan should emphasize functional skills required on the job, at home, and in the community. Participation of the parent/guardian is viewed as critical, and this model calls for parent education activities to improve the background information and skill effectiveness of parents as they participate in transition planning. Interagency cooperation is also an aspect of the planning phase. It requires the involvement and cooperation of various agencies that will be involved with the student during the period of transition. Finally, this model presents several employment outcomes that provide alternative employment approaches to handicapped persons, including competitive employment, supported competitive employment, enclaves, and specialized industrial training.

Other Transition Models

Several other transition models have been developed in various states including Missouri, Minnesota, Pennsylvania, Washington, and Oregon. Some, like the

OSERS and VCU models described above, emphasize the issue of employment and see employment as being the "heart" of the transition process. Others view transition from a broader perspective and see employment as being but one component of the overall transition effort.

Halpern (1985) has developed a model that emphasizes the nonvocational aspects of transition. He views successful community adjustment as the goal of transition and believes that quality of life and social and interpersonal issues are just as important as employment. Through research conducted in Washington, Oregon, California, and Colorado, Halpern has concluded that success in employment does not necessarily correlate with success in other areas of life. Consequently, he advocates programs that consider all dimensions when determining need for services.

The use of a functional curriculum, with emphasis placed on vocational and career as well as life-skills issues, is inherent in most transition models. Brolin (1986) has developed a "Life-Centered Career Education (LCCE) Model for the Transition from School to Work," which emphasizes the inclusion of career-oriented education even at the preschool level. Brolin presents 12 propositions, generated from research in a variety of areas, that he believes will facilitate the training of handicapped individuals and will assist in their acquiring the skills necessary to become self-sufficient adults. Included in these propositions are: the integration of career education in all areas of instruction: "hands-on" learning experiences wherever possible; active partnership among schools, parents/guardians, business, and industry and community agencies; and the creation of a position for a Training Resource Coordinator who would assume responsibility for transition services. Brolin describes this as a total-person approach that emphasizes all aspects of the individual's development—not just vocational development.

Finally, some concern exists among transition advocates that the current Excellence in Education Movement may hamper efforts to get functional curriculums into classrooms where they are perceived as being needed. This education movement calls for a set number of credits in English, Mathematics, Science, Social Studies, and other areas. Not only are many of the courses in these areas not necessarily "functional" for all students, but the requirement that all students be subjected to such an academically oriented curriculum could take time away from functional, life skill, and vocational instruction. Relatedly, many professionals are currently recognizing the need for alternative diplomas that would indicate the specialized instruction the student has received and would reflect the student's accomplishments more adequately than a certificate of attendance, which is the current alternative to a regular diploma. Although these issues are as yet unresolved, they will most certainly influence transitioning efforts in the coming years.

Working with Parents

> Any effort at improving the school to work transition for handicapped youth that fails to incorporate parental involvement as a major component of the process will have limited success. . . . A mutual trust relationship between parents and professionals needs to be nourished. . . . The parent/student will have to choose the type of activity or service outcome that is important to them. Preferably this sort of decision making should not be done in isolation, but more appropriately through the participation of the parent, client, professional team. (Pennsylvania Transition from School to the Workplace, 1986; p. 83)

Research involving the impact of parental participation has indeed shown that the role of the family in the transition process is critical. In studying moderately and severely handicapped individuals, Schalock et al. (1986) found that students whose families were moderately to highly involved in their programming were more successful on employment outcome measures than were students whose families had low involvement. Further findings indicated that those who had high family involvement received higher wages and worked more hours/weeks than did those with low family involvement. Schalock and Lilley (1986) reported that family involvement is repeatedly shown to be related to successful living and employment. Hasazi et al. (1985), in studying educably and trainably mentally retarded individuals, found that 61% secured employment through a self-family-friend network. In a similar study, Hasazi, Gordon, and Roe (1985) found that among all handicapped postschool individuals, 84% had found work through the self-family-friend network. The value of active family involvement in achieving successful transition appears to be well documented.

Unfortunately, there is some indication that as a child grows older, the family typically becomes less involved in the educational planning process. Johnson, Bruininks, and Thurlow (1987) cite a 1982 study by Lynch and Stein which found that parents of older students participated in Individual Education Planning conferences significantly less often than did parents of younger children.

Teachers are apparently dissatisfied with such decreased parental involvement and desire more collaboration with parents. Benz and Halpern (1987) reported on the results of questionnaires sent to administrators, teachers, and parents in the state of Oregon, and found that 36% of the responding teachers indicated that they were dissatisfied or very dissatisfied with parental support received and 44% indicated that they would like more communication and parent involvement in classroom activities. Over half of the parents indicated contact with their child's teacher once per term or less. Relatedly, one third of the parents indicated that they had no idea what their children would be doing in terms of employment either 1 year or 10 years following high school, and one quarter of them had no idea where their children would be living 1 or 10 years after school. It is apparent that the role of the parent in regard to educational and transitional planning must be expanded.

The involvement of the parent in the educational process must begin early in the child's life. It is highly unlikely that a parent who has not been involved in the child's educational planning prior to adolescence will suddenly become involved at the time of transition. It is important that "vocational awareness" on the part of the parent begin early in the child's academic career and be ongoing throughout the child's life. The parent must recognize that the purpose of education is to prepare the child academically, socially, and vocationally for adulthood. The professional must assist the parent in seeing education from a multidimensional perspective. As Fine has noted elsewhere in this volume, the professional must assume multiple roles when assisting parents. Among these roles are the roles of therapist, expert, and advocate.

Therapist

Professionals must be aware that even at the level of transition, many parents continue to experience guilt regarding their child's handicap. Likewise, parents are frequently apprehensive and fearful about their child's future. In fact, many parents who have successfully dealt with these feelings while the child was in school experience renewed guilt and anxiety when they realize that their child is ready to begin life as an adult. There are also some parents who never fully accept the idea that their child is handicapped; these parents keep expecting that at some point in time their child will be "normal." These feelings and issues can frequently present obstacles to objective and realistic decision making on the part of parents and hence jeopardize collaborative transitional programming. As such, they must be identified and resolved by the professional before additional programming is initiated. In some cases, short-term therapy may be necessary to resolve these issues.

Expert

The role of expert requires that the professional assume both an educational and problem-solving perspective when working with parents in transitioning. As an expert, the professional must educate parents about the kinds of decisions they and their children must make, and the type of information that must be considered if one is to make realistic and informed vocational decisions. The types of decisions that must be made vary, but include such things as what vocational training program should the child be enrolled in, what type of job placement services should be initiated, what type of job should be sought, what on-the-job assistance or modifications will be necessary, etc. The type of information the professional must provide to parents in order to facilitate such decision making is two-fold: (1) information about their child (i.e., their abilities, interests, values, personality characteristics, etc.) and (2) information about the world of work (i.e., the rewards, requirements, and demands of different training programs and jobs). The former can be gleaned via books, periodicals, and other reference materials. Although it is the professional's responsibility to insure that this information is available to the parent, the professional should encourage the parents to gather as much of this information as they can on their own. Once this information is available, the parent and professional can jointly assume a problem-solving perspective in making the necessary vocational decisions.

Advocate

As mentioned throughout this chapter, the transition process is complex and often confusing to parents. Many different professionals and agencies are often involved and assume different roles in the process. To complicate matters, agencies frequently use different criteria to determine eligibility for services, and professionals often disagree. As an advocate for the parent and their child, it is the professional's responsibility to sort through this confusion, to identify all services to which the child is entitled, and to attempt to clarify and resolve all disagreements among professionals. As an advocate, the professional should attempt to organize all information and present this information to the parent in a highly ordered and coherent fashion. Obviously, then, in addition to preserving the rights and privileges of the parent and child, the role of advocate also assumes that the professional will act as a liaison between the parent and other involved agencies and professionals. The importance of this role will become clear when team planning is discussed in the next section of this chapter.

Team Planning

In an effort to provide better-organized transition services to handicapped individuals, many states have developed interagency agreements. These agreements involve educational and vocational rehabilitation personnel and other adult service providers who function as a team in facilitating the transition process. Typically, such teams will consist of any combination of teachers (regular education, vocational education, and special education), psychologists (school and clinical), counselors (school and vocational rehabilitation), vocational evaluators, social workers, and administrators. There are three primary types of teams with which the professional should be familiar. First, there is the multidisciplinary team in which each professional independently makes recommendations and these recommendations are collected by one team member who is responsible for generating a final report. Second, there is the interdisciplinary team in which the client is evaluated by a variety of professionals who then make decisions by group consensus. Finally, there is the transdisciplinary team in which professionals continue to be involved after the initial assessment in terms of interaction, evaluation, and assessment, but one professional assumes the responsibility of carrying out the recommendations and working directly with the client/family (Pennsylvania Departments of Education & Labor and Industry, 1987).

In terms of working with client/families, and in view of the ongoing nature of the transition process, the transdisciplinary team approach offers numerous advantages over other team planning models. Although most Individual Education Plans are completed by interdisciplinary teams, the transdisciplinary team may be better for the following reasons:

1. It is easy for a client/family to be intimidated in an interdisciplinary team meeting. When many "experts" are discussing what is "best," it is easy for the feelings of the client or client's parents to be overlooked. By utilizing a transdisciplinary approach and having one professional function as the main contact person between the client/family and the team, this can be avoided.

2. The transition process is an ongoing one—as both educators and adult service providers have large case loads, it is more economical to use the transdisciplinary model.

3. The transdisciplinary model is less confusing for the client/family—if there are questions or concerns, they know exactly who to contact.

4. The "responsibility" for the transition plan rests primarily in the hands of one individual—there is less likelihood of "buck passing" if one person bears the primary responsibility for overseeing the plan.

5. Unfortunately, there are issues regarding "turf" and "territory" that frequently arise when a team approach such as this is used. When a client/family becomes involved in these issues, the outcome is never positive. Utilizing a transdisciplinary model can help to avoid involving clients in these issues.

Individual Planning

Philosophically, professionals should view themselves as advocates for the client and the client's family, and should attempt to facilitate realistic and informed vocational decision making. To the maximum extent possible, responsibility for decision making should rest with the client and/or the client's family. The professional's role should be one in which he or she provides the client with the information neccesary for realistic and informed decision making and attempts to remove obstacles (such as guilt, anxiety, etc.) that may impede such decision making.

The individual professional working with a client/family to facilitate successful transition from school to work must be knowledgeable about a number of topics that cross several major disciplines including psychology, vocational education, vocational rehabilitation, and special education. Although these topics cannot be described in detail within this chapter, the professional working as a member of a transdisciplinary transitioning team should have a general understanding of three such topics: vocational assessment, vocational instruction, and vocational placement options and considerations.

Vocational assessment. In order to identify realistic vocational objectives for clients, and to plan appropriately the services neccessary for clients to eventually attain these objectives, information must be gathered relative to a client's vocational strengths and weaknesses. Vocational assessment is the process by which such information is acquired. Typically, vocational assessments are completed by multidisciplinary teams which include vocational evaluators, psychologists, teachers, and guidance counselors. Comprehensive vocational assessments include measures of mental ability, academic achievement, small/large motor coordination, personality, vocational interests, vocational aptitudes, vocational adaptive behavior (appropriateness of behavior in the work setting), and functional life skills (Hohenshil, Levinson, & Buckland-Heer, 1985). A variety of assessment techniques are utilized to complete such assessments, including observation, interviews, paper-pencil tests, performance tests, work samples (specific job functions from a single occupation or a group of occupations which are performed under observations of a trained evaluator), simulated work experience, and work experience. Generally, it has been advocated that such assessments be completed as part of a handicapped student's triennial reevaluation (which is required by law), and that such assessments be initiated early in a handicapped student's school career (as early as the 6th grade) (Levinson & Capps, 1985). The results of such assessments should form the foundation for planning and initiating vocational education and instruction and should be shared with the client and his or her family as part of the vocational decision-making process.

Vocational education/instruction. As alluded to earlier, a functional skills approach to instruction should be advocated by professionals involved in transitioning efforts with handicapped clients. Vocational assessment results should be used to determine what functional life skills (including academic skills in reading, writing, and computation) necessary for independent functioning in the community and on the job need to be taught. Similarly, vocational assessment results should provide the professional with some preliminary information relative to the appropriateness of training in various occupational areas. Having identified realistic vocational training options for a client, training should initially focus on facilitating acquisition of skills necessary for entry-level employment in the occupational area and gradually introduce advanced skills needed for higher-level jobs. For more severely handicapped clients, instruction should be a continual process of teaching a skill, testing to assess acquisition, and teaching until mastery. Once mastery is reached, the next sequential skill leading to entry level employment would be taught. In order to facilitate generalization of skills from training to the job, it is often advocated that training be conducted on the job. For more information on Life-Centered Career Education, Functional Community Based Special Education, Work Adjustment Training Programs, and other organized training programs designed to accomplish the goals listed above, the reader is referred to Levinson, Peterson, and Elston (in press).

Vocational Placement Options/Considerations

The vocational placement options for handicapped individuals are many and varied and are expanding as vocational services for this population improve. Options can be categorized as competitive employment, in which individuals are placed in competitively salaried community jobs without ongoing support services; supported employment, in which individuals are placed in jobs with special assistance from "job coaches" who provide ongoing support (including training, retraining, problem resolution, etc.); and sheltered employment, in which individuals are placed in businesses, operated by human service agencies, typically termed "sheltered workshops" or "work activity centers."

A variety of approaches can be used to facilitate the job placement of handicapped individuals, including job-seeking skills training, job matching and referral services, job adaptation, and community-based training and supported employment. Job-seeking skills training teaches individuals (usually via classes) the skills necessary to obtain and keep a job (skills such as résumé preparation, interviewing, etc.) after which individuals assume responsibility for seeking out their own jobs. Job matching and referral services are placement resources in which job openings are collected and matched to the interests and capabilities of job applicants. This service is frequently used in combination with other services. Job modification is a type of selective placement approach that focuses on adaptation of job tasks and the working environment in order to accommodate the needs and limitations of the individual. Community-based training and supported employment, including on-the-job training and work-study programs, is a placement process in which training is provided by an employer and vocational counselors or job coaches monitor client progress and assist in remediating job-related difficulties. Selection of an appropriate job-placement strategy should be made in consultation with the client and/or client's family and will depend on the individual needs and characteristics of the client.

In addition to possessing knowledge in the previously identified areas, the professional involved in transitioning must:

1. Be knowledgeable about the roles, responsibilities, and expertise of the other transitioning "team" professionals and be able to refer the client and his or her parents to these other professionals when appropriate.
2. Be knowledgeable about the support service agencies available in the local community and establish liaison relationships with these agencies.
3. Be knowledgeable about the employment options and occupational training alternatives that exist in the local community so that this information can be used by the professional in collaboration with the client and parent during decision making.
4. Be knowledgeable about local job market trends and consider how such trends may eventually alter the occupational training and placement options currently available.

Summary

As the full impact of recent federal and state initiatives aimed at facilitating transitioning of handicapped individuals is experienced, it is likely that an increased number of mental health and social service workers will become involved in transitioning efforts. The success of these efforts may ultimately influence the overall quality of life experienced by the handicapped individual with whom the professional is working. For this reason, transitioning presents a new and critically important challenge to the professional working with handicapped individuals and their parents. This chapter has reviewed several different transition models and the various pieces of federal legislation that have spurred development of these models. The roles of professionals in facilitating transitioning efforts have been reviewed, particularly in regard to the responsibilities these professionals have to parents throughout the transitioning process. The chapter concluded with a brief discussion of knowledge across the disciplines of special education, vocational education, and vocational rehabilitation necessary for successful transitional programming. It is the hope of the authors that the chapter has provided an initial base of information pertinent to a professional's involvement in transitional programming.

References

Anderson, W. T. (1982). *Job satisfaction among school psychologists.* Doctoral dissertation, Virginia Polytechnic Institute and State University, Blacksburg, VA.

Batsche, C. (1982). *Handbook for vocational school psychology.* Des Moines, IA: Iowa Department of Public Instruction.

Bedeian, A. G., & Marbert, L. D. (1979). Individual differences in self-perception and the job-life satisfaction relationship. *Journal of Social Psychology, 109,* 111-118.

Benz, M. R., & Halpern, A. S. (1987). Transition services for secondary students with mild disabilities: A statewide perspective. *Exceptional Children, 53*(6), 507-514.

Brolin, D. E. (1986) A model for providing comprehensive transitional services: The role of special education. In J. Chadsey-Rusch & C. Hanley-Maxwell (Eds.), *Enhancing transition from school to the workplace for handicapped youth: Personnel preparation implications* (pp. 116-128). Champaign, IL: National Network for Professional Development in Vocational Special Education.

Dore, R., & Meachum, M. (1973). Self-concept and interests related to job satisfaction of managers. *Personnel Psychology, 26,* 49-59.

Edgar, E. (1987). Secondary programs in special education: Are many of them justifiable? *Exceptional Children, 53*(6), 555-561.

Fardig, D. B., Algozzine, R. F., Schwartz, S. E., Hensel, J. E., & Westling, D. L. (1985). Postsecondary vocational adjustment of rural, mildly handicapped students. *Exceptional Children, 52*(2), 115-121.

Greenhaus, J. H. (1981). Self-esteem as an influence on occupational choice and occupational satisfaction. *Journal of Vocational Behavior, 1,* 75-83

Haavio-Mannila, E. (1971). Satisfaction with family, work, leisure, and life among men and women. *Human Relations, 24*(6), 585-601.

Halpern, A. S. (1985). Transition: A look at the foundations. *Exceptional Children, 51*(6), 479-486.

Hasazi, S. B., Gordon, L. R., & Roe, C. A. (1985). Factors associated with the employment status of handicapped youth exiting high school from 1979 to 1983. *Exceptional Children, 51*(6), 455-469.

Hasazi, S. B., Gordon, L. R., Roe, C. A., Hull, M., Finck, K., & Salembier, G. (1985). A statewide follow-up on post high school employment and residential status of students labeled "mentally retarded." *Education and Training of the Mentally Retarded, 20*(4), 222-235.

Hohenshil, T. H., Levinson, E. M., & Buckland-Heer, K. (1985). Vocational assessment practices for school psychologists. In A. Thomas & J. Grimes (Eds.), *Best practices in school psychology manual* (pp. 215-228). Kent, OH: National Association of School Psychologists.

Iris, B., & Barrett, G. V. (1972). Some relations between job and life satisfaction and job importance. *Journal of Applied Psychology, 56*(4), 301-307.

Johnson, D. R., Bruininks, R. H., & Thurlow, M. L. (1987). Meeting the challenge of transition service planning through improved interagency cooperation. *Exceptional Children, 53*(6), 522-530.

Kalanidi, M. S., & Deivasenapathy, P. (1980). Self-concept and job satisfaction among the self-employed. *Psychological Studies, 25,* 39-41.

Kornhauser, A. W. (1965). *Mental health of the industrial worker.* New York: Wiley.

Levinson, E. M., & Capps, C. F. (1985). Vocational assessment and special education triennial reevaluations at the secondary school level. *Psychology in the Schools, 22*(3), 283-292.

Levinson, E. M., Peterson, M., & Elston, R. (in press). Vocational counseling with the mentally retarded. In D. C. Strohmer & H. T. Prout (Eds.), *Counseling and psychotherapy with mentally retarded persons.* Brandon, VT: Clinical Psychology.

Mithaug, D.E., Horiuchi, C. N., & Fanning, P. N. (1985). A report on the Colorado statewide follow-up survey of special education students. *Exceptional Children, 51*(5), 397-404.

Orphen, C. (1978). Work and non-work satisfaction: A causal correlational analysis. *Journal of Applied Psychology, 63*(4), 530-532.

O'Toole, J. (Ed.). (1973). *Work in America: Report of a special task force to the Secretary of Health, Education, and Welfare.* Cambridge, MA: MIT Press.

Pennsylvania Departments of Education & Labor and Industry. (1986). *Pennsylvania Transition from School to the Workplace* (pp. 3, 7, 83). Harrisburg, PA: Author.

Poplin, P. (1981). The development and execution of the IEP: Who does what, when, to whom? In T. H. Hohenshil & W. T. Anderson (Eds.), *School psychological services in secondary vocational education: Roles in programs for handicapped students* (pp. 26-39). Blacksburg, VA: Virginia Tech. (ERIC Reproduction No. 215245)

Portigal, A. H. (1976). *Towards the measurement of work satisfaction.* Paris: Organization for Economic Cooperation and Development.

Public Law 88-210, the Vocational Education Act of 1963.

Public Law 90-576, Vocational Education Amendments of 1968.

Public Law 93-112, the Vocational Rehabilitation Act of 1973.

Public Law 94-142, the Education for All Handicapped Children Act of 1975.

Public Law 94-482, the Education Amendments of 1976.

Public Law 95-602, the Vocational Rehabilitation Amendments of 1978.

Public Law 98-199, the Education Amendments of 1983.

Public Law 98-524, the Carl D. Perkins Vocational and Technical Act of 1984.

Rusch, F. R., & Phelps, L. A. (1987). Secondary special education and transition from school to work: A national priority. *Exceptional Children, 53*(6), 487-492.

Schalock, R. L., & Lilley, M. A. (1986). Placement from community-based mental retardation programs: How well do clients do after 8 to 10 years? *American Journal of Mental Deficiency, 90*(6), 669-676.

Schalock, R. L., Wolzen, B., Ross, I., Elliot, B., Werbel, G., & Peterson, K. (1986). Post-secondary community placement of handicapped students: A five-year follow up. *Learning Disability Quarterly, 9,* 295-303.

Schmitt, N., & Mellon, P. M. (1980). Life and job satisfaction: Is the job central? *Journal of Vocational Behavior, 16*(1), 51-58.

Silvestri, G. T., Lukasiewicz, J. M. (1987). A look at occupational employment trends to the year 2000. *Monthly Labor Review, 110*(9), 46-63.

Snyder, C. D., & Ferguson, L. W. (1976). Self-concept and job satisfaction. *Psychological Reports, 38,* 603-610.

Super, D. (1957). *The psychology of careers.* New York: Harper.

Wehman, P. (1986). Transition for handicapped youth from school to work. In J. Chadsey-Rusch & C. Hanley-Maxwell (Eds.), *Enhancing transition from school to the workplace for handicapped youth: Personnel preparation implications* (pp. 26-43). Champaign, IL: National Network for Professional Development in Vocational Special Education.

Will, M. (1986). OSERS programming for the transition of youth with disabilities: Bridges from school to working life. In J. Chadsey-Rusch & C. Hanley-Maxwell (Eds.), *Enhancing transition from school to the workplace for handicapped youth: Personnel preparation implications* (pp. 9-24). Champaign, IL: National Network for Professional Development in Vocational Special Education.

17

PREPARING PARENTS TO PARTICIPATE: ADVOCACY AND EDUCATION

Craig R. Fiedler

The Education for All Handicapped Children Act of 1975, Public Law 94-142, and the recent P.L. 99-457, which expands services for younger children, place a high value on parental participation in educational planning and decision making. With these laws, parents of exceptional children were given participatory rights with regard to their children's education—rights that the public schools never before had to recognize or allow. Some of these include parents' right to: be a part of the process for evaluating their child; challenge the process for evaluating their child; challenge the accuracy of their child's evaluation, program, or placement; give or withhold consent to initial evaluations or placement; have access to school records; participate in public hearings on the state special education plan; and plan their child's educational program (i.e., participate in writing the IEP) (Turnbull, 1986).

It is clear that Congress intended parents to be active advocates for their children's best interests and that parents were viewed as the ultimate educational decision makers (Turnbull, Turnbull, & Wheat, 1982). However, merely passing a law that establishes an opportunity for parents to participate in educational planning and decision making does not ensure that such participation will automatically occur, especially if parents and professionals alike do not actively embrace the spirit of this new partnership (Turnbull & Turnbull, 1982). This new role perception of parents has created an expectation and need for parent education and support to enhance their advocacy efforts and participation in the educational planning process. Indeed, parents who do participate in the educational process and understand their children's rights have a far better chance of securing an appropriate education for their child than do those parents who remain uninvolved, unprepared, and uninformed (Herr, 1983).

This chapter will address this critically important issue of how professionals can prepare parents of exceptional children to participate, to whatever extent they can, in their children's education. Instead of a professional attitude that considers parental participation as troublesome and irrelevant, a new vision is required, one in which professionals respond to parents as potential partners and collaborators. This collaborative concept of parent participation in educational matters essentially attempts to empower and enable parents to work actively on behalf of their exceptional child. This new partnership and collaboration require the advocacy efforts of parents and professionais alike. Specifically, this chapter identifies barriers to more active parent participation; describes what is meant by educational advocacy; presents specific strategies/considerations for enhancing parental participation in IEP conferences (while adhering to the belief that parents should be allowed to participate in their children's education according to their preferences); outlines the basic skills required of both parents and professionals in their advocacy efforts; and discusses pertinent considerations in resolving, in a nonadversarial fashion, parent–professional conflict which, at times, arises from assertive advocacy. Finally, examples of specific programs and intervention strategies that individual professional educators and entire school districts might employ to enhance parent participation will be highlighted.

Barriers to Parent Participation

Before reviewing several identified barriers to parent participation in educational decision making, a consideration of the extent to which parents of exceptional children participate in the decision-making process of IEP conferences will be reviewed. Most of the research on parent participation has focused on levels of participation at IEP conferences because those meetings represent the most typical and crucial interactions between parents and educators as envisioned by P.L. 94-142.

Research on Parent Participation in IEP Conferences

A review of research clearly indicates that although parent attendance at IEP meetings is fairly high (Goldstein, Strickland, Turnbull, & Curry, 1980; Marver & David, 1978), parent participation in actual decision making is limited. Goldstein et al. (1980) observed the IEP conferences of 14 elementary students with mild disabilities. This study examined the topics of discussion, frequency of contributions by each conference participant, and overall satisfaction with conference participation and decisions made. Goldstein et al. concluded that parents were by no means equal participants or actively involved in the decision-making process even though parents reported a high degree of satisfaction with those conferences and their role.

Another study interviewed 32 parents of elementary learning disabilities students to assess their involvement in the development and implementation of their child's IEP (McKinney & Hocutt, 1982). Essentially, this study found that the majority of parents reported they did not participate fully in the IEP development and only 16% could specify the contribution they made. Parent participation in the implementation and monitoring of the IEP was negligible.

Lynch and Stein (1982) surveyed over 400 parents of students representing a variety of exceptionalities, ages, and ethnic backgrounds. A follow-up study was conducted to include a greater representation of Hispanic parents (Lynch & Stein, 1987). Coinciding with earlier studies, findings by Lynch and Stein confirm that most parents report satisfaction with their child's special education program even though parent participation in IEP conferences was quite passive. Hispanic parents indicated that they felt significantly less involved than did Anglo parents, but not significantly less involved than Black parents. Also, both Hispanic and Black parents offered significantly fewer suggestions at the IEP meetings than did Anglo parents. These findings are especially pertinent given the increasing racial and ethnic diversity in this country.

Turnbull (1983) concluded that the current level of parent participation in IEP conferences can more accurately be described as passive rather than active. Also, parents generally reported satisfaction with both their child's special education program and their relatively low degree of involvement in IEP development. Fiedler (1986) offered two explanations for these research findings. One explanation is that minimal or passive parent participation in their child's education may reflect genuine preferences for the amount of participation parents can offer at any given moment. The implications of this reality on parent–professional interactions will be discussed later in this chapter. A second explanation for passive parent participation in IEP conferences is that numerous barriers have precluded them from more active participation.

Barriers to Active Parent Participation

For parents to become productive participants and advocates in their children's education, professionals must recognize the barriers currently operating that prevent active parent participation. These barriers operate either indirectly by damaging parent–professional interactions and, ultimately, their relationship; or these barriers have a direct adverse impact on parents' participation by limiting their time, energy, knowledge, and psychological support which are necessary for active parent participation and advocacy. Turnbull and Turnbull (1986) identified these typical barriers, which are summarized in Table 17.1.

A review of the barriers enumerated in Table 17.1 reveals the importance of professionals' attitudes and interpersonal skills. In respect to professional attitudes Fiedler (1986) noted:

> More positive attitudes and assumptions toward parents are promoted by emphasizing the role of parents as family members. This role is based on the premise that successful family life requires that the needs of all family members, including parents, must be identified and addressed. This premise adheres to basic principles incorporated in family systems theory, which views the family as a social system with unique characteristics and needs. Accordingly, underlying family systems theory is the basic belief that the individual members of a family are so interrelated that events affecting one member will inevitably affect all family members. (pp. 1-2)

Undoubtedly, parent–professional interactions that address the needs of the entire family unit will provide the foundation for more positive relations between the two and the establishment of a true partnership as envisioned in P.L. 94-142. In addition to developing more appropriate and positive professional attitudes toward parents, parent–professional collaboration and partnership are largely dependent upon interpersonal factors. Four interpersonal factors are fundamental in establishing collaborative and productive parent–professional relationships: (a) willingness to listen; (b) recognition of trust as a basic element of cooperation; (c) knowledge and acceptance of individual values; and (d) willingness to accommodate a partnership relationship (Simpson & Fiedler, 1989).

Willingness to listen. Listening to parents is the most fundamental way in which professionals can communicate interest and willingness to accept parents as educational partners. Active listening enables professionals to develop greater understanding of and empathy for parental issues and stressors, and, thus, professionals will be better equipped to offer appropriate support, whether it be informational, educational, psychological, or simply a referral to another agency or resource. Also, listening communicates respect and encourages parents to become more actively involved in educational planning and decision-making discussions.

Recognition of trust. Trust is an essential ingredient in parent–professional relationships. Indeed, parents who do not trust professionals will be disinclined to form a productive partnership and will not be as actively involved in their children's education. Simpson (1982) identified seven requirements for developing

Table 17.1
Barriers to Parent Participation and Productive Parent–Professional Interactions

General category	Example	Effect on parent participation and/or parent–professional interactions
1. Psychological	Different perceptions among parents and professionals	Parents concerned about what is best for their one child; professionals' concern must extend to all children—often leads to tension/antagonism in parent–professional interactions.
2. Attitudinal	a. The Parent as Vulnerable Client	Parents might feel vulnerable when asking for help; unequal power distribution between parent and professional.
	b. The Parent and Professional Distance	Professionals fail to express empathy—failure to establish foundation of trust required for parent–professional partnership.
	c. The Parent as Patient	Professional attitude that parent is in need of treatment—this undermines notion of parent–professional partnership.
	d. The Parent as Responsible for the Child's Condition	Parents made to feel guilty; hinders development of trust in parent–professional relationship.
	e. The Parent as Less Observant, Less Perceptive, and Less Intelligent	Professional attitude which dismisses validity/importance of parent opinions and impressions.
	f. The Parent as Adversary	Competitive atmosphere develops between parent and professional.
	g. The Parent as Pushy, Angry, Denying, Resistant, or Anxious	Professional labeling of parents who disagree with them; this establishes a poor foundation for parent–professional interactions by ascribing negative characteristics to potentially valid concerns.
3. Cultural/Ideological	Ethnic background and cultural heritage influences personal and family values.	Parent and professional values may collide causing lack of sensitivity and understanding, and communication breakdowns.

Table 17.1 (*Continued*)

General category	Example	Effect on parent participation and/or parent–professional interactions
4. Parent-Identified Barriers	a. Logistical (e.g., lack of transportation, child care, time conflicts)	Parents have many demands on their time, attention, and energy; not always able to devote to exceptional child's education.
	b. Communication Problems	Parent–professional understanding is essential for productive interactions; language (too much professional jargon) and cultural barriers.
	c. Lack of Understanding of the School System	Lack of parent understanding of legal rights, special education procedures, classroom practices; parents often feel ill prepared to participate in educational planning and decision making.
	d. Uncertainty About the Child's Exceptionality	Affects parents' feelings of competence and ability to contribute information and participate in decision making.
	e. Feelings of Inferiority	Feeling intimidated; gives parents a diminished sense of status or power in decision making.
5. Professional-Identified Barriers	a. Parental Apathy	Professionals becoming negative toward parents who do not participate according to their levels of expectations; leads only to worsening of parent–professional relationship.
	b. Professional Time Constraints	Competing time and energy demands on professionals.
	c. Professional Expertise Constraints	Lack of appropriate professional training in knowing how to support and work with parents.

Note. Adapted from Turnbull and Turnbull (1986).

parent–professional trust: (a) willingness to be involved in the educational process, (b) acceptance that both parents and educators have a commitment to children, (c) willingness to serve as a child advocate, (d) positive outlook, (e) willingness on the part of parents and professionals to reinforce and confront one another, (f) sensitivity to individual needs and emotions, and (g) desire to trust.

Acceptance of individual values. Personal values determine many of our decisions and much of our behavior. Professionals must not presume that their values are more acceptable than those of parents. Simpson and Fiedler (1989) cautioned that:

> ... when attempting to make value-based decisions, professionals should anticipate differences of opinion. Such differences should not be perceived as problematic; however, they do require that parents as well as educators recognize their own values and accept that others will often have different goals and beliefs. (p. 163)

Accommodation of partnership relationship. Finally, professionals must actively promote and accept parents as participants in the educational process. This requirement cannot be legislated; it must be demonstrated by words and actions. Professionals who actively seek to eliminate or minimize barriers to parent participation, who are willing to listen to parents, who develop mutual trust, and who acknowledge and accept individual values will be promoting and supporting parents as active participants in the educational process.

Educational Advocacy

Advocacy is the representation of rights and interests of oneself (or others) in an effort to bring about change and to eliminate barriers to meeting identified needs (Haggerty, 1976). In ensuring an appropriate education for exceptional children, advocacy takes two forms: (a) the responsibility of professionals themselves to serve as advocates for exceptional children and (b) professionals' obligation to prepare parents adequately to fulfill their advocacy role.

Child Advocacy

With respect to child advocacy, Fiedler (1986) noted that "special education professionals have historically avoided advocacy responsibility because of insufficient training, legal ramifications, pressure from superiors, and competing time and energy demands" (p. 7). However, it has now been recognized by the

American Association on Mental Retardation (Antonak, Mallory, & Thede, 1986) and the Council for Exceptional Children (1983) that special education and developmental disabilities professionals have advocacy responsibilities to the children they serve, including the following:

1. Professionals should seek to improve government provisions for the education of exceptional children.
2. Professionals must work cooperatively with and encourage other providers to improve the provision of special education and related services to exceptional children.
3. Professionals should document and objectively report to their supervisors inadequacies in resources and promote appropriate corrective action.
4. Professionals should monitor for inappropriate placements in special education and intervene at the appropriate level to correct the situation when inappropriate placement exists.
5. Professionals must follow laws and regulations that mandate a free, appropriate public education to exceptional students and the protection of the rights of exceptional persons to equal opportunities in society.

Parent Advocacy

Professional support of parent educational advocacy efforts should focus on two broad topics: legal rights and enhancing parent participation in the IEP process. Both will be discussed briefly.

Providing information on legal rights. It is not sufficient that professionals merely provide parents with a written notice describing their child's educational rights. Indeed, Yoshida, Fenton, Kaufman, and Maxwell (1978) found that many parents do not receive adequate notice of their procedural safeguards as accorded by P.L. 94-142. Perhaps part of the problem related to ensuring adequate notice to parents about their legal rights and procedures is the rather high readability level of the disseminated material. Thus a nationwide survey of state departments of education (McLoughlin, Edge, Petrosko, & Strenecky, 1981) revealed that materials disseminated to parents consistently had a 14th- to 15th-grade level readability rate. Such a high readability level restricts access to information by parents with limited educational backgrounds. Roit and Pfohl (1984) also expressed concern that parent information materials distributed by educational agencies may not be comprehensible to a large number of parents of exceptional children. In addition, these authors suggested that school personnel assume greater responsibility for evaluating the knowledge acquired by parents through the disseminated materials. This admonition seems particularly pertinent when considering the Council for

Exceptional Children's (1983) ethical mandate that professionals should inform parents of the educational rights of their children and of any proposed or actual practices that violate those rights.

On what legal rights and educational procedures should professionals ensure that parents have been sufficiently informed? As an example, the questions in an action guide to the rights of people with disabilities prepared by the Wisconsin Coalition for Advocacy (1986) should be addressed and covered with parents. These questions are presented in Table 17.2. This information could be disseminated to parents via a workshop format or in an informational packet developed by the school district. In either format, ensuring parent understanding should be an affirmative professional obligation.

Enhancing parent participation in the IEP process. Educational programs should involve parents to the maximum extent possible, while at the same time acknowledging the parents' rights to choose minimal participation. More participa-

Table 17.2
Sample of Relevant Questions on Legal Rights and Educational Procedures

---

What is special education?
How does the school find children who need special education?
What happens when the school is told about a disabled child?
How does the school decide if a child has exceptional educational needs (EEN)?
How does the M-team do its evaluation?
What kinds of tests can the M-team use to find out about the child's disability?
What kind of child gets special education?
What if the parents do not agree with the M-team report?
What happens after the M-team makes its report?
What happens after the IEP is finished?
What does "least restrictive environment" mean?
Where will the child go to school?
What about school activities outside the classroom?
What special services will be given at the school besides classroom teaching?
What about transportation?
What reports will the school send to the parent, and which ones must the parent sign?
What if the parent disagrees with a decision by the school?
What is a parent support group?
What are formal complaint procedures?
How do I write a letter of complaint?
What is a due process hearing?
What rights does a parent have at a due process hearing?
How do I appeal a decision after the due process hearing?

---

tion is not necessarily better participation (Turnbull & Turnbull, 1982). Adhering to the family systems perspective, professionals should tolerate and encourage a range of parent participation options matched to the needs and interests of each family.

As an example of the range of parental participation options, seven potential parent participation levels will be briefly discussed. Professionals, in close collaboration with parents, should identify the needs, interests, and abilities of parents and then match family resources to a preferred level of parent participation. Parent participation options include the following (Fiedler, 1986).

1. Attendance and approval of teacher priorities: Parents attend IEP meetings, receive feedback about their child, and receive and approve proposed IEP goals.
2. Sharing information: Parents provide information to the educational staff regarding, for example, their child's current level of functioning within the family, effective and ineffective teaching strategies, preferred and nonpreferred activities, and so forth.
3. Suggesting goals: Parents suggest specific skills or goals that they would like to see incorporated into the educational program.
4. Negotiating goals: When differences of opinion arise, parents and educational staff negotiate to agreement on IEP goals and implementation strategies.
5. Collaboratively analyzing and monitoring implementation: After reaching agreement on the IEP, parents help monitor day-to-day performance to assure achievement of goals, help include new goals when performance criteria are met, and reexamine goals that are not being met for respecification of goals or procedures.
6. Joint programming: Parents select specific IEP goals that they will implement in the home and/or community settings, simultaneously and in cooperation with the school's implementation of the goals.
7. Independent programming: Parents undertake training of educational goals in the home or community. (p. 6)

After an acceptable level of parent participation has been chosen, parents should receive information and support on how to function at that level. This information and support may be provided via reading materials made available to parents, formal workshop sessions, or through the establishment of parent support groups. Table 17.3 summarizes the skills to be trained within each of the seven parent participation levels (Simpson & Fiedler, 1988). Considerations for each level of participation are provided for three phases: prior to the IEP conference, during the conference, and after the IEP conference.

Table 17.3
Considerations for Parent IEP Participation

	Phase of participation		
Levels of involvement	Pre-IEP conference	During IEP conference	Post-IEP conference

Attendance and approval	1) Plan for the meeting:
	  a) Determine the site of the conference
	  b) plan to arrive on time
	  c) identify a baby-sitter to avoid having to bring young children to the meeting
	  d) determine how much time has been alloted for the conference
	  e) attempt to identify who will attend the meeting.
	2) Consider bringing a friend or relative to the meeting if you are uncomfortable attending alone.
	3) Develop a positive attitude regarding the meeting as opposed to assuming an adversarial position.
	4) Familiarize yourself with legal and legislative special education mandates. In particular, review handbooks and pamphlets relating to P.L. 94-142.
		1) Maintain a positive attitude during the conference.
		2) Maintain a businesslike demeanor:
		  a) dress in a business-like manner
		  b) bring writing materials
		  c) avoid isolation via the seating arrangement
		  d) listen carefully
		  e) introduce yourself and request that others at the meeting do the same, including specifying their role.
		3) Be willing to accept responsibility for problems that are outside school. Similarly, do not expect school personnel to solve your personal or family problems. However, you may seek referrals from school personnel for such services.
			1) Be willing to attend future meetings and to offer support and approval.

Table 17.3 (Continued)

	Phase of participation		
Levels of involvement	Pre-IEP conference	During IEP conference	Post-IEP conference
Sharing Information	In addition to the above,	In addition to the above,	In addition to the above,
	5) Maintain and organize developmental, school, and clinical records on your children and review these records (including previous IEPs) prior to conferences.	4) Bring background information and other information that you may wish to share at the conference.	2) Obtain and file a copy of the IEP and any other information needed for future reference.
	6) Develop a list of information and other data you wish to share at IEP conferences. Write this information down because you may not remember it at conference time.		3) Family members, including the child about whom the meeting was held (if appropriate), should be provided conference information.
Suggesting Goals	In addition to the above,	In addition to the above,	In addition to the above,
	7) Identify with family members (including the child about whom the conference will be held) prioritized goals for the child.	5) Assertively maintain a participatory status during the conference. Ask for clarification about items and concepts which you fail to understand and which are not explained; solicit input and feedback from individuals who might not otherwise share information;	4) Prepare notes about the meeting following the conference. These notes should reflect happenings during the conference and should be filed with the student's IEP.
			5) Contact the appropriate personnel if clarification or

	make suggestions you consider important; request a copy of the completed IEP; and request additional meeting time if the allotted schedule is insufficient for completing the IEP. 6) Present to IEP participants parent and family goals for the child.		additional information is required. 6) Reinforce educators for their work, for example, through letters and phone calls following the IEP conference.
Negotiating goals	In addition to the above, 7) Positively and assertively work with educators during the IEP conference. Present and advocate for priority goals. However, avoid arguing over minor details or attempting to dominate the meeting.	In addition to the above, 8) Consider enrolling in assertiveness training and problem-solving workshops.	Same as above.
Monitor Implementation	In addition to the above, 8) Establish the manner in which goals and objectives will be monitored and how this information will be communicated to educators.	In addition to the above, 9) Consider enrolling in workshops on child and program assessment and evaluation.	In addition to the above, 7) Maintain an ongoing record of IEP progress and skill development.

Table 17.3 *(Continued)*

Levels of involvement	Phase of participation		
	Pre-IEP conference	During IEP conference	Post-IEP conference
Engage in joint programming	In addition to the above, 10) Familiarize yourself with teaching strategies and behavior management procedures.	In addition to the above, 9) Establish the manner in which goals and objectives will be monitored and how this information will be communicated to educators.	Same as above.
Engage in independent programming	In addition to the above, 11) Develop proficiency in independently carrying out teaching strategies and behavior management procedures.	In addition to the above, 10) Establish the conditions under which goals and objectives will be independently pursued by parents and the manner in which this information will be communicated.	Same as above.

Note. From R. L. Simpson and C. R. Fiedler, in *The Second Handbook on Parent Education: Contemporary Perspectives* by M. J. Fine (Ed.), 1989, San Diego, CA: Academic Press. Copyright 1989 by Academic Press. Adapted by permission.

In addition to recognizing and supporting parents in efforts to determine a comfortable and realistic level of parent participation, professionals should consider the following guidelines for enhancing parent–professional partnerships.

1. *Inventory parent preferences for the IEP conference.* Turnbull and Turnbull (1986) devised a questionnaire to solicit parent preferences on the following questions pertaining to an IEP conference:

> What people would you like to bring with you to the conference?
> What professionals do you want to attend the conference?
> What time would be convenient to hold the meeting?
> Where should the meeting be held?
> Do you need any child care or transportation assistance?
> What kind of information would you like to receive prior to the conference?
> Do you want to share information with the school in advance of the conference?

2. *Allow enough time for meetings.* The single most important contribution to effective conferences is allowing enough time. Assess the agenda, allow time for discussion and reaching consensus, set realistic time estimates, and schedule accordingly.

3. *Make preliminary contacts informal and welcoming.* Parents will respond more favorably if they have had opportunities to chat informally with professionals prior to attending a formal meeting such as an IEP conference.

4. *Assign a conference liaison to the parents.* Parents need to know that there is one person who is principally knowledgeable about their child's educational experience and can answer their questions.

5. *Divide the evaluation and IEP components of the decision-making process into separate conferences.* Especially for parents new to the special education system, receiving both evaluation information and making educational decisions in one meeting is intellectually and emotionally overwhelming.

6. *Avoid premature solutions.* Professionals should remain flexible and not get narrowly locked into only one solution for a perceived problem.

7. *Don't wait.* If a child has a problem or the professional is aware of a particular parental concern, do not wait until the formal conference to raise the issue or problem initially.

8. *Avoid jargon.*

9. *Learn from the parents.* Acknowledge the parents' expertise about their child's interests, behaviors, and history.

10. *Encourage open, honest communication.*

11. *Evaluate the IEP conference.* Ask parents to evaluate their conference experiences and use their feedback to make conferences more responsive to parents' needs.

Basic Advocacy Skills

This chapter has taken a position that educational advocacy (from both professionals and parents, whenever possible) for exceptional children is often necessary to ensure them an appropriate education. What are the basic character-istics of a good advocate? Cutler (1981) delineated the following traits.

1. Greater concern for the child's best interests than for the concerns or interests of the school system.
2. Long-term commitment to the child's welfare and to being the child's advocate.
3. Knowledge of the present needs of the child or the ability to recognize those needs.
4. Assertiveness in pointing out the child's needs to the people responsible for meeting those needs.
5. Ability to work with others to develop appropriate and beneficial educational goals and plans for the child.
6. Ability to find and use information, allies, and resources to put the needed educational plans to work.

Effective advocacy is an ongoing process that requires a number of specific skills. Paul, Neufeld, and Pelosi (1977) suggested a number of skills required of an effective advocate. Among the skills are: (a) ability to communicate; (b) understanding of legal rights; (c) knowledge of within-system procedures, negotia-tion procedures, and data collection methods; (d) understanding of special education methods and procedures; and (e) facility in monitoring educational progress and use of the media. Effective educational advocacy and the use of the above-mentioned skills may inevitably, at times, lead to parent–professional conflict. The methods that parents and professionals use to conceptualize and resolve conflict are important determinants of whether conflict may be settled constructively, in a nonadversarial fashion, or whether the conflict must be resolved by the formal, adversarial, due process hearing system.

A Nonadversarial Approach to Parent–Professional Conflict

In an investigation of the conflict-handling modes of behavior of parents and school personnel, Fiedler (1985) concluded that both parents and school personnel engaged in relatively low levels of collaboration. As Fiedler (1986) noted:

> This result is disconcerting because it suggests that parent–school conflict can be expected to continue as long as parents and school personnel fail to recognize the value of collaboration and fail to use effective problem-solving techniques in their interpersonal interactions. (p. 6)

In an effort to collaborate and resolve conflict in a nonadversarial manner, parents and professionals should (a) arrange to get together as soon as concerns arise; (b) share information and feelings clearly, vividly, and sensitively (avoid blaming one another or presenting a single solution early); (c) listen to the other's view; (d) try to agree on a definition of the problem; (e) if there is disagreement, clarify what each is seeing/experiencing (ask for specific examples); and (f) decide on next steps—who is going to do what and by when (Braun & Swap, 1987).

One example of an interesting and creative conflict resolution technique, called "Creating a Vision," was suggested by Braun and Swap (1987). Oftentimes parent–professional conflict is generated because they do not share a common vision of what is most important for the child to learn. For example, a parent may want a child to master college preparation academic skills, while the professional may see vocational training as most important. This difference in vision generally leads to parent–professional mistrust and outright conflict. In order for parents to enlist the support of professionals, it is important to share a "vision" of the child. Braun and Swap suggest the following questions to help parents articulate their hopes and long-term goals for their child:

1. What are your hopes and dreams for your child? What do you see your child doing in 5 years? in 10 years?
2. Can you tell an anecdote about your child that communicates your vision in a compelling way?
3. Why is this accomplishment important to you? What gives it special meaning for you?

Collaboration or mutual problem solving is the most highly recommended method for effective conflict resolution (Araki, 1983; Deutsch, 1973; Fisher & Ury, 1981; Simpson, 1982). Collaboration leads to constructive, nonadversarial conflict resolution with the distinct advantage of "providing a means for meeting both the parents' and educators' needs while serving the best interests of the child" (Simpson, 1982, p. 278). Generally, the problem-solving process is composed of the steps outlined in Table 17.4.

Table 17.4
The Problem-Solving Process

---

1. Define the problem (from both parties' perspective)
2. Generate possible solutions
3. Choose a solution—weigh possible risks, gains, likelihood of success, costs
4. Implement the chosen solution
5. Evaluate the solution

Examples of School-Based Advocacy Programs/Interventions

Educational advocacy and enhancement of parental participation in their children's education can take many forms. The following programs/interventions are merely illustrative of some of the activities that individual professionals and entire school districts might consider.

Special Education Parent Facilitator/Host Family Program

Lynch and Stein (1987) describe a support service whereby parents of exceptional children themselves are trained by the school district to serve as liaisons between the school district and other parents of exceptional children. These Special Education Parent Facilitators are paid by the school district as paraprofessionals and provide support, information, and training to other parents. A similar program was advocated by Braun and Swap (1987) where volunteer parents would serve as host families for parents new to the school district or new to special education procedures. These host families were available for both emotional and informational support.

Internal Advocacy System

An internal advocate or ombudsman program established by school districts would assist parents in presenting their complaints to the appropriate school officials. As detailed by Creekmore and Creekmore (1981), an internal advocate would "assume an intermediary role between the placement committee and the building principal, communicating to the senior administrative officer extraordinary happenings during the decision-making process. The advocate's role here is that of compliance officer for the child and family" (p. 10). Additionally, the internal advocate would monitor implementation of the child's IEP, provide in-class consultation, secure helpful materials, and disseminate inservice information.

Parent Information Center

A meeting place for parents located within a school building could provide social, emotional, and informational support. Parents could obtain reading materials on child development, special education diagnostic and instructional methods, and special education rights and procedures, among other topics. A special education staff member could be available to answer parent questions.

Parent Support Groups

Professionals working in schools could organize parent groups. These groups would have an inherent social/emotional focus but could also focus on specific informational issues such as behavior management, planning for your child's future, sibling issues, teaching your child academic skills, or legal issues/rights. Ideally, professionals should initiate these parent groups and then as quickly as possible turn their operation over to the parents themselves.

Transition Services

Parents of exceptional children typically experience transition stress as their child changes from early childhood to school age, or from school age to adolescence, or from adolescence to adulthood. Professionals must be sensitive to this transition stress and support parents in a variety of ways. Professionals can help parents think ahead to next year or 5 years from now by discussing instructional objectives in terms of the child's future needs. Turnbull and Turnbull (1986) suggested other strategies: "[V]isits to new classrooms or community programs such as group homes, meetings with future teachers, talks with parents of older children with similar exceptionalities, can all help to reduce the fear of the future by making it less unknown" (p. 109). In essence, school transition support should build bridges for parents to make life cycle changes less stressful.

Summary

Public Laws 94-142 and 99-457 legislate parental participation in the educational decision-making process. This chapter attempted to suggest how professionals can turn that legislative mandate into a practice reality by recognizing the barriers that have historically precluded active parent participation, by assuming the responsibilities of becoming an educational advocate for exceptional children and their parents, by taking actions to enhance parental participation in IEP conferences, by actively practicing the skills of effective advocacy, and by working to resolve parent–professional conflict in a nonadversarial manner. Truly supportive and effective professionals recognize that their client responsibilities extend beyond the individual child they are serving and encompass responsibilities to that child's parents and entire family unit. This ecological perspective is essential in realizing one's potential as an effective professional in the 1990s and beyond.

References

Antonak, R. F., Mallory, B. L., & Thede, D. L. (1986). A proposed set of ethical principles for developmental disabilities professionals. *Mental Retardation Systems, 3*(1), 12-22.

Araki, C. T. (1983). A practical approach to conflict resolution. *Educational Perspective, 22*(1), 11-16.

Braun, L. A., & Swap, S. M. (1987). *Building home-school partnerships with America's changing families.* Boston: Wheelock College.

Council for Exceptional Children. (1983). Code of ethics and standards for professional practice. *Exceptional Children, 50,* 205-209.

Creekmore, W. N., & Creekmore, N. N. (1981). The internal advocacy system: An alternative strategy for teacher and child. *Focus on Exceptional Children, 14*(1), 1-16.

Cutler, B. C. (1981). *Unraveling the special education maze: An action guide for parents.* Champaign, IL: Research Press.

Deutsch, N. (1973). *The resolution of conflict: Constructive and destructive processes.* New Haven: Yale University Press.

Fiedler, C. R. (1985). *Conflict prevention, containment, and resolution in special education due process disputes: Parents' and school personnel's perceptions of variables associated with the development and escalation of due process conflict.* Unpublished doctoral dissertation, University of Kansas, Lawrence.

Fiedler, C. R. (1986). Enhancing parent-school personnel partnerships. *Focus on Autistic Behavior, 1*(4), 1-8.

Fisher, R., & Ury, W. (1981). *Getting to yes: Negotiating agreement without giving in.* Boston: Houghton-Mifflin.

Goldstein, S., Strickland, B., Turnbull, A.P., & Curry, L. (1980). An observational analysis of the IEP conference. *Exceptional Children, 46*(4), 278-286.

Haggerty, D. E. (1976). Definitional aspects of advocacy and protective services. In G. J. Bensberg & C. Rude (Eds.), *Advocacy systems for the developmentally disabled* (pp. 43-50). Lubbock, TX: Texas Tech University Research and Training Center in Mental Retardation.

Herr, S. S. (1983). *Rights and advocacy for retarded people.* Lexington, MA: D.C. Heath.

Lynch, E. W., & Stein, R. C. (1982). Perspectives on parent participation in special education. *Exceptional Education Quarterly, 3*(2), 56-63.

Lynch, E., & Stein, R. C. (1987). Parent participation by ethnicity: A comparison of Hispanic, black, and Anglo families. *Exceptional Children, 54*(2), 105-111.

Marver, J. D., & David, J. L. (1978). *The implementation of individualized education program requirements of P.L. 94-142.* Trends Park, CA: SRI International.

McKinney, J. D., & Hocutt, A. M. (1982). Public school involvement of parents of learning disabled children and average achievers. *Exeptional Education Quarterly, 3*(2), 64-83.

McLoughlin, J. A., Edge, D., Petrosko, J., & Strenecky, B. (1981). P.L. 94-142 and information dissemination: A step forward. *Journal of Special Education Technology, 4*(4), 50-56.

Paul, J. L., Neufeld, G. R, & Pelosi, J. W. (Eds.). (1977). *Child advocacy within the system.* Syracuse, NY: Syracuse University Press.

Public Law 94-142, The Education for All Handicapped Act of 1975.

Public Law 99-457, The Education for All Handicapped Act of 1986.

Roit, M. L., & Pfohl, W. (1984). The readability of P.L. 94-142 parent materials: Are parents truly informed? *Exceptional Children, 50*(6), 496-505.

Simpson, R. L. (1982). *Conferencing parents of exceptional children.* Rockville, MD: Aspen.

Simpson, R. L, & Fiedler, C. R. (1989). Parent participation in individualized education program (IEP) conferences: A case for individualization. In M. J. Fine (Ed.), *The second handbook on parent education: Contemporary perspectives* (pp. 145-170). New York: Academic Press.

Turnbull, A. P. (1983). Parental participation in the IEP process. In J. A. Mulick & S. M. Pueschel (Eds.), *Parent-professional participation in developmental disabilities services: Foundations and prospects* (pp. 107-123). Cambridge, MA: The Ware Press.

Turnbull, A. P., & Turnbull, H. R. (1982). Parent involvement in the education of handicapped children: A critique. *Mental Retardation, 20,* 115-122.

Turnbull, A. P., & Turnbull, H. R. (1986). *Families, professionals, and exceptionality: A special partnership.* Columbus, OH: Merrill.

Turnbull, H. R. (1986). *Free appropriate public education: The law and children with disabilities.* Denver: Love.

Turnbull, H. R., Turnbull, A. P., & Wheat, M. (1982). Assumptions about parental participation: A legislative history. *Exceptional Education Quarterly, 3*(2), 1-8.

Wisconsin Coalition for Advocacy. (1986). *Rights and reality: An action guide to the rights of people with disabilities in Wisconsin.* Madison, WI: Governor's Committee for People with Disabilities and the Wisconsin Coalition for Advocacy.

Yoshida, R. K., Fenton, K., Kaufman, M. J., & Maxwell, J. P. (1978). Parental involvement in the special education pupil planning process: The school's perspective. *Exceptional Children, 44,* 531-534.

Subject Index

Author Index

343